'Colin Cooper's book is a masterpiece of lucidity and a must-have for students, researchers, and practitioners alike. Psychological testing can be a challenging topic, given the mathematical underpinnings of the field, and Cooper deftly navigates the territory between technical details and approachable exposition. A valuable and comprehensive resource, fully updated in its second edition, and well-suited as a textbook for university courses in psychological assessment.'

Robert F. Krueger, PhD, *Distinguished McKnight University Professor, University of Minnesota*

'Colin Cooper is a leading authority on psychometrics with an uncanny ability to convey high-level technical concepts. To this day, I keep learning from his texts and so I am delighted to welcome the publication of this – substantially updated – second edition. It is the first textbook I recommend to anyone wishing to get acquainted with the science of psychometrics.'

K. V. Petrides, *Professor of Psychology and Psychometrics (UCL)*

'Colin Cooper's book is superb – the work of a true expert in psychometrics. Not only is it comprehensive and rigorous, it tackles often neglected issues (e.g., the role played by factor analysis and the conceptual nature of psychological measurement). It is practical, too, with data sets and exercises provided. Cooper's wit infuses the pages which makes for an enjoyable read.'

Philip J. Corr, *Professor of Psychology, School of Health and Psychological Sciences, University of London*

'Professor Colin Cooper taught students the principles of psychometrics and psychological testing for 30 years. Also, he edited related journals for almost as long. It has resulted in this extremely valuable book which is characterized by unique and quality content, natural flow, substance, and expert knowledge. It will be invaluable to both undergraduate and postgraduate students, as well as practitioners who are seeking emphatically not a statistics text.'

Małgorzata Fajkowska, *Head of the Laboratory of Personality Psychology, Institute of Psychology, Polish Academy of Sciences*

AN INTRODUCTION TO PSYCHOMETRICS AND PSYCHOLOGICAL ASSESSMENT

An Introduction to Psychometrics and Psychological Assessment is the successor to Cooper's prize-winning book *Psychological Testing: Theory and Practice*. This expanded and updated volume shows how psychological questionnaires and tests can be chosen, administered, scored, interpreted and developed. In providing students, researchers, test users, test developers and practitioners in the social sciences, education and health with an evaluative guide to choosing, using, interpreting and developing tests, it provides readers a thorough grasp of the principles (and limitations) of testing, together with the necessary methodological detail.

This book has three distinctive features. First, it stresses the basic logic of psychological assessment without getting bogged down with mathematics; the spreadsheet simulations and utilities which are integrated into the text allow users to explore how numbers behave, rather than reading equations. Readers will "learn by doing". Second, it covers both the theory behind psychological assessment and the practicalities of locating, designing and using tests and interpreting their scores. Finally, it is evaluative. Rather than just describing concepts such as test reliability or adaptive testing, it stresses the underlying principles, merits and drawbacks of each approach to assessment, and methods of developing and evaluating questionnaires and tests. Unusually for an introductory text, it includes coverage of several cutting-edge techniques, and this new edition expands the discussion on measurement invariance, methods of detecting/quantifying bias and hierarchical factor models, and features added sections on:

- Best practices for translation of tests into other languages and problems of cultural bias
- Automatic item generation
- The advantages, drawbacks and practicalities of internet-based testing
- Generalizability theory
- Network analysis
- Dangerous assumptions made when scoring tests
- The accuracy of tests used for assessing individuals
- The two-way relationship between psychometrics and psychological theory.

Aimed at non-mathematicians, this friendly and engaging text will help you to understand the fundamental principles of psychometrics that underpin the measurement of any human characteristic using any psychological test. Written by a leading figure in the field and accompanied by additional resources, including a set of spreadsheets which use simulated data and other techniques to illustrate important issues, this is an essential introduction for all students of psychology and related disciplines. It assumes very little statistical background and is written for students studying psychological assessment or psychometrics, and for researchers and practitioners who use questionnaires and tests to measure personality, cognitive abilities, educational attainment, mood or motivation.

A proud Cornishman, **Colin Cooper** obtained his BSc and PhD degrees in psychology from the University of Exeter in the UK. He worked on developing methods for selecting pilots and for assessing flexible thinking in senior officers before taking a lectureship at the University of Ulster in Coleraine, Northern Ireland. He moved to Queen's University, Belfast, where he taught and researched individual differences, psychometrics and statistics for 20 years. He took early retirement in 2012 and emigrated to Ontario, Canada, where he is currently editor-in-chief of two journals and president of the International Society for the Study of Individual Differences. He has published extensively in the areas of individual differences and psychometrics, and in his spare time he enjoys classical music, writing, travel and walking.

An Introduction to Psychometrics and Psychological Assessment

USING, INTERPRETING AND DEVELOPING TESTS

COLIN COOPER

SECOND EDITION

Routledge
Taylor & Francis Group

LONDON AND NEW YORK

Cover image: © Getty

Second edition published 2023
by Routledge
4 Park Square, Milton Park, Abingdon, Oxon OX14 4RN

and by Routledge
605 Third Avenue, New York, NY 10158

Routledge is an imprint of the Taylor & Francis Group, an informa business

© 2023 Colin Cooper

The right of Colin Cooper to be identified as author of this work has been asserted in accordance with sections 77 and 78 of the Copyright, Designs and Patents Act 1988.

All rights reserved. No part of this book may be reprinted or reproduced or utilised in any form or by any electronic, mechanical, or other means, now known or hereafter invented, including photocopying and recording, or in any information storage or retrieval system, without permission in writing from the publishers.

Trademark notice: Product or corporate names may be trademarks or registered trademarks, and are used only for identification and explanation without intent to infringe.

First edition published by Routledge 2018

British Library Cataloguing-in-Publication Data
A catalogue record for this book is available from the British Library

ISBN: 978-1-032-14616-4 (hbk)
ISBN: 978-1-032-14617-1 (pbk)
ISBN: 978-1-003-24018-1 (ebk)

DOI: 10.4324/9781003240181

Typeset in Avenir, Bell and Bembo
by Apex CoVantage, LLC

Access the Support Material: https://www.routledge.com/9781032146164

DEDICATION
To Wesley

CONTENTS

Preface   xi

1   INTRODUCTION TO PSYCHOMETRICS   1

2   TESTS, SCALES AND TESTING   21

3   THE MEANING OF MEASUREMENT   47

4   ADMINISTERING AND SCORING QUESTIONNAIRES AND TESTS   61

5   INTERPRETING SCORES   99

6   CORRELATIONS   117

7   RANDOM ERRORS OF MEASUREMENT   137

8   SYSTEMATIC INFLUENCES AND GENERALISABILITY THEORY   165

9   TEST VALIDITY, BIAS AND INVARIANCE   185

10   INTRODUCTION TO FACTOR ANALYSIS   211

11   PERFORMING AND INTERPRETING FACTOR ANALYSES   229

12   ALTERNATIVE FACTOR ANALYSIS DESIGNS   263

13   DEVELOPMENTS IN FACTOR ANALYSIS   283

14   NETWORK ANALYSIS   305

15   ITEM RESPONSE THEORY   321

16   TEST AND SCALE CONSTRUCTION   347

17   PROBLEMS WITH TEST SCORES   377

18   PSYCHOMETRICS IN CONTEXT   395

References   403
Index   421

PREFACE

This book is designed to give anyone who uses or develops tests a sound and up-to-date grasp of the principles of psychological assessment – and to show how tests may best be used in practice. It is written for everyone who needs to understand use or develop psychological questionnaires, tests and assessments. Thus the likely readership will include students of psychology and other disciplines, test users and professionals – particularly those involved in personnel selection and placement.

Understanding these issues is important, as psychological tests are everywhere. Job applicants complete personality tests and have their cognitive abilities or leadership skills assessed. Health professionals use them to assess dementia and other clinical conditions. Children may be assessed for dyslexia, developmental difficulties or behavioural problems. Researchers in psychology, medicine, education and other disciplines routinely measure personality, cognitive abilities, attitudes, moods, emotional states and a whole host of other characteristics; whilst the rest of us read (and occasionally marvel at) these studies, we sometimes need to check whether their assessments and inferences are likely to be accurate. And we even complete tests and questionnaires in our spare time, to try to learn more about ourselves. But how can we decide which tests say something meaningful, and which are no more useful than reading tea leaves?

Psychometrics is a brave attempt to quantify all that is essentially human – our personality, mental abilities, moods and motives. What could be more important for the science and practice of psychology than that? Unusually, this book covers both the theory and practice of psychometric testing. The practical aspects include how to find (or construct) a test or questionnaire, put it on the internet, check the quality of the data, score it, and interpret the scores. The book also explains modern approaches to reliability theory, factor analysis, item response theory, network analysis and other key methodologies, and shows how tests and questionnaires may be validated. It also considers (and attempts to evaluate) some devastating criticisms of the whole rationale of psychological assessment made by Joel Michell and others.

What makes this book unique is its "hands-on" approach. Rather than showing equations (which experience tells me 9 of 10 students will ignore), most chapters are accompanied by some simple-to-use spreadsheets for Open Office and Microsoft Excel. They have three purposes. Some of them show how commonly used techniques work; the spreadsheet which performs VARIMAX factor rotation in factor analysis, for example. Some use simulated data to demonstrate an important point – for example, to show how test length influences reliability. And some of the spreadsheets are utilities; they compute statistics and perform analyses which most statistical packages ignore. Thus one spreadsheet computes a whole range of different types of correlations between dichotomous (two-valued) variables. Another scores questionnaires. A third performs item analysis to identify and remove underperforming items. All the spreadsheets are integrated into the text in the form of exercises with clear instructions and learning outcomes.

Having read this book and worked through the exercises, students and researchers should have a sound grasp of the principles of modern psychological assessment methods. They should be able to find tests and questionnaires, administer and score them, analyse their psychometric properties and interpret their meaning – whilst being alert to the strengths and weaknesses of questionnaires, tests and rating scales. They should also be able to design and validate a scale or test measuring personality mood or some cognitive ability. That is my hope, anyway.

Thanks are due to several people. Several generations of undergraduate and graduate students at Queen's University, Belfast, taught me how to teach psychometrics whilst I was trying to teach them psychometrics, and thanks are also due to Adam Woods at Routledge, and to Scott Coello for the cover.

And of course, special thanks to Wesley – for his unflagging support, love and help – aided and abetted by Lucky and PussPuss.

Colin Cooper
London, Ontario
September 2022

SPREADSHEETS AND SOFTWARE

The spreadsheets which accompany this book use either Open Office or Microsoft Excel. Open Office is free to download and use, and runs on most platforms including MacOS, Windows and Linux. It may be downloaded from www.openoffice.org/. The spreadsheets and links to other software referenced in the text may be downloaded from routledge.com/9781032146164. The spreadsheets do not use macros, ActiveX or other extensions, and so should run in most environments. Some run perfectly well on mobile devices, whilst those which involve heavy computation or interactive graphics will need a laptop or desktop machine.

CHAPTER 1
INTRODUCTION TO PSYCHOMETRICS

Psychometrics translates as "the measurement of the human spirit", and it is hard to think of any more ambitious project than this – nor one which is of more practical use. Students, researchers, practitioners, clinicians, educators and others need to measure a bewildering measure of personality, cognitive abilities, interests, motivation, mood, educational attainment and such like using questionnaires, tests or measures of human or animal performance. Despite the wide range of characteristics being measured by tests, most test users need to know the same basic things:

- Is it possible to measure psychological concepts (anxiety, intelligence etc.) using tests?
- If so, what kinds of things are measured by tests?
- What *types* of tests are there?
- How can I find a test?
- How should tests be administered and scored?
- How should these scores be interpreted? For example, how can I tell whether a score of 20 on a particular test is low, average or above average?
- How confident can I be that the test measures what it *claims* to measure? For example, do people's scores on a test of anxiety accurately reflect their true levels of anxiety, and not something else?
- How much measurement error is associated with people's scores on the test? If a test shows that someone has an IQ of 110, how likely is it that their true IQ might be as high as 130? Or as low as 95?
- Are the scores on this test influenced by other things? For example, if a personality test is given to job applicants, will they try to distort their scores in order to get the job?
- How can I develop a test myself?
- What is factor analysis and how is it used?
- Is it possible to give people different items yet still be able to compare their scores?

DOI: 10.4324/9781003240181-1

This book is written to help students, researchers, test administrators, test users and practitioners to gain a conceptual understanding of all of these issues. It will also be useful for those seeking to obtain professional qualifications in test use. The aim of the book is to allow readers to identify a test or other measurement instrument appropriate for their needs, evaluate its technical merits, administer and score it. It also suggests how tests of personality, abilities, mood and motivation may be developed and validated. Finally, readers will then be guided in how the test scores may be used for a number of practical applications.

Unusually, perhaps, this book also alerts readers to Michell's (1997) devastating critique of psychological assessment which argues that test construction (by any method) has no sound scientific basis, and that test scores are essentially meaningless; they have the mere pretence of being a science. It also considers Cattell's (1973) comments regarding "source traits", and whether it is possible to identify traits which correspond to real individual differences in the way in which people function (perhaps caused by differences in development, biological make-up or social experiences) rather than personality traits which are social constructions and are *assumed* to exist without any real evidence.

Having taught the principles of psychological assessment to students for 30 years, and having edited journals for almost as long, three things stand out in my memory.

First, psychologists and other test users generally do not love mathematics or statistics. This is unfortunate, as psychometrics is essentially a rather specialised branch of statistics: journals such as *Psychometrika* and *Applied Psychological Measurement* contain cutting-edge papers which require considerable mathematical sophistication, and most psychometric texts also contain enough formulae to thoroughly frighten most psychologists and test users. This book therefore contains as few formulae as possible and is emphatically not a statistics text. It instead aims to give readers a conceptual grasp of the main issues. Whilst it does assume that readers have at some stage been exposed to correlations, t-tests, multiple regression, analysis of variance and so on, it does not require a detailed knowledge of these techniques.

Second, it often seemed to me that students only really understood psychometric concepts when they rolled up their sleeves, got their hands dirty and actually analysed some data. I have tried to follow the same approach when writing this book. For this reason, the book should be read in conjunction with specially prepared spreadsheets. Rather than showing formulae in the text, it is far more interesting to allow readers to see for themselves how numbers behave. My feeling is that this will give a deeper level of understanding than most of us could acquire from examining (or more probably, ignoring) a printed formula. Some of these spreadsheets may also be useful for everyday analyses – although no guarantee is given as to their freedom from error.

Finally, when reporting the results of their analyses many students and researchers repeat phrases without showing an understanding of what they imply. For example, they may have been taught to say "the reliability of a test was above 0.7, which is acceptable" without really understanding what (if anything) this means. Or because their favourite statistic package produces such statistics, they may say "Bartlett's test of sphericity showed that the data were suitable for analysis" without appreciating that this statistic is known to be deeply flawed. I hope that having read this book, readers will have a grasp of the basic logic of psychological testing and so will understand what they are doing and why.

WHO NEEDS TESTS?

Psychological tests and assessments are widely used by practitioners – professionals such as clinical, educational, occupational, sport and forensic psychologists. They are also widely used by researchers and students in psychology and other disciplines, and by organisations seeking to select the most promising applicants or candidates for promotion.

Different types of test users face different issues when selecting, administering, scoring and interpreting the results from tests, and the following pages outline a little about how tests are used in the real world – along with some mention of the pitfalls which test users will encounter.

PRACTITIONERS

Tests may be used for the guidance and assessment of individuals, often in medical, clinical or educational settings. An educational psychologist may use a test to help them determine whether a child's verbal skills are substantially weaker than their other reasoning skills, which may suggest a diagnosis of dyslexia. A clinical psychologist may ask the carers of children with behavioural problems to rate their behaviour using a standard checklist in order to determine the areas of concern and their severity. Or the psychologist may give a screening test to help them determine whether a child shows signs of autism. A physician may use a screening test to help them evaluate whether an elderly patient shows signs of cognitive decline, or symptoms of depression. And (controversially) a teacher may try to assess the preferred learning styles of children in their class in an attempt to identify which children are "linguistic", which are "spatial", which are "kinaesthetic" and so on, so that the style of teaching to which each child is exposed is chosen to match their learning style. Sports psychologists try to assess motivation, mental toughness, self-efficacy (self-belief) and so on. Health psychologists may need to measure how much pain a person experiences, or how well they understand the information given them by a medical practitioner.

Occupational psychologists (sometimes called "industrial psychologists" or "organisational psychologists") will often use tests to perform in-depth assessments of individuals for development purposes, or to determine whether selecting the wrong person for the job would have major financial or other consequences. Senior executives may be hauled away to an assessment centre where assessments of their leadership styles, creativity and a host of other characteristics may help the practitioner determine whether they become the next chief executive officer or president of a company.

Forensic psychologists also use tests, for example, in order to determine whether someone who is accused of a crime is able to distinguish between right and wrong, or whether they are likely to be able to understand the court proceedings, give instructions to their legal representative and so on – "fitness to plead" in English law. They may also try to use tests to help them make difficult decisions about individuals, such as whether a dangerous prisoner has reformed enough to be freed. This is problematical, as one of the main characteristics of psychopaths is their tendency to lie!

The key point is that all of these practitioners will seek to make accurate assessments of individuals using data which they have probably collected themselves. They will almost invariably compare an individual's scores with "norms" to determine (for example) whether a person's score on a test measuring depression is in the "normal range", or so high that they may wish to discuss therapy or some other intervention. Such practitioners will probably use only widely known, well-constructed tests whose content, foibles, limitations and properties are well-documented (but see also Chapter 17). They will also follow guidelines as to which instruments are suitable for the person being assessed (in terms of age, language skills, freedom from bias, acceptability etc.) and will usually assess individuals face to face, one-on-one – an expensive and often time-consuming process.

These test users will need to attend courses approved by the test publisher and/or undergo a period of supervision to train them in the administration, scoring and interpretation of the tests which they plan to use; evidence of such training is normally required before test materials will be sold to them.

There are good reasons for this requirement. For example, if part of a test times how long it takes a child to assemble a four-piece jigsaw, it is obvious that the four pieces need to be presented to every child in the same initial positions, otherwise the test will be easier for some children than for others: test users will need to be trained so that children's scores may be compared, no matter by whom they are tested. Or suppose that vocabulary is assessed using an item such as "What is a kitten?" It might seem obvious that the correct answer is "a young cat" – but what should the test administrator do if the child says "a sort of cat" or "a cat"? If some administrators treat "a sort of cat" as being correct, whilst others treat it is incorrect, or if some administrators encourage the child to elaborate their answer whereas others do not, then it should be obvious that the scores on the test will not be accurate for all children. Tests such as these require specific training.

However, these practitioners will need a general understanding of the logic of how psychological assessments work with particular focus on issues such as scaling (converting scores on an ability test into an "IQ", for example), the accuracy of assessments, and issues such as cultural sensitivity, which is why they have an interest in this book. All these test users will want to know something about issues such as "reliability", "validity" and "bias"; the principles for selecting and using administering and scoring a test; and the merits and limitations of psychometric assessment

A note of caution is needed, however, as just looking at a test cannot always reveal whether it measures anything useful. During my consultancy work I have seen several tests which have been sold to government departments and private businesses which are slickly presented (and *very* expensive) but which lack evidence to suggest that they actually measure anything of worth. On the other hand, well-designed tests can be enormously useful to organisations. Kanfer et al. (1995, p. 597) suggest that

> companies have unarguably saved billions of dollars by using ability tests to assure a merit-based selection process. . . . Overall, tests of intellectual abilities are the single most predictive element in employee selection . . . and certainly more valid than the use of personal interviews . . . in predicting training and on-the-job success.

However, some degree of technical knowledge coupled with a healthy scepticism is essential. Caveat emptor – let the buyer beware!

RESEARCHERS AND STUDENTS WHO RELATE TEST SCORES TO BEHAVIOUR

The second group of test users are students or researchers who do not claim to be experts in the psychology of individual differences. Their prime interest might be in social psychology – for example, studying whether being a member of a minority group affects feelings of self-worth. They will therefore need to find some way of measuring "self-worth". They might be geneticists, health or medical researchers, perhaps linking variations in DNA (at the molecular level) to individual differences in depression, aggression or perfectionism. Or they could be developmental psychologists keen to determine whether a programme of environmental enrichment improves scores on some trait (intelligence or anxiety, perhaps) relative to the scores of a control group. Another researcher may wish to test whether stimulating an area of the brain with a substantial magnetic field (transcranial magnetic stimulation) has an effect on some aspect of cognitive performance, and so will need to be able to measure the appropriate cognitive abilities as accurately as possible. Even behaviourists sometimes use tests; personality scales have been developed which supposedly measure how quickly a person will condition following positive and negative reinforcement. Others may want to determine whether stand-up comedians differ from the rest of us in terms of several personality traits, whether romantic partners tend to have similar personalities, whether children who are bullied in childhood lack self-confidence as adults, or whether caffeine improves working memory.

Tests may also be used to measure transient moods or emotions – "states" rather than traits. For example, tests measuring moods may be administered to examine how life events such as diagnosis of cancer affect mood, stress and so on.

The key point is that almost all psychological research involves some kind of psychological questionnaire, test or assessment. If these measurements are not accurate, then either the research will fail to show anything, or the conclusions may be misleading.

These researchers all link scores on a test to behaviour or life events. They are not interested in assessing or understanding individuals; they instead want to determine whether scores on some psychological test differ significantly between groups of people; for example, whether the environmental enrichment programme improves children's levels of intelligence, relative to a control group of children who do not receive the intervention.

Such researchers are in a more difficult position than the practitioners. Practitioners use top-quality commercial tests which are widely used and are capable of providing accurate assessments when properly administered to appropriate individuals. However, many of the tests which are available to measure other aspects of individual differences will not have gone through so much in the way of quality control. The test items will often be printed as appendices to journal articles, and it is up to the individual researcher to evaluate the quality of the test before using it. How can one know whether a test of conscientiousness developed using 60-year-old residents of Chicago 20 years ago will give sensible results if it is administered to British job applicants? No-one can know for sure, and so the researcher will need to perform some analyses on the data they collect to check whether all (or at least some) of the test items seem to perform satisfactorily.

All too often, it seems that the main reason for using a particular test is because other researchers do so, which can lead to the continued and uncritical use of some really rather suspect measures, particularly in social psychology. Readers who are in this position will want to use this book to help them identify for themselves whether a particular test is likely to measure what it claims to, whether it is likely to be useful for a particular application with a particular sample of people, how to check whether it performs properly when used in a different context, and how the scores should be interpreted.

RESEARCHERS WHO RELATE TEST SCORES TO OTHER TEST SCORES

Members of the third group are psychologists, often personality psychologists or social psychologists, who are mainly interested in the interrelationship between two or more traits, each of which is measured by some scale or test. These test users relate scores on one test to scores on other tests rather than to more objective measures, such as DNA variations, school achievement or age. For example, they might study the link between self-concept and cheerfulness (both measured by questionnaires), or whether high levels of creativity are found in people who show slight signs of schizophrenia ("schizotypy"). Sometimes the concepts are rather less clear, and several variables may be involved. For example, a researcher might study whether "sense of self-empowerment" influences "feelings of self-esteem", and whether depression influences both of these.

The tests used by these researchers are generally not administered one-to-one. Instead they often involve questionnaires which may be administered online, on sheets of paper to a group of students in a lecture, or by telephone. There is always a trade-off between the amount of time taken to assess a variable and the accuracy of assessment, as will be shown in Chapter 7.

In this type of research

- The test scores are not being used to make potentially life-changing decisions about individuals but will be related to the scores of other people using correlations, structural equation modelling or other techniques.
- Participants usually volunteer to take part in such research or are coerced into doing so for some form of course credit and will often complete the questionnaires

anonymously. Thus they have little to lose by not fully engaging with this "low-stakes" research, as their answers will not affect their lives in any way. This may be a problem.
- The researcher is often not present to answer any queries, suggest a rest break, encourage the participant to perform their best or otherwise do their best to ensure that the questionnaires or tests are being answered carefully and honestly.
- It is not uncommon for participants to be given a whole sheaf of questionnaires (or their electronic equivalent) to complete in one session, which can be a grisly experience. It has been found that participants may start to respond randomly towards the end of a long testing session (Weirich et al., 2017), so it may be better to use shorter, potentially less accurate assessments rather than involving participants in a long assessment session. How short can they become?

Because these researchers relate test scores to other test scores, they encounter a rather different set of problems to those who relate scores on a test to behaviour. First, by definition, they need to assess more than one psychological variable – which means that the assessment session will generally be longer. This can lead to the problems with concentration, co-operation etc. noted previously.

Second, it is quite possible that something other than the trait which the test is supposed to measure might influence scores on both tests. Suppose that a researcher administers tests measuring social independence and verbal ability to a sample of teenagers and finds that there is a positive correlation. This could lead them to develop a complex theory about why verbal skills can help adolescents to develop individual identities through deeper interactions with others, or it could just be because the researcher used adolescents with a wide range of ages (say 12–18). The younger children will have lower levels of verbal skills and will also still be more dependent on their families. So the only reason that the correlation appears might be that the participants in the study differ widely with respect to age. If the researcher had tested a narrower age group (or somehow corrected statistically for the effects of age, using techniques such as partial correlation, path analysis or structural equation modelling), then they might well find that in reality there is zero correlation between social independence and verbal ability.

It is very, very easy to fool yourself (and others) when relating scores on one test to scores on other tests – either through correlations or more complex statistical techniques. When interpreting the results from studies which involve correlating different questionnaires, one needs to be alert for problems such as these.

In the previous example, it was quite straightforward to identify that there may be a problem. The "Method" section of a journal article will report the age range of the participants, and an alert reader could realise that there might be an alternative (and simpler) explanation for the results. However, sometimes there is little or no evidence that something is amiss because the variable which influences scores on both tests is psychological, rather than physical. Suppose that a researcher examines the correlation between scores on a test measuring how highly people rate their own sense of humour, and scores on a test measuring their scores on a personality trait known as Psychoticism – which basically involves enjoying hurting others, being indifferent to others' feelings etc. Suppose too that there is a significant correlation; people high on Psychoticism may tend to be humourless. What can one make of this?

The problem here might be that some people in the sample may try to give a good impression of themselves, whereas others will not (this is discussed in Chapter 8). This former group will probably report having an excellent sense of humour and also will claim not to have violent fantasies, hallucinations, enjoy teasing animals etc. and so will have low scores on the Psychoticism scale. A person's tendency to give socially desirable answers may very well affect the way they respond to the items on both of these scales. So it *might* be the case that the correlation between sense of humour and Psychoticism is found only because both are influenced by social desirability. If (as is likely) the researcher has not chosen to measure social desirability as part of the study, there is little chance that this problem will ever be detected.

My point is that many personality psychologists and social psychologists build up ever more complex models, using ever more complex statistical tools, but without always being alert to the possibility that they are building these theories on a foundation of straw. For this reason, I advocate studies which relate scores on a questionnaire to some aspect of behaviour rather than to scores on other questionnaires.

There is yet another issue which is widespread in the social psychology literature when researchers correlate (or perform more fancy analyses) on several scales. What if two scales contain items that are very similar? The Rosenberg self-esteem scale (Rosenberg, 1965) is a very widely used test in social psychology. So too are the Harter scales (Harter, 1988). One of the 10 items from the Rosenberg scale reads "On the whole, I am satisfied with myself", and respondents are asked to rate how much they agree with that statement. One of the five items in the global self-worth section of the Harter scale (adolescent form) is "[some] teenagers are pretty pleased with themselves"; respondents are asked to rate how true that statement is for them.

As far as I can see, these items essentially ask the same question. How could someone who agreed with the question from the Rosenberg scale possibly disagree with the question from the Harter scale? Yet they are supposed to measure quite different things, and several researchers blindly correlate the scales together and interpret the correlation as if it measured something interesting. One does not need to be a psychometrician to appreciate that this is patent nonsense. If the same item appears in two different questionnaires, then this will almost certainly result in the two scales being correlated (assuming that the two scales have high *reliability*, a term which will be discussed in Chapter 7).

This is a real problem which frequently escapes the notice of journal editors and reviewers. At the time of writing, 20+ studies have examined the correlations between the Harter and Rosenberg scales, and these have been cited over 470 times in total. There are 470 published papers that have cited a finding which is fundamentally misleading because their authors lack an understanding of basic psychometric principles. There are plenty of other examples, too. Scales measuring depression also contain items that are very similar to the two mentioned previously (the 10-item Beck Depression Inventory contains the item "I do not feel like a failure", for example) – and so any research linking scores on *this* questionnaire to the Rosenberg and Harter scales must surely also be flawed. There are 244 papers that mention the Beck and the Harter and/or Rosenberg scales, and just one of these has been cited over 200 times.

The literature is full of studies using other scales where scores on questionnaires are correlated and interpreted without considering what items are asked. More surprisingly still this problem is little recognised. It is time to shout that the emperor wears no clothes!

But how big an issue is item overlap in practice? If one has two tests which measure quite different things (that is, should correlate 0.0), how large does the correlation between them become if they share one or more items? Now might be as good a time as any to introduce a spreadsheet to help explore what sort of effect having one (or more) items in common can have on the correlation between two tests.

Spreadsheet name: Spreadsheet 1.1: Correlations caused by shared items

Download from: routledge.com/9781032146164

Purpose: To explore how large the correlation between two tests can become if they contain one or more items with identical meanings.

Contents of spreadsheet: Simulated data from 110 people, with a normal distribution of scores on two uncorrelated scales.

Suggested activity:

- Decide how many "items" there should be in test 1 and test 2, and enter these values in the green cells. These numbers should be 20 or fewer.
- Check that the total score, shown to the right of each blue area, is calculated correctly.
- Set the number of shared items to zero.

- The yellow box shows the correlation between the total scores on test 1 and test 2, based on 110 simulated people.
- To generate a new set of simulated data, press F9 (Windows or Linux) or Fn + F9 or Ctrl + Shift + F9 (MacOS). Repeat 10 or so times, and note the typical value for the correlation.
- Change the number of shared items – e.g., to 1 or 2. Generate another 10–20 or so sets of random data, and note the correlation.
- Explore how changing the length of the tests influences the size of the correlation between two tests which share 1 or more items.
- How large would the correlation between two tests (one containing 5 items, the other 10 items) typically be if they have one item in common?

Points to note:

- In all spreadsheets in this book, experiment by changing entries in the *green* areas. Results are in the *yellow* areas.
- Simply download another copy if you accidentally change formulae.
- The simulated data representing these items appears in the blue shaded areas.
- The spreadsheet always generates data from 110 "people".
- Correlations which are less than −0.19 or greater than 0.19 are statistically significant ($p < 0.05$).
- The spreadsheets are not sophisticated or user-proof. For example, strange things will happen if the number of shared items is set to be larger than the number of items in a test.
- Readers who are familiar with the concept of "reliability" may wish to experiment by changing the value of this parameter. Otherwise it is safe to leave it at the default value of 0.7.
- Readers who want to explore how the spreadsheet operates should click the "calculations" tab at the bottom of the spreadsheet.

Learning outcomes: Readers should now be able to:

- Appreciate how scales which share items can appear to be spuriously correlated.
- Recognise that the problem can be very severe with short scales or several overlapping items.

PSYCHOMETRICIANS

The fourth group of people with an interest in testing are not psychology practitioners or researchers at all. Theoretical psychometricians typically have one or more mathematics or statistics degrees and will be keen on developing new methods of analysing data. Their work fills journals such as *Psychometrika* and *Applied Psychological*

Measurement and will be of interest to those who want to start programming or exploring cutting-edge techniques. Although the psychometrics literature up until the 1990s was often fairly accessible to those without mathematics degrees, readers without a strong mathematical background are likely to find modern contributions challenging, if not incomprehensible.

This book does not set out to be a detailed, up-to-the-minute account of sophisticated techniques for constructing, developing, administering, scoring or evaluating tests. But whilst it covers the old, simple, tried and tested methodology which has a proven track record in helping practitioners and researchers measure abilities, personality, mood and so on, it also serves as an introduction to newer developments which seem to me to be important – such as alternatives to "coefficient alpha" for measuring reliability, Mokken scaling, network analysis and item response theory. However, this is not a book on the formal, mathematical basis of psychometric theory. Although this underpins much of the content and spreadsheets, statistical formulae are kept to a bare minimum.

It also deals with topics (such as how to write good test items, and how to use test scores in practice) which psychometricians generally eschew. Whilst it is all very well developing wonderful new ways of analysing responses to test items, if the raw data are meaningless because of poorly written items, or if the data from questionnaires are simply inappropriate for this type of analysis, the whole thing is rather pointless. This book will, however, give psychologists and others a basic understanding of the main issues in psychological assessment which will allow the more mathematically sophisticated reader to explore modern developments in psychometric theory.

THOSE SEEKING SELF-KNOWLEDGE

The final group of test users will probably not read this book, though I mention them for the sake of completeness. Many books, newspapers, magazines and websites contain personality tests, quizzes and tests, and whilst some of these are obviously frivolous ("Which type of dog do you most resemble?") others claim to assess personality, intelligence and so on. Whilst some such tests are properly constructed and may give accurate results when taken under appropriate conditions (e.g., Eysenck & Wilson, 1976), the technical details which allow most such tests to be evaluated are simply not available, and so they should be treated with extreme caution. Online intelligence (IQ) tests are a particular problem, as large random samples of the population need to be tested in order to interpret the scores – and it is difficult to see how a free-to-use online site could possibly gather such data. We did so when developing the BBC's "Test the Nation" IQ tests, but that was a long, expensive process using a market-research agency to find and test a large random sample of the population in advance of the television show.

Unless the provenance of a test is well known, it is best to be very sceptical of claims such as "this pop star has an IQ of 180" for reasons which will be explained in Chapter 5, and to be wary of tests which claim to analyse personality through investigating which colours you prefer, your name or suchlike. Are these tests properly designed, and so potentially capable of giving some accurate insights? Or are they written by a journalist without any proper development at all – which begs the question of why we bother taking them. It is possible that these assessments could actually prove harmful; if a vulnerable person or a child were to take one of these tests and feel upset about their results or be teased by others, the consequences could be tragic.

PSYCHOLOGY AND PSYCHOMETRICS

All decent tests should be linked to some kind of theory of individual differences in psychology, biology, developmental psychology, neuroscience, sociology or some other area. The researcher who studies state-dependent memory (whether recall is easier if the person is in the same mood state that they were when they learned the material) needs to know what the main mood states are before they can try to measure them. They also need to know what type of memory process they should measure. For this, it is necessary to turn to previous research; just devising a test off the top of one's head is unlikely to be well received by one's peers or by journal editors. Likewise, if we want to measure a child's cognitive performance to help us decide if they are dyslexic, we need to know how many distinct cognitive abilities there are, and which patterns of cognitive abilities reflect dyslexia in order to draw any valid conclusions about the child.

There is a two-way relationship between psychological theory and psychometrics. Sometimes psychological concepts arise from speculation, personal experience, clinical observation or some other process which is not based on the careful analyses of data. The now-popular notion of emotional intelligence originated from a "theoretical and philosophical framework" developed in Wayne Payne's PhD thesis, rather than hard data. Likewise, Howard Gardner's model of multiple intelligences is based on a literature review which sought to identify groups of cognitive skills which appeared to resemble each other in terms of their developmental history, all being affected by damage to a particular area of the brain, and so on. And there are numerous theories of personality which have their roots in clinical observation rather than any statistical analysis; Carl Jung's "analytical psychology" (a form of psychoanalysis) led him to suppose that people can be classified as introverts or extraverts, for example. Whilst psychometrics did not help to develop these theories, it can be used to devise measurement instruments. For example, the techniques outlined in this book have been used to develop questionnaires to measure emotional intelligence, verbal and non-verbal intelligence, depression, extraversion, anxiety and a huge range of other important characteristics.

Can we perform the same trick backwards? Can we use psychometric techniques to analyse a wide range of behaviours, and develop a theory from this? The answer is "perhaps". Some psychometric techniques (notably factor analysis) have been used to develop theories about personality and mental abilities. For example, the analysis of the relationships between various tests have led Spearman, Thurstone, Cattell and Horn, and Carroll (amongst others) to develop theories about the number and nature of human cognitive abilities and personality.

Few psychologists claim that psychometric analyses alone are enough to develop a "model" of human behaviour. Take general intelligence as an example. It has been known for over a century that performance on all tasks which involve thought tend to correlate together positively, even if they seem to involve quite different cognitive processes. Why *is* it that people who have above-average short-term memory (for example) are also generally better than average at visualising shapes, coming up with creative solutions to problems, solving puzzles requiring logic, and identifying whether two briefly presented shapes are the same or different? Psychometric analysis tells us that this is the case; it does not give us any understanding of why this happens, and this is what is needed for any proper science of psychology. In much the same way that psychologists discovered general intelligence, our prehistoric ancestors living away from the equator no doubt noticed that at some times of the year days seemed longer than others, which coincided with warmer weather etc. However, they did not have any understanding of why this happened; for this they had to wait for Copernicus and Kepler.

In order to gain a proper scientific understanding of the variables identified by psychometric techniques it is often necessary to perform laboratory studies to try to build up a picture of what social, developmental, genetic, cognitive and physiological processes cause people to behave in this way. The only exception is when questionnaires and tests can be developed to measure "low-level" building blocks; for example, it has been claimed that questionnaires can measure behavioural inhibition, approach/avoidance behaviour etc. (Corr, 2008). But in general, using psychometric techniques really is just the very first step in understanding what is going on. Psychometric analyses can help psychologists identify that something interesting is there which merits study; they are unlikely to be able to show what causes it.

Although there is considerable interplay between psychometrics and theories of cognitive ability, personality, mood and motivation, this book does not attempt to cover these theories; it is not a textbook on individual differences, though some readers might wish to read it alongside books such as Cooper (2015; 2021), which do explore such issues. Nor is it necessary to know anything about psychological theory in order to grasp the principles laid out in this book, for although I will occasionally refer to some characteristic such as "anxiety", "depression" or "intelligence" when giving examples of how a psychometric technique might be used, the examples I use are those with which every reader of this book is likely to be familiar. Thus readers from disciplines other than psychology should find few problems following the principles laid out in the following chapters.

WHAT DO TESTS MEASURE?

Tests have been developed to measure a wide range of variables, from aesthetic taste to pain sensitivity, attitudes, personality, cognitive abilities, interpersonal skills, emotional sensitivity – the list is almost endless. Fortunately, it is possible to categorise them and to use similar techniques to develop and evaluate them.

TRAITS

The **trait** is an important concept in psychology. A trait is simply a disposition – a characteristic which is fairly stable over time, and fairly stable from situation to situation. For example, it has been found through research that some people are more anxious than others. If we took 20 people in the same situation (e.g., having coffee with friends) and ranked them in order of anxiety from 1 (least anxious) to 20 (most anxious), the idea of a trait suggests that if we were to go back and test these people in a few weeks or a few years later, the person ranked 20th should still have a ranking of 20 (or nearby); they certainly should not be ranked 1 or 2. Note that this does *not* imply that situations do not affect how a person acts or feels. When put in a stressful situation, everyone's level of anxiety will rise; when relaxing at home, everyone's anxiety levels will fall. But what the idea of a trait does imply is that within each situation, the rank-ordering of people will stay roughly constant.

There are two types of traits. **Personality traits**, such as anxiety, refer to the manner in which people behave; their personal style, if you like. Thus someone with high anxiety is likely to sweat more than someone with low anxiety, to talk faster, to be more wary of snakes, spiders etc., and generally to be more alert to signs of danger in the environment. Personality traits describe the way in which a person behaves, not the level of performance which they can achieve; asking if a person "is good at anxiety" makes no sense.

Ability traits instead reflect level of performance on unfamiliar tasks, or those which have not involved training. Solving an anagram or reading the emotion in a stranger's face would be abilities. Psychologists are usually interested in *cognitive* abilities, and so focus on abilities which require thinking for their successful performance. The key thing about all ability traits is that the quality of performance can be assessed, in principle, at any rate. It should be possible to determine how quickly people can solve anagrams, or how accurately they can recognise which emotions a person is experiencing from studying a video of their face. Asking if a person "is good at solving anagrams" is a perfectly sensible question.

Questionnaires and tests which measure personality traits and abilities are all constructed quite similarly. However, there is one important point to bear in mind. Abilities are usually measured through assessing behaviour. Questions are administered which are answered correctly or incorrectly. It is only possible to obtain a high score on such a test if one has a high level of the ability (or if one cheats!). Personality tests, and the ability tests used by Howard Gardner and his followers (Armstrong, 1994; Shearer, 2007) rely on **self-report**. Typical items would be "I panic easily" (which measures neuroticism), "I am skilled at handling social situations" (extraversion), "I can easily remember a tune I have heard once" (musical intelligence) and so on. Participants are usually asked to rate themselves or are rated by parents, friends, teachers etc. by choosing a phrase such as "very true of me" or "somewhat true of me" for each item in the test. There are obvious problems with this approach. People may simply lie. They may want to portray themself (or the person whom they are rating) in a particular way. They may make erroneous judgements; a colleague of mine was quite alone in thinking that they were musically gifted! Or they may be confused about how the **rating scale** works; does everyone apply the same criterion when deciding that a statement is "somewhat true", for example? What do "usually" and "often" mean? All of these issues are well known but pose a mighty problem for rating scales. This might be part of the reason that ability tests tend to have rather stronger links to behaviour than personality tests, or ability tests based on rating scales.

ATTAINMENTS

It is also possible to measure **attainments**. Unlike ability traits or personality traits, attainment tests measure performance in one particular area and are not expected to generalise to other areas. They are usually used to measure some fairly narrow skill, competency or knowledge following a course of instruction or training. For example, they may be used to measure an electrician's knowledge of safety codes, or their ability to turn an architect's schematic drawing into a safe installation. However, it is impossible to generalise this knowledge; our electrician's performance does not allow us to predict how much they are likely to know about plumbing, jazz or gardening. A child who performs well on a test of French vocabulary may or may not perform well in other areas. It all depends on what they have been taught, their motivation to study the subject, their ability to learn and recall information, the amount of time they have spent revising and so on. Attainments are influenced by knowledge, experience and training, as well as by abilities, personality, moods and motivation. A person's performance on an attainment task is therefore a mixture of several different things – which is why psychologists tend not to focus on them, though they are clearly of considerable practical use.

STATES

Unlike traits, **states** are short-lived and vary over time; they may also depend greatly on life events, thoughts or physiological effects. For example, I may experience great fear if a driver nearly kills me when driving on the highway; a few minutes later my fear will have returned to its normal (trait) level, and in a few hours I will probably have forgotten about the whole event. I am writing this late in the afternoon and I feel hungry (a state) and so will need to prepare dinner sooner rather than later; after dinner I will have no interest in food for a few hours. Thus states may be altered by external and/or internal (physiological states) events; cognitions may also be important in determining motivation (e.g., the realisation that you are not providing for your family, which may incentivise you to earn more).

As you will have gathered from these examples, psychologists normally identify two types of states: **mood states** (or emotion states) and **motivational states**. One might expect a person's average state to correspond to their level of a trait, as proposed by Cattell (1973) – and indeed it does (Hepburn & Eysenck, 1989).

There are several ways of measuring states. Most psychologists simply use self-report questionnaires; items measuring traits ask "How do you usually behave [or feel]?" or "How well does this phrase describe you?" However, scales measuring moods instead ask people to reflect on how they feel "right now" (in which case, being asked to answer these silly questions will have altered their mood state) or at some other time, such as when they arrived at work this morning (in which case, their memory might be faulty). Readers may detect a certain cynicism here. But regardless of the questions asked, it is necessary to ensure that items such as these really do measure states (and not traits), as discussed in Chapter 12.

ATTITUDES

Attitude measurement has a long history in psychology. It is possible to assess **attitudes** by behavioural techniques; for example, counting the number of times a person nods or shakes their head when listening to a statement which might be taken as a measure of their strength of feeling – positive or negative – towards the topic. Physiological measures might also be used, as when measuring a paedophile's degree of pupil dilation when viewing images of young children.

It is also possible to measure attitudes by indirect methods. For example, if a reasoned argument produces a conclusion with which a person disagrees, they are likely to be more critical and more aware of the assumptions made and flaws of logic than if they agree with the conclusion. If we were to ask people whether they agreed with the conclusion reached here:

People who are smart succeed in life.

People who are smart do not need to work hard.

Therefore, if people want to succeed in life, they do not need to work hard.

those who do not have a particularly positive attitude to work might be more likely to agree with the conclusion than someone who believes that hard work produces results.

There are other indirect methods too: people tend to like others who share similar attitudes, so one approach to measuring someone's attitudes would be to present them with descriptions of several people and ask them which person they would like to meet. There are also several tasks which use reaction times to assess attitudes (e.g., Roddy et al., 2010).

However, the easiest way to measure attitudes is via rating scales – and as these are similar to personality scales (presenting several statements and asking participants to choose the one which best describes how they feel) and suffer from the same problems, such as social desirability effects, much of what is said about personality tests in the following chapters also applies to the assessment of attitudes.

ASSUMPTIONS MADE WHEN MEASURING TRAITS OR STATES

Unfortunately, it is all too easy to overlook the sorts of assumptions which are being made when using or devising a test or questionnaire.

ASSUMPTION 1: THE CHARACTERISTIC EXISTS

Psychiatrists once used terms such as "degree of Oedipal fixation" to differentiate between people, but most would now agree that this is meaningless. It is all too easy to invent a term which we *think* describes an important way in which people differ, but which has little or no basis in reality. It is also very easy for psychologists and others to construct tests which do not measure what they expect. The Repression-Sensitisation Scale developed by Byrne (1961) supposedly measures how people deal with threat – repressors avoid or deny it, whilst sensitisers are alert to signs of danger, which they confront. This all sounded perfectly plausible, reputations were formed and the scale was widely used until it was discovered that scores on this scale correlated over 0.9 with anxiety – showing that repression-sensitisation was not a new concept at all (Slough et al., 1984). We return to issues such as this in Chapter 9 when discussing the validity of tests.

ASSUMPTION 2: SITUATIONS, NOT PERSONALITY, ABILITY ETC. MIGHT DETERMINE HOW PEOPLE BEHAVE

It obviously makes no sense to categorise people as anxious versus relaxed (for example) without considering the **situation** in which anxiety is measured. In some settings – such as just before an examination or sitting in a dentist's waiting room – almost everyone will feel anxious, whilst very few people would feel anxious whilst meditating or taking a long, hot bath. Sternberg has taken much the same view with regard to intelligence; he points out that children may be able to solve problems in situations where the outcomes matter to them yet may perform dismally when exactly the same problem is presented in a different context in school (Sternberg, 2004).

This has led some social psychologists such as Mischel (1968) to suggest that situations determine how people behave; we may be fooling ourselves entirely whenever we think that people behave consistently. Traits may not exist, and so we should not bother trying to measure them. However, three types of evidence seem to suggest that this argument is not entirely correct. First, if traits do not exist, scores on questionnaires and tests measuring them could not predict how people behave, yet authors such as Roberts and Yoon (2022) and Schmidt and Hunter (2004) show that scores on tests measuring traits can predict many real-life behaviours. Second, scores on traits measured by questionnaires correlate (sometimes substantially) with biological markers. For example, traits such as general intelligence are highly heritable, indicating that they reflect individual differences in people's biological make-up. This simply could not be true if the test scores were substantially influenced by situational factors. Third, studies such as Conley (1984) and Deary et al. (2000) show that scores on questionnaires and tests are extremely consistent over time, which is unlikely to be the case if responses were situationally determined.

ASSUMPTION 3: TEST SCORES ALLOW US TO MEASURE TRAITS OR STATES

What do we mean by "measurement"? And just because we generate numbers by calculating people's scores on tests, can we then be confident that we have measured their behaviour? This potentially damning problem has been raised by several philosophers of science (Maraun, 1998; Michell, 1997) who point out that the numbers which arise from scoring psychological tests are very different from the numbers which arise from physical (or other proper scientific) measurements and cannot be presumed to behave in the same way or be suitable for the same statistical analyses. Psychological characteristics simply may not be quantifiable – or at least there may be no *evidence* that they are quantifiable. We can *count* the number of problems which people solve correctly when taking an ability test, or add together people's self-ratings, but this may not be measurement as such. The usual statistical methods may therefore be inappropriate. We return to this important issue in Chapter 3, but note that most psychologists simply ignore it.

SUMMARY

This chapter outlined the aims and objectives of this book and made the point that psychological tests and assessments are very widely used by practitioners: for example, in clinical, forensic, health and sport psychology; by researchers in areas other than cognitive psychology who need to relate behaviour to some form of psychological measure; and by individual difference and social psychologists who explore the relationships between the scores which people obtain on two or more psychological tests. It is argued that this last form of research is difficult and problematical, and it is demonstrated that several commonly used tests may share the same item or may be influenced by the same response style (such as portraying oneself in a good light). This can create huge problems for the interpretation of such analyses. The chapter also introduced a spreadsheet so that readers can explore the effect of overlapping items on the correlation between tests of various lengths.

The chapter then mentioned the interplay between psychological assessment/psychometrics and psychological theory, noting that it can work two ways. Tests can be constructed to measure characteristics which have been identified through medical research etc. In addition, psychometric analyses of behaviour can show how we might usefully describe the way in which people behave, feel and act – but not why they do so. To gain a proper scientific understanding of this will probably require laboratory studies.

The chapter introduced two important concepts: traits, which are rather stable aspects of personality or ability; and mood and motivational states, which are short-lived and often influenced by internal events (e.g., physiological changes, thoughts) or the environment. The concept of attitude is also briefly introduced.

Finally, we considered some rather fundamental assumptions made whenever attempting to use any scale to measure anything. One of these suggests that assigning numbers to people's responses to test items involves counting, not measurement as such.

CHAPTER 2
TESTS, SCALES AND TESTING

So far, we have used terms like "test", "scale", "questionnaire" and "item" without really specifying what they mean. This chapter will clarify these terms, outline the general logic of testing, and give some general information about the principles of testing and test administration together with some practical guidance about how to locate tests and scales.

TESTS AND SCALES

For historical reasons, a set of items measuring a cognitive ability or knowledge is usually called a **test**. We might talk about a test of short-term memory, or vocabulary. It is usual to refer to a collection of items measuring a single personality trait, or a mood or motivational state, as a **scale**. We thus speak of a scale measuring extraversion, positive affect or drive to succeed.

A **questionnaire** consists of one or more scales. For example, the NEO-PI(R) is a widely used personality questionnaire which bundles five different personality scales. However, there is nothing hard and fast about these definitions; you will sometimes read of a "personality test", for example.

> EXERCISE
>
> Before reading the rest of this chapter, you will find it useful to assess your own personality by using a reputable questionnaire such as https://hexaco.org/hexaco-online, and you might also like to assess your cognitive abilities using one or more of the sample tests at https://icar-project.com/ (free registration required). As you are reading this book, it is probable that you will use tests similar to these at some stage of your studies or career, and so it is good to understand what your participants will experience; it will also help you understand the issues discussed in this chapter and the next.
>
> To see what the scales mean, click on the "scale descriptions" button on the home page. To interpret your **HEXACO** score, look at your own score on the honesty-humility, emotionality, extraversion, agreeableness and conscientiousness scales. (You can safely ignore the other rows.) The final column of the output shows the

DOI: 10.4324/9781003240181-2

> "normal range" for each of these traits; if your score is higher or lower than this range then this is significant. For example, if your score on openness to experience is 4.5 and the range in the final column is 2.5 to 4.13, you are more open to new experiences than most people.

WHAT IS A PSYCHOMETRIC ASSESSMENT?

The term **psychometric assessment** strikes terror into the heart of many job applicants who, like so many others, think that tests offer some deep insights into the soul which cannot be obtained by any other means. Reality is very different. A questionnaire or test of any sort is simply a standardised way of gathering information about a person. By **standardised** we mean that any person, anywhere in the world, has exactly the same experience – no matter who administers the test or questionnaire, or when, or where it is administered. *Everything* should be standardised: the instructions, the environment (as far as possible), the amount of time given to answer the items, the size and brightness of items on the screen or test booklet, the wording of the items, the way that answers are recorded etc. This is because altering any of these may affect the test's accuracy.

Each test also comes with instructions for scoring it in a standardised method, which in practice usually means turning the responses which the participant makes into some type of numerical scores. These scores can be compared with the scores obtained by other persons, correlated with other variables (such as electrical activity in some part of the brain), or correlated with other scores from scales or tests. It turns out that the rationale for scoring tests is more complex than it may seem, and so this will be considered in Chapter 4; the present chapter provides a general introduction to test items and testing procedures.

TESTS AS SAMPLES OF ITEMS

Let us start off with a very simple example. Suppose that a teacher wants to measure how many historical dates her pupils can remember, after a year of instruction. The pupils have been given a book containing 400 dates and should have memorised them all. (I sincerely hope that history is no longer taught like this – but this example is easy to visualise.) The range of possible items which could be measured is called the **domain** – an important term in psychometrics. The teacher wants to test their knowledge of this domain of 400 items. How should she do so?

One approach would be to prepare a test in which students were tested on all 400 of the dates which were mentioned in the book, using items such as "What year did . . . happen?" In theory, this is both the simplest and best approach: it allows the extent of each child's knowledge of dates on the day of the test to be determined exactly. There is no estimation involved: their score on all of the items in the domain (all the items which could possibly have been asked) is their **true score**. This is another important term to bear in mind.

But testing all 400 items would take a long time and be tedious for everyone involved. It would also probably be necessary to split the testing over several occasions to prevent the children becoming bored or fatigued, and hence answering carelessly towards the end of the test. In practice, it might be better to measure performance on a smaller number of questions and hope that the children's scores on the short test will give a good estimate of how they would have performed on the 400-item test.

How then should the teacher sample items from the textbook? What she should most certainly *not* do is select the items from the same part of the book: if all of the items were selected from the very last pages, this would underestimate the ability of those children who had not quite read the entire book but who knew the earlier pages well. Likewise, taking all the questions from the first pages would not be a good idea, as this would overestimate the scores of students who never read any further! Selecting the items on one topic would not be a good idea either, as some children may be interested in (say) medieval history but nothing earlier and nothing later. If the test were to consist of items which covered the medieval period only, then these children's knowledge would be overestimated. Conversely if the teacher asked *no* questions from this period, then the ability of these children would be underestimated.

The best approach is therefore to draw a proper random or stratified sample of items (without replacement, so that each item appears only once) from the book – for example, drawing one date at random from each page of the textbook. This will ensure that the items which are to be given to the children are representative of all 400 items in the domain: they will not all be on the same topic, or from the same part of the textbook, and so they should give an unbiased estimate of each child's knowledge.

I have used the example of a history test because it is easy to specify what the domain of knowledge is, and because it is easy to visualise how the teacher might select items from the domain. Other types of items (those measuring personality, mood, motivation, cognitive abilities etc.) are much more common, and these will be introduced later in this chapter. The key thing to remember is that all items which form a scale or test are assumed to represent some domain of interest. This domain can sometimes be very narrow, for example, all of the single-digit addition problems. Or it can be extremely broad in nature; for example, the domain of all types of puzzles which require thought for their successful solution. These might include anagrams, identifying which shape might come next in a series, visualising what an object would look like from another position, assembling a jigsaw within a particular time limit – the list of possible puzzles is almost endless. In the field of personality the domain might include all items that could possibly be written to assess anxiety. In these examples the number of potential items is so large as to be almost infinite, and there is no obvious way of drawing a random sample of them, as was the case with the history textbook. However, the principle that a test or questionnaire represents a selection of items from a domain turns out to be surprisingly useful, as discussed in Chapter 7 and in what follows.

THE ORDER OF ITEMS

When putting together a personality questionnaire to measure several different traits, it is usual to mix up the order of the items. A personality questionnaire may set out to measure extraversion, neuroticism, openness to experience, conscientiousness and agreeableness. These are five different scales, each containing several items which are scored separately, yielding scores on the five traits. If a person was presented with all of the extraversion items first ("Do you like lively parties?", "Do you make friends easily?", "Can you easily persuade other people to do what you want?" etc.) followed by a block of neuroticism items ("Do you worry a lot?", "Do you sometimes feel unhappy for no obvious reason?", "Are you afraid of any harmless animals, such as birds or moths?" etc.), some people taking the test will probably realise what it is intended to measure. If they say that they like lively parties, they may then feel that they *have* to agree with the next two items (which also measure extraversion) just to appear consistent. For this reason, tests which consist of several different scales usually have the items presented in a random order. In the earlier example, a neuroticism item might be followed by an extraversion item, then a conscientiousness item, an openness item, perhaps another conscientiousness item, an agreeableness item and so on. This makes it harder for participants to guess what the items measure and how they form scales.

There is some empirical evidence that randomising the order of items makes questionnaires more accurate (Franke, 1997), although the literature is inconsistent, as some researchers (e.g., Schell & Oswald, 2013) find that the ordering of items does not much influence the structure of personality questionnaires. However, there seems to be no reason *not* to randomise the order of items, and to ensure that "carry over" effects from one item to the next are the same for each person, it might be wise to use the same randomised order for everyone.

Ability tests are treated differently. Although there are exceptions such as the AH-series (Heim et al., 1970) tests that measure more than one ability usually present blocks of similar items – for example, 20 items measuring short-term memory, 20 items measuring visualisation and so on. The reason is simple: different types of items usually require different instructions to make sure that the participant knows what they are being asked to do. These are often followed by **practice items** (items which the participant completes and is then told the correct answer). It is thus necessary to present blocks of similar items, as each block will require different instructions.

TESTS, SCALES AND TESTING

Within each block items are usually ordered in terms of difficulty (as determined by giving the items to a sample of people in a **pilot study**), with the easiest items coming first. Encountering an easy item at the start of the test will show participants that they have understood what to do and give them confidence that they can solve the problems. If the items were randomly ordered in terms of difficulty, a low-ability participant might give up if they could not solve the first few items. Finally, as the items measure *performance* rather than an opinion, it does not really matter if participants know what the items measure. A person's score on a test of short-term memory is unlikely to change much whether they are told in advance what the test measures, whereas a person's score on a scale measuring self-centredness might well change, as some people might try to project an image of themselves instead of answering the items honestly.

SINGLE-ITEM TESTS

It is possible, though unusual, to measure personality, attainment, ability, mood or any other characteristic using a **single-item test**. For example, see Table 2.1.

The first problem with doing so is that by using a single question, it is possible that momentary loss of attention, problems understanding the meaning of some of the words in the question, or some other transient problem may affect the way in which a person responds to that single question. Suppose that a respondent has a completely unrealistic view of how depressed other people are: they may feel that everyone else in the world is completely happy and they alone feel miserable. Or they might take offence and choose not to label themselves as "depressed" even though they probably are. Either or both of these will distort the way in which this person responds to the single item. At least asking multiple questions may avoid the problem of momentary lapsed attention (it is unlikely that a person will be distracted or take issue with the wording of *all* questions, and averaging the scores on several questions should therefore produce more accurate estimates of a person's level of the trait). Thus it seems likely that multi-item scales might lead to more accurate assessments than single-item measures. That said, several psychologists propose using single items to measure traits (e.g., Konstabel et al., 2012), particularly when administration time is short.

There is another reason for avoiding single-item tests, too. We have seen that psychologists often measure quite broad traits such as depression. Psychiatrists

Table 2.1 A single-item test measuring depression

| How depressed are you? | Extremely | Quite | Average | Not very | Not at all |

recognise several signs that a person may be depressed; the *Diagnostic and Statistical Manual* (American Psychiatric Association, 2022) shows that sleep disturbance, lack of interest in previously enjoyed activity, weight change, indecisiveness and several other behaviours can all indicate depression. If a trait such as this has several different symptoms, or facets, then asking just one question ("How depressed are you?", for example) ignores all the other pieces of evidence which may point to depression. It is quite possible that a person may not wish to admit to feeling depressed but might freely say that they had sleep problems, weight fluctuations etc. By measuring the whole range of indicators, the scale is much more likely to give an accurate measurement of a person's level of depression.

Third, when a multi-item scale is administered, it is possible to test whether or not all of the items measure the same characteristic within a sample of people. It will show whether respondents answer items at random, for example, as doing so will reduce the correlations between items. It might be worthwhile knowing this if a questionnaire is included towards the end of a long session (fatigue), if participants are completing an experiment for money or course credit (low motivation to answer honestly), or if a questionnaire is likely to be used in a setting where participants might be tempted to give socially desirable answers, such as when applying for a job.

Fourth, the more items in a scale, the larger the range of potential scores. This is perhaps most obvious in the case of ability items: a single ability item can yield a score of 0 or 1 (incorrectly or correctly answered), which is not particularly useful for making fine distinctions between people; increasing the number of items to 20 and working out each person's total score obviously gives a range of possible scores between 0 and 20. Thus a scale made up of many items has the potential to draw finer distinctions between people than do short scales, or those which are scored as correct/incorrect.

There is a lively literature about personality assessment using single items. Single-item tests work best when the scale is so narrow in content that it merely consists of several paraphrases of the same item. As Robins et al. (2001) observe, "In our experience, even when the . . . items are interspersed with items from other scales, participants frequently write comments such as, 'I have already answered this question!'". So perhaps it is not surprising that if the domain of items is extremely narrow, asking a question once is almost as effective as asking (almost) the same question 10 times! Thus single-item scales may be useful when measuring something as narrow in scope as self-esteem or happiness. On the other hand, measuring broader traits such as extraversion using single items seems to be less effective (Gosling et al., 2003), as might perhaps be expected. Although it may sometimes be expedient to try to measure a trait using just one item, this cannot really be recommended – largely because it is impossible to tell how accurately that item measures the trait, other than by measuring the consistency of scores over time, as discussed in Chapter 7.

THE IMPORTANCE OF UNIDIMENSIONAL SCALES

A scale consists of group of items whose scores are combined. It should be obvious that all of the items which form a scale should measure the same trait or state; for example, a scale measuring depression could usefully consist of an item measuring low mood, another about weight changes, another about sleeping patterns and so on, as all of these are known indicators of depression.

In Table 2.2 the answers indicating depression are shaded; they would not be in a real questionnaire, of course. So if each "depressed" answer is awarded 1 point, and the other answer 0 points, it is obvious that each person's score on this scale must be between 0 and 4, with a larger score indicating a greater level of depression.

However, this approach only makes sense if we somehow know that all of these items measure the same thing – that they are all indicators of depression, in other words. The term for this is that they are **unidimensional**: they measure a single dimension of personality or ability. In the case of depression this is easy because the clinical symptoms are well-documented. It would be much less obvious if someone wanted to measure creativity. Is the ability to think of novel uses for objects (for example, "What useful object could you make from two pencils, a rubber band and some paper?") related to the ease with which people can think of new ideas ("How many different uses can you think of for a brick?"), for example? Should ability to write a poem be included? Or inventing a novel game involving playing cards? It is important to know this, because it would make little sense to put items together in the same scale if they measured different things.

Suppose that we add another four items to the depression scale – items that measure extraversion (how sociable and outgoing someone is) versus introversion, with these items being scored so that a high score indicates extraversion. It should be obvious that someone who scores 8/8 on this scale must be both depressed and extraverted: someone who scores 0/8 likewise has to be an introvert who is low on depression.

Table 2.2 Four items measuring depression

1	Do you often feel "down" for no good reason?	Yes	No
2	Do you sleep well?	Yes	No
3	Has your weight gone up or down by more than 5 kg in the last 6 months?	Yes	No
4	Do you have much energy?	Yes	No

But what of someone who scores 4/8? They could be depressed and introverted. Or not depressed and extraverted. Or have moderate degrees of both introversion and depression. These are clearly very different people, yet they would all obtain the same score (4) on the questionnaire, which makes little sense. It is for this reason that psychologists and others take great care to ensure that the items which form scales all measure the same thing, generally using a technique known as **factor analysis** (discussed in Chapters 10–13) for this purpose. Factor analysis would reveal that items 1–4 measure one trait, whilst items 5–8 measure something completely different. This would indicate that the eight-item questionnaire consists of two scales, which need to be scored and interpreted separately.

HOW LONG SHOULD A SCALE BE?

The fun starts when we try to ascertain how many items are needed in a scale. We earlier discussed a hypothetical test where the domain consisted of 400 historical dates which needed to be remembered. When constructing a test to measure knowledge of dates, would 100 items give a good enough approximation to people's true scores? Perhaps 50 items might suffice? Or even 10? It is probably intuitively obvious that long scales are likely to be more accurate than short ones. For example, finding the percentage of items answered correctly on a 50-item scale will give a better estimate of each child's knowledge than finding the percentage answered correctly using a 10-item scale. How do we know this? Suppose a particular child knows the answers to half of the questions in the domain of knowledge. If the scale was just 10 items long, it *could* be that all of the dates in the scale just happened to be ones which they knew. However, it is far less likely that all the items in the 50-item scale just happened to be the ones that this student knew: they would have to be lucky much more often to obtain full marks in a longer test than in a shorter one. So longer scales are generally more accurate than short ones, though if a scale is *too* long, participants might feel fatigued or bored, and so start to answer randomly – and this will reduce the accuracy of the assessment.

The aim of any scale is to estimate a person's true score, the score which they would obtain if they answered all possible items in the domain. It turns out to be surprisingly easy to estimate how well scores on a particular scale will correlate with the true score. This may sound like an impossibility. As a domain could contain near-infinite number of items (all the important dates in history, for example – not just the 400 listed in the book), it would clearly be impossible to test anyone's knowledge of all of them. But suppose that we have two scales, both built from the same number of items from the same near infinitely large domain – two 50-item scales measuring performance on randomly chosen historical facts, perhaps. We do not know the correlation of either scale with the true score. However, we can easily find out the correlation between the two scales, simply by giving both scales to a large sample of children. If each scale consists of a random selection of items, carefully sampled to cover the whole domain, and the scales are the same length, each scale should have the same correlation with the true score. If both of the scales are long, then the correlation between them will be fairly similar, no matter which particular items are put into each scale. (Take this on trust, for now.) As will be shown in Chapter 7, it is quite easy to estimate the size of the correlation between each scale and the true score from the knowledge of the correlation between the two scales.

The length that a scale should be therefore depends on the purpose for which it is to be used. A scale which is used to help a practitioner make a potentially life-changing decision about an individual will need to be extremely accurate and therefore probably quite long. In other settings it may be more cost-effective to use a short scale and accept that the scores will not be extremely accurate. The length of a scale also depends crucially on the quality of the items. Some scales contain items which correlate quite substantially with the true score, and so a few items will be able to estimate the true score quite accurately. However, in real life it is quite common for the correlation between each item and the true score to be as low as 0.3 or so. As will be seen in Chapter 7, if the quality of the items is poor, more of them need to be added together in order to measure a trait with the desired degree of precision.

ABILITY TESTS

TYPES OF ITEMS FOR ABILITY TESTS

Several types of items have been devised to measure abilities and attainment.

In conventional assessments the participant is given a problem to solve or a question to answer. This problem/question is sometimes known as the **stem**. There are several different ways in which participants can indicate their response.

Free response items

These are sometimes used for ability or knowledge assessments. **Free response items** involve participants giving their answer in their own words (writing, speaking or typing the response) or by making any other type of response which does not involve choosing between alternatives. For example, a vocabulary test for a young child might involve a child being asked to "name something that is blue" and speaking their response. They might be given a set of coloured blocks and be asked to arrange them to replicate a design shown in a booklet. Essays such as "What were the causes of World War I?" can be regarded as free response items – albeit ones which involve long responses which will be challenging to score accurately. A respondent might be asked to type the answer to a problem such as "How far is Winnipeg from Montreal?", asked to draw the shape which comes next in a series, or asked to "sing the tune which I just played you", "tell me who is the prime minister", "draw a picture of a bicycle" – the number of possible formats is huge.

Free response items have several advantages over other types of items discussed later. First, they cannot "lead" the participant towards the right answer; as soon as one presents a person with several different answers and asks them to choose between them, there is the possibility that someone who does not know the answer might be able to eliminate all but one, and so work out what must be the correct answer without actually *knowing* the correct answer at all. For example, if someone was asked "How many sides does a pentangle have?" and were given the alternatives (a) 3, (b) 4 or (c) 5, they might have absolutely no idea what the correct answer was. However, if they know that a three-sided figure is called a triangle, and a four-sided figure is a rectangle, it is unlikely that either of these can be the correct answer. Thus they will arrive at the correct answer by a process of elimination – which is presumably not what the person who set the test intended. Free response items – asking each person to simply write what they think the answer is – overcomes this problem.

Second, free response items can be given verbally, which may be particularly useful when testing young children or those with limited reading or writing skills (e.g., many prisoners, those with eyesight problems or Parkinson's disease).

Third, free response items sometimes seem to be the only possible choice – e.g., when assessing how accurately a person can draw a familiar object from memory. Anagrams are another form of item which is difficult to assess by any other means. If a person was asked to rearrange the letters in "rat heel" to form a single word, and given four choices: "athlete", "reheats", "leather" and "armhole", the astute individual would simply check to see which of the four alternatives contained all of the letters in "rat heel". Comparing letters is a different (and probably much easier) task than solving the anagram – and so if one wants to assess how well people can solve the anagram rather than comparing letters, a free response format would seem to be the best option.

They also have several disadvantages.

First, answers can be ambiguous and therefore hard to score. For example, if someone attempts to "sing the tune they just heard" but the sound they make is horrible, is this because they cannot remember the tune or because they just have a terrible singing voice? It can be hard to know whether to mark this as correct or incorrect.

Second, the practicalities of scoring free response items are appreciable. A human eye and brain is almost always needed, and these are both slow and expensive. Execrable handwriting, spelling etc. may cause problems for the person who reads the answer; a correct answer may be misinterpreted, and vice versa. Even the responses that are not handwritten, oral etc. may need some human judgement. If someone uses a keyboard, which sounds as if it should be a fairly safe way of recording their response, it is possible that someone will insert a comma after the "thousand" when typing a large number or use the letter "O" instead of a zero. Or they may just make a random typing error which a human would spot but a computer program probably would not. If the answers are written on sheets of paper which are then scanned and run through a handwriting recognition program, there are still more opportunities for errors to creep in. Poor handwriting, crossings-out and so on might lead to inaccurate interpretations of what has been written. Scoring free response items really requires human input.

Multiple-choice items

Most ability or attainment tests involve multiple-choice items, purely for ease of scoring. Here the respondent is shown both the stem and a list of options, only one of which is correct. For example, "World War I started in (a) 1066, (b) 1812, (c) 1914, (d) 1939". The respondent then chooses one of the options – normally by clicking a mouse or ticking a box on an answer sheet.

There are several problems with such items, and Gierl et al. (2017) give an excellent discussion for readers who need to know more. It is important to evaluate distractors, to ensure that none of them is so obviously incorrect that no-one chooses them. It is also important to check that none of the distractors can possibly be correct. For example, in a geography test, one might ask "Exeter is in . . . (a) Canada, (b) the UK, (c) Norway, (d) Peru". The problem is that there *is* an Exeter in Canada, so the item has two correct answers. Multiple-choice tests have other problems, too.

- Respondents who do not know the correct answer will sometimes choose the correct answer by chance if they guess an answer at random. This causes problems for some techniques used to estimate people's abilities – notably Rasch scaling, which is discussed in Chapter 15.
- Inventing plausible but incorrect answers (known as **distractors**) is difficult, as discussed in Chapter 16. It requires some insight as to what might confuse respondents, and/or how they might go about eliminating incorrect answers to arrive at the correct one. This may involve analysing students' incorrect responses to free response items, or some lateral thinking; in the aforementioned item, you might feel that "Exeter" does not sound like a Spanish or Norwegian word, and so (c) and (d) are unlikely to be correct and would probably not be good distractors to use.
- Guessing (and the use of strategies to eliminate obviously incorrect answers) mean that the response to the item does not *just* reflect the ability or knowledge being assessed; it also reflects luck to some extent, along with the ability to identifying an efficient strategy for eliminating some distractors. If someone is unsure of the

answer, multiple-choice items involve knowledge and cognitive processes which are very different from those involved in writing the answer in a free response format.
- How many distractors should there be? I cannot offhand think of any commercial test which offers respondents more than eight choices of answer, and four is probably the most common number. The reason for this is rarely articulated, but having just two alternatives would obviously mean that each person has a 50% chance of correctly guessing correctly if they chose an answer at random. The scale would therefore need to be longer than if there were more distractors, to compensate for the effects of lucky guessing. On the other hand, showing a person a large number of distractors will make each item much longer to solve, and the extra reading involved will slow down the assessment process. In addition, Miller's (1956) work suggests that if there are more than about five alternatives, some respondents might find it difficult to keep them all in mind and will need to keep checking the page or screen – again slowing some (but not all) respondents and introducing random error into the scores on the item. There is a surprisingly large literature on this issue, summarised by Gierl et al. (2017). Empirical studies and mathematical considerations suggest that three, perhaps four choices are best for multiple-choice tests.
- The number and choice of distractors determines how easy the item is – and once again, this is an arbitrary choice made as the item is being constructed. For example, it is probable that had we chosen the years 1915, 1916 and 1917 as distractors, the item would be harder than using the widely spread dates shown previously, because some people would have had the vague idea that World War I took place early in the 20th century, but not know the precise date.
- What should participants be told about guessing or omitting answers? Many multiple-choice ability tests urge participants to guess if they are unsure of the correct answer – so what should be done with those who nonetheless do not guess, but leave an answer blank? The safest plan is to make a random guess, or statistically estimate how many of the unanswered items they would probably have answered correctly, considering their performance on the items which they *did* attempt. A few tests ask participants *not* to guess and warn them that incorrect answers will be penalised. However, this introduces a whole new problem. What if participants use different criteria for deciding whether they think that their answer is correct? One person might be terrified of being penalised for an incorrect answer, and so will leave an item blank if they are not 100% positive that their answer is correct, whilst someone else might take a chance and only leave the item blank if they cannot eliminate any of the distractors. These different strategies will influence the scores which the participants obtain and will probably make them less accurate. It is probably best to ask participants to guess if unsure, but in any case, it is vital that participants should be told precisely what to do if they do not know the answer to a question – even though the way in which they define "know" will probably vary from person to person.

- It can be difficult to measure some higher-order problem-solving and reasoning skills using multiple-choice tests. For example, suppose that an organisation wanted to assess how well an applicant for a senior position could draw up a development plan to move a company forward from some (hypothetical) financial calamity. It is not really obvious how one could measure this sort of skill using multiple-choice items.
- If someone finds an item difficult, should they spend a long time on it, or move on to the next and (perhaps) be allowed to revisit it later?
- A respondent who is not fully engaged with the assessment process will sometimes just tick boxes randomly in order to end the assessment as quickly as possible. It is much harder to spot that this has occurred with a multiple-choice test than with a free response test, where the respondent would need to leave each item unanswered or (perhaps) write some word which has no connection with the question.

It is clear that measuring abilities or attainments using multiple-choice tests is not as straightforward as it might appear, and that the test instructions should make it clear how much time is available, what someone should do if they are "stuck" on an item, and whether they should guess an answer if unsure.

TIME LIMITS, SPEEDED AND POWER TESTS

A **power test** of imposes few (if any) time limits. The difficulty of the items is what allows power tests to differentiate between people. A power test based on anagrams would involve items which varied considerably in difficulty level; participants would be asked to solve the list of anagrams, taking as long as they want to do so.[1] As ability items are almost always ordered in terms of difficulty, most participants will only encounter impossibly hard items towards the middle or end of the test, which should prevent them from becoming demotivated.

The test instructions should try to ensure that everyone approaches the test with the same strategy in mind. Most tests ask people to work through items at their chosen speed – "work as quickly and accurately as you can" being a typical instruction. Without such guidance, some people may rush through the test making many mistakes, whilst others are more cautious. In this case the scale risks measuring caution as well as ability; it may not be unidimensional. In addition, if time limits are so "tight" that many people do not have the chance to attempt every item, the test will assess speed of responding (as well as the ability which the test sets out to measure, and cautiousness). For this reason, time limits are usually quite generous.

If participants are asked to guess the answers when they are unsure, it is sensible to show them exactly how much time they have left to complete the test so that they can spend the last couple of minutes going back and marking their best guesses, rather than leaving items blank.

Computerised testing also allows time limits to be imposed for individual items; a person may be given 15 seconds to solve each problem, and after that time they are moved on to the next item whether or not they managed to attempt an answer. However, unless the time given to solve each item is fairly generous, participants who work slowly (for whatever reason) will run out of time for every item, which they will find frustrating and their score of zero would underestimate their true ability. If they are allowed to work at their own pace, they may be able to answer *some* items.

A **speeded test** is one where participants need to work quickly – for example, to cross out every "a" in a passage of text, where the text is so long that virtually no-one would be able to finish the task in the time allowed. The task is easy and almost everyone could score 100% correct if they were given unlimited time. It is this which distinguishes a speeded test from a power test. For a speeded test the key question is how many items can be answered in a given time. Tasks such as "in two minutes, write as many words as possible which might be used to describe a brown wooden bench" (a measure of flexible thinking) is a common example of a speeded test.

Strategies and motivation will have a large influence on performance on speeded tests (see, for example, Ranger et al., 2021). For example, should one work slowly and carefully, or is it better to work fast and make some mistakes (e.g., crossing out some letters other than a's)? How much error-checking should be carried out? How important is it to achieve a high score?

Whether one chooses a power test or a speeded test depends, to some extent, on what the test is supposed to measure. Creativity is sometimes defined as the ability to think of many different ideas quickly; perceptual speed is the speed with which strings of characters can be compared to determine whether they are the same or different. Both of these can only be measured by speeded tests. But otherwise it is probably advisable to use power tests where possible, instructing participants to work as fast as they can without sacrificing accuracy.

We return to all these issues in Chapter 16.

ADAPTIVE TESTS

One problem with conventional ability tests is that they need to be designed for a specific range of abilities. There are several versions of many ability tests (e.g., the Weschler series of tests) which offer versions designed for preschool children, older children and adults. The items in a reasoning test for 7-year-olds would obviously need to be much easier than those in a test for adults, as reasoning skills develop over time. In addition, university graduates probably show higher levels of abstract reasoning than the population in general, as these skills would have been developed during their education. One thus needs to have a rough idea of the ability levels of the people who one will be testing, so that one can choose a test containing items which most participants will find challenging but not impossible. A test which contains many items which are trivially easy will lead to boredom, and perhaps careless responding; think of an adult being given reasoning questions designed for 7-year-olds. A test which contains many items that are impossibly difficult may lead to the person being assessed to lose motivation or give up completely. However, it is sometimes difficult to estimate the ability range that one will encounter. For example, it has been found that whilst surgeons generally score well on intelligence tests (their scores are high, and the range of scores is quite small), manual labourers have scores below the national average – but the range of scores is much larger, as some highly intelligent people may choose or be forced to take up manual jobs (e.g., Reynolds et al., 1987). It is thus important to select a test which matches both the level and the range of abilities of the people being assessed. If there is no previous literature, how can one know this in advance? How can one decide which test to buy?

Adaptive tests offer a way round this conundrum. After making some very strong assumptions about the ways in which items and people behave (as discussed in Chapter 3), an adaptive test is administered by a computer program which monitors each person's performance and continually estimates their ability. They are initially given an item of moderate difficulty, chosen at random. The difficulty of the next item that a person is given will depend on their previous performance; someone who consistently solves easy, moderately difficult items, but not the difficult items, will be administered moderately difficult or difficult items, which they should find challenging but not impossible to solve. Someone who can only manage the easy to moderately difficult items will be given items in this range of difficulty. This means that people are administered different sets of items, and as these items vary in difficulty the test cannot be scored by simply adding up the number which are answered correctly. It is however possible to compare people's abilities, even if they have been given completely different sets of items, using a mathematical technique called **item response theory** (see Chapter 15).

PERSONALITY, MOOD, MOTIVATION AND ATTITUDE SCALES

The most popular format for personality and other questionnaires is the rating scale (sometimes called the **Likert scale**, after the social psychologist who first devised it). Respondents are shown a statement ("stem") and are asked how much they agree with it, how well it applies to them, or something similar. Historically, several other methods have been tried, including projective tests (where participants make their own interpretation of some ambiguous stimulus, such as a picture or inkblot) and "objective tests" – tests where the participant is either unable to modify their behaviour, or where they do not know which aspect of their behaviour is being assessed. However, as these techniques are highly specialised (and frequently ineffective) they will not be considered further. In the following discussion I will assume that items are administered as a conventional personality questionnaire.

Likert scales can be used to measure states or traits; the stem for a personality item (a trait) will ask how people normally behave, whilst scales measuring mood or motivation states will ask how they feel right at this moment.

As there can be no correct or incorrect answers to these types of questions, participants are usually asked to rate how well each statement describes them (or the person being rated), how much they agree with a statement, or something similar. For example, they might be asked to fill in one of the circles in order to answer each of the items in Table 2.3.

More recently, there have been attempts to develop more enjoyable alternatives ("gamification"). For example, it may be possible to assess personality by tracing the choices that a person makes when they play an online game. Wariness of other characters might indicate neuroticism, for example. The problem is that such assessments are not (yet) very accurate (e.g., McCord et al., 2019).

SELF-RATINGS

Some scales are completed by the participant, who describes how they think, feel, or behave. These are (unsurprisingly) known as **self-report scales**. Self-report scales rely on the participant being motivated to answer truthfully – and also having the self-knowledge to allow them to do so.

Asking participants to complete research studies anonymously might be expected to produce more honest responses and so improve the quality of the data. However, several studies (e.g., Butler, 1973; Francis, 1981) suggest that respondents often behave no differently under anonymous/named conditions. The only real problem with anonymous data is that it is difficult to assess people on more than one occasion, where their answers on two or more measures will need to be matched up. This can be overcome with a little ingenuity – for example, giving each person a code to memorise (or a set of stickers to put on paper questionnaires), or asking them to generate the same code on each occasion using well-known information

TESTS, SCALES AND TESTING

Table 2.3 Items using Likert scales

	Strongly agree	Agree	Neutral	Disagree	Strongly disagree
I am the life and soul of the party	○	○	○	○	○
Global warming will destroy the planet	○	○	○	○	○
The benefits of recreational drugs outweigh their risks	○	○	○	○	○

	Definitely	Probably	Neutral/ unsure	Probably not	Definitely not
My mother was smarter than me	○	○	○	○	○

	Very much	Some-what	Unsure/ neutral	Not much	Not at all
How much do you enjoy travelling to new places?	○	○	○	○	○

	Very much better than other brands	Better than other brands	No better or worse than other brands	Worse than other brands	Much worse than other brands
Gleemy Chompers toothpaste cleans my teeth	○	○	○	○	○

(e.g., the first initial of their first pet followed by the house number where they grew up followed by the last two digits of the number plate of their first car). The context in which the data are gathered is also important, as discussed in Chapter 8. Using self-report scales as part of an employment selection process may lead to some respondents denying having any characteristics which may be viewed negatively.

Q-data and Q'-data

A major problem with personality scales is that people will happily rate almost anything. An old personality questionnaire contained the item "I see things or animals or people around me that others do not see". But how could anyone *know for certain* that other people did not see what they saw? This brings us to an important issue: whether we should believe what people say when they answer questions using rating scales. If someone strongly agrees that they see things or animals or people around them that others do not see, this could indicate that they do, in fact, have visual hallucinations. Or it could be the case that statistical analyses show that *saying* that one has visual hallucinations is one aspect of a particular personality disorder.

In the first case, we believe what the respondent says. In the second, we do not – but rely on statistical analyses to help us determine what (if anything) responding this way indicates about a person. For example, it might be found that people who strongly agree with this statement might go on to develop symptoms of schizophrenia – so the fact that a person says that they experience hallucinations may have some useful diagnostic value. It does not matter a jot whether the person really *does* experience hallucinations – all that matters is that they *say* that they do.

This is an important point to bear in mind; an item may be useful for assessing personality no matter how stupid or irrelevant it appears to be. All that really matters is whether the way people answer this and other items allows us to describe or predict their personality, attitudes etc. based on statistical analyses, such as those described in Chapters 10, 14 and 15. It may be naïve to assume that responses to self-rating scales say something useful about how the individual truly feels or behaves, though social psychologists regularly make this strong assumption when measuring attitudes.

Because of this, Cattell (1946) suggested that two different terms should be used to describe data from questionnaires. He suggested that responses to questions which are treated as revealing some insight about the individual (such as attitude questionnaires) should be termed **Q'-data**, the "Q" being short for "questionnaire". Data which are not taken at face value but which are simply used because they have been found empirically to predict behaviour or to show useful associations with other responses are known as **Q-data**. It is important to bear this distinction in mind when analysing responses from questionnaires. Treating responses as Q-data means that even bizarre items ("How much do you agree with the statement 'I am the smartest person in town'?" – another genuine item) may be useful. If the statement were interpreted as Q'-data it would imply that the person was intelligent; if interpreted as Q-data it might, perhaps, indicate hubris – but this would need to be determined empirically. Throughout the rest of this book we treat all responses to items as being Q-data, for the statistical analyses which allow us to check how accurately items and scales measure what they claim to assess do not require us to take responses at face value.

Other problems with self-ratings

The second problem with self-report questionnaires is that people might compare themselves to different groups. For example, an item whose stem is "I am more intelligent than most people" is almost impossible to answer unless the person is told which reference group to use. Should a student rate their intelligence relative to the rest of their class at university? Given that the correlation between intelligence and academic performance is over 0.8 (Calvin et al., 2010), if students at a good university rated themselves relative to their classmates, they would seriously underestimate their scores, because their classmates would almost all be above average intelligence. Thus someone who correctly perceived that they were appreciably less intelligent than their classmates could be well above average intelligence when compared to the population as a whole.

It would, in theory, be possible to specify the norm group: "Thinking about all the people in your school, would you say that you are more intelligent than most of them?" might work if participants had gone through an education system which did not rely on academic selection. But this makes the stem rather long, and most psychologists do not think about such issues carefully enough when writing items.

The third problem is self-knowledge. Most people think they have an above-average sense of humour, intelligence and are more popular than they really are; indeed psychologists and sociologists study this as the "Lake Wobegon effect" or "illusory superiority", which is the tendency to overestimate one's capabilities or knowledge (Kruger, 1999). This is not the place to explore the literature, but suffice it to say that people do seem to exaggerate their strengths without meaning to, whilst others do not. This is unfortunate, for if everyone exaggerated to the same extent it would not matter in the slightest. If everyone's score on a question was 1 point higher than it should be, this would not affect the correlation between the score on that question and anything else. However, if some people's responses to an item are higher or lower than they should be whilst other people's scores are accurate, then responses to that item become tainted with measurement error.

Fourth, there may be individual differences in the way in which people use the rating scales. There is also a well-researched tendency for some people to tend to agree with personality items, whatever they are, for example. Others try to give a good impression of themselves. Yet others see complex issues as clear-cut and strongly agree or strongly disagree with everything. We return to these issues in Chapter 8.

Fifth, there is the problem of random responding. It is common to find that some respondents tick the same alternative (often the centre, "neutral" answer) for many items in succession, suggesting that they may be responding randomly; however it is hard to be certain of this. If respondents just tick a different box each time without reading the item, this would be difficult to detect by eye. However, it is possible to find pairs of items which correlate very substantially; if a person gives very different responses to items in such pairs, this may indicate that they are responding randomly, and some questionnaires incorporate scoring techniques which allow such random responding to be detected.

Finally, in the case of personality questionnaires, it is normal to ask participants to answer each question, and this is normally stressed during the instructions for these scales. But what should be done if someone leaves blanks? We consider the problem of missing data in Chapter 4.

RATINGS BY OTHERS

Rather than rating oneself, it is also possible to obtain ratings from line managers, teachers, friends or others who know the individual well. These **peer ratings** can sometimes produce similar results to self-reports, although it has been argued that self-ratings may be more accurate for the reasons discussed later. It can be interesting to explore the reasons why discrepancies arise when married couples (who presumably know each other fairly well) rate each other (McCrae et al., 1998).

There are several issues associated with the use of ratings of other people, rather than self-reports.

- It is difficult to be sure how well raters actually know the people who are being assessed – particularly if the ratings are performed at work, where a manager may need to rate a great number of people.
- One advantage of using ratings is that if each rater assesses several people they know, it is possible to correct for any bias that the raters may show – for example, rating everyone favourably (or unfavourably) – by standardising each rater's scores.
- It is possible that rating others may yield more objective results than rating oneself; it eliminates the problem of self-delusion.
- Of course it is possible that the raters will not be objective. They may want a colleague, a student or a friend to get a job, or just to appear in a good light.
- There are also areas of each person's life which the rater may not be qualified to judge; a work colleague may have only observed someone in a very restricted range of settings, and it is quite possible that they may view a colleague as supremely confident, whereas the ratee might acknowledge that this is just an act, and they truly feel insecure much of the time.
- There may also be a "halo effect". If the rater rates someone highly on some desirable trait, they may also tend to rate them highly on all other desirable traits, as discussed in Chapter 8.
- Finally, it is possible that the raters use the questionnaire to show which

TESTS, SCALES AND TESTING

characteristics they *think* go together – not how the individuals actually behave. For example, the rater may believe that religious people are tolerant, so having rated a colleague as being strongly religious, they may then rate them as tolerant, completely ignoring all the evidence which suggests the exact opposite.

A more formal discussion of some of these issues with reference to the literature is given by Paunonen and O'Neill (2010). Self-report and peer-ratings of behaviour each have their merits and disadvantages – however the vast majority of research uses self-report scales and questionnaires simply because they are so much more convenient. Suppose that you want to research the link between some aspect of personality and smoking behaviour. To gather data using self-report one merely needs to put a questionnaire online measuring personality and smoking behaviour and encourage people to visit the link. If personality is to be rated rather than self-assessed, the person who completed the smoking questionnaire would then need to nominate someone who knows them well – they would need to be contracted and agree to participate – and it would be necessary to match the smoking data with the personality ratings for each person. This is not a trivial task, especially if the smoking data are collected anonymously (so that names cannot be used to match rater and ratee).

FORCED-ALTERNATIVE ITEMS

Not all self-reports use Likert scales. With **forced-alternative items**, respondents are given two or more alternatives and are asked which of them best describes them, which one they are most likely to adopt or something similar (see Table 2.4).

Unlike Likert scales, each of the possible responses to a forced-alternative item represents a *different* scale. The number of alternative answers for each item is usually equal to the number of scales in the test. The two items shown were designed to measure three scales: neuroticism, extraversion and openness to experience (three

Table 2.4 Examples of forced-alternative items measuring neuroticism, extraversion and openness to experience

In each scenario, choose the ONE phrase which best describes how you would behave.			
If I won the lottery I would . . .	move house in case my family was held to ransom	host a huge party for my family and friends	travel to better understand other cultures
When travelling, my priority is to . . .	always ensure I know where my passport is	make lots of new friends	tour art galleries and museums

important personality factors). Each stem is therefore followed by three options – one indicating neuroticism, one indicating extraversion and one indicating openness to experience. Someone who chose the third alternative to both stems would value cultural activities and would therefore have a high score on openness to experience; someone who chose the first alternative for question 1 and the second for question 2 would be somewhat extraverted and somewhat neurotic and so on. In practice, of course, the order of the answers is randomised so that it less obvious to the respondent that the choices reflect the same three scales.

One obvious problem with this approach is that it is only appropriate for questionnaires which measure more than one trait.

A second difficulty is that if one option is hugely more attractive than the others, then almost everyone will choose it, regardless of their personality. Thus when these tests are being developed, the items are normally given to a large sample of people who are asked to rate each alternative for its level of **social desirability**. Three items from different scales having similar social desirability are then used as the alternative answers for each stem. Unfortunately, however, social desirability is likely to vary from sample to sample and culture to culture (Ryan et al., 2021), as well as over time; what was socially desirable for a group of elderly Pennsylvanian churchgoers in the 1990s might not be the same as what is socially desirable for psychology students in the 21st century! Thus there is a danger that tests which are designed in this way may lose their effectiveness over time, or when used with groups different from the ones used to develop it.

Finally, as will be shown in Chapter 5, interpreting the scores from these tests is very difficult indeed; standard statistical techniques for evaluating tests and scales may be inappropriate, and so those who select or use these tests need to be very cautious.

Some gamified personality tests follow this format: if a person is given three choices of action on encountering a dragon, one of these might indicate neuroticism, one extraversion and another conscientiousness, for example. The same difficulties apply to the interpretation of scores from these measures (e.g., Harman & Brown, 2022; McCord et al., 2019), although as they are generally developed by computer scientists rather than psychometricians, the problem generally seems to be unrecognised.

ADAPTIVE TESTS

It is also possible to use adaptive testing for personality tests, and a few studies do so (e.g., Reise & Henson, 2000). Whilst this should, in theory, speed up the testing process, these authors question whether the extra complexity is worth the effort.

OVERVIEW OF TESTING PROCEDURES

More detail about test administration is given in Chapters 4 and 16. The paramount consideration is that no-one should be harmed by taking a test. All possible steps must therefore be taken to ensure that answers (and scores on the test) remain confidential to each participant; other participants must not be able to see which responses are made, or even *whether* a response has been made, to avoid bullying, embarrassment, name-calling etc. If many people are being tested in the same room, this means keeping good separation between them, with no opportunity for answer sheets, screens etc. to be viewed by others.

A risk assessment should also be carried out – particularly in the case of assessments which might deal with sensitive issues. The use of anatomically detailed dolls in forensic interviews or an item asking about attitudes to abortion might trigger painful memories for some participants, and a proper evaluation of the risks/benefits (to the individual) of testing is needed. As well as signing a form which gives their informed consent to filling in the questionnaires or taking the test, participants should always be reminded that they are free to withdraw their consent and leave at any time, and be provided with contact details (such as a business card) so that they may raise any queries or concerns with the researcher or professional at a later date.

The next important consideration is that the experience of taking the test should be exactly the same, no matter who in the world administers it to which person. This sounds straightforward, but in practice it may not be. Each commercial test normally comes with a manual, which specifies precisely what instructions the participants will be given; these need to be read verbatim – stilted though this sometimes appears – in order to ensure that everyone taking the test has the same experience. It would otherwise be impossible to compare people's scores. Some of the factors which need to be controlled are:

- The testing environment should be free from distractions, noise, talking etc. with no opportunity for collaboration, cheating or copying. This is fairly easy to arrange when questionnaires, ability tests or attainment tests are completed using pen and paper in a large room, such as a lecture hall. It is much harder to ensure that the environment is suitable when a test is administered via the internet. If anonymous participants complete an internet questionnaire or ability test, then there is no guarantee that the testing conditions are optimal. The test could be taken on a mobile phone with a dirty, cracked screen which cannot display high-resolution graphics over an internet connection which is so slow that pages take a long time to load. The items might be answered by a group of people working together, perhaps accessing other websites to help them find the correct answers. Or there might be loud music or conversations in the background, which would affect concentration. It is in any case extraordinarily difficult to ensure that the person

actually taking the test or questionnaire is who they say they are, though a webcam may be of use here. They might even be a "bot", as discussed in Chapter 4.
- The test instructions ensure that all participants understand what they are being asked to do when completing each scale of the test; examples are given in Chapter 16. They should be read (or displayed on screen) without making any alterations. Some ability tests have practice items – easy items to make sure that participants understand what to do, and how to record their responses. Once again, it is important to make sure that these are administered exactly according to the instructions.
- If a test has time limits, these should be imposed strictly, to ensure that scores are comparable from study to study.

LOCATING TESTS

Identifying the "best" test for a particular application is not straightforward. Researchers and practitioners will need to bear in mind the context in which the test is used (as a test which works with well-motivated students may not work when used as part of a job-selection procedure), the characteristics of the sample (age, cultural background, reading-skills etc.), as well as the psychometric qualities of the tests. Giving suggestions as to which tests might be appropriate for each ability, trait and state which has been studied in the last century would make the book both enormous and excruciatingly dull and it would be out of date almost immediately. However, readers will need to locate tests from time to time, and so here some suggestions which may be useful.

Some tests are well-known commercial products, and psychologists and others who need to find a test measuring anxiety, general intelligence or virtually any other trait or state should first turn to the Buros Organisation's **Mental Measurements Yearbooks**. These books list commercially published tests and questionnaires by topic and (crucially) also review many of them in some detail. Few of us would buy a washing machine without reading an independent review by an expert, and the same principle applies to tests. Test reviews can also be purchased from the website www.buros.org. Independent reviews such as these really are essential for identifying good, well-constructed tests which may be worth the substantial price sometimes charged by test publishers.

Test publishers' catalogues are another option. However useful these may be for finding out what tests are available, it is important to remember that these are marketing tools and are unlikely to offer balanced evaluations of tests. It is essential to consult the literature to determine whether a particular test seems to measure what it claims to measure using a sample which is fairly similar to the one which you propose to use. Publishers are unlikely to mention that a particular test is technically flawed, so selecting a test from a publisher's catalogue alone is a courageous act. It is necessary to read the research literature to determine whether the test is likely to be useful; guidance about the desirable properties that a test should show is given later in this book. Several commercial tests present precisely zero evidence that they measure what they claim.

If one wants to measure a fairly well-researched aspect or personality or cognitive ability, Lew Goldberg has an excellent selection of personality scales known as the **International Personality Item Pool (IPIP)** (http://ipip.ori.org; Goldberg, 1999). These are free to use for any purpose. The **International Cognitive Ability Resource (ICAR)** provides a free-to-use set of cognitive ability tests (https://icar-project.com/; Condon & Revelle, 2014). Both websites are strongly recommended; they also contain information about the psychometric properties of the tests and scales.

The Educational Testing Service maintains a substantial database listing commercial and non-commercial tests, which anyone can search at https://www.ets.org/test-collection.html/. It allows keyword search (so that one can search for scales measuring anxiety, for example), author search etc. and gives details of where each test may be obtained; in the case of recent unpublished tests this may include the e-mail address of the author. This database includes details of some very old tests, as well as up-to-date ones, and is warmly recommended.

Members of the American Psychological Association (or those whose universities have purchased access to their databases) can access a database known as Psychtests at www.apa.org/pubs/databases/psyctests/, which mainly lists unpublished tests and questionnaires. It is possible to search for tests using this, and sometimes download tests and supporting documentation directly – for a fee.

Many tests used in psychology appear as appendices to journal articles. A literature search using keywords such as "anxiety", "Mexic*" and "child*" in a bibliographic database for locating journal articles (Web of Science, PsychINFO or the like – not a simple internet search) will identify journal articles which have studied anxiety in Mexican children, for example. It is then necessary to read these journal articles to find out which tests were used, which will be listed in the reference section. This paper will very often contain the test items.

If the author of a test is known, and there is reason to believe that the test may be published in the back of a journal article, a citation search can be useful. Papers containing tests tend to be heavily cited by others and so are easy to find.

It is also vital to critically evaluate the test for oneself, in order to determine whether it was soundly constructed and is likely to be suitable for use for your application with your sample. All too often, researchers seem to assume that because others have used a particular test, it must be well constructed and measure what it claims to assess. If the test was developed in a different country or a long time ago, it will be necessary to check that it measures what it claims to measure (see Chapter 9) before it is used for any serious purpose. Above all, it is important to read through the items, and convince yourself that they are (a) different in meaning from each other, (b) they completely cover the domain of interest and (c) they are appropriate for the sample with whom they are to be used (language, difficulty, cultural assumptions etc.). It may also be necessary to check that the items behave as they should, as described in Chapters 7 and 16.

Finally, it is important to bear copyright considerations in mind when administering scales in *any* format. Whilst items from the IPIP and the ICAR are free to be used however one wishes, most commercial tests explicitly forbid the photocopying of test booklets or answer sheets, and do not permit test items to be administered by other means (e.g., using survey software). There is something of a grey area when items are published as an appendix to articles in commercial scientific journals.

SUMMARY

This chapter introduced some key terms and described the basic logic of psychological assessment – that items in a scale must be selected so that the sample all the items that could possibly be written to measure some trait or state (the "domain" of items). It then examined various types of items used in tests of ability, personality etc. and gave a critical evaluation of each format. This reveals that the commonly used Likert scale format has a surprising number of problems. The chapter then outlined the importance of administering tests in a standardised way and outlined some advantages and pitfalls of various methods of test administration. The chapter concluded with some practical guidance on how to find a test for a particular application.

NOTE

1 This is not quite true. Many tests impose some sort of generous time limit, otherwise some dedicated or obsessional participants will wrestle with the more difficult items until doomsday. However these limits are usually set so that 90% or more of the participants normally complete all items in the time allowed.

CHAPTER 3
THE MEANING OF MEASUREMENT

Chapter 2 showed several different types of items and suggested that items measuring the same trait should be grouped together to form scales and that responses to test items should be turned into numbers. For example, we might award people 1 point if they answer an ability item correctly and 0 points if they do not. We might award 5 points if someone strongly agrees with a statement, 4 points if they agree, 3 points if they are neutral, 2 points if they disagree and 1 point if they strongly disagree. Then we calculate a score for each person on the items in that scale by adding up their scores on the items. This is such common practice that it is hard to see what (if anything) is wrong with it. This chapter questions whether it is legitimate to use numbers to represent individual differences in personality, abilities etc.

It is arguably the most important (and conceptually the most difficult) chapter in this book, and my suspicion is that many readers will be advised to skip over it. This would be a great shame. Unless we can show that test scores reflect real, measurable properties of the individual (things like brain electrical activity or developmental changes), we make a case that psychological questionnaires and tests cannot "measure" anything. Many or all of the numbers which psychometricians analyse may well be meaningless.

This is not a popular view, particularly amongst those who have invested years of their lives in researching individual differences, for it suggests that much or all of such research may be worthless. Paul Barrett has pointed out that most researchers simply refuse to accept that there is a problem in an attempt to reduce their cognitive dissonance.

> As Michell notes in his target article, the response from psychologists and psychometricians alike has been largely silence. From my own attempts to relay his thesis in papers, conferences, and academic seminars, I have been met with a mixture of disbelief, disinterest, anger, accusations of intellectual nihilism, ridicule, and generally a steadfast refusal to seriously question the facts. And, make no mistake, Michell deals with facts about measurement.
>
> (Barrett, 2008)

DOI: 10.4324/9781003240181-3

Those who feel that I am overstating the problem may like to consider this quotation which argues that individual differences research is fatally flawed because of the

> conviction that psychological attributes – such as cognitive abilities, personality traits, and social attitudes – are quantitative. Survey the psychometric literature: It reveals a body of theories, methods, and applications premised upon the proposition that psychological attributes are quantitative but is devoid of serious attempts to consider relevant evidence for that premise. The theories proposed (such as the factor-analytic theories of cognitive abilities and personality) are typically quantitative; mainstream psychometricians typically believe that they are able to measure abilities, personality traits, and social attitudes using psychological tests; and within applied psychometrics, tests are typically promoted using the rhetoric of measurement. Yet, there is little acknowledgment that this premise might not be true: No research programs that I know of are dedicated to testing it; no body of evidence is marshaled in its support (indeed, as far as I know, none exists); and no attempt has been made to devise methods for diagnosing the difference between quantitative and merely ordinal attributes. Psychometrics is premised upon psychological attributes being quantitative, but this premise is rarely treated as raising questions, usually only as answering them.
>
> (Michell, 2008)

In short, the numbers which result from scoring psychological tests may be meaningless. This is a serious concern, and the debate about what psychological measurement is (and is not) is still current. This chapter is included because readers need to be aware of the controversy. If true, the philosophers' comments about psychological measurement may invalidate most of what we do. It is certainly an issue to which all test users need to give serious consideration.

MEASUREMENT IN SCIENCE

In physics it has been claimed that "whether or not a thing is measurable is not something to be decided *a priori* by thought alone, but something that can be decided only by experiment" (Feynman et al., 1963 sec 16–1). It is difficult to imagine how physics or chemistry would have developed if it were not possible to measure temperature, mass, voltage, time etc., as the "laws" that have been developed (such as Ohm's law, gravitational attraction, the gas laws in chemistry) are formulae which demonstrate how basic measurements of physical objects are related. For example, Boyle's law points out that if the volume of container of gas is halved (think of a bicycle pump), the pressure of the gas inside it doubles, provided temperature is kept constant. Volume is measured by combining several measures of length; pressure can be measured by measuring force exerted over a particular area (length again!). The discovery of this mathematical relationship led to the kinetic theory of gases, and discovering that the theory sometimes did not work (for example, carbon dioxide becomes solid at low temperature and high pressure) led to extensions of the theory.

This is an example of how quantitative theories can drive science forward; we measure properties of substances, find a mathematical relationship between these properties, explore the conditions under which this relationship holds (constant temperature, pressure not too high, temperature not too low) and extend the underlying theory to account for these discrepancies. The key point is that the numbers that we use represent a basic physical property of the thing being measured. It is only because of this that numbers are useful.

In physics, there is a clear relationship between the numbers assigned to a construct (e.g., temperature) and some basic property of the thing being measured. Fundamentally there has to be a **unit of measurement**, such as an inch, mile, degree Celsius or second. If this is the case, we can infer that the distance between the reading of "14" and "16" on a measuring instrument (such as a tape measure or thermometer) is the same as the distance between the "5" and "7", and that the distance between the "2" and "16" readings is exactly twice the distance between the "1" and "8" readings. This is known as **concatenation**.

MEASUREMENT IN PSYCHOLOGY

Joel Michell (1997) provided a devastating critique of psychological measurement theory; his paper should be read by all test users. Michell's conclusion is simple: psychological assessments involving questionnaires and tests do not constitute proper scientific measurement. This may come as rather a surprise. After all, questionnaires generally produce numerical scores, and the complicated statistical methods used to develop and refine tests almost invariably assume that these numbers correspond to real levels of traits. Structural equation modelling, factor analysis and other sophisticated mathematical techniques are used to develop and refine theories based on test scores – it all certainly *looks* like science. Given the wealth of statistical theory which underpins psychological assessments, and the objective statistical analyses which are used, how can anyone possibly claim that psychological tests are scientifically worthless?

Michell approaches the problem from the viewpoint of the philosophy of science. He argues that proper scientific measurement is only possible when the thing being measured (an **attribute**) has been shown to have **quantitative structure**. This is an empirical issue. Length, time and temperature are examples of quantitative attributes. The specific instance of a quantity is known as its **magnitude**. Thus (for example) the number of seconds taken to read this chapter is a magnitude of the attribute "time".

So what is the problem? Why not define "intelligence" as an attribute, and "score on Form 3 of the Cattell Culture Fair Test" as its magnitude? This is essentially what generations of psychologists have done – and the problem is that they have not demonstrated that the attribute (intelligence) is itself quantitative before rushing in, assigning numbers to behaviours, and performing mathematical operations on them. Wonderful though it is, mathematics only makes sense when the numbers which are being manipulated obey certain axioms which define a quantitative variable. Otherwise, the numbers which are generated by any statistical procedure are meaningless.

In psychology it is perfectly sensible to use numbers to represent reaction times, to show the power of various frequency bands in a person's electroencephalogram or report the concentration of cortisol in their blood as these are based on real properties of the person (measurements of time and voltage, measurements of volume and mass) which are widely used in science and which are universally applicable. The voltage measured from someone's head via their electroencephalogram is only quantitatively different from the voltage which surges through a long-distance power line. Both refer to the amount of energy needed to move electrical charge from one place (the surface of the skull, or the power plant) to another (such as the ground). The point is that physical basis of these processes is well understood.

Unfortunately, most psychology "measurements" are not like this.

Much of the problem seems to lie with S. S. Stevens' (1946) contribution in which he defined measurement as the process of assigning numbers to objects. He developed the idea of scales of measurement. **Ratio scales** (such as mass, length, or the Kelvin scale of temperature) have a zero point and equal intervals between numbers. Unfortunately, Stevens also suggested that an **ordinal scale** (rank-ordering) was a form of measurement, and this turns out to be a major problem.

In Lewis Carroll's *Through the Looking-Glass*, Humpty Dumpty says "When I use a word . . . it means just what I choose it to mean – neither more nor less". This is precisely what Stevens did with numbers. One can assign numbers to ranks ("ordinal data"). One can use numbers to represent categories, and Stevens suggested that it was reasonable to both of these things. The problem is that when they are used like this, numbers do not behave the same way that we are accustomed to, and we cannot claim to have "measured" something just because we have assigned a number (rather than a letter or a shape) to it. All we are doing is counting. Whilst we can say that Jane solves twice as many problems as Karl, we cannot say that Jane is twice as intelligent as Karl – even if there is such a thing as intelligence, and it is quantitative.

The definition of what makes an attribute quantitative becomes somewhat technical; Hölder's seven rules for this are translated from German in Michell and Ernst (1996). But the bottom line is that if an attribute is quantitative, it is possible to calculate the ratio between any two magnitudes of that attribute, which expresses one magnitude in units of the other. For example, I can establish that my desk is 50 inches wide – a proper scientific measurement of the width of my desk, using an inch as marked on a tape measure as the standard unit of measurement. (Of course this choice is arbitrary – I could measure my desk in matchbox widths, if I chose.) The key thing is that knowing that my desk is 50 inches wide and that the alcove in my office is 60 inches wide tells me that the desk will fit into the alcove with 5 inches to spare on either side. I could not perform this sort of operation using scores on psychological tests.

The characteristics of people which are measured by psychological tests are (generally) inferred, not observable. They do not exist as physical objects whose properties such as length or weight can be measured. Of course, not all variables in the physical world can be measured either, and Michell gives the example of density, which cannot itself be measured directly. This turns out to be a good analogy with psychological tests. For one way in which we can determine the density of a solid directly is through determining whether it floats or sinks in a number of (arbitrarily selected) liquids. We could count the number of liquids in which it sinks, and this would give us a measure of its density. We could even construct tables of norms (see Chapter 4) showing the number of solid substances which sink in our selection of liquids; this would allow us to discover that (for example) only 10% of the solids which we have tested are denser than iron.

This whole process is directly analogous to psychological assessment, where we give different people arbitrarily selected items to solve or answer. We count the number which they solve correctly (or their scores on Likert scales), and this is our measure of their ability, or level of the trait. However, just as density is not a fundamental property of physical objects (it does not follow that an object which sinks in four of the liquids is twice as dense as one which sinks in two of them, for example), scores on psychological scales simply do not behave in the same way as the measurements with which we are familiar.

Suppose that you score 20 on a scale measuring extraversion (sociability) whilst your partner scores 40. We *can* calculate the ratio, and he might tell all his friends that their score is twice yours. But what does that actually mean? Does it follow that someone who scores 80 on the test is four times as extraverted as you, and twice as extraverted as your partner? If someone else scores 60 on the test, does it mean anything to say that the difference between their level of extraversion and your partner's (20) is the same as the difference between your partner and you? The problem for psychology is that the numbers which are used to represent scores on psychological tests simply do not behave in the same sort of way as numbers which represent quantitative attributes. And although we can perform whatever fancy statistical operations that we choose on those numbers, the results from these analyses might well be meaningless. Michell (2000) called psychometrics "a pathology of science" for this reason. It *looks* like science (involving what appears to be quantification, and complicated mathematical techniques being applied to what look like quantities) but in reality, it can go nowhere – "Garbage in, garbage out," as our computer science colleagues say. For it is certainly true that it is hard to imagine that laws such as Newton's laws of motion could emerge from relating scores on tests to other variables. The best that one can hope for seems to be a non-parametric correlation, under ideal conditions.

Matters become murkier when we consider **interval scales**, ordinal scales and nominal scales. Heat reflects the amount of molecular jiggling in a substance; when all of the molecules are all at rest, the temperature is known as absolute zero. However, the thermometers that we use in our everyday lives do not represent this basic physical property. Setting my oven to 110 degrees Celsius does not mean that it is twice as hot as when I set it to 220 degrees. The amount of molecular jiggling does not double, because the "zero point" of the Celsius scale is set at an arbitrary level (the amount of jiggling which happens to represent the freezing point of water, rather than zero jiggling). This is an example of an "interval scale". It is also possible to recognise that some ovens are hotter than others, but not to be able to quantify by how much; this is an **ordinal scale**).

The incoherence of Stevens' arguments, and especially his suggestion that counting (e.g., the number of items answered correctly) can lead to ratio scales, was recognised quite early on.

> Nowhere in Stevens' writings can one find a qualification that only certain kinds of objects or events produce ratio scales when counted, or that counting produces ratio scales only in certain situations. . . . If counting produces ratio scales, then psychology must be rife with ratio scales because psychologists so often count – and not only rife, but in a position to augment the number of ratio scales by means of the effortless expedient of converting scales in current use into counts. Rather than computing IQ, for example (an ordinal scale according to Stevens, 1951, p. 27), the psychologist could merely revert to counting the number of questions answered correctly (which should be a ratio scale because it is a count).
> (Prytulak, 1975)

They still receive attention.

> The psychological sciences have adopted practices where psychological quantities may be invented at the will of the researcher and attention is then focused upon ever more creative and technical means to impose "real number" mathematics upon psychological attributes with little to no theoretical justification for doing so.
> (McGrane, 2015)

Psychologists are not as cautious as (other) scientists, and they use numbers to represent psychological concepts without considering whether the characteristics which these numbers attempt to quantify actually exist. Even if they do exist, are they quantifiable, or are they subjective experiences which cannot be measured using numbers? More importantly, can we ever *demonstrate* that scores on tests represent real characteristics of people?

Michell has suggested that because numbers are so fundamentally important for the development of physical sciences, and psychologists are desperate to have their measurements classed as "science", they have rushed headlong into using numbers to represent levels of psychological variables *without first checking that the numbers that they use correspond to any real property of the person*. The psychology of individual differences may thus have the appearance (but not the reality) of being a science. Michell suggests that psychologists pretend that they are measuring personality, abilities etc. because they are desperate to have the appearance of "doing science", along with the funding opportunities and prestige which this affords. Paul Barrett (2008) summarises the issues beautifully and simply, concluding:

> Something about the way we go about construing psychological variables, their measurement, and their presumed causal relations is wrong. That's where our efforts should be concentrated as scientists, not on yet more questionnaire item test theory and assumption-laden structural latent variable models that ignore the fundamental issues of quantitative measurement. We might seriously consider whether psychology might be, for all intents and purposes, a nonquantitative science.

We earlier considered how Boyle's law in physics leads to accurate predictions, and ultimately to a theory of how and why gases behave in the way they do. There are no comparable laws in the psychology of individual differences as far as I am aware. Even if there is such a thing as an anxiety system in the human body, we cannot predict that someone will show a particular level of skin resistance (anxious sweating) in a particular situation, or that a particular dose of a particular drug will reduce their score from 11 to 4. At best, we can gather data from many people, and calculate correlations – although these correlations are often woefully small and of trivial importance, showing only very weak (albeit non-zero) relationships between the variables.

It is as if we are trying to measure length using a ruler where the distances between the numbers vary randomly – and where every test involves using a different version of the ruler. In addition, there is likely to be a lot of random error which affects the accuracy with which we can read the ruler's markings. This does not sound much like precise, scientific measurement.

The fundamental issue is that scores on psychological tests do not represent basic properties of the thing being measured; they do not have a "unit of measurement". Even if traits such as anxiety exist and are quantitative, our scales and questionnaires do a fairly feeble job of assessing it and are unlikely to be able to develop proper quantitative laws.

Michell (2008) summarises the issue succinctly.

1. Psychometricians claim to be able to measure psychological attributes.
2. In this, they employ theories presuming that these attributes are quantitative.
3. There is, however, no hard evidence that these attributes are quantitative.
4. So their claim to be able to measure these attributes is at best premature, at worst, false.

All the clever psychometric methods described in the rest of this book *assume* that the numbers that are generated when people respond to test items or questionnaires represent levels of personality, intelligence etc. in much the same way as numbers in physics or other sciences represent length, mass, time, and other fundamental or derived units of measurement. The key word here is *assume*.

There are two basic issues here. First, can psychological measures *in* principle ever be quantitative? Second, if so, is it ever possible to *demonstrate* that they are quantitative?

These issues are complex, at least for those of us with a limited knowledge of the philosophy of science. Part of the problem is that psychological constructs may be social constructions. We argued earlier that "beauty" cannot be an intrinsic property of humans. Instead we choose to regard certain characteristics as beautiful – but what these are will probably vary from culture to culture and time to time. The paintings of Rubens show that fuller figures were seen as more beautiful in the 17th century than they are now, whilst time and culture determines whether we regard tanned skin as attractive. Beauty is a "social construction" – a characteristic which we attribute to an object or a person, rather than a property of the object or person. Whilst we can develop scales to measure it, scores on such scales do not reflect any real property of the object or person. This causes problems.

> How can an attribute that is constructed by humans be a quantity, or a *real* property at all? Even if one accepts that such attributes can be modelled as quantities, they are surely resistant to standard techniques of (physical) empirical manipulation such as concatenation, which arguably eliminates them as candidates for "fundamental" measurement.
>
> (Maul et al., 2016)

Anything which is a social construction cannot be measured, and part of the problem is that we cannot easily tell whether our constructs ('intelligence", "anxiety", "need for approval", "self-esteem" etc.) represent real characteristics of people, or social constructions – ideas which come from us, rather than being characteristics of people.

This means that there is no way of ensuring that the numbers produced by questionnaires or tests have any basis in reality. They *might* perhaps reflect some real property of the person, but they might not. Indeed it is often found that there is a large disparity between what people *say* they will do when answering questions in questionnaires and their actual behaviour (e.g., Sheeran & Webb, 2016). If responses to items do not reflect how people actually behave, and there is no way of tying the responses to some detailed underlying theory (such as underpins measurement of voltage), then perhaps we have not "measured" anything at all.

That said, some psychological characteristics may not be social constructions. Anxiety and depression may have their roots in people's experiences and biological make-up. Intelligence is known to be highly heritable in adulthood and adolescence (LaBuda et al., 1987). Scores on intelligence tests therefore indicate (to some extent) some sort of biological characteristics of our nervous systems. However, it does not follow that intelligence is measurable. The distinction is between measurement and counting the number of items that are answered correctly when someone takes an intelligence test.

COUNTING AND MEASUREMENT

Counting is different from measurement. I can count the number of houses between my house and the park, but as the width of each garden is different (and there are roads to cross), I have not *measured* the distance between my house and the park. If there are 20 houses between my house and the park (counting), and I have passed 10 of them, I cannot conclude that I am halfway there (measurement). This is because there is no unit of distance. If all the houses were the same width, and there were no roads in the way, then counting would be equivalent to measuring. But to achieve this measurement we would have to *demonstrate* that all of the houses were the same width (by measuring them) – in other words, showing that the things we are counting are the same size. And to do this, we need a way of measuring the attribute. We need to show that the intervals between the numbers in our scale (the count of the number of houses I have passed) corresponds to distance; each number may represent a length of (say) 30 metres. Such measurement involves the use of ratio scales.

In the case of intelligence items, the problem is that we cannot demonstrate that someone who gets 80% of the items correct has twice the level of ability as someone who gets 40% of them correct. Items will probably vary in difficulty; if 40% of the items in an intelligence test are trivially easy for a child of a certain age but the remainder are really difficult, a child who scores (say) 50% correct might have twice the level of intelligence as one who scores 40% correct; we have no way of telling whether or not this is the case.

Some researchers claim that psychometric techniques can overcome this problem. However, it is uncertain whether techniques such as conjoint measurement and Rasch scaling can do so. See, for example, Trendler (2009; 2019) and Michell (2019). These papers are classics but are not particularly easy; Saint-Mont (2012) and Barrett (2011) offer more accessible summaries for those who are interested.

TEST SCORES AS ORDINAL DATA

We might reluctantly accept that scores on psychological scales may not provide measurements (as used in physics) and so cannot be used to develop quantitative laws, similar to Boyle's gas law discussed earlier. However, if we are prepared to make the risky assumption that a trait or state is quantitative, perhaps we can use test scores to rank-order people and treat scores on psychological tests as "ordinal data" – whereby we can say that one person has a higher level of a trait than another, but we cannot tell how much higher it is. Such data can be analysed using non-parametric statistics. Even this is not without its problems, for it is not obvious how we should decide that one person's score is higher than another's.

Suppose that Adam and Eve completed the obsessionality questionnaire shown in Table 3.1. These are not particularly good or bad items; they resemble those found in thousands of personality questionnaires. A high rating means that the person agrees with the statement, and a low rating means that they disagree.

Psychologists would normally add up scores on several items, each measuring a different aspect of obsessionality, to estimate how obsessional a person is. Adam scores 11, Eve scores 9, so Eve seems to be less obsessional than Adam. You might argue that although this is not a ratio scale, the numbers tell us something useful; they may perhaps form an interval or ordinal scale. We might therefore conclude that Adam is more obsessional than Eve – even though we cannot be sure by how much.

Table 3.1 Responses of two people items measuring obsessionality using a 7-point rating scale (after Kline, 1968)

	Adam	Eve
Do you insist on paying back even small, trivial debts?	2	3
There's nothing more infuriating than people who don't keep appointments.	6	1
Do you have a special place for important documents?	2	3
Can you usually put your hand on anything you want in your desk or room?	1	2

Perhaps we should look instead at the responses to the individual items. Eve's responses to items 1, 3 and 4 suggest that she is *more* obsessional than Adam on three out of the four items. So is Eve more or less obsessional than Adam? It is almost impossible to tell. Because the numbers which emerge when people's responses to questionnaires and tests are scored do not correspond to any known psychological or physical processes, we cannot know how (or whether) it is appropriate to add them up or otherwise combine them to say anything sensible about a person's level of a trait.

PRAGMATIC ATTEMPTS AT PSYCHOLOGICAL MEASUREMENT

Although Hölder's axioms are used to demonstrate that an attribute must be quantitative, it is perhaps possible that some attributes might be quantitative even though they cannot be shown to meet all these criteria. One way of justifying the use of psychological test scores as measurements would be to show that test scores (or some transformation of them) were proportional to some real, measurable property of people. Suppose that we found a psychological test, the scores of which correlated very substantially with a measure which was genuinely quantitative, such as hormone levels, genetic make-up, or cerebral blood flow. It could be argued that scores on such tests may be quantitative, as they correlate substantially with truly quantitative measures.

The best example I know concerns intelligence. We first have to assume that individual differences in intelligence exist. Then we need to assume that it is quantitative — that people's levels of intelligence can be represented by numbers. Next, we need to develop some kind of test which measures intelligence. And finally, we need a theory linking intelligence to some type of physical measurement.

Some psychologists have suggested that intelligence is just speed of information processing; some people may have nervous systems which just transmit information faster than others. Then we need to find a way of measuring this, such as inspection time (Nettelbeck, 1982), which is the amount of time a person needs in order to recognise (encode) a simple shape or sound. Numerous studies have shown inspection time to be strongly correlated with scores on an intelligence test; a correlation of 1.0 indicates that the two variables are exactly proportional. If the correlation was 1.0, this would mean that a person's score on the intelligence test is exactly proportional to the speed with which they can process information (as measured by the inspection time task). We could use regression to link people's scores on the intelligence test to their inspection time in milliseconds — and we could derive a formula such as

inspection time = (score on a particular intelligence test) × 8.7 + 23 to tell what a person's inspection time (in milliseconds) would be, based on their intelligence test score.

As we know, time is measured on a ratio scale; this means that we could estimate people's inspection time using a standard intelligence test and say that because Zoe has a score which is twice as high as Helen's, Zoe's inspection time is twice as fast as Helen's, and so Zoe is twice as intelligent as Helen. We are essentially using inspection time (which we know is a ratio-scaled variable) to calibrate our intelligence test scores.

The problem is that the correlation between inspection time and intelligence is, at best, about 0.6, meaning that scores on intelligence tests only explain about a third of the person-to-person variability in intelligence. Although there is a relationship between scores on intelligence tests and a physical property of the individual, this is not substantial enough for us to treat the intelligence test score as a proxy for inspection time. In addition, it is highly unlikely that the relationship between inspection time and test score will be linear; this will depend on the distribution of the difficulty of the test items. We will also need to make some rather unlikely assumptions about the way people respond – see the discussion of Guttman scales in Chapter 4.

SUMMARY

This chapter is meant to shock and worry readers. It suggests that psychological scales and tests may not measure real characteristics of people, and that it is quite wrong to *assume* that test scores are measurements of anything. At best, we can count the number of responses made to test items. Likert scales are particularly problematical. We have shown using the obsessionality example that combining the scores on several items can produce different answers, depending on the (arbitrary) scoring system used. We cannot claim to have measured individual differences unless there is clear evidence linking scores on tests to behaviours which are genuinely quantitative (not scores on other tests). Given that most psychologists have zero interest in relating scores on tests to any real property of the individual, the outlook for psychological measurements may be bleak. It certainly casts doubt on the legitimacy of ever more complex psychometric techniques that *assume* that data are quantitative.

Most psychologists simply ignore the issues discussed in this chapter, if they are even aware of them, and I appreciate that most readers of this book will be required to explore and understand the psychometric methods and techniques in the following chapters without regard to the issues discussed earlier. It is much easier to press ahead and perform complex analyses than to worry too much about what the numbers that one analyses actually mean. But please treat this chapter as a sort of "health warning".

Worry about what you are measuring. Ask yourself whether more complex techniques introduced near the end of this book are always going to be appropriate for your data. Where possible, use non-parametric measures. But bear in mind that whatever it is you are trying to measure may not be quantitative at all.

CHAPTER 4
ADMINISTERING AND SCORING QUESTIONNAIRES AND TESTS

Questionnaires and tests can be administered in several ways. Specialised clinical and diagnostic instruments are administered face to face by a trained psychologist to ensure the greatest possible accuracy and motivation. Tests and questionnaires may be administered to groups of people in a room, under supervision – for example, when using a test or questionnaire as part of a selection process, where specialised equipment is involved, or when gathering data from student volunteers in a lecture theatre. Or tests may be put on the internet. Once there, they can either be administered to known individuals (for example, student volunteers or patients) who are individually invited to take part in the study. Alternatively, online platforms may be used to recruit volunteers. It is possible to specify the types of participants one wants using these platforms, which appears to make it straightforward to recruit participants from any desired population. However, this may not be possible in practice, as discussed later.

This chapter considers how tests may be administered and how responses to tests may be translated into numbers for statistical analyses.

ADMINISTERING TESTS AND QUESTIONNAIRES

There are two main options for administering the types of questionnaires and tests discussed in Chapter 2. The items can be administered using a computer – either as a stand-alone application or over the internet. Stand-alone applications are more common for cognitive tasks which may require high-quality graphics, special peripherals (such as joysticks or response boxes) or rely on accurate time measurement, which can be challenging to achieve over the internet. It is much more straightforward to administer questionnaires over the internet by inviting known participants from a "subject pool" to visit a website which is not publicised, by seeking volunteers from social media websites or by recruiting participants who are paid for their efforts via

DOI: 10.4324/9781003240181-4

commercial sites such as Mechanical Turk (MTurk) or Prolific. Alternatively, data can be gathered in the old-fashioned way, using paper booklets and answer sheets.

PUTTING ITEMS ONLINE

These days most questionnaires and some cognitive tests are administered over the internet. If any serious psychometric analyses are to be performed on the data from online questionnaires or tests, then it is important that the responses to individual items are made available – not just the total score for each scale. Check this, as these data may not be available when using commercial systems.

For multiple-choice ability tests, it is important to know whether each item was answered correctly or not and to differentiate between items that were answered incorrectly and those which were not attempted (e.g., because they were near the end of a test, and time ran out). If you are developing such a test, it is also important to know which alternative was chosen for each item to see whether any of the incorrect alternatives ("distractors") were unduly popular or unpopular. It is therefore important to know which answer was chosen for each item – not just whether or not the item was answered correctly.

The main advantages of computer administration are that:

1. Timings for sections of the test (or indeed for individual items) can be imposed.
2. It is possible to measure a wide range of responses. For example, it is possible to measure how long it takes for each person to answer each item, to measure mouse or joystick movements, to record what a person says.
3. It is possible to test remotely – for example, allowing someone to take an aptitude test at home rather than in an assessment centre. (That said, the obvious difficulties are ensuring that the person taking the test is who they say they are and that they do not have any help from other people or electronic devices when taking the test.)
4. It is possible to implement **adaptive** ability tests (see Chapter 15), where the difficulty of the items administered varies for each participant, so that each participant is given items which are taxing but not impossible.
5. Scores may be obtained immediately, allowing for feedback to be given.

Using internet-based assessments from a test publisher's site

Some test publishers (e.g., Pearson Assessments) offer online versions of some commercial questionnaires and tests. They may also offer computer-generated "narrative feedback" based on the test scores; these are reports designed for personnel managers or for feedback to the people who took the test; for example, "John is a little more anxious than most applicants". These will be useful for psychologists who give feedback to job applicants etc. but will generally be of little interest to researchers who focus on the relationships between item responses and scale scores, rather than trying to understand individuals' personalities.

The other problem is that rather few good commercial questionnaires and tests are available for online use – and it is rare to be given access to responses to individual items. This limits the analyses which can be performed. In a very few cases the test publisher may claim that the method of scoring responses is "commercially sensitive" and so will not reveal how the responses are translated into numbers – which means that it is difficult or impossible to check how well the test works in a particular culture, age group or application. Such assessments should be avoided if at all possible.

The assessments are often expensive, and it may not be possible to integrate them into a "package" of several scales or tests for administration using MTurk etc. In addition, as there are good-quality free alternatives to many commercial questionnaires, it is unlikely that many researchers or students will choose to use test publishers' offerings – though those who are involved in personnel assessment and training may find them useful.

Developing internet-based measures

It is extremely straightforward to put questionnaire items online using a free site such as https://surveymonkey.com. Although designed for surveys, the format can be used for Likert scales (or multiple-choice responses). Another advantage of this "do-it-yourself" approach is that several scales can be combined into the same survey. It is also possible to obtain responses to individual items, thus facilitating psychometric analyses.

This approach should not be used for commercial tests, the items of which are copyrighted. However, the https://ipip.ori.org site mentioned in Chapter 2 holds a great many personality scales which are free to use for any purpose.

Putting together internet-based cognitive ability tests is more difficult, as displaying complex graphics, timing responses etc. can be challenging. However, free experiment generator packages such as Pavlovia, Tatool or the PsyToolkit (Stoet, 2010) may be useful. These sites come with libraries of cognitive tests which may perhaps provide what you require, and it is also possible to amend these or design new ones from scratch. These systems can produce cognitive experiments which can be integrated into systems such as Prolific (see later). There are others, too, including commercial ones such as Gorilla or Inquisit.

Administering internet-based measures

Most research in individual differences is based on data from internet volunteers, who are paid small amounts for completing questionnaires and tests. Mechanical Turk and Prolific are two popular sites which have databases of volunteer workers. You can specify the population you want (e.g., 500 female Australians aged 18–40), generate the questionnaire/test using SurveyMonkey, PsyToolkit or other platforms, and these systems will recruit volunteers and collate their responses; the process is usually very speedy. The advantages of this method are that:

- Data can be collected from large samples very quickly and with minimal effort – which explains its popularity.
- It is possible to specify a target population, rather than relying on student volunteers, which used to be commonplace.
- Item-level responses from all participants may be retrieved as a spreadsheet. It may be possible to automatically score the responses, but if not, the methods described in the next section may be used.
- It is possible to specify whether respondents should use a PC or mobile device.

The technique is so popular that its drawbacks tend to be ignored. Recent research suggests that despite the claims of the site operators, the problems with this methodology may be so severe that studies based on samples of people from the internet may be worthless unless extreme care is taken to screen the data.

The problem of lack of control

The obvious issue with recruiting participants over the internet is that one has no idea about the conditions under which the data are collected. Are participants alone, or in a public place where others can see their answers? Is the device which they are using suitable, or small/old/cracked? Are they sober, drunk or drugged? Are they focusing their complete attention on the task or are they trying do something else at the same time, such as working or playing a computer game? Are they genuinely trying to advance science by participating, or are they clicking more or less at random in order to earn as much money as possible from as little effort as possible?

The problem of deliberate misrepresentation

A major problem with such research is that there is no way of telling whether people misrepresent themselves. You may *ask* for Australian women aged 18–40, but how can you tell whether the person completing your questionnaire or test really does fall into this category? Whilst participants are only paid modest amounts of money (by

Western standards) for completing tasks, these amounts may be significant for those in developing economies. Completing such tasks may be a useful source of income for some. Misrepresenting oneself in order to be included in studies is widespread. Wessling et al. (2017) found that between 24% and 83% of mechanical Turk respondents misrepresented themselves when completing questionnaires. It seems clear that it is naive to assume that participants in online studies are who they claim to be.

It is normal to include some screening questions in an attempt to guard against such deception – but online fora have developed which explicitly advise participants and programmers how to evade such checks (Wessling et al., 2017). Chmielewski and Kucker (2020) outline some possible screening techniques – but as these are now published and known to unscrupulous participants, they are probably now ineffective.

The problem of careless or malicious responding

Some participants may not pay much attention to the meaning of the questions or the nature of the cognitive tasks which they perform. This may be due to lapses of attention (tiredness, attempts at multi-tasking) or they may be malicious (pressing keys at random in order to obtain payment for minimal effort). There are several ways of identifying inattentive or malicious responding by people, and there is a considerable literature on this (e.g., Desimone et al., 2015). If a person's data is identified as "suspect", none of their answers should be included in any analyses. How might one detect inattentive or malicious responding?

- One can include items such as "leave this item unanswered" – so that if an answer is given, one can probably assume that the respondent is not paying attention or that they are a bot.
- Response times to items can sometimes be measured. Are they within the "normal" range? Too fast? Too slow? Too variable (perhaps indicating that the participant is doing two things at once)?
- If two items are very similar in meaning (e.g., "Are you a nervous person?", "Do you usually feel anxious?"), it is possible to check whether they are answered similarly. If a respondent agrees with one item and disagrees with the other, they are probably responding randomly. It is possible to develop more complicated techniques like this, based on several items (Curran, 2016) – people whose patterns of responses are unusual are dropped.
- Statistical models may be used to try to classify each participant as a "likely genuine participant", "likely random responder" etc. Details of some approaches are given in Roman et al. (2022) and Schneider et al. (2018). Such approaches require an advanced understanding of statistical techniques.

Some sites such as MTurk have "premium members" who have strong approval ratings and who are paid more for each study. One might expect them to produce better quality data. Unfortunately, this does not seem to be the case (Rouse, 2020).

The problem of bots

If the earlier issues were not bad enough, it has very recently become clear that **bots** (malicious computer programs which pretend to be real people) are being used to take online studies in order to generate income for their programmers (Godinho et al., 2020; Ilagan & Falk, 2022). They may answer items at randomly or be programmed to give answers with a particular frequency distribution. The responses made by bots are likely to be similar to those made by inattentive or malicious humans and will generally tend to reduce correlations between test items and add measurement error to scores on scales. If a questionnaire is attacked by multiple bots, the data may be completely meaningless, and any results from its analysis may mislead other researchers.

Detecting bots is not easy, as shown by Storozuk et al. (2020) who describe their experiences and evaluate several methods for identifying answers made by bots. This paper is essential reading for anyone contemplating online data collection. Surprisingly, perhaps, obvious techniques such as inserting CAPTCHA images into the survey, checking whether IP addresses were from the country at which the study was aimed, or using photographs of text (rather than machine-readable text) were not particularly effective. These authors advise against publicising the survey on social media (Facebook, Twitter etc.), as this is where many bots may find targets to attack.

The extent of the problem

How big a problem *is* inattentive or malicious responding? It is hard to be sure, as the extent of the problem will presumably depend on the size of the financial reward and the topic (questionnaires perhaps being easier to fake than tasks requiring continuous input). The amount of bad data found will also clearly depend on the effectiveness of the method used to detect it. Without knowing the number of respondents who are bots or careless responders, it is difficult to tell the effectiveness of methods for detecting them or to know the number of "false positives" (careful respondents who are wrongly identified as malicious).

It has been found that a surprisingly small percentage (6%) of bad data can seriously affect the results of psychometric analyses (Arias et al., 2022), and so the problem is probably quite serious. One study (Pozzar et al., 2020) found that 94% of data obtained in an internet study was fraudulent, where people misrepresented themselves, or produced low-quality data, and 16% of the "respondents" were clearly identified as bots. These figures are alarming.

Although administering questionnaires online via websites such as Mechanical Turk is tremendously quick and convenient for researchers and students, it is clear that considerable effort *must* be spent on identifying participants who are lying about their credentials and participants/bots who produce flawed data. It may be preferable to administer any online questionnaires or tests to individuals who can be trusted to provide usable data – such as other students or members of a "research panel" of known volunteers who participate for no reward. See Shamon and Berning (2020). The other alternative is to administer the questionnaire or test in a supervised environment, such as a computer laboratory. The presence of research staff may discourage random responding; it would be obvious if someone was rushing thoughtlessly through the items. The common practice of administering questionnaires and tests to anonymous paid volunteers is, however, inviting trouble.

PAPER-AND-PENCIL TESTING

In olden days people completed questionnaires and tests using paper test booklets, and sometimes a separate answer sheet (so that the test booklet could be reused as some commercial booklets are very expensive). Some commercial questionnaires and tests such as Cattell's 16PF (Cattell et al., 1994) and Raven's Matrices (Raven et al., 2003) are only available as paper booklets, and given the problems with internet testing outlined previously, it is clear that this older method of administration still has its advantages.

Questionnaires may be administered to groups of people or given/posted to people to complete at their leisure. Cognitive tests generally have time limits, and so these are normally only administered to groups of people. The advantages of paper-and-pencil testing of groups of people are that:

- The data unequivocally come from real people, not bots.
- Participants may put more effort into responding when dealing with a researcher in person, rather than an impersonal internet request.
- It can be easy to test quite large groups – e.g., in a university lecture hall.
- Participants can ask if there is something which they do not understand.
- It is possible to see whether a participant is behaving oddly – such as responding very quickly or not reading items before responding.
- Market research agencies can provide validated samples of people – e.g., a sample of the general population stratified by age, sex and educational qualifications.
- Familiarity with computer hardware will not impact performance when testing older people.

The drawbacks are that:

- It is difficult and expensive to recruit "special" groups of participants – e.g., those from a different country.
- The data need to be scored as described later.
- Requiring participants to attend at a particular time and place may reduce the number of volunteers available.
- It is not possible to time individual items (for cognitive tests), and it may be difficult to impose strict time limits for entire tests as some people may continue to work after being asked to stop.

TELEPHONE ADMINISTRATION

Market researchers and others sometimes administer brief questionnaires by telephone. However, this approach imposes memory demands as the participant must remember the entire stem of the questionnaire item. This is presents problems for older participants (Lang et al., 2011). Poor literacy or language skills may also lead to poor quality data (Sutin et al., 2013).

SCORING TESTS AND QUESTIONNAIRES

The vast majority of scales involve some form of scoring process in order to translate performance on the test items into some sort of numerical score. For example, the teacher scoring the attainment test which measured knowledge of historical dates (see Chapter 2) would probably give students 1 point for each answer that is correct. As this is a free response test, guessing is unlikely to be much of an issue. Each child's score on the test would then be calculated by adding up the number of items correctly answered.

Free response ability tests are usually scored in a similar way, with 1 point being awarded for each correct answer. However, matters become a little more complicated for multiple-choice tests, where participants have to choose the one correct answer from a number of possible options, and where time limits are involved.

Likert scales (introduced in Chapter 2) are commonly used to measure personality, attitudes and moods. A Likert scale is simply a rating scale where people are asked to rate how well a statement describes them, how much they agree with a statement, or something similar. If the scale has five levels of response (strongly agree/agree/neutral/disagree/strongly agree, for example), these responses are scored by assigning the numbers such as 1/2/3/4/5 or 5/4/3/2/1 to the various responses. A high score represents a high level of the trait or state.

Table 4.1 Three items measuring extraversion showing the answer sheet and marking key

		Strongly agree	Agree	Neutral	Disagree	Strongly disagree
1	I am the life and soul of the party	O	O	O	O	O
2	I would rather sit by myself than socialise	O	O	O	O	O
3	I have more friends than most people	O	O	O	O	O
	Marking key for items 1–3					
		Strongly agree	Agree	Neutral	Disagree	Strongly disagree
1	I am the life and soul of the party	5	4	3	2	1
2	I would rather sit by myself than socialise	1	2	3	4	5
3	I have more friends than most people	5	4	3	2	1

For example, suppose that the items in Table 4.1 were used to measure extraversion, or sociability. The first rows show the answer sheet, and the bottom of the table shows which marks would be awarded for the various answers. So someone high on this trait would strongly agree with item 1, strongly disagree with item 2, and strongly agree with item 3.

It does not matter which numbers are used, as long as the difference between adjacent numbers (1, in the example) is always the same.

This would work, as the scores from psychological scales are normally correlated with other things – for example, scores on *other* psychological scales, some aspect of behaviour such as simple reaction time. The important thing about correlations is that they are insensitive to the scale of measurement. So it does not matter whether the "low" score for an item starts at 0, 1, or 1,199,816 – or anything else. The correlation

Table 4.2 Marking key where responses are equally spaced, although starting at different (arbitrary) numbers

		Strongly agree	Agree	Neutral	Disagree	Strongly disagree
1	I am the life and soul of the party	11	13	15	17	19
2	I would rather sit by myself than socialise	9	7	5	3	1
3	I have more friends than most people	2	4	6	8	10

between scores on the test and anything else will be exactly the same whatever the starting point. See Spreadsheet 4.1 if you need to be convinced of this.

> **Spreadsheet name:** Spreadsheet 4.1: Correlations
>
> **Download from:** https://routledge.com/9781032146164/
>
> **Purpose:** To show that correlations are unaffected by the scale of measurement, or the starting value.
>
> **Contents of spreadsheet:**
>
> - Section A shows the responses that five people make to the items in Table 4.1. Each person places an "x" in the box which best describes them.
> - Section B shows the scoring key – the table which converts the "x's" into numbers. When freshly downloaded, this shows that for item 1 anyone strongly agreeing with the statement is awarded 5 points, 4 points if they agree and so on. For item 2 (where strongly *disagreeing* with the items represents a high level of extraversion), strongly agreeing is awarded 1 point, agreeing 2 points and so on.
> - Section C shows the scores which each of the five people obtained on some other scale. It also shows the scored responses, obtained by applying the scoring key to the responses in section A, plus each person's total score on the three items.
> - Section D shows the correlation between the total score and the score on the other scale.
>
> **Suggested activity:**
>
> - Check that you understand how the scoring key translates each person's response to each item into a number. Perhaps alter some of the responses (deleting one "x" and inserting another on the same line) to check.

- To convince yourself that the correlations in section D are not influenced by whether the values in the scoring key start at 1, 0 or some other number, try adding a constant to all the numbers in the scoring key for one of the items – add 10 to each value of the scoring key for item 1, perhaps. The correlation between the total score and the score on the other test does not change – though of course the total score increases.
- You might also like to change the interval between adjacent categories for all items. Perhaps use the values in Table 4.2. Again, the correlation does not change.
- However, if the interval between adjacent categories in the scoring key are not all the same, the correlation *will* change. Try the values in Table 4.3, or any other values which you choose.

Points to note:

- Experiment by changing entries in the *green* areas.
- Results are in the *yellow* areas.
- Simply download another copy if you accidentally change formulae.

Learning outcomes: Readers should now be able to:

- Show an understanding of how Likert scales are scored using a scoring key.
- Appreciate that as long as the interval between adjacent categories is the same within and between items, the correlation between scores on a test and another variable remain the same.
- Appreciate that it does not matter whether the interval between adjacent categories is large or small.

You might feel that the example in Table 4.3 would not work for two reasons: first, the difference between the marks awarded to adjacent statements is not constant (in item 1); second, the difference between adjacent cells is not the same for every item (scores for item 2 increase by 1 from low to high; scores for item 3 increase by 2).

Table 4.3 Marking key where the difference between adjacent categories is not always identical and where there are also differences *between* items

		Strongly agree	Agree	Neutral	Disagree	Strongly disagree
1	I am the life and soul of the party	1	3	4	6	9
2	I would rather sit by myself than socialise	5	4	3	2	1
3	I have more friends than most people	1	3	5	7	9

The problem is that, as we saw in Chapter 3, there is absolutely no way of telling whether the numbers 5/4/3/2/1 for "strongly agree", "agree" etc. are any more appropriate than (say) 9/8/6/3/1. We cannot know whether the numbers that we use should be equally spaced — that is, whether the step of moving from "strongly agree" to "agree" on the response scale measures the same amount of change in extraversion as moving from "neutral" to "disagree" — because, after all, the words used to define the numbers are arbitrary. In Table 4.3, if we had used the words "describes me perfectly", "strongly agree", "agree", "strongly disagree" and "nothing like me", you can see that the gap between the words "agree" and "strongly disagree" *looks* like a larger change in extraversion than moving from (say) "describes me perfectly" to "strongly agree". But there is no way of telling. Likert scales almost always use numbers that are equally spaced — but it is by no means certain that this will always be appropriate, even if the attribute being measured is quantitative.

THE PRACTICALITIES OF SCORING TESTS

LIKERT-SCALED ITEMS MARKED ON A TEST BOOKLET OR ANSWER SHEET

It is still common practice to gather data using paper questionnaires (and sometimes separate answer sheets) similar to those shown in what follows. Unlike the example in Table 4.1, the items in Figure 4.1 measure two different traits; items 1 and 3 measure extraversion (sociability and optimism), whilst items 2 and 4 measure neuroticism.

There is one transparent acetate sheet for each scale. Each shows many marks should be awarded for a particular response, and which responses should be added together. In the example, when the extraversion scoring template is placed over the answer sheet, this individual obtains a score of 4 points for question 1 and 5 points for question 3. Items 2 and 4 do not contribute to the extraversion score. If the neuroticism scoring template is placed over the answer sheet, scores of 2 and 1 would be awarded for items 2 and 4, respectively. Thus this person would obtain a score of 9 for extraversion and 3 for anxiety.

MARKING BY HAND

There is plenty of scope for errors to creep in when scoring tests manually using templates — typically because the acetate scoring sheet is not correctly placed over the paper answer sheet, or because the person scoring the test makes an arithmetic slip

ADMINISTERING AND SCORING QUESTIONNAIRES AND TESTS

Item	Practice items	Strongly agree	Agree	Neutral/ unsure	Disagree	Strongly disagree
P1	I understand how to mark my answers to the items in this questionnaire	●	○	○	○	○
P2	I will be try to be honest when giving my answers	○	○	○	○	○
Item	Main test	Strongly agree	Agree	Neutral/ unsure	Disagree	Strongly disagree
1	I find it easy to talk about myself	○	○	○	○	○
2	I rarely feel 'down'	○	○	○	○	○
3	I'm a pessimist at heart	○	○	○	○	○
4	I worry a lot	○	○	○	○	○
etc.						

Item	Strongly agree	Agree	Neutral/ unsure	Disagree	Strongly disagree
P1	●	○	○	○	○
P2	○	●	○	○	○
Item	Strongly agree	Agree	Neutral/ unsure	Disagree	Strongly disagree
1	○	●	○	○	○
2	○	●	○	○	○
3	○	○	○	○	●
4	○	○	○	○	●
etc.					

Figure 4.1 Typical format of a personality test booklet and (optional) completed answer sheet. This scoring template would normally be printed on a transparent acetate sheet which is placed over the answer sheet (or question booklet) so that the marked response is visible.

when adding together the scores for the individual items (which is normally done using mental arithmetic, without writing down anything but the final score for a trait). Errors could also creep in if the respondent does something strange – for example, marking two answers for a question, one of which was correct, or crossing out a correct answer but not marking any other choice. In this sort of setting, it is quite possible that two

A scoring template for Extraversion						A scoring template for Neuroticism					
Item	Strongly agree	Agree	Neutral/ unsure	Disagree	Strongly disagree	Item	Strongly agree	Agree	Neutral/ unsure	Disagree	Strongly disagree
P1						P1					
P2						P2					
Item	Strongly agree	Agree	Neutral/ unsure	Disagree	Strongly disagree	Item	Strongly agree	Agree	Neutral/ unsure	Disagree	Strongly disagree
1	5	4	3	2	1	1					
2						2	1	2	3	4	5
3	1	2	3	4	5	3					
4						4	5	4	3	2	1

Figure 4.2 Transparent scoring templates for extraversion and neuroticism scales for use with the answer sheets shown in Figure 4.1

scorers might sometimes reach different conclusions about whether or not an answer was correct. However, the great advantages of scoring tests this way are:

1. The ability to test large groups of people at once – either using test booklets or test items presented using a data projector – without having to set up large numbers of computers
2. Speed of setup: answer sheets and marking templates can be prepared in a few minutes
3. Costs are minimal, whereas optical scanners (see what follows) are expensive, and the answer sheets used with them may need to be purchased or specially printed rather than photocopied.

The main disadvantages are that:

1. The whole process is slow and tedious to perform.
2. It requires mental arithmetic skills from the person scoring the test.
3. The only output is each person's total score on each scale of the test. It is surprising how often one needs a record of precisely which response was made to each item – for example, to check the internal consistency of the test (see Chapter 7), identify which responses were most popular, perform a factor analysis to check that all of the items measure the same trait (see Chapter 10), or identify items which were not

attempted. My advice is always to record the responses to individual items even if scoring templates are available because it is extremely likely that this information will be needed at some stage during the analysis. Rather than scoring the items, just enter characters from the keyboard to represent the responses that were made. The characters which you use are arbitrary (but should obviously be the same for all items in a scale); if items have five possible responses, you could use 1/2/3/4/5 or z/x/c/v/b or anything else you like. Items that are unanswered or spoilt might be left blank or coded 9.

MARKING BY SCANNER

What of optical scanners? These use specially designed answer sheets and commercial software. They scan responses to multiple-choice items, and the associated software also scores the items. This is probably much safer than relying on the mental arithmetic prowess of a human, who may have spent several hours sleepily scoring responses. Furthermore, if the system detects a problem with any items (for example, if two responses are marked for the same item or a coffee stain covers part of the answer sheet) it will normally flag that sheet as requiring human intervention to decide what should be done. Here the degree of accuracy is likely to be high, and it is quick and easy to check this by scanning and scoring sheets twice. The software provides an abundance of information, including the total scores for each person, scores for individual items and various statistical breakdowns. Some commercial test publishers still provide a scanning service for users, but I have always found that manually entering data into a spreadsheet is quick, and the effort in setting up and printing answer sheets for optical scanners is not worthwhile for a questionnaire which one designs oneself.

MARKING BY SPREADSHEET

An alternative to using templates to score responses to multiple-choice tests answered on paper involves simply entering a codes identifying which boxes were ticked into a spreadsheet and using this to score the items and test. For example, a mark in the "strongly disagree" box could be coded as "1", "disagree" as "2" and so on using adjacent keys on a QWERTY keyboard, which makes data entry much faster than if responses were coded "a", "b", "c" etc. It is then necessary to reverse the scores on some items. This solution is likely to be faster and more accurate than marking answer sheets manually, using templates. Like the optical scanner it provides the full item-by-item breakdown of results.

Spreadsheet 4.2 scores Likert scales, produces some simple item statistics and helps one decide which values to use for any missing data. If there are no missing data, it also calculates the total score for each person on each scale. It might be of some practical use, though as before, no guarantee can be given as to its accuracy.

> **Spreadsheet name:** Spreadsheet 4.2: Simple Likert scorer
>
> **Download from:** https://routledge.com/9781032146164/
>
> **Purpose:** To show Likert-scaled data may be scored using a spreadsheet.
>
> **Contents of spreadsheet:** Sample data from seven people on two scales, with one piece of missing data.
>
> **Suggested activity:**
>
> - After entering some basic information in the "Raw_Data" tab, section A specifies the names for the scales, and how the items should be scored. A "1" indicates which scale each item measures; there should therefore only be one "1" in each column. Missing data should be left blank.
> - Section B contains raw data – indicating which box each person ticked (1 for the leftmost box etc.). Each person *must* be given a name or code in column A.
> - The "Scored_Items" tab holds the scored data, which can be copied and pasted into another program. If desired, it is also possible to sort these data so that all of the items in the same scale are next to each other. Missing data appear as blanks.
> - The "Scores" tab shows the mean and standard deviation for each item *based just on those people who answered the item*. This can be useful when deciding which value to use for missing data.
> - As the mean of the other participants is 4 for item 3, it might be useful to go back to the "Raw_Data" tab and replace the blank with 4.
> - As there are now no missing data, the scores of each person on each scale are shown in the "Scores" tab.
>
> **Points to note:**
>
> - Experiment by changing entries in the *green* areas.
> - Results are in the *yellow* areas.
> - Simply download another copy if you accidentally change formulae.
>
> **Learning outcomes: Readers should now be able to:**
>
> - Score a Likert-scaled questionnaire.

IPSATISED SCALES

So far, each item in a scale has attempted to measure a person's position along a single trait. For example, each item correctly answered on a test of memory would normally increase a person's score by 1 point; strongly agreeing with a statement such as "I suffer from 'nerves'" will increase the individual's anxiety score. **Ipsatised (or ipsative) scales** are different. Instead of measuring the extent to which a person agrees with statements measuring various levels of one trait (**normative scales**), an ipsative scale provides respondents with several different statements, *each measuring quite different traits*, and requires them to choose which statement best describes them and which is most untrue of how they feel, think or act. We gave a somewhat different example of an ipsative scale in Chapter 2; they both suffer from the same problem.

These tests are usually scored by counting the number of times that a person says that a particular trait describes them well minus the number of times that they say that the trait describes them badly. An example may make this clearer.

Suppose that a researcher is interested in measuring four different traits; the extent to which they blame others when things go wrong, their level of depression, their belief in luck and their inability to focus their thoughts. It would be possible to devise several items, such as those in Table 4.4.

In this example, the participant chose the "neurotic" answer twice (blaming themselves and feeling like crying), they did not blame others ("the test is unfair") and they did not have problems focusing their thoughts. When this scale is scored, they would therefore have a score of 2 for neuroticism, 0 for belief in luck, −1 for blaming others, and −1 for inability to focus their thoughts.

This all looks very appealing, and several published tests use this sort of format (mostly in education and occupational/organisational psychology), including the Schwartz Value Survey, the Defense Mechanisms Inventory and the Occupational Personality Questionnaire. However, there are well-documented problems with this approach. Those who defend the use of ipsative tests (Baron, 1996; Bartram, 1996) against their critics (Johnson et al., 1988; Meade, 2004) tend to have a vested interest in their use. I certainly have very major reservations about the techniques. The reasons for this are several.

THEY CANNOT SAY ANYTHING ABOUT HOW ONE PERSON'S *LEVEL* OF A TRAIT COMPARES WITH ANOTHER'S

Psychologists are usually interested in determining a person's level of a trait relative to others; for example, to determine how neurotic, extraverted or intelligent they are, or

Table 4.4 Example of two ipsative items

			Best answer	Worst answer
Each item outlines a scenario and offers you four possible reactions. For each item, simply choose the ONE answer which best describes how you would think, feel or act, and put a mark in the "Best answer" column. Please also identify the ONE answer which is unlike how you would think, feel or act, and mark the "Worst answer" column.				
1	If I perform badly in a test, it is	because the test is unfair.		x
		my own fault for not studying hard enough.	x	
		just bad luck.		
		because I couldn't concentrate.		
2	If I lock myself out of my car,	it's because the locking system is badly designed.		
		I feel like crying.	x	
		it's because everyone makes mistakes sometimes!		
		it's probably because my mind wandered.		x
etc.				

to correlate their scores on some scale with other things. This is more or less essential in many applied settings; for example, to help a personnel manager decide whether a job applicant shows sufficient evidence of leadership ability to be appointable.

Ipsatised tests cannot provide any such information. All they might say is whether a person's (self-reported) level of one trait is lower or higher than their own self-reported score on another trait. But they cannot show whether any of that person's scores are low or high relative to those of other people. So whilst they may perhaps be of some use when counselling individuals, it makes little sense to try to use ipsatised scales for anything else.

To see why, consider how two people might respond to one of the items from the previous example (see Table 4.5).

Table 4.5 Two respondents with very different levels of agreement produce the same responses to an ipsatised item

		Person A			Person B		
Item	Possible answers to item		Best	Worst		Best	Worst
If I perform badly on a test, it is	because the test is unfair.	Agree		x	Very strongly disagree		x
	my own fault for not studying hard enough.	Very strongly agree	x		Disagree	x	
	just bad luck.	Strongly agree			Strongly disagree		
	because I couldn't concentrate.	Strongly agree			Strongly disagree		

This table shows how two people feel about each possible answer. It can be seen that they have nothing much in common. Person A tends to think that all of the answers describe them quite well, whilst person B feels that none of them does so. Yet based on their responses to that item, they both end up with exactly the same score on the four scales measured by the test. This is because this format ensures that each person's score on a scale (such as neuroticism) *is relative to their scores on the other scales*. If all of the scales measure different things (i.e., are uncorrelated), this makes little sense conceptually. Why *should* a person's level of extraversion affect their score on the neuroticism scale? It is hard to justify this on any grounds.

ALL THE SCALES ARE NEGATIVELY CORRELATED – EVEN WHEN PEOPLE RESPOND RANDOMLY

Because each question in the questionnaire gives a respondent 1 point for one trait and takes away 1 point from another trait, any person's total score (summed across all traits) will always be the same. So a person who has a high score on one trait (neuroticism, say) *must* have low scores on the other traits. This means that all of the traits will be negatively correlated together.

Spreadsheet name: Spreadsheet 4.3: Correlations between ipsative scales from random data

Download from: https://routledge.com/9781032146164/

Purpose: To show that ipsative scales are negatively correlated. To explore how the number of scales, the number of items, and the number of people in the sample influence these correlations.

Contents of spreadsheet: This is the first spreadsheet which simulates data. It simulates how people would respond randomly to items such as those in Table 4.4 and shows the correlations between the scales.

Suggested activity:

- Start by setting the number of scales to 4 and the number of items to 2 in section A. Set the number of simulated people to 250. This represents the scores of 250 people who respond entirely randomly to the two items in Table 4.4. In section B, note the correlations between scales (and the average correlation). Generate another set of random data by pressing F9 (Windows or Linux) or Fn + F9 or Ctrl + Shift + F9 (MacOS); repeat several (perhaps 10) times in order to establish what the correlations between the scales typically are.
- Try altering the number of scales (perhaps using 3, 5 and 8), and for each condition try altering the number of people (perhaps 20 and 250) and the number of items (perhaps 2, 10 and 20). What influences the size of the correlations between the scales? What influences the standard deviation – in other words, the amount of variation between the correlations?
- Try to produce the largest correlation you can between a pair of scales.
- Using a calculator, work out $-1/(\text{number of scales} - 1)$. Does this resemble the correlation you find?

Points to note:

- Experiment by changing entries in the *green* areas.
- Results are in the *yellow* areas.
- Simply download another copy if you accidentally change formulae.
- Pay particular attention to how small numbers of people result in correlations which vary considerably – though the average size of the correlation stays roughly the same. Also note that correlations between the scales get larger as the number of scales decreases. So a small sample with few scales will produce some very appreciable (negative) correlations between scales. It would be easy to interpret these as being of psychological interest, even though they mean nothing, as they stem from random numbers.

- For those who wish to delve deeper, the simulated data are shown below the correlations. Each participant's data consists of two lines – the first line containing the responses which they classify as "like me" and the second row those responses which they feel do not describe them. (The two items are obviously different!) Then each scale is scored by adding up the number of times an item is marked "like me" minus the number of times it is marked "unlike me". These scores are shown to the right of the data. It is these scores which are correlated together.

Learning outcomes: Readers should now be able to:

- Show some familiarity with the idea of using simulated data to understand statistical issues.
- Appreciate that ipsative scales show substantial negative correlations – even when there is really no relationship between the scales at all (i.e., when the responses are completely random).

If participants filled in the answers to several Likert scales randomly, the correlations between the scales would be close to zero. This makes sense; a correlation of zero implies that there is no relationship between the scores on one scale and the scores on another scale, and when people respond at random, then of course there *should* be no relationship between the scores on the various scales. That is what randomness implies.

It should be obvious that this is not the case for these ipsatised scales. These scales are negatively correlated – even when people respond at random. This poses several problems for statistical analyses described in subsequent chapters. For example, techniques such as factor analysis and reliability analysis simply will not yield sensible results (Cornwell & Dunlap, 1994); although techniques have been developed to allow the factor analysis of ipsative data (e.g., Yu et al., 2005), these are complex and not implemented by any statistical package of which I am aware.

THE WORDING OF AN ITEM INFLUENCES THE SCORES OBTAINED ON ALL SCALES

Suppose that an item was phrased in such a way that almost everyone would choose the answer which corresponded to that scale. For example, in question 2 in Table 4.4, if the second alternative was changed from "I'd feel like crying" to "I'd feel a little upset", then almost everyone would choose that answer – which of course would increase everybody's neuroticism score and decrease their scores on the other scales. The way in which one item is worded can affect the scores obtained on different scales. To get round this, advocates of ipsative testing recommend ensuring that all alternatives are equally popular. This can be attempted as the test is being developed by asking people to rate themselves on Likert-scaled versions of the items; for example, "On a scale of 1–5, if you lock yourself out of your car, how likely are you to feel like crying?" Only phrases measuring different traits which are rated similarly are put together as alternative answers for an item. However, this begs the question of how similar the scores need to be – and it involves a lot of extra work, and ultimately produces a scale which is difficult or impossible to analyse.

CLEANING DATA

One problem which is frequently encountered is that of missing or corrupted data. If participants complete a questionnaire by hand, some individuals will inevitably leave some questions unanswered, mark two answers to the same item, or something similar. In other cases, participants may decide to respond randomly – perhaps by ticking the same box for every item on the page.

When answering items in an ability of attainment test, some participants will mark more than one answer for an item or leave some items unanswered. This is a particular problem if the test instructions ask respondents to guess if they do not know the answer to a question. If a questionnaire or test is administered via computer, then this may not be an issue, provided that the program or website requires that participants make a response before seeing the next item/problem or proceeding to the next page. Some websites (such as SurveyMonkey) can make this straightforward to implement; however it is necessary to ensure that the person who sets up the questionnaire actually does so. (The default for SurveyMonkey is to allow participants to skip questions if they wish.)

As discussed, detecting malicious responding and bots is both technical and complex; papers such as Chmielewski and Kucker (2020) and Storozuk et al. (2020) are warmly recommended to those who plan to choose to gather data from paid internet participants.

However the data are collected, it is unwise to simply take the scores at face value until one has performed some quality control. Ideally, the research protocol should specify how missing data are to be treated before any data are collected. In practice it is more likely that many researchers will not have thought this through and may be faced with a stack of questionnaires with missing values scattered through them. How should one proceed?

RANDOM RESPONDING ON LIKERT SCALES

If participants are not motivated to take the questionnaire or test seriously, it is possible that they may tick boxes at random or make the same response to each of the items on an answer sheet. It clearly makes sense to try to identify and eliminate such individuals before performing any statistical analyses on the data, as random responses will generally reduce the size of any correlations, t-tests or other statistical tests which are performed using the test scores. If test-takers are more highly motivated (for example, if the scale is administered as part of a selection procedure), then this is less likely to be a problem. Identifying random responding is not always straightforward, however.

First, it makes sense just to look at the answer sheets (or the coded responses) *before* the items are scored, in order to check whether each individual seems to have chosen the same response to many consecutive items; this may (perhaps) indicate that they are not answering the questions honestly. This interpretation could be incorrect; someone who ticks the "neutral" or "unsure" box to all the items in a Likert scale might genuinely have problems formulating an answer to the questions which are posed. Nevertheless, if a person strongly agrees (or disagrees) with each item or chooses the same alternative for every item in an ability test, then it might make sense to consider discarding their data.

Some questionnaires include a random-responding scale. In Chapter 1, I bemoaned the fact that many scales in common use essentially paraphrase the same item many times. Whilst being deplorable for measuring personality traits, such items may be useful when checking for random responses. For if someone strongly agrees that they feel anxious, and also strongly agrees that they feel calm and relaxed, it seems probable that they have either misread a question or are ticking boxes at random. Some personality questionnaires contain a random-responding scale to check whether individuals give discrepant responses like these, and it is not too arduous a job to construct one oneself, if necessary, by identifying pairs of items which have a very high positive or negative correlation (above 0.7 or below −0.7, say), and using these items to form a random-responding scale. It does not matter at all if the pairs of items measure quite different traits or states.

For example, suppose that previous analyses had shown that items 1 and 3 in the questionnaire shown in Table 4.6 correlated 0.8, whilst items 2 and 4 correlated −0.7. It would be possible to construct a random-responding scale based on these items by using the scoring key shown in the table.

If someone is behaving consistently then their score on item 1 should be the same as their score on item 3. Likewise, their score on item 2 should be the same as their score on item 4 (which is reverse-scored, as the correlation between item 2 and item 4 is large and *negative*). A random-responding scale could therefore be constructed by adding together a person's scores on one item of each highly correlated pair and subtracting the scores from the remaining item in the pair. In this case one could calculate the score on item 1 minus the score on item 3 and add this to the score on item 2 minus the score on item 4. The closer this number is to zero, the more consistent a person is.

Table 4.6 Four items which may be useful for detecting random responding

		Strongly agree	Agree	Neutral	Disagree	Strongly disagree
1	I prefer my own company to being in large gatherings	1	2	3	4	5
2	I feel on top of the world	1	2	3	4	5
3	There's nothing worse than a large party	1	2	3	4	5
4	I feel sad	5	4	3	2	1

But what should one do if a person's score on a random-responding scale is high? This is a difficult decision. If the assessment is being made for the purpose of individual assessment (for clinical purposes, for example), then raising the issue with the participant might give some insight as to whether and why they intentionally responded in this way. If the data are being gathered as part of a norming exercise (see what follows), then it makes sense to not eliminate anyone, as other samples of people will probably also contain a similar proportion of people who respond randomly. However, if the data are being gathered for research purposes (for example, to correlate scores on a scale with some other variable(s)), then it might be acceptable to remove a small percentage of people from the sample if there is clear evidence of random responding – although this should obviously be done before performing any statistical analyses, otherwise it might be tempting to simply remove cases in order to increase the size of the correlation, improve model fit and so on.

MISSING DATA FROM LIKERT SCALES

What if some items are left unanswered? Several options are available. These include ignoring the missing data, dropping anyone with missing data from the sample, and trying to estimate what the missing data might have been.

Ignoring missing data from a Likert scale is a very bad idea. Assuming that the items are scored 1–7 (or something similar), simply ignoring missing items (essentially giving them a score of 0) will result in the individual having a lower score than they should for the scale. Dropping anyone with missing data from the analysis is much more defensible, but much depends on how much data is missing and how long the scales are. There are no hard and fast rules, but if someone omits just one item from a 50-item, 7-point Likert scale, it should be clear that estimating their score on that item might be a sensible option. With so many items in the scale the standard deviation of scores within the sample is likely to be quite large, and even if the estimate is terribly inaccurate it will not greatly affect their score on the scale. If more than a few percent of data are missing from any participant, it might be better to drop that participant from the sample and not use their scores on any of the other scales or measures either. This is sometimes called "listwise deletion of data".

Listwise deletion of data is not a panacea, however. First, it might lead to biased samples. Suppose that some individuals chose not to answer an item asking about attitudes to abortion, for example. Might they have strong views which they choose not to disclose? If so, dropping them might make the sample less representative of the population than it would otherwise be. Second (and more pragmatically) listwise deletion of data can sometimes lead to a drastic decrease in the size of the sample.

The next option is to drop only the person's score on the scale which is affected by missing data. Thus if 100 people complete three scales (Scale A, Scale B and Scale C), suppose that five people omit one or more items from Scale A, and three different people omit one or more items from Scale B. Everybody answers every question in Scale C. The correlation between Scales A and B would be based on 92 people, the correlation between Scales A and C would be based on 95 people, and the correlation between Scales B and C would be based on 97 people. The disadvantages of this approach are first that the correlations might, in extreme cases and in theory, be based on completely different samples of people. And it means that the correlations differ in their statistical power, which could complicate the interpretation of the results. Yet if the sample size is large and only a few percent of data are missing for any variable, this "pairwise deletion" procedure can be the most practical.

Estimation of scores is another option – and this is where life can become needlessly complicated in my opinion. Suppose that an item has a 7-point Likert scale, giving scores between 1 and 7. If someone declines to answer this item, what score should they be given? One possibility would be to give them the midpoint score (4 in this case). Why this and not (say) 1 or 7? If we estimate their score as 4, then the worst-case scenario is that the person would have answered the item with a 1 or 7 had they attempted it – meaning that we have overestimated or underestimated their score by 3. If we estimate their score to be 1, then the discrepancy could be as large as $7 - 1 = 6$. Hence, it is safer to choose the midpoint.

But suppose that everyone else in the sample obtains a score of 1 or 2 on this item. The scale could ask people how much they agree with some extreme view – capital punishment for minor offences, for example. In this case estimating missing data as a 4 might not seem so sensible; it might be safer to look at the modal score (the most popular score) given by the people who *did* answer that question and use this as our estimate of the missing data. There is a lot to be said for this simple technique.

Finally, it is possible to estimate what a person's score on the scale (or missing item) might have been, based on their responses to those items which are not missing. This is fairly straightforward using techniques such as multiple regression, and there is a substantial literature on the topic. Newman (2014) gives some useful practical guidelines, and computer programs such as SPSS allow missing data to be estimated ("imputed") with ease. There are several other mathematical techniques which can be used to estimate missing data, and there is a substantial literature on the subject.

The reason I do not propose going into detail about such methods is that (a) they are potentially dangerous and (b) if the amount of missing data is small, then it should not matter much how the missing data are estimated. So why are the techniques dangerous? Missing-data estimation techniques will always ensure that a person's estimates are broadly in line with their responses to other, similar items. Suppose that a person strongly agrees with nine statements such as "Immigrants should be repatriated", "The courts are too lenient" and other items indicating a right-wing political attitude, but they fail to answer a 10th item. We will never know why, but any imputation method will assume that the person would have answered this item in line with the others. But suppose that the item was "Homosexuality is against Bible teaching", and the person with missing data was themselves gay. They might well have disagreed with such a statement, and this might be why they left it unanswered. Second-guessing how an individual might have responded, based on the responses made by different individuals, will not always be accurate. It might also affect the results of other statistical analyses. For given that any imputation method based on regression or similar techniques will assume that the response to a missing item is consistent with a person's other responses, the estimation of missing data will inevitably overestimate the consistency of people's responses. This will make the correlations between items somewhat higher than they ought to be, and this in turn will affect important properties of the scale, such as its reliability and factor structure – terms which we explore in later chapters.

The bottom line is that if large amounts of data are estimated, there is a real risk that the scale will appear to show better psychometric properties than it really has. And as soon as we start to estimate values, we move away from reality. Whatever its faults and challenges, psychometrics is based upon the responses made by real people to a standard set of items. Once one starts estimating data, this is no longer the case, and this should be a cause for concern. Statisticians delight in the challenge of using ever more complex mathematical models to estimate missing values – but just because one can, should one do so? It is hard to have much faith in any results from a dataset which is riddled with missing data.

In terms of practical guidelines, I would be wary of estimating more than 5%–10% of the items from a scale; for short scales this would mean no estimation at all. I would also seriously consider dropping participants who omit items from several scales. If the data have been gathered from a carefully constructed sample, rather than a convenience sample, it would be necessary to check their demographics against the remainder of the sample to ensure that the people who omit several items are not similar in terms of age, location, background, gender, scores on those scales which they *did* complete etc. If this analysis shows that the people who omitted items do not form a random subset of the original sample, there is a problem with no real solution, as removing these individuals will bias the sample. One possibility might be to remove the individuals with missing data and also remove *other* people to keep the sample balanced. So if 20 men showed unacceptable levels of missing data, one approach might be to remove both them and 20 women (with similar age, locations, background, scores on the non-missing scales etc.) to ensure that the sample remains balanced.

MISSING SCORES ON MULTIPLE-CHOICE ABILITY AND ATTAINMENT SCALES

Ability scales usually impose some sort of time limit. As discussed in Chapter 2, speeded tests have short time limits. Virtually nobody will have time to complete all the items, and the score on a scale will be the number of items correctly answered within the time limit. Unanswered items are simply ignored when scoring these tests. Power tests have more generous time limits, and the items generally start by being hard and then become more difficult as the scale progresses. Each person progresses through the easy items to a set of items which they find taxing, whilst the later items in the scale will be difficult or impossible for almost everyone. But what should people do if they do not know the answer? The test instructions need to make this clear and should also specify whether incorrect guesses are penalised. If the instructions do not specify whether participants should guess if they do not know the correct answer, there is a risk that scores on the test will be confounded by willingness to guess; those who do so would have a higher score than others of equal ability who did not guess, because some of the guesses would turn out to be correct.

What if the instructions specify that wrong answers will be penalised? This is hardly a panacea either, as some participants might risk a guess if they manage to eliminate a few of the alternative answers to a question, whilst others might be more risk-averse. So once again, there is a danger that the scores on the scale will be influenced by willingness to take a risk. Some tests urge participants to guess if they are unsure of the answer. This will inevitably add some random "noise" to each person's score, and this will reduce the size of correlations between the items, which becomes important for many analyses. Someone who knows the answers to only four items of a 20-item scale will have to guess the answers to 16 items, whilst someone who knows the answers to

16 items will only have to guess the answers to four of them. Worryingly, it will mean that the scores of the lower-ability individuals are likely to be less accurate than the scores of higher-ability individuals, as they will have guessed more answers.

If this is not obvious, look at Spreadsheet 4.4.

> **Spreadsheet name:** Spreadsheet 4.4: Guessing in ability tests
>
> **Download from:** https://routledge.com/9781032146164/
>
> **Purpose:** To show that asking participants to guess can increase the range of scores of low-ability participants.
>
> **Contents of spreadsheet:** Simulated data from low-ability and high-ability respondents to a 20-item ability test.
>
> **Suggested activity:**
>
> - Scroll down to see the data in section B: 40 high-ability participants score 16/20 correct and guess the remaining four answers at random; 40 low-ability participants score 4/20 and guess the rest.
> - The graph shows the frequency distribution of the total scores obtained by all 80 participants. Generate several new sets of data (F9, Fn + F9 or Ctrl + Shift + F9) to show this is not a fluke.
>
> **Points to note:**
>
> - Note that the range of scores is larger for the low-ability participants because they have guessed more answers.
>
> **Learning outcomes: Readers should now be able to:**
>
> - Appreciate that guessing increases the standard deviation of test scores, as some people's luck is better than others when they guess.

This finding has some rather unpleasant implications for statistics (such as the Pearson correlation, analysis of variance and regression), which assume that the amount of scatter is roughly the same at each level of ability. *It is fair to say that if most psychologists are aware of this problem, they ignore it.*

That said, if a test requires participants to guess if they are unsure of an answer and despite this some items are left unanswered, it is necessary to guess on their behalf. Of course, if participants were to guess, it is probable that they would be able to eliminate some incorrect responses – but as we cannot know what strategies an individual would have used to answer an item which they did not attempt, it is normal to assume that they would have just guessed answers at random. This is less than ideal, but it is hard to think of a better solution without becoming bogged down with complex estimation procedures.

Missing data is a problem with no good solution, and it is advisable to make every attempt to ensure that each participant in a study follows the instructions and attempts all items of a Likert scale, and all items of a test where the instructions ask them to guess if unsure. One otherwise has to make difficult decisions as to whether to drop participants, or to enter the realms of fantasy land by second-guessing why participants did not answer certain questions, and deciding what to do about the situation. Although much has been written about the estimation of missing data, in my opinion, if one needs to worry about whether one estimation method is markedly better than another, then one has so much missing data that *any* analysis will be unsafe. Meade and Craig (2012) and Gallitto and Leth-Steensen (2015) provide useful guidelines for dealing with missing data *in extremis*.

GUESSING AND SPEED FOR TIMED MULTIPLE-CHOICE ABILITY TESTS

Ability test instructions normally specify what people should do if they do not know the correct answer to an item. Some ask them to make their best guess. Some ask participants to leave it unanswered. And in an attempt to discourage guessing, some tests warn participants that if they answer an item incorrectly, they will be penalised.

Suppose that we have a test made up of vocabulary items, such as:

Item 1. A drumlin is a:

(a) musical instrument (b) type of toad, (c) round hill, (d) Japanese pen

Item 2. A peon is a:

(a) labourer (b) flower (c) anthill (d) example of excellence

How would *you* approach these items if you did not know the answers? For item 1, if you did not know that the answer is (c), you might argue that as a drum is a musical instrument, (a) might be correct. You might think that "drumlin" does not sound like a very Japanese word, so conclude that (d) is unlikely. You may know nothing about toads or types of hills, and so you would probably choose (a) as your answer – perhaps (b) or (c), but definitely not (d).

Likewise, for item 2, two of the distractors were written to confuse the unwary – peon sounds rather like "peony" (the flower), and it might also be confused with "paragon" (d). Unlike item 1, it is not obvious that any answer is impossible, so most people would probably choose more or less randomly between the four alternatives, perhaps favouring (b) over the others.

I give these examples to show that we cannot assume that people guess at random when they do not know the answers to multiple-choice items. Highly intelligent test-takers might be able to eliminate some alternatives as unlikely, and so may be able to make more accurate guesses than lower-ability participants, who are more likely to guess at random.

For multiple-choice ability tests:

- Highly able people will probably know many of the answers – by definition.
- They will therefore have to guess the answers to fewer items.
- When they *do* guess, these guesses might be more accurate than the guesses of low-ability participants.

Both the amount of guessing and the *quality* of guessing are likely to depend on cognitive ability. The two variables are confounded, and we cannot tell whether a person obtains a high score because they are good at solving that particular type of problem or because they are good at eliminating alternatives to arrive at the correct answer. As far as I am aware, there has been rather little research in this area, other than in the context of item response theory (see Chapter 15).

What if the test instructions ask participants to guess if they are unsure, but some people do not? This is a fairly common situation. Sometimes participants leave an item blank meaning to return to it later but forgetting to do so. Some tests have time limits which are so short that participants do not have time to attempt all the questions. What should happen if someone has not attempted all the items, despite having been asked to guess if unsure? Despite the issues raised above (intelligent people being able to make better guesses), the best solution is probably to randomly guess answers on behalf of the participant for those items which are left blank. The score of the participant would otherwise be underestimated, as some of the guesses to multiple-choice items will probably be correct.

DERIVING AND INTERPRETING SCORES

The guidelines for scoring tests given earlier are very straightforward; after all, how else *could* one sensibly score tests other than by giving 1 point for each correct answer? We have all been so accustomed to this procedure, used when assessing school performance, in game shows on television and in numerous other contexts that it seems to be second nature. In fact, it makes some quite substantial assumptions about the relationship between performance on individual items and ability, though these are rarely considered or made explicit.

Consider an ability test whose items differ in difficulty. For example, 10 items might ask participants to solve anagrams whose lengths vary from 4 to 12 letters. (We will assume that all the words are equally common, so that the length of the word is what determines the difficulty of the item). Suppose that two people score five of these correct within the allocated time period of 3 minutes.

If 1 point is awarded for each correct answer, these people have equal levels of ability. But what if one person correctly solved all of the easy items (4–8 letters long) whilst the other person got some of these wrong but correctly solved several of the harder items? Would it still be sensible to regard these people as having the same level of ability?

"Of course", readers will exclaim at this point, "this is highly unlikely for it is obvious that anyone who solves a hard item will also be able to solve all items which are easier, too". And this is quite possibly correct; my purpose in mentioning it is to point out that whenever scores on items are added together, there is an assumption that (almost) everyone who correctly solves a difficult ability item will be able to solve all (or almost all) of the easier ones. It otherwise makes little sense to add together the scores on several items.

Louis Guttman suggested a very simple model linking people's abilities to item difficulties. He argues that it should be able to plot these on a graph, as shown in Figure 4.3.

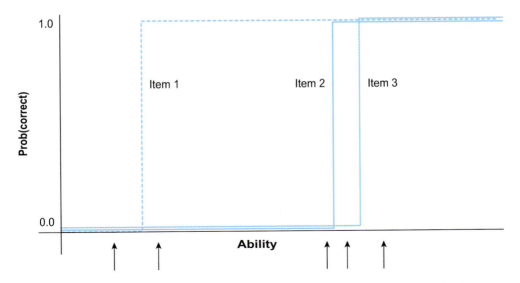

Figure 4.3 Item characteristic curves for three items forming a Guttman scale. Arrows represent people whose levels of ability will result in scores of 0, 1, 1, 2 and 3.

The vertical axis shows the probability of getting an item correct, which Guttman argued should be either zero (assuming a free response rather than a multiple-choice item) or 1.0. The horizontal axis represents to abilities of the people taking the items; the four arrows represent four people with various levels of ability. The lines (**item characteristic curves [ICCs]** – an important term) show the probability that someone with a particular level of ability will pass each of the items.

Someone with a very low level of ability (leftmost arrow) would have a zero probability of correctly answering any item. People with slightly higher ability (second and third arrows) would answer item 1 correctly but are bound to answer items 2 and 3 incorrectly. The fourth person will answer the first two items correctly but will fail the third. The final person will answer all three items correctly. Guttman's model makes explicit the assumption that we make when adding together scores on items – that everyone who answers a difficult item correctly also answers all easier items correctly. If we do not make this assumption, then it makes little sense to treat the total score as a measure of a person's ability.

The good thing about Guttman's model is that it is empirically testable and needs nothing in the way of fancy statistics – although it does assume that people either agree/disagree with a statement or answer an ability item correctly or incorrectly.

Suppose that five people respond to three ability items as shown in Table 4.7; 1 represents a correct answer and 0 an incorrect answer. The total scores for each person and for each item are also shown.

To determine whether the items form a Guttman scale, all that is necessary is to first sort the data by the total score per person, so that the person with the lowest score appears in the first row, the person with the next highest total score appears in the second row and so on (see Table 4.8).

Next, sort the *columns* by the total for each *item* – so that the first column of data shows an item which most people got correct, the second column shows the next most difficult item and so on (see Table 4.9).

Just inspecting this last table will show whether the items form a Guttman scale. Read across the rows for each person. It can be seen that a zero is *never* followed by a 1. This means that a person who answers an item incorrectly *never* goes on to answer an easier item correctly. Thus these items form a perfect Guttman scale.

This all sounds very straightforward – but like many good ideas it does not work well in practice. It does not really apply to Likert scales, although Likert items could be rephrased in order to undergo Guttman scaling. So the item "Do you like large social

Table 4.7 Scored responses of five people to three ability items (1 = correct)

	Item 1	Item 2	Item 3	Total
Person 1	0	0	0	0
Person 2	0	0	1	1
Person 3	1	1	1	3
Person 4	1	0	1	2
Person 5	0	0	1	1
Total for item	2	1	4	

Table 4.8 Guttman scaling: sorting rows by total score

	Item 1	Item 2	Item 3	Total for person
Person 1	0	0	0	0
Person 2	0	0	1	1
Person 5	0	0	1	1
Person 4	1	0	1	2
Person 3	1	1	1	3
Total for item	2	1	4	

Table 4.9 Guttman scaling: sorting columns by total correct

	Item 3	Item 1	Item 2	Total for person
Person 1	0	0	0	0
Person 2	1	0	0	1
Person 5	1	0	0	1
Person 4	1	1	0	2
Person 3	1	1	1	3
Total for item	4	2	1	

gatherings? (a) Very much (b) Quite a lot (c) Not particularly (e) Not at all" could become four items: "Do you very much enjoy social gatherings?", "Do you quite enjoy social gatherings?" etc. for the purposes of Likert scaling. However, the obvious problem with this approach is that participants will check back to make sure they are acting consistently, and so it would be amazing if these items did not form a Guttman scale (unless, of course, the items are separated by other items asking quite different questions, which would make the checking process harder).

It is often claimed that social distance measures form Guttman scales. These involve items such as:

1   I would happily share a house with a person of a different ethnic background to my own.
2   I would not mind living next door to someone from a different ethnic background to my own.
3   I would not mind living in a town where there are significant numbers of people from a different ethnic background to my own.

The rationale for constructing these items is that if a person agrees with the first statement, then their lack of prejudice also suggests that they should agree with the other statements, too. Thus the items will form a Guttman scale.

This sounds very encouraging – but the problem really is that this "scale" is more a psychometric exercise than anything else. As discussed in Chapter 1, the content of these items is terribly narrow in scope, and so a scale such as this is unlikely to reveal any unexpected insights about human personality, attitudes and so forth. Each item assesses whether or not a person would feel comfortable living at a certain level of proximity to members of other ethnic backgrounds, and one might as well measure this with a single item as this scale. In addition, there is no guarantee that the way in which people answer such questions predicts how they would actually behave, whilst it could be argued that the questions are silly anyway; it is quite possible that people might be prejudiced against some ethnic groups but not others. Implicit prejudice and other types of evidence for prejudice (e.g., Pettigrew & Meertens, 1995) are not considered at all. So it is hard to see that scores on this scale can say much on their own. They would need to be combined with other evidence in order to be useful – see "hierarchical models" in Chapter 13.

The good thing about Guttman scaling is that it can be related to how we measure objects in the physical world. Suppose that we want to measure the height of trees. Imagine that the horizontal axis in Figure 4.3 measures height, and the items in the test are:

1   Is the tree more than 2 metres high?
2   Is the tree more than 7 metres high?
3   Is the tree more than 9 metres high?

You wander through a wood, measuring a random sample of trees and giving each tree a score based on the answers to the questions shown previously – where answering "yes" to a question achieves a score of 1 and "no" is scored as 0. Thus a tree 8 metres high would be given a score of 2 on this scale.

These items form a Guttman scale as shown in Figure 4.3, as every object which is over 9 metres high is also over 7 metres high and over 2 metres high. You might wonder why I chose these particular values of height. I chose them more or less at random, based only on the intuition that some of the trees might be quite small (under 2 metres) whilst others will be more than 9 metres high. But within these limits my choice of heights was arbitrary; I could have chosen 1, 3 and 8 metres if I wanted to. The appropriate values of height (item difficulty) depend on the objects (people) one wants to measure. The reason why I chose these random values (rather than, say, neatly spacing the distances at 3, 6 and 9 metres) is that when writing items for a psychological scale, one certainly cannot assume that they are equally spaced. In the prejudice example, one cannot assume that the difference in prejudice between item (a) and item (b) is the same as the difference between item (b) and item (c). We just write our items using our intuition (or results of previous research) to try to ensure that not everybody will answer all of the items the same way – in much the same way that when measuring trees we do not have items such as "Is the tree more than 1 cm high?" (as they all will be) or "Is the tree more than 100 m high?" (none will be).

It should be clear from all this that adding together scores on items from Guttman scales can only tell us which objects are taller than which other objects, or which people are more able than which other people. It does not allow us to tell how *large* the differences between people are. A tree which scores 1 on the tree test (and is thus between 0 and 2 metres high) is not half the size of one which scores 2 (between 7 and 9 metres high). Likewise, though Figure 4.3 shows us that one person scores 0, two score 1, one scores 2 and one scores 3, it does not allow us to quantify the *size* of the difference between people. In other words, even if items can be found which fit the model, the Guttman scaling procedure only allows us to determine the rank-order of objects (people), rather them putting them on a useful metric such as height in metres.

Very few ability items actually do form Guttman scales – and those which do tend to vary so drastically in difficulty that they are unlikely to be of much practical use for making fine discriminations between people. For example, the following free response knowledge-based items would probably form a Guttman scale:

Item 1. What is a cat?

Item 2. When would you use an umbrella?

Item 3. Why do countries explore outer space?

However, adding additional items of intermediate difficulty would, in practice, result in the data not fitting the model (Kline, 2000a). If a model does not fit the data, the obvious thing to do is to modify it slightly. Perhaps rather than showing a sudden increase from 0 to 1, the lines should show a gradual increase in probability over a range of abilities. And perhaps the steepness of the lines should be allowed to vary, from item to item, rather as shown in Figure 4.4.

Here the probability of answering an item correctly does not suddenly flip from zero to 1. Instead, the probability of answering an item correctly gradually increases as people's ability increases. The responses to any ability items will reflect both the ability of the people to whom the item was administered plus some random "noise", as some people who know the answer will press the wrong button on the computer keyboard, some people who do not know the answer may make a lucky guess or may suffer a mental blank and therefore answer an easy item incorrectly. This form of scaling turns out to be very useful indeed, and we return to it in Chapter 15.

The key point to bear in mind is that when we write items for an ability test (or personality test), we have no guidelines for deciding how hard the items should be

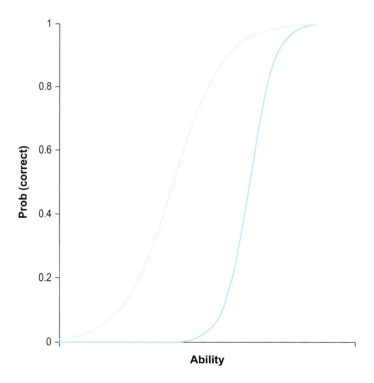

Figure 4.4 Probability of passing each of two items as a function of ability; compare with Figure 4.3

(or, in the case of Likert scales, how high or low the mean score should be). We just write items which look as if they will differentiate between people in the sort of sample with whom we plan to use them. If a test contains many items which are difficult but few which are easy for a sample of people, this will allow the test to make fine differentiations between people of high ability but will be less able to draw distinctions between people of low ability. This is because few of the item characteristic curves will move from zero to 1 at the "low" end of the ability scale, rather as shown in Figure 4.3. Whilst item 2 and item 3 have ICCs which are fairly close to each other, there is a large gap between the ICCs for item 1 and item 2. Thus people whose ability falls in the range between item 1 and item 2 will all get the same score (1) on the test. ICCs which rise up close to each other are capable of making more precise discriminations between people than are ICCs which are far apart.

There are thus two problems with adding up scores on items and using this total score as a measure of ability. First, doing so only makes sense if people who pass an item of a particular difficulty level also pass all easier items. Otherwise two people with different levels of ability could have identical scores, if one of them fails some easy items. The second problem is that item difficulty is always going to be arbitrary. It will depend on the cognitive demands of an ability problem and the extremity with which a personality item is phrased; for example, "Do you sometimes feel nervous when . . . ?" versus "Do you always feel terrified when . . . ?" The ICCs will therefore be random distances apart, and as shown with the physical length example, this means that the total score can only ever show us that one person's score is higher or lower than another person's. It cannot tell us by how much, for in order to do so the ICCs would need to be evenly spaced. It is becoming clear that scores on psychological tests do not seem to measure things in the same way that rulers, weighing scales etc. operate – much as discussed in Chapter 3.

SUMMARY

This chapter discussed how tests may be administered and has revealed some alarming shortcomings with the popular method of administering questionnaires and tests over the internet. It seems that respondents are often not who they say they are, random or careless responding is commonplace, and significant numbers of responses may come from "bots" (computer programs) rather than people. The chapter then showed how responses to questionnaires may be translated into numbers, which is the usual precursor to interpreting what they mean and/or performing statistical analyses on them. Whilst it is straightforward to add up scores on Likert scales and ability items, it is shown that scoring ipsatised scales poses major – perhaps insurmountable – problems. Finally, the idea of Guttman scales and item characteristic curves was introduced. This shows that adding together scores on test items requires some sort of model about the relationship between a person's level of the trait being assessed and the way in which they respond to items in the scale. These are important concepts which will be developed later.

CHAPTER 5
INTERPRETING SCORES

Scores on tests can be used in two ways. As we have seen in Chapter 3, most researchers simply treat test scores in the same way as they treat "real" properties of people, such as measures of reaction time, brain voltage and so on. Whilst researchers normally just correlate scores on various scales with other things as described in Chapter 1, practitioners need to determine what an individual's score on a scale implies about them, which is the focus of this chapter.

Whilst it is undeniable that scores on psychological tests may sometimes be of practical use (e.g., in personnel selection), their lack of quantitative structure arguably makes them unsuitable for most of the complex analyses which are normally performed on them – and theories of human personality, abilities, prejudice, group dynamics, attraction, social cognition, and the self are just a few of those which may be fatally flawed. That said, most readers of this book will be keen to learn how to use tests, whatever the rights and wrongs of the testing procedure, and so it would be wrong to end the book here. The concerns raised in Chapter 3 are, however, very real and will not go away, no matter how much we collectively choose to ignore them.

INTERPRETING AN INDIVIDUAL'S SCORE ON A SCALE

This section explores how one might interpret one person's score on a particular test. This is the way that tests are usually used by clinical psychologists, educational psychologists and other professionals who administer a scale to one person and seek to draw some inference about that person's intelligence, position on the autistic spectrum, level of dementia, suitability for employment, or something similar. These psychologists use tests to help them understand individuals, and to do so it is necessary to use **norms**. These are simply tables which show the frequency distribution of scores on a particular scale.

Of course, not everyone needs to interpret individual people's scores. If a researcher just wants to determine whether level of anxiety (as measured by a questionnaire) is

DOI: 10.4324/9781003240181-5

related to performance at work, for example, then all they need to do is correlate the scores on the anxiety questionnaire with some measure of job performance. Because correlations are insensitive to the scale on which anxiety and job performance are measured (in other words, the mean and standard deviation of either set of scores do not influence the correlation), this correlation will show whether there is a linear relationship between anxiety and job performance. There is no need to use norms at all.[1] They can simply correlate scores together or use multiple regression, analysis of variance, factor analysis, structural equation modelling or other exotic techniques in order to establish how scores on tests are related to scores on other tests, or to other things.

Whether or not norms are used, it is necessary to assume that adding together the scores on various items is able to tell us something sensible about an individual's level of a particular trait or state – which is a major problem, as shown in Chapters 3 and 4.

NORMS

Whilst calculating total scores on tests is simple and intuitive, we have shown that numbers which result will not behave in the same way as numbers in the physical world. Even if the items form a Guttman scale (which is unlikely, unless they differ drastically in difficulty), the total score on a test will only allow us to rank-order people, because the distances between the ICCs vary, rather than corresponding to a particular metric such as length. It is not possible to say that someone who scores 20 on a particular test measuring extraversion is half as extraverted as someone who scores 40 on the same test. Nor can we tell whether a score of 20 represents a high, medium or low level of extraversion; it all depends on how the questions are phrased. This is why one needs to use norms. Norms are simply tables which show the frequency distribution of scores on some scale within some group of people. If the sample is large and carefully constructed, it is then possible to extrapolate and claim that the table of norms is a good estimate of the distribution of scores within a particular population – for example, UK adults aged over 18.

It is obviously crucially important to use an appropriate normative sample to make sense of a person's scores. Using norms gathered from 18-year-old university students to interpret the score of an 8-year-old on an ability test would obviously be nonsensical, as levels of ability improve with age until late adolescence. In order to interpret the 8-year-old's score, it would be necessary to gather data from others of a similar age.

It follows that constructing tables of norms is a time-consuming and extremely expensive task. The norms for tests such as the Wechsler ability scales involve gathering data on a representative sample of people; the **stratified sampling** technique means that the sample resembles the population of the country in terms of age, geographical location, gender balance, educational qualifications, ethnic background etc. Some interesting dilemmas emerge when deciding who to exclude from the group. Should prisoners, hospital patients etc. be excluded when gathering normative data from adults? How about elderly patients with dementia, who will almost certainly obtain low scores on the test? Testing these individuals might prove taxing in the extreme, yet if they are omitted from the normative group, this will lead to the scores of seniors being overestimated.

To give a concrete example to illustrate how norms are constructed and used, suppose that 2035 people were administered a 20-item free response ability test. Scores on this test can therefore range from 0 to 20. The number of people obtaining each score can be shown in a table such as Table 5.1.

The first column shows each possible score on the test. The second column shows the number of people who obtained each score. The third column shows the number of people who obtained each score *or less*. The fourth column converts column 3 into a percentage: the percentage of people who obtain each score or less. This is known as the **percentile** – an important term. The remaining terms will be introduced later.

In order to interpret an individual's score, it is usual to use the percentile figure in the table of norms. In the example only about 20% of the normative group obtain a score of 12 or less. Assuming that the table of norms is appropriate for use with the individual and adequately represents the scores of the population, we can infer that someone who scores 12 on the test is in the bottom 20% or so of the population.

All commercial tests designed for use on individuals will have a table of norms; many will have separate tables for different nationalities, ages, and (perhaps) different clinical or occupational groups. However, care must be taken when choosing which norms to use, and selecting the wrong ones may result in legal challenges. For example, in many countries it may be illegal to use separate norms for males and females or (sometimes) for members of different minority groups. It might be necessary to compare a man's scores against the scores obtained by the population as a whole – not just the scores from other men.

This can cause problems. For example, there are clear sex differences in some psychological variables, such as Psychopathy (the tendency to be cruel, violent and callous). Men generally score higher than women on such scales. It would therefore seem sensible to compare a man's scores against other men's scores. If they were compared against the population, then a man who was low on Psychopathy (by men's standards) would appear to be average, as including the women's scores would lower the median.

Table 5.1 Norms from 2035 people on a 20-item free response test. The average score is 14.46, standard deviation 3.21.

Score	Number of people with this score	Number of people with this score or lower	Percentile	Stanine	Quartile
0	3	3	100 × 3/2035 = 0.15	1	1
1	2	3 + 2 = 5	100 × 5/2035 = 0.25	1	1
2	6	3 + 2 + 6 = 11	0.54	1	1
3	8	19	0.93	1	1
4	8	27	1.33	1	1
5	13	40	1.97	1	1
6	17	57	2.80	1	1
7	23	80	3.93	1	1
8	25	105	5.16	2	1
9	33	138	6.78	2	1
10	57	195	9.58	2	1
11	87	282	13.86	3	1
12	133	415	20.39	3	1
13	201	616	30.27	4	2
14	293	909	44.67	5	2
15	357	1266	62.21	5	3
16	270	1536	75.48	6	3
17	198	1734	85.21	7	4
18	126	1860	91.40	8	4
19	100	1960	96.31	8	4
20	75	2035	100.00	9	4

We have mentioned that scores on ability tests will increase from early childhood until (at least) late adolescence, and so separate norms need to be developed for each age band. Tests such as the **Wechsler Intelligence Scales for Children** report norms for each 3-month age band, so that children can be compared with others of very similar age. The width of these age bands will obviously depend on the degree to which scores on the scale change with age.

Gathering norms from thousands of children for 50 or more 3-month age bands would clearly be prohibitively expensive. It is thus necessary to use smaller groups at each age band, and/or test fewer age bands and perform some interpolation to estimate what the scores of intermediate age groups might look like. For example, if a score of 15 represents the 50th percentile for children aged between 8y0m and 8y3m and the 40th percentile for children aged between 8y6m and 8y9m, if we assume that there is a gradual increase in test scores with age, then a score of 15 should be approximately the 45th percentile for children aged between 8y3m and 8y6m. If data have been gathered for a small sample of children of these ages and suggest that a score of 15 should correspond to the 55th percentile, then there might be a case for moving this figure closer to 45 if the adjacent norms are based on larger samples. There are more sophisticated ways of performing such analyses too (fitting curves to represent how the mean scores change over a large range of ages, and also estimating how the shape of the distribution changes smoothly over a large range of ages), but it is unlikely that many readers of this book will need to explore these issues in detail. All the hard work is done by the test publishers.

A perennial problem of norms is whether or not they transfer across cultures, or from group to group, an issue known as **invariance**. Invariance has several meanings (Widaman & Reise, 1997), ranging from whether or not the items in a questionnaire form the same scales in two different populations to much more restrictive definitions – for example, whether the correlations between items and the means and the standard deviations of the items are the same in each group.

For example, suppose that a British university found despite offering a wide range of support options, some 25% of engineering students fail their course at the end of the first year because of a limited grasp of mathematics. The obvious solution would be to give applicants a mathematics test, so that they could tell for themselves whether or not they are likely to encounter problems, and perhaps reconsider applying (or possibly so that the university could decide to only admit those who scored above some criterion). Suppose that such a test was available – but it had been developed using Australian technical college students. Perhaps it showed that a score of 45 indicated that someone was at the 25th percentile (i.e., a score below 45 indicates that someone is in the lowest 25%). Is it possible to use these norms to help to make decisions about the British students? The Australians may have gone through a different system of mathematics education at school, we may not be told much about how the sample was collected, the gender balance might be different etc.; it is terribly hard to know whether or not norms collected in one setting will apply in another without gathering data and checking for measurement invariance (Jiang et al., 2017).

Unless one uses a high-quality commercial test in the same country where the norms were developed, it will be necessary to norm the test oneself. In the case of the engineering applicants, this would involve gathering data from applicants, casting these data into a table such as Table 5.1, checking that the test scores do indeed indicate which students have problems completing the course, then determining where the cut-off points might be so that students in subsequent years could be advised whether or not they have the necessary skills.

Ipsative scales cannot use norms (Closs, 1996) – which is a strong reason for not using them for individual assessment or guidance. This is because a person's score on one scale will also depend on how they score on other scales measured by the test (Cooper & Kline, 1982).

AGE NORMS

When testing children, some tests still use **age norms**. Here a child's score is compared with the average scores obtained by children of other ages. For example, if the average score of the large, representative normative sample of 9-year-olds on a scale is 20, and an 8-year-old child also scores 20, that child scores as well as the average 9-year-old. So the child whose chronological age (CA) is 8 has a **mental age** (MA) of 9 on that scale. Indeed, a child's intelligence quotient (IQ) used to be defined in this way. According to that outmoded definition the **ratio IQ** is

$$IQ = 100 \times \frac{MA}{CA}$$

which in this example would be 112.5.

There are several good reasons for not using this type of norm. First, it assumes that there is a steady increase in scores from year to year. Given that the difficulty of items in a test is essentially arbitrary, there can be no guarantee that this assumption is sensible. It might be the case that there is a huge jump in scores between ages 8 and 9, but a much smaller increase in scores between ages 9 and 10. Second, it might be that the increase in performance with age is not linear (as the definition of IQ assumes) but follows a curve. Third, it is sometimes impossible to calculate age-related norms. Suppose that *no* group of younger or older children or adults ever scores an average as high as 10 on that difficult test. It is clearly impossible to interpret the scores of the child who scores 10. Age-related norms are best avoided.

PROBLEMS USING NORMS

Large, representative samples are necessary in order to construct tables of norms. "Large" is generally taken to mean several hundred individuals, and we have already touched on the problem of ensuring that the normative group is appropriate. However, one issue which is rarely discussed is the relationship between the size of the normative group and the ability of the individual being assessed.

Suppose that a test is normed using a sample of 1000 people. This sounds as if it ought to be ample. For example, 200 people will have scores within a quarter of a standard deviation either side of the average, and so there are no problems using the table of norms with people of near-average ability. But consider what happens at the very end of the distribution. Suppose that Harry has a z-score of 2.58 – a very high score, and one which you would expect to find in only 1% of the population (as you may care to check, using a table showing the normal distribution). The problem is that if only 1% of the population obtain a score this large, only about 1% of the normative sample (10 people) will have a score this high. So really, when deciding whether Harry's score places them in the top 1% of the population, one is really only using a tiny sample of people to do so. We cannot be sure that the tiny sample of 10 people truly represents the distribution of scores in the population; when gathering the normative data, we may have been unlucky and some of these 10 people may have been much more (or less) able than we assumed. As a result of this, one cannot expect estimates to be particularly accurate when interpreting very high or very low scores using norms.

This is a real problem, as users of psychometric tests are generally more interested in scores near the extremes than at the middle of the distribution – for example, to determine whether a child shows significant problems with their verbal or non-verbal reasoning skills, or to identify a genius or a psychopath. Thus this issue is of great practical significance. The best advice that we can give is to ensure that the size of the normative sample is large and that it is sampled with exquisite care. Even then users should be very careful when using norms to interpret extreme scores. There are plenty of urban myths out there; for example, the pop singer whose IQ is supposedly 180 (five standard deviations above the mean). Is this likely to be true? Such a score would place her in the top 0.000005% of the population. However, it should be clear from what has been said here that even if the intelligence test is completely accurate, it is impossible to be sure whether a very high score places a person in the top 0.01%, 0.005% or 0.000005% of the population. To do so would require a set of norms comprising literally billions of people because only very large samples will provide enough people at the "tails" of the distribution to allow us to draw inferences about the meaning of a score. Even if a sample of a million people were used, we would expect no-one to obtain a score as large as our pop idol's. Without a sample large enough to provide tens of people (at least) with adjacent scores to those of our pop star, the best that one could sensibly say is that their score is high – and perhaps the size of the normative sample might allow one to say that they were likely to be in the top 1%. But inferring anything more extreme would be silly and impossible to justify.

SCALING SCORES

Different scales have different means and standard deviations – even if they supposedly measure the same thing. This is because scales contain different numbers of items which vary in their difficulty. For example, one scale measuring extraversion might have scores which are **normally distributed** in the population (i.e., follow a bell-shaped curve) with an average of 20 and a standard deviation of 5. Another, much longer test might have an average score of 40 and a standard deviation of 10. So it is impossible to tell what a score of (say) 30 on a particular test tells us about a person without knowing the mean and standard deviation of scores on the scale and performing a few mental mathematical gymnastics. It is therefore common practice to scale the scores so that they may be more easily interpreted. That way anyone looking at a person's score on any test will be able to see how it compares with their score on any other test, and how it compares with the scores of other people.

Z-SCORES

Sometimes a psychologist may not have access to a table of norms, such as those in Table 5.1. When a scale is published in a scientific journal, its authors usually only quote its mean and standard deviation, some information about the sample, and a claim that the scores were normally distributed – in other words, that the scores follow a bell-shaped distribution rather as shown in Figure 5.1.

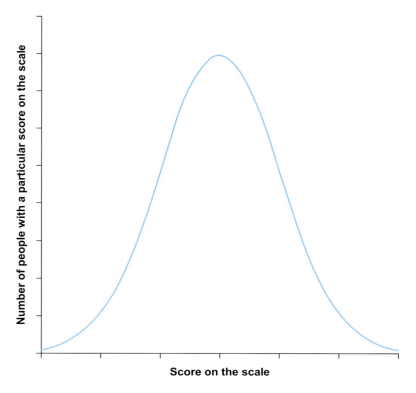

Figure 5.1 A normal distribution of scores on a psychological scale

INTERPRETING SCORES

This is less than ideal. To start with, the sample may not resemble the sample whose data you have collected. The claim that the data are normally distributed may or may not be entirely accurate. But in some cases, one may have no choice other than to try to interpret test scores by using the original researcher's norms – perhaps one has such a small or unrepresentative sample that it makes little sense to construct norms based on the data that one has collected oneself.

Suppose that the authors of a scale report that the average score is 14.46, and the standard deviation of the scores within that sample is 3.21 (the standard deviation shows how widely the data are spread either side of the average).

By taking each person's score on that test, subtracting the average and dividing by the standard deviation, it is possible to convert the score on any normally distributed scale into a **standardised score** or **z-score**. These correspond to a normal distribution having a mean of zero and a standard deviation of 1. For example, a score of 20 on the scale shown in Table 5.1 which has a mean of 14.46 and a standard deviation of 3.21 will correspond to a z-score of (20 − 14.46)/3.21, or 1.72.

Why bother? The advantage of z-scores is that it is possible to interpret a person's score on any test quickly. For example, if someone has a z-score of 0, it follows that their score is average – no matter what the mean and the standard deviation of the original test scores happened to be. If someone has the same z-score on two very different scales, their performance is equally extreme on each of the scales. Furthermore, it is possible to interpret the test scores by consulting a table showing the "cumulative standard normal distribution", rather than having to consult a separate table of norms for each scale. This table of the cumulative normal distribution can be found in virtually any statistics text or online. Alternatively you may wish to use Spreadsheet 5.1.

> **Spreadsheet name:** Spreadsheet 5.1: z-Scores
>
> **Download from:** https://routledge.com/9781032146164/
>
> **Purpose:** To calculate a person's z-score and show what percentage of the normative group are likely to have a lower score than this individual's score.
>
> **Contents of spreadsheet:**
> - Section A calculates a z-score, assuming that the normative group follows a normal distribution.
> - Section B uses that z-score to estimate what percentage of people will have a lower score than this individual.
>
> **Suggested activity:**
>
> - In section A, enter a score from Table 5.1, together with the mean and standard deviation shown at the bottom of that table. Note the value of z.

- In section B, enter the value of z. Note the proportion of people estimated to have a score which is less than this.

Points to note:

- Percentiles allow the meaning of a score to be interpreted, no matter what the mean and standard deviation of the test may be, provided that the scores follow a normal distribution.

Learning outcomes: Readers should now be able to:

- Calculate and interpret a percentile score.

Whichever method is used, this technique will show what proportion (or percentage, when multiplied by 100) of people obtain a particular z-score or less. You may wish to use the spreadsheet to check that 95.8% of people will obtain a z-score which is less than the standardised score (1.72) of the person mentioned. Their score places them in the top 4% or so of the population.

This approach will only be accurate when the scores on the test really *do* follow a normal distribution – and this may well not be the case. You may have noticed that the mean and standard deviation shown here are those from Table 5.1. We have seen from the fourth column of Table 5.1 that a score of 19 on this test corresponds to a percentile score of 95.7; the person is in the top 4%. Yet when we estimate the percentile using z-scores, a score of 20 (not 19) places a person in the top 4%. The reason for this discrepancy is that the data shown in Table 5.1 do not follow a perfect normal distribution. Sometimes, assuming of normality may be the only option available; however interpreting performance using z-scores will only ever be a rough approximation, because one never really knows how closely the scores follow a normal distribution. Use it with caution for this reason.

Converting test scores to z-scores merely alters the mean and standard deviation of the scores on the test; it is what is known as a "linear transformation" because it involves subtracting the same number (the mean) from everyone's test score, and then dividing everyone's score on this variable by the same number (the standard deviation of the scores). As correlations are not influenced by either the mean or the standard deviation of the scores, it follows that the correlation between the raw scores and some other variable will be exactly the same as the correlation between the z-scores and that variable.

T-SCORES

z-Scores are often negative, and this confuses some simple-minded practitioners – particularly in education. To avoid this problem, they developed something called the **T-score**; note that this has nothing to do with the t-test in statistics or T-scaling (described later). Whereas z-scores have a mean of zero and a standard deviation of 1, T-scores have a mean of 50 and a standard deviation of 10. To convert a z-score on a test to a T-score, one simply multiplies it by 10 and adds 50. This value is then rounded to the nearest integer. So a z-score of −1.39 (for example) corresponds to a T-score of −13.9 + 50 = 36. There is no good reason for using T-scores, other than because some non-specialists may be accustomed to them.

Once again, as T-scores merely change the mean and standard deviation of the scores, the correlation between the raw scores and some other variable will be exactly the same as the correlation between T-scores and that variable.

IQ

The **IQ** (or **intelligence quotient**) is a widely used transformation for the interpretation of tests measuring intelligence or cognitive performance. IQ scores are sometimes known as **deviation IQ**s to distinguish them from the obsolete age-based "ratio IQ" discussed earlier. The definition of the deviation IQ is similar to that of T-scaling – but instead of producing scores with a mean of 50 and a standard deviation of 10, IQ scores have a mean of 100 and a standard deviation which is usually 15, though some tests use a standard deviation of 16 (e.g., the Stanford-Binet series of intelligence tests) or even 24 (Cattell's "Culture Fair Intelligence Test"). Thus in order to interpret an IQ, great care must be taken to determine what standard deviation the test developer used. A person's IQ of 115 on most tests would be equivalent to an IQ of 124 on the Cattell scales.

To convert a z-score to an IQ (with standard deviation of 15), all one does is multiply the z-score by 15 and add 100. Hence, a z-score of 1.0 corresponds to an IQ of 115.

To interpret what a particular IQ score tells us about somebody, it is just necessary to perform the same trick backwards. Suppose someone has an IQ of 80. Their z-score is (80 − 100)/15 or −1.33. The cumulative standard normal distribution shows that about 91% of people perform better than this.

Once again, the correlation between IQ scores and some other variable will be the same as the correlation between the raw scores and that variable.

STANINES

Stanines are sometimes used in educational and occupational/organisational psychology as an alternative to z-scores. The term **stanine** is a portmanteau word for "standard nine", as stanines divide the population into nine groups, the width of each of which is half a standard deviation. This is shown in Figure 5.2, which indicates the percentage of people who fall into each stanine (assuming that the data follow a normal distribution). To understand why they are convenient, knowing that a person falls in the first stanine tells you that they are in the lowest-scoring 4% of the population. If they are in the second stanine, they are in the lowest 4% + 7% = 11%. If in the third stanine, they are in the lowest-scoring 23% and so on. It is easy to remember these figures, and so rather than having to look up the cumulative standard normal distribution in order to interpret each individual's z-score, it is rather more straightforward to categorise people into groups (stanines) in order to interpret their scores.

So someone with a stanine score of 5 has a score which is close to the average, someone with a stanine score of 3 is below average and someone with a stanine score of 9 is well above average. In many practical situations this sort of crude categorisation is all one needs, for there is little point in obsessing about small distinctions between people in much applied work.

If one does not wish to assume that the test scores are normally distributed, it would also be possible to determine which test scores correspond to which stanine score simply by looking at the percentile scores in the table of norms. For we can see from Figure 5.2 that 4% of the scores should fall into the first stanine. Turning back to Table 5.1, it can

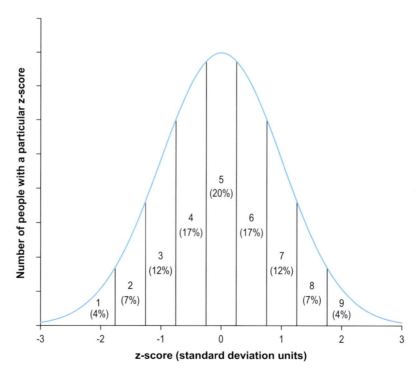

Figure 5.2 Stanines numbered 1–9. Numbers in brackets show the percentage of the sample in each stanine, assuming that the data follow a normal distribution.

be seen that 4% of the participants obtain scores of 7 or fewer on that scale. Hence, a score of 7 or fewer on that scale corresponds to a stanine score of 1. Table 5.1 also shows the rest of the stanine scores calculated by this method.

As the stanine scores involve grouping people into categories (rather than using their raw scores), the correlations between stanine scores and some other variable will not be quite the same as the correlation between raw scores and that variable – though they should be very similar.

STENS

The advantage of stanines is that the fifth stanine represents an average score, as shown. Nevertheless, Raymond Cattell and his co-workers have developed a similar system based on 10 groups of people, called the **sten** ("standard 10"). Once again, each group is half a standard deviation wide, and so the first stanine represents z-scores of −2 or less, the second stanine corresponds to z-scores between −2 and −1.5 and so on. Not having a single central (average) category presents some problems for the use and interpretation of stens, which is probably why they are rarely used.

QUARTILES

Quartiles are more sometimes used when one seeks to classify people into four groups: well below average, slightly below average, slightly above average, or well above average. Unlike stanines or stens, there are roughly equal numbers of people in each group. Thus in Table 5.1, some 25% of people have scores between 0 and 12, another 25% have scores of 13 or 14, another 25% have scores of 15 or 16, and another 25% have scores of 17 or more. These quartile scores are shown in the final column of that table. The advantage of using quartiles is that one can easily see how a person's score compares with those of other people – a quartile score of 1 shows that someone is in the bottom 25% and so on. Beware of performing statistical analyses using quartile scores, though. As there are equal numbers of people in each group, the frequency distribution of quartile scores will follow what is known as a rectangular distribution – not a normal distribution. This can cause seriously misleading results if the quartile scores are correlated with other data which are normally distributed, are used as the dependent variable in t-tests etc.

T-SCALING

Sometimes one constructs a test and discovers that the scores are not normally distributed. In the case of an ability test, merely including more easy items than difficult ones will lead to a skewed distribution of scores – and when writing items, one does not know other than by intuition what difficulty level will be appropriate for a particular population.

Likewise, when constructing a personality inventory, it is quite possible that more respondents will agree with items rather than disagreeing with them (or vice versa). This will lead to a skewed distribution of scores rather than a normal curve.

T-scaling (not to be confused with t-tests or T-scores) is a little-known technique by McCall (1939) which attempts to make a non-normal distribution more normal in shape. It cannot achieve miracles. In particular, it will be unsuccessful if the distribution of scores on a test is J-shaped, or very flat. But it can be useful if the distribution of scores is skewed – and this is perhaps the most common reason for non-normality.

For example, suppose that a group of people produce the following scores on a test.

Table 5.2 Frequency distribution of data for T-scaling

Score	0	1	2	3	4	5	6	7	8
No. of people with score	3	5	10	19	17	13	10	6	4

When these are transformed into z-scores and plotted as a graph in Figure 5.3, it is clear that the distribution is a little skewed.

In Figure 5.3, all of the points are equally spaced along the x-axis; the intervals between the various scores on the test (0, 1, 2 etc.) are equal on the graph. T-scaling works by moving some of the data points to the left or right in order to produce a better approximation of the normal curve. In this case it moves the peak of the curve slightly to the right, as shown in Figure 5.4.

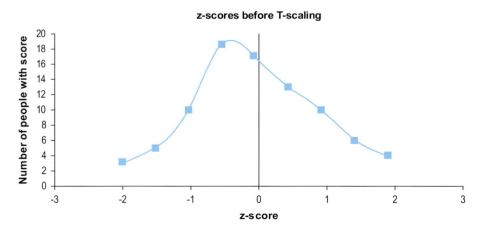

Figure 5.3 Frequency distribution of data from Table 5.2

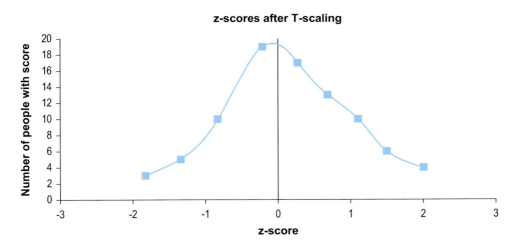

Figure 5.4 Data from Table 5.2 after performing T-scaling

If the technique is to be used in earnest on real data, it might make sense to smooth the frequency distribution before T-scaling – however a discussion of these methods is beyond the scope of this book. See Kolen and Brennan (2014) if interested.

T-scaling may be useful where one needs to perform analyses which assume that the data are normally distributed (but where they manifestly are not) – although there is a literature which suggests that many statistical procedures are not unduly influenced by breaking the assumption of normality. In any case, non-parametric methods are often available for even more advanced methods, and as we argued earlier in this chapter, scores on psychological tests are probably better regarded as ordinal data than interval data – in other words, the scores might perhaps show which individuals score higher than which other but cannot show by how much.

Because T-scaling moves some points a greater distance along the x-axis than others, it is not a linear transformation of the data. The correlation between T-scaled scores and another variable will not be the same as the correlation between the raw scores and that variable, although they will almost certainly be very similar.

Spreadsheet name: Spreadsheet 5.2: T-scaling

Download from: https://routledge.com/9781032146164/

Purpose: To perform T-scaling on up to 60 variables.

Contents of spreadsheet: Sample data showing how many people obtained each score on a 20-item scale.

Suggested activity:

- Change the frequencies in column B; these represent the number of people having each score on the scale. Perhaps use the data from Table 5.1.
- Note that T-scaling suggests that you should replace the original scores with those shown in the final column when performing further analyses: frequencies do not change.
- Try entering more values in column B to discover which sorts of frequency distributions T-scaling can make more normal. For example, try one which is very "peaked" in the middle, another which is very flat, and one where the tail of the normal distribution goes down then up again. For example, 8, 3, 1, 5, 9, 14, 17, 25, 29, 36, 38, 42, 46, 47, 52, 50, 43, 35, 26, 11, 4.
- To use with a scale having more (or fewer) scores, simply add or remove values in columns A and B.

Points to note:

- The first column shows the various scores of the test, and the second column shows the number of people with each score.
- The final column shows the rescaled scores. The scores in the final column should be used instead of the scores in the first column if the scaled scores are to be used for any statistical analyses.
- The scores in the final column have the same mean and standard deviation as the original data.

Learning outcomes: Readers should now be able to:

- Perform T-scaling.
- Appreciate which types of frequency distribution it can make more normal, and which it cannot.

Because T-scaling alters the test scores, it follows that it should *not* be used when either developing tables of norms or interpreting scores using tables of norms. As these tables show the actual percentile scores, non-normality of the data distribution is not an issue. T-scaling is useful for making a distribution of scores look more normal, and this may facilitate the interpretation of these scores or make them better suited for parametric statistical analyses – but that is all.

SUMMARY

This chapter began with a stern warning that scores on psychological scales cannot be used to quantify traits, which should be a major concern for all those who believe that psychometrics is akin to scientific measurement. Michell has argued that it is inappropriate to treat scores on tests as representing proper, scientific measures – and so the potential of psychology to discover mathematically sound laws and principles based on test scores is limited. That said, it is possible that despite their crudeness, scores on tests may have some practical value. The remainder of the chapter therefore examined how scores on scales may be transformed and interpreted, and how the shape of the distribution of scores can be changed through various forms of scaling.

NOTE

1 Doing so will make the distribution of scores rectangular, rather than bell-shaped, which might cause problems for the analysis.

CHAPTER 6
CORRELATIONS

This book is not a statistics text; it focuses on how tests are devised and used, and how scores on tests may be used to help to draw inferences about personality, intelligence and so on. However, at this stage it is necessary to digress slightly and consider how **correlations** can be used (and misused) when analysing responses to items. This is important because most of the techniques discussed in the following sections are based on correlations. There are many different types of correlations, and many things which can affect their values, which means that there are plenty of traps for the unwary! This brief chapter therefore introduces the humble correlation coefficient and shows how it can be used and abused. I would strongly advise that readers should not skip this brief chapter even if they are quite confident about their statistical skills, as it contains material which is not normally taught in statistics courses, plus many useful techniques for dealing with issues encountered when analysing scores from psychological tests.

INTRODUCTION TO CORRELATIONS

Correlations are statistics which show the extent to which scores on one variable are proportional to scores on a second variable. For example, they may be used to show the extent to which people's height is related to their weight, or whether scores on a questionnaire measuring anxiety are related to scores on a questionnaire measuring depression. The square of any correlation is particularly useful; it shows how much variance the two variables have in common. A correlation of 0.7 between two tests thus indicates that about half (0.7 × 0.7 = 0.49) of the person-to-person variability in the scores on one test can be predicted by knowing people's scores on the other test. This holds true no matter how large or small the sample may be.

Correlations are numbers which can be any value between −1.0 and +1.0. A positive correlation (i.e., one greater than zero) shows that if someone has an above-average score on one variable, their score on the other variable will also probably be above average. If one score is near average, the other will probably be near average too and so on. Height and weight show a positive correlation. A negative correlation (one between −1 and 0) indicates that a high score on one variable tends to accompany a

DOI: 10.4324/9781003240181-6

low score on the other. And of course a correlation of zero implies that people's scores on one variable are completely unrelated to their scores on the other variable.

It is also possible to test whether a correlation is significantly different from some other value (such as zero or the value of a correlation found in another person's study). As this is a psychometrics text and not a statistical one, we shall not explore this in much detail – however a statistical "teaser" might be in order here. Suppose that two researchers report correlations which, by some amazing coincidence, are significant at exactly the same probability level: $p = 0.000022$. One of these results is based on a sample of 200 people. The other is based on a sample of 2000 people. Which is the more interesting finding?

The correlation which is based on the large sample will be smaller than the correlation which is based on the large sample. For the example in the previous paragraph, a correlation of 0.3 based on a sample size (N) of 200 is significant with $p = 0.000022$. A correlation of 0.083 with $N = 2000$ is significant with $p = 0.000022$. The first correlation shows that the two variables share 9% of their variance; the second correlation shows that they are virtually unrelated. I make this point because (a) many researchers seem to believe that results from a huge sample are always more important than results from a moderate-sized sample and (b) because researchers sometimes report correlations which are so tiny that they can have no relevance to any real-world behaviour. À propos this, I recently read a published paper which attached great importance to a (statistically significant) correlation of 0.1. The fact that this is significant tells us that with their huge sample, there is evidence that the true value of the correlation is unlikely to be zero. These authors believed that explaining $0.1 \times 0.1 = 0.01 = 1\%$ of the overlap between two variables was interesting; choosing to overlook that 99% of the person-to-person variation in scores was due to other things. There is much to be said for focusing on the size of the square of the correlation, as well as its statistical significance. That way one gets a feel for the size of the effect, as well as whether it is unlikely to have arisen by chance.

This brief chapter is highly selective, and there is a considerable amount of new research into how best to quantify the relations between variables. Choi et al. (2010) and Lalla (2017) give excellent introductions to those seeking a modern overview of the use of correlations to analyse interval-scaled data (which is, arguably, what scores on psychological scales represent) whilst Olkin and Finn (1995) provide a reasonably modern account of how differences between correlations may be calculated, and they include a number of useful guides – for example, how to test whether two multiple correlations (from different samples) are different. Birnbaum (1973) is still essential reading for those who worry about whether it is appropriate to assume a linear (i.e., straight line) relationship between the variables – and the consequence of getting this decision wrong.

TYPES OF CORRELATIONS

Psychometricians correlate many different types of data and use these correlations as the basis for many different purposes – e.g., reliability analysis, establishing the validity of tests, factor analysis and other techniques to be explored later in this book. The types of variables which are correlated also vary considerably. Everyone reading this will be familiar with the idea of correlating two continuous variables, such as the ratio of the lengths of the second and fourth fingers (thought by some to be related to the extent to which an individual was exposed to androgens in the womb) and simple reaction time. Some transformations may be necessary to make the distributions roughly normal, but at least these variables are proper quantities.

More often than non-psychologists correlate responses to test items, scores on tests, or ratings of behaviour. They may *choose* to treat these as being quantitative variables, but as we demonstrated in Chapters 3 and 4 this is an act of faith which may have little empirical or scientific basis. Sometimes psychologists correlate ordinal data – based on rankings. And in some cases, psychologists need to correlate variables which have only two values, such as whether or not an item was answered correctly. These all raise their own issues and will be considered here in turn.

TWO CONTINUOUS VARIABLES

Two continuous variables, such as annual income and years spent in the education system, may be plotted against each other (a scatter diagram, or scatterplot) showing each person's data on the two variables as a dot. The correlation shows how closely the points cluster around a line running from bottom-left to top-right (for a positive correlation) or top-left to bottom-right (for a negative correlation). Inspecting this diagram can show whether the data are more or less normally distributed; if they are, there will be more data points towards the centre of the graph than at the extreme values. Looking at the graph can also show whether the variance (spread) of the data is proportional to one of the variables. It seems sensible to begin by simply looking at some correlations because most statistics textbooks include scatter diagrams showing a perfect correlation, a large positive correlation, a large negative correlation, and a zero correlation – but nothing in between. Thus researchers may become overexcited when interpreting the statistical significance of rather small correlations. Simply examining the correlations can bring one down to earth.

Looking at the data is essential for detecting **outliers,** which can cause major problems when calculating correlations. An outlier is a data point which lies well away from the "swarm"; they may represent genuine scores, but more often than not they arise because a score has been wrongly entered (for example, typing 77 instead of 7 when entering data) or because missing data have not been treated sensibly. For example, unanswered items from Likert scales may have been given scores of zero rather than being estimated as outlined in Chapter 4. Sometimes missing data are coded as 9 or 99, with the intention of telling SPSS or whichever statistical package is being used to treat such data as being missing, but then forgetting to do so. It is essential to examine the frequency distributions of each variable to check for aberrant values before calculating correlations, for outliers can have a truly massive influence on the correlation. Just one outlier can easily turn a correlation of 0 into a correlation of 0.7, which will wreak havoc with any statistical procedure (reliability analysis, factor analysis etc.) which is based on correlations.

Spreadsheet name: Spreadsheet 6.1: Pearson correlations

Download from: https://routledge.com/9781032146164/

Purpose: To show scatter diagrams of correlations.

Contents of spreadsheet: Simulated scores on two normal variables, from 6 to 200 people.

Suggested activity:

- Adjust the bottom slider to give a sample size of 100.
- Adjust the top slider to see what a correlation of (roughly) 0.2, 0.3 or 0.4 actually looks like.
- With sample sizes of (say) 20, 100 and 200, adjust the slider to see what a statistically significant correlation ($p < 0.05$) looks like.

Points to note:

- It will be necessary to move the top slider to and fro in order to generate the appropriate correlation.
- As both variables are normally distributed, there are more data points towards the centre of the graph than at the periphery.
- Even though the correlation of 0.2 is statistically significant (i.e., we can be fairly sure that the data are not random), there is only 0.2 × 0.2 = 4% overlap between the two variables, and it is very hard to see any relationship between the two variables by eye – or even see whether the correlation is positive or negative.

Learning outcomes: Readers should now be able to:

- "Eyeball" data and roughly estimate correlations.

Correlations are not influenced by either the mean (the level of scores) or the standard deviation (the scale of measurement) of the variables being correlated. Thus adding the same arbitrary number to each participant's score and/or multiplying each person's score by another arbitrary number will not change the correlation at all. In practical terms this is useful. It does not matter whether we measure reaction time in microseconds, milliseconds, seconds or years; it does not matter if the responses to a 5-point Likert scale are coded 0/1/2/3/4, 5/7/9/11/13 or −37/−20/−3/14/31 – the correlation will be unchanged.

If this is not obvious, click on the "scaling" tab at the bottom of Spreadsheet 6.1. This shows a scatter diagram based on two variables – Var1 and Var2 – along with the mean, standard deviation and the correlation between Var1 and Var2. It also allows you to rescale Var 1 and/or Var 2 by adding a constant (any number) to each person's score on either of these two variables, and then multiplying the result by any constant. For example, one could add 47 to everyone's score on Var 1 then multiply this total by 6. The spreadsheet shows the rescaled scores, along with the scatter diagram, mean, standard deviation and correlation. It can be seen that the correlation does not change, no matter what number is added to the scores or what multiplier is used.

Textbooks usually stress that the correlation coefficient can be any number between −1 and +1. This is not quite true, even if the measurements which are being correlated are completely error-free. The **Pearson correlation** can only be exactly 1.0 (or −1.0) if the two variables have the same frequency distribution. For example, the correlation can only be −1 or +1 if both variables follow a normal distribution, or if both follow a **rectangular distribution** (where equal numbers of people obtain each score on a measure) or if both follow some other distribution. If one of the variables follows a normal distribution and the other follows a rectangular distribution, or is **skewed**, the correlation cannot be 1.0. Some textbooks mention this; however they do not consider say how much of a problem this is likely to be in practice. Spreadsheet 6.2 allows this to be explored.

> **Spreadsheet name:** Spreadsheet 6.2: Pearson correlations with skewed data
>
> **Download from:** https://routledge.com/9781032146164/
>
> **Purpose:** To show how skew affects the maximum possible correlation between two variables.
>
> **Contents of spreadsheet:** Simulated data from 1000 people forming skewed, normal and rectangular distributions.
>
> **Suggested activity:**
>
> - Choose the same level of skew for both skewed distributions (e.g., means of 5). Scroll down to inspect the correlations between the two skewed distributions.

Also note the correlation between the normal and skewed, the normal and rectangular, and the skewed and rectangular distributions.
- Generate several sets of data (press f9 etc.) and note the typical values for these correlations.
- Change the skew on one of the distributions (e.g., to 15). Note the size of the correlations between the skewed distributions for several sets of data.
- Repeat for other, more extreme differences in skew.

Points to note:

- The data in this simulation make the correlations as large as possible; the "person" with the lowest score on one distribution also has the lowest score on all other distributions etc.
- This spreadsheet involves quite a lot of computation, so there may be a pause of a few seconds after pressing f9.

Learning outcomes: Readers should now be able to:

- Appreciate that if two variables have equal skew, their correlation can be 1.
- Appreciate that if distributions differ, correlations are marginally less than 1, but that is unlikely to be a major problem unless variables are heavily skewed in opposite directions.

This exercise shows that the maximum possible correlation is not *much* less than 1.0 unless the variables differ enormously in skew. When calculating correlations between two variables which have many possible values, one probably does not need to worry too much about the frequency distributions of variables being correlated unless they are severely skewed in opposite directions.

TWO TWO-VALUED (DICHOTOMOUS) VARIABLES

Psychologists often need to correlate scores which have only two values – the most obvious case being where responses to an ability test item are coded as correct or incorrect, or where performance is coded as pass/fail. In order to perform reliability analysis, factor analysis etc., as described in later chapters these items need to be correlated together – and mathematically there is nothing wrong with doing so. When the usual (Pearson) correlation is calculated between two **dichotomous** (two-valued) variables, it is usually known as the **phi coefficient**. However, interpreting phi coefficients is difficult.

It is usual to summarise dichotomous variables using a table such as Table 6.1, simply because it is more convenient that showing many rows of data containing 0s and 1s (or whatever other codes are used – the correlation will be the same however the categories are coded).

Table 6.1 Two datasets showing the number of people answering two ability items correctly (1) and incorrectly (0)

		Dataset A			Dataset B		
		Variable 1			Variable 1		
		0	1	Total	0	1	Total
Variable 2	0	20	10	30	48	48	96
	1	6	40	46	12	12	24
	Total	26	50	76	60	60	120

Dataset A simply shows that 20 people scored 0 on both variable 1 and variable 2, six scored 0 on variable 1 and 1 on variable 2 and so on. Phi simply shows the correlation that is obtained by calculating the Pearson correlation from a table of data containing 20 rows of "0 0", five rows of "0 1" etc., as shown in Table 6.1. A phi of 0.552 looks sensible, as people tend to generally either score 1 for both items or score 0 for both, which should result in a positive correlation. But what if the items differ in drastically their difficulty, as shown in dataset B?

Spreadsheet name: Spreadsheet 6.3: Correlations from dichotomous data

Download from: https://routledge.com/9781032146164/

Purpose: A utility to compute several different correlations from dichotomous (two-valued) data.

Contents of spreadsheet: Data from Table 6.1.

Suggested activity:

- Enter the numbers from dataset B from Table 6.1 into the spreadsheet; 50% of people score 1 on variable 1 and 20% score 1 on variable 2. Spend no more than a minute or two entering any numbers you like in the green cells trying to obtain a correlation of +1 *whilst keeping the proportion who score 1 on variable 1 at 0.5 and the proportion who score 1 on variable 2 as anything other than 0.5.*

Points to note:

- It is impossible to achieve a correlation of 1.0 unless the same proportion of people scoring 1 is the same for both items.
- It is possible to calculate many other different statistics from dichotomous data, each of which is another form of correlation coefficient. Several of these will be referenced in later chapters.

Learning outcomes: Readers should now be able to:

- Appreciate that dichotomous variables can only correlate perfectly if the same proportion of people score 1 on each variable.
- Use the spreadsheet to calculate a range of different correlation coefficients.

It turns out that it is mathematically possible to obtain a correlation of +1 (or −1) only if both items happen to have exactly the same level of difficulty (the same proportion of people scoring 1, otherwise known as the **p -value**).[1] Figure 6.1 shows what the maximum possible value of phi is if one variable has a *p*-value of 0.5 and the other has a different *p*-value. It can be seen from this graph that if the difficulty value of the second item is 0.2 (as with dataset B), then it is mathematically impossible for phi to be any larger than 0.5 (Ferguson, 1941). The spreadsheet shows the maximum value of phi ("phimax") which is possible for any pair of variables.

This creates a major problem. The *p*-values of the variables cannot (usually) be changed to make them equal. For example, some ability test items will invariably be harder than

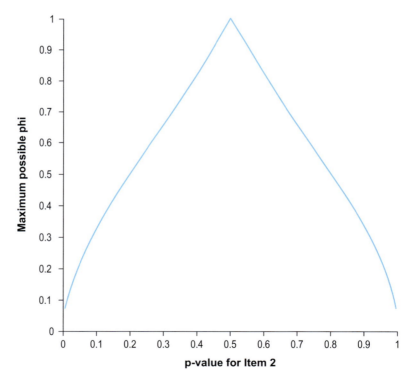

Figure 6.1 Maximum possible correlation between an item having difficulty of 0.5 and other items of varying difficulties (*p*-values)

others. Therefore, the correlation between two items generally can never equal 1.0, which poses some interesting questions about how one should interpret it. For how *does* one interpret a correlation of 0.5 between two items? It could (as in dataset A) mean that there is a moderate relationship between variables of similar difficulty. Or it could (as in dataset B) suggest a relationship which is as strong as it can be, given that the items have different *p*-values. The problem is that statistical techniques which use correlations (such as factor analysis) do not "know" where the correlations have come from, and so cannot intuit that sometimes the correlation is bound to be less than 1.0. It will cause major problems for such techniques.

One (old) solution suggested dividing a correlation by its maximum possible value. This ensures that every correlation lies between −1 and 1. However, this introduces a host of other problems, too (Davenport & Elsanhurry, 1991), so it cannot really be recommended, although it is commonly used in Mokken scaling (see Chapter 15). It is therefore very dangerous to calculate the usual Pearson correlation ("phi") from two-valued data, unless the two variables have very similar difficulty levels.

Before leaving phi, we should note in passing that it is related to the chi-square statistic with which many readers will be familiar; details are given on the spreadsheet. Indeed, phi is calculated twice there – once using the Pearson formula and once from chi-square.

Rather than using phi, it is possible to calculate other types of correlation from this sort of data. Several have been proposed; the spreadsheet computes **Goodman-Kruskal gamma** (also known as Yule's Q), the **contingency coefficient**, the **G-index** and **kappa**, just for information. (The computational formulae are quite simple and may be deduced from the spreadsheet.) Readers may find it interesting to explore how or whether these differ from phi, especially when the *p*-values of the items are both similar and different. All of these coefficients seek to get around the problems of the phi coefficient and are sometimes used when checking whether two people can rate behaviour similarly. However, they are rarely (if ever) used as the basis for reliability analysis, for factor analysis etc., although it is possible to use some of these for factor analysis in the R environment. The exception is the G-index, which can be used to correlate people together and is the basis for Q-factor analysis, discussed in Chapter 12 (Holley, 1973; Vegelius, 1973).

In some cases we can imagine that the variables which are being analysed represent arbitrary "cutting points" of some normally distributed continuous variable. For example, an item measuring whether or not a person understands the meaning of the word "chair" presumably measures some underlying variable of verbal comprehension. So in correlating the responses to that item with an item measuring mathematical ability (for example, "What is 463 × 3?"), we really want to know what the correlation between the two underlying, continuous, traits is. If it can be assumed that both of the two-valued variables represent points along some normally distributed trait (such as verbal comprehension or numerical ability), then it is possible to estimate what this correlation might be using something called the **tetrachoric** correlation. It is *not* sensible to calculate this when one or both of the variables represent a genuine categorical variable, such as gender.

The tetrachoric correlation is difficult to calculate exactly (Olsson, 1979) and several approximations have been developed – the spreadsheet shows two of them. Matrices of tetrachoric correlations can be calculated using the Factor program introduced in Chapter 11 (Lorenzo-Seva & Ferrando, 2006) by specifying the **polychoric** option, or from within the R statistical environment (R Core Team, 2013). They may be used for factor analysis, as discussed in Chapters 10–13, and (controversially) for reliability calculations, as discussed in Chapter 7. Tetrachoric correlations are generally larger than phi correlations, and so produce larger estimates of reliability, larger factor loadings and so on. This probably accounts for their popularity. However, they should *only* be used if both of the variables represent some continuous trait which just happens to have been coded as 0/1.

For example, an applied psychologist might calculate the tetrachoric correlation between whether or not trainee pilots have passed a test measuring visualisation skills, and whether or not they successfully qualify as pilots. Both could be reasonably supposed to represent normally distributed variables – but it would be far safer to correlate scores on the visualisation test with some outcome score on the piloting variable, rather than risk introducing error by calculating the tetrachoric correlation.

Should it be necessary to find the statistical significance of a tetrachoric correlation, see Guilford and Lyons (1942).

ONE CONTINUOUS AND ONE DICHOTOMOUS VARIABLE

It is sometimes necessary to calculate the correlation between one dichotomous variable and one continuous variable. For example, it is possible that in the previous example there *is* no detailed information available about why individuals passed or failed the piloting course, whereas scores on the visualisation test are a continuous variable. What happens when a Pearson correlation is calculated between a two-valued (dichotomous) variable and a continuous variable?

For historical reasons this is known as the **point-biserial correlation** – and it suffers from much the same problem as the phi coefficient. The point-biserial correlation can never be 1.0 because (by definition) the two variables have differently shaped distributions – one being continuous and the other two-valued. At best, the correlation

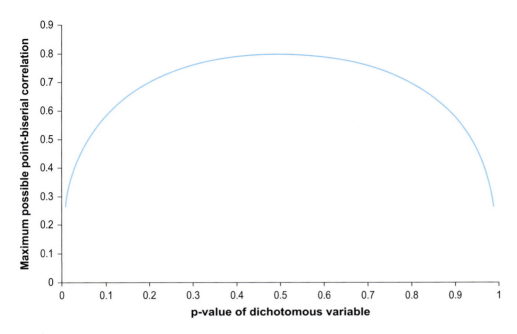

Figure 6.2 Maximum possible correlation when a two-valued ("dichotomous") variable is correlated with a normally distributed continuous variable

between them can be about 0.8, as shown in Figure 6.2. However, the good news is that the maximum correlation is between 0.6 and 0.8 as long as the *p*-value of the dichotomous variable is between about −0.2 and 0.2 – that is, as long as the dichotomous variable is neither very easy nor very difficult.

It is also possible to calculate a statistic known as the **biserial correlation**, which adjusts for the problem that the point-biserial correlation can never equal 1.0. It assumes that the dichotomous variable represents a score on some underlying normally distributed variable, for example, level of performance during flying training. Although we have only access to these data after they have been coded as pass/fail, we know that they come from a continuous distribution, which we can probably assume to be normal in shape. The biserial correlation boosts the point-biserial to give a correlation which can range from −1 to 1 for any *p*-value of the dichotomous variable. It is simply necessary to know the point-biserial correlation (or the Pearson correlation, which is the same thing) and the difficulty of the dichotomous item (the proportion of people who answer it in a particular direction). For example, if the point-biserial correlation is 0.4 and 20% of people pass an item (making its *p*-value 0.2). Spreadsheet 6.4 shows that the biserial correlation is 0.57.

> **Spreadsheet name:** Spreadsheet 6.4: Biserial correlation
>
> **Download from:** https://routledge.com/9781032146164/
>
> **Purpose:** To calculate a biserial correlation.
>
> **Contents of spreadsheet:** A point biserial correlation and a *p*-value for the dichotomous variable.
>
> **Suggested activity:**
>
> - This is a utility, as biserial correlations are rarely calculated by statistical packages.
>
> **Points to note:**
>
> - The biserial correlation can be *appreciably* larger than the point-biserial.
>
> **Learning outcomes: Readers should now be able to:**
>
> - Compute a biserial correlation.

The same caveats apply as with the tetrachoric correlation. Computing the biserial correlation if the dichotomous variable is categorical (e.g., gender) is nonsensical. And it is far better to try to measure both variables on a continuous scale than to use a dichotomised variable. However, if there genuinely is no alternative, the biserial correlation can be useful. The statistical significance of the biserial correlation cannot be tested using the same formulae as for the Pearson correlation unless the sample size is large (Alf & Abrahams, 1971).

TWO ORDINAL VARIABLES

Readers will be familiar with **Spearman's rho** and **Kendall's tau** as non–parametric measures of correlation. Spearman's rho is often presented using a rather arcane formula; however the same result may be obtained by simply ranking both variables from smallest to largest and calculating a Pearson correlation on the two sets of ranks. As Spearman's correlation can be calculated using the usual formula for a Pearson correlation (only performed on ranks, not the original numbers) there can be little doubts as to its suitability for use in factor analysis etc. Given the concerns with the nature of psychological variables outlined in Chapter 3, it is surprising that this is not more common; this might just be because SPSS does not present it as an option.

There is another statistic known as the polychoric correlation, which resembles the tetrachoric correlation only with two *or more* levels of each variable. Again, it is necessary to assume that the numbers being correlated come from some underlying normally distributed continuous variable, but unlike the Pearson correlation, the polychoric correlation does not assume that the distance between a rating of 1 and 3 (for example) is the same as the distance between 4 and 6 on the underlying variable. This makes the polychoric correlation a sort of compromise between the ordinal Spearman correlation and the more stringent assumptions of the Pearson correlation. It is thus quite widely used – particularly in areas such as factor analysis. Calculating the polychoric correlation and its statistical significance is even more unpleasant than the tetrachoric correlation, and so there is no spreadsheet here to do so. The Factor program (Lorenzo-Seva & Ferrando, 2006) or the Psych package in the R environment (Revelle, 2017c) will allow them to be calculated.

CORRELATIONS AND GROUP DIFFERENCES

Most psychologists ignore the possibility that their data may contain sub-groups of individuals who respond differently to test items or other measures. The temptation is simply to plough ahead and calculate correlations. However, this can be dangerous. Consider the data in Table 6.2 and try to estimate (by eye) what the correlation between the two variables might be.

Few readers would have much of a problem correlating these two variables together. The correlation between variable 1 and variable 2 is 0.34, so most people would infer that this represents some sort of positive relationship – albeit one which is not statistically significant with this sample.

Table 6.2 Scores on two variables (plus gender)

	Gender	Variable 1	Variable 2
Jack	M	7	9
Oliver	M	8	7
Ben	M	8	8
Gabriel	M	6	9
Nora	F	7	4
Violet	F	5	5
Emma	F	6	5
Susan	F	5	6

However, look again at these data. For in this fictitious example there is a huge *negative* correlation between the two variables for the men ($r = -0.82$) and a huge *negative* correlation between the variables for the women ($r = -.85$), as you might care to verify. The only reason that there appears to be a positive correlation when the entire sample is used to calculate the correlation is because there is a substantial difference in the average scores of the men and women. This is not uncommon in psychology. For example, men score about 0.7 of a standard deviation higher than women on the personality trait of Psychoticism (Eysenck et al., 1985). The purpose of this analysis is to show that the presence of group differences can have a massive effect on correlations. It is therefore advisable to check for group differences wherever possible before calculating correlations or performing any more detailed analysis – factor analysis or reliability analysis, for example. The results can otherwise be meaningless.

This issue is obvious if one simply plots the scores of the men and women separately for all pairs of variables, as some computer packages allow. A quick glance will reveal gross group differences. Or else t-tests, analysis of variance etc. can be used to check that none of the group differences is appreciable (*appreciable* rather than statistically significant).

If group differences *are* found on some variables, there are several options available. If the sample is large, it is safest to analyse data for each group separately. However, if the

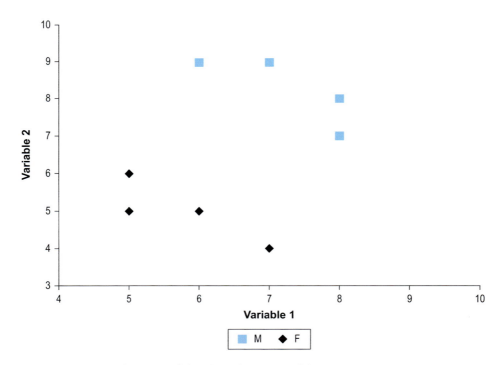

Figure 6.3 Scatter diagram of the data shown in Table 6.2

sample contains several different group types (e.g., male/female, young/middle-aged/elderly, addicts/non-addicts), this is clearly unlikely to be feasible unless the sample is *very* large. Other options include standardising the data in order to eliminate any group differences or using partial correlation to control for the effects of differences between groups. However, this is statistics, not psychometrics, so it would be inappropriate to explore the issue further. The important point is to recognise that group differences can wreak havoc with correlations. When researching variables which might show group differences, these *must* be explored before computing them – though research papers which do so are the exception rather than the rule.

CORRECTING CORRELATIONS FOR UNRELIABILITY

We can never measure anything accurately, and the effect of measurement error will be to reduce the size of the correlation between two variables (i.e., bring it closer to zero). It is tempting to ask what the correlation might be had the variables been measured with greater accuracy. As will be shown in Chapter 7, a scale's **reliability** is a statistic which estimates how accurate its scores are. For example, Chapter 7 shows that the square root of a statistic called **coefficient alpha** estimates the correlation between people's scores on a test and their true score. It is thus possible to derive a formula to estimate what the correlation between two tests would be if both were measured completely accurately.

This can obviously be dangerous. If the best-available tests have been used to measure some trait (and if not, why not?), it would never be possible to measure the trait with greater accuracy. Correcting for reliability thus leads us away from real data into fantasy land. We look at the relationship between theoretical concepts (which will always be larger than the correlations between variables) and ignore the inconvenient problem that these cannot show what correlations between real tests can ever look like.

Spreadsheet 6.5 shows how correlations may be corrected for measurement error. One simply enters the correlation which has been found, the reliability of each of the variables (e.g., coefficient alpha, or test-retest reliability), and it estimates what the correlation between the variables *would* be if both of them were completely free from measurement error.

CORRECTING CORRELATIONS FOR RESTRICTION OF RANGE

A common problem arises when using tests, or other criteria, for selection purposes. How can these tests be validated, in order to check that they work properly? For example, suppose that a university selects students entirely on the basis of their grade point average, A-level grades, or some other measure of achievement in school. Do these measures of school achievement predict how well the students will perform at university? Or if a firm uses some form of ability test to screen potential employees, how well do scores on that test relate to job performance? The problem with both of these scenarios is that because the people who are accepted into the organisation must all have passed the selection procedure, the range of scores on the selection test (or the range of grade point averages, A-level grades or whatever) will be smaller than in the population from which the people were selected. This implies that the standard deviation of the scores in the "selected" group will be smaller than in the population.

A consequence of this is that the correlation between scores on the selection test and any other variable will be smaller than they would be if the correlation had been based on a random sample of people from the population. The validity of the selection measure (its correlation with performance) will be underestimated.

There are three ways round this problem.

1 One can administer the test to applicants but not use it (or anything similar) to select people. Thus the people who are selected will form a random sample of the population with respect to their scores on the test; the correlation between the test and the outcome measure will not need to be corrected. This is unlikely to be feasible in practice. If the organisation believes that the existing test has any merit whatsoever for selecting people, it is unlikely to agree to abandon it temporarily for the purpose of research.
2 The usual solution is to correct for "restriction of range". If one knows the standard deviation of scores in the population (from the test scores of the pool of job applicants, or the national average of school performance indicators) and the standard deviation of the scores in the selected group, it is possible to correct the correlation by estimating what it would be if the standard deviation of the selected group was the same as that of the applicants. Spreadsheet 6.5 does this. For example, if the correlation between test scores and job performance is 0.3, the standard deviation of test scores in the sample is 10 and the standard deviation of test scores in the population is 20, then the "corrected" estimate for the correlation is 0.53. This formula may also be used to reduce the correlation if a sample standard deviation is larger than in the population – for example, if a researcher puts together a sample which consists of more university students and people with special educational needs than would be found in the population, when performing research on intelligence. This will overestimate the correlation between an intelligence test and anything else.
3 A much better solution was put forward by Dobson (1988), but it is rarely cited. It is unrealistic to correct the correlation by making the standard deviations of the sample equivalent to the standard deviation of the population in the scenarios

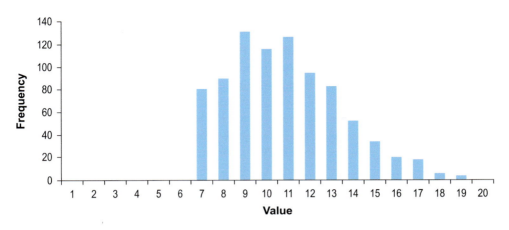

Figure 6.4 A truncated normal distribution of test scores from employees who were only selected for employment if they had a test score of over 6

mentioned, because the reason why people are not selected is because of their low scores on the selection test. The test scores of the selection test will therefore probably follow a "truncated normal distribution" as shown in Figure 6.4, rather than a normal distribution which is narrower than in the population. Spreadsheet 6.5 performs this correction too. All that is needed is to enter the observed correlation between, for example, school performance and university performance, and the proportion of people selected from the population based on their school performance. For example, if a university department selected the best 200 of 2000 applicants, this figure (the "selection ratio") would be 200/2000 or 0.1. If the correlation between school performance and university performance for this group was found to be 0.2, correcting it gives a figure of 0.44, as you might care to verify.

A more detailed discussion of these issues is given by Sackett and Yang (2000).

SIGNIFICANCE TESTING

Is a correlation different from zero? Is a correlation different from some other value? Is a correlation different from another correlation? The first question is, of course, just a test of the statistical significance of the correlation; it will be shown by any statistical package. The second and third questions should perhaps be addressed more often than they are. For example, if one researcher discovers that the correlation between two traits is 0.3 and someone else finds that it is 0.2, is there reason to believe that this difference is real, or might it have occurred by chance?

What one *cannot* do is infer that because the correlation of 0.3 is statistically significant (i.e., likely to be different from 0) whilst the correlation of 0.2 is *not* statistically significant, the two correlations are different. For it might be the case that one correlation is significant with $p = 0.049$ and the other just fails to reach significance ($p = 0.051$) – even though the correlations are virtually the same size (I assume that the sample sizes are equal). It is instead necessary to test the significance of the *difference* between the correlations from two different samples. Spreadsheet 6.5 does so. It is occasionally necessary to calculate the difference between correlations when the same sample is tested twice; if so, see Howell (2012), for example.

AVERAGING CORRELATIONS

It may sometimes be useful to average correlations – for example, when drawing some conclusion about several studies where the raw data are not available to be reanalysed. Strictly speaking, one should not simply average correlation coefficients, as the average one obtains will be a biased estimate; however if the correlations are between −0.7 and +0.7, it does not matter too much, other than to obsessional journal referees. If the correlations are larger, it is necessary to perform what is known as a "Fisher transformation" before averaging. This converts the correlation into a variable having a roughly normal distribution. After averaging these Fisher transformations, the result is converted back into a correlation. Spreadsheet 6.5 performs this analysis, averaging up to six correlations.

> **Spreadsheet name:** Spreadsheet 6.5: Correlation utilities
>
> **Download from:** https://routledge.com/9781032146164/
>
> **Purpose:** To correct correlations for unreliability and restriction of range. To average correlations. To test whether two correlations differ.
>
> **Contents of spreadsheet:** Various sample data.
>
> **Suggested activity:**
>
> - Reliabilities of 0.7–0.8 are quite common. Enter a correlation, and then note how much it increases when corrected for unreliability. Try several different values of correlation, and several different values for reliability (between 0 and 1).
> - Check how changing the proportion of people selected alters the correlation that is corrected for attenuation using Dobson's method.
> - Convince yourself that if the sample standard deviation is smaller than the standard deviation in the population, the correction for restriction of range increases the size of the correlation. What happens if the standard deviation in the sample is *larger* than in the population?

- Try averaging some correlations. Note that the Fisher method (used here) gives similar results to a simple average unless the correlations are larger than about 0.8.

Points to note:

- These utilities are hard to find and are brought together for convenience. Although they are believed to be accurate, these formulae are intended for educational (rather than research) purposes.

Learning outcomes: Readers should now be able to:

- Perform a range of corrections and significance tests.

SUMMARY

Many psychometric analyses are based on correlations. If these are inappropriate for the data being analysed (e.g., if dichotomous data are simply treated as if they are continuous) or if care is not taken to check for group differences or outliers, the sophisticated analyses described in the following chapters are meaningless as well as scientifically and practically worthless. The issue of group differences is the one which I would single out for special attention. It is all too easy to rush ahead and calculate correlations for a diverse group of people without recognising that if the sample consists of two or more subgroups of people with different mean scores, the size and sign of the correlation can be massively influenced by such differences. Few psychologists appreciate this point.

It can also be difficult to track down techniques for correcting correlations for the effects of restriction of range and unreliability, and so the spreadsheets may be of use to practitioners who need to perform such corrections.

NOTE

1 This has nothing to do with the use of the term "p-value" in statistical significance testing.

CHAPTER 7
RANDOM ERRORS OF MEASUREMENT

This chapter and the next consider the accuracy of test scores. This chapter deals with random errors of measurement. It shows how a branch of psychometrics known as "reliability theory" can be used to estimate how accurately a scale or test can estimate each person's true score, provided that certain assumptions are met.

No measurement is ever perfectly accurate. If I measure the length of a piece of paper using a ruler, it is probable that I will overestimate or underestimate its length by a millimetre or two just because of problems aligning the end of the ruler with the end of the paper and reading the length corresponding to the other end of the piece of paper, plus possible problems with the rulers themselves; my selection of cheap, dollar-store rulers might be inaccurate. But if I measure the same piece of paper using the same ruler on many occasions, or assume that a cheap ruler is as likely to underestimate as overestimate a length, it should be intuitively obvious that the average of all these measurements is likely to be close to the true length of the piece of paper. By taking multiple measurements the errors should cancel each other out.

For example, if I measured the same piece of paper on 15 occasions, the lengths (in millimetres) might be as shown in Table 7.1.

We can plot these lengths as a bar chart (see Figure 7.1), and both experiment and statistical theory (something called the central limit theorem) tell us that the distribution of these scores follows a normal distribution. In other words, (a) we are as likely to overestimate as underestimate a measurement and (b) we are more likely to underestimate or overestimate the measurement by a small amount than a large amount.

Table 7.1 Fifteen measurements of a piece of paper

Occasion	1	2	3	4	5	6	7	8	9	10	11	12	13	14	15
Measurement	92	93	91	90	92	92	92	93	92	94	91	92	91	92	93
Error	0	1	−1	−2	0	0	0	1	0	2	−1	0	−1	0	1

DOI: 10.4324/9781003240181-7

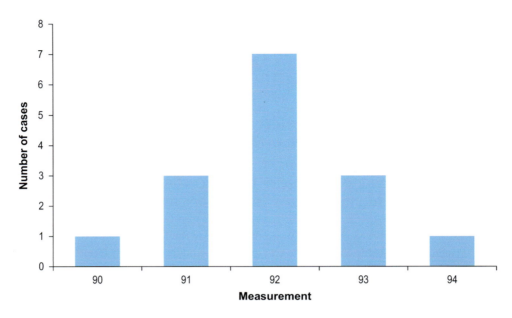

Figure 7.1 Frequency distribution of measurements from Table 7.1

Taken together, (a) and (b) imply that the average error will be zero – as we are likely to overestimate the length as often as we underestimate it, and by a similar amount. If the average error is zero, it follows that we can average all the measurements to obtain an estimate of the true score, −92.0. This is the best estimate that we have of the true length of the piece of paper. In order to estimate this true score accurately we need to make a very large number of measurements – otherwise we might be unlucky and make some measurements which all just happen to be too large or too small. It should be obvious that as the number of measurements increases, the more likely our estimate of the true score, obtained by averaging repeated observations, is likely to be accurate.

WHY PSYCHOLOGICAL MEASURES ARE DIFFERENT FROM PHYSICAL MEASURES

Comparing psychological measurements with physical measurements like this has some appeal, but it falls down in three main respects.

First, as we noted in Chapter 3, there is no guarantee that the trait or state which the test is designed to measure is quantitative at all – in which case all attempts to measure it using numbers, adding together scores on items etc. will not be appropriate. And as items vary in their difficulty (or for Likert-scaled items, how extreme a level of the trait they represent), it is not reasonable to treat sums of responses to these items as anything better than interval-scaled data. This suggests that the best that any test can do under ideal circumstances is rank-order people.

Second, in psychology we cannot ask the same question over and over again when trying to measure some trait, as respondents will simply remember their previous answer and repeat it. It is therefore necessary to devise different items, each of which measures the same trait but by different means. If a scale is designed to measure vocabulary, one might assemble a selection of words of appropriate difficulty (perhaps by randomly sampling words which occur in the written language within a certain band of frequency). Or if we try to measure a trait such as depression, we could ask questions each of which relates to a different aspect of depression, such as weight change, feelings of hopelessness, inability to concentrate etc. The basic principle still holds: if we assume that the measurement errors are random, our best estimate of the true score is a person's total score on the scale.

Third, the instruments used to measure physical quantities are generally fairly accurate. The reading on the ruler is influenced by the length of the object being measured – not time of day, atmospheric pressure, distance from the equator or anything else – and so only a very few readings are needed to achieve an accurate measurement. On the other hand, items in psychological scales are almost invariably affected by many different traits, and so the correlation between responses to an item and the "true score" (a person's level of the trait being assessed) is usually feeble. It is possible to estimate this in several different ways, but a correlation of 0.3–0.4 would be common, whilst a correlation of 0.5 would be surprisingly large. In other words, most test items are only feebly related to the trait which they purport to measure; bear in mind that even a correlation of 0.5 implies that only 25% of the variation in people's responses to the item is due to the influence of the trait being assessed!

Why is this? "Do you enjoy lively parties?" is an item which has been shown to measure extraversion. But think about what else might affect how a person responds to this item. Age might affect it – I certainly enjoy parties less than I used to. Even if I hate parties I might *say* I enjoy them because I think it is expected of me. I might have decided to focus on my work instead of partying. Even a highly extraverted person might disagree with this item if they do not enjoy interacting with drunken people, if they have been to so many parties recently that they abhor the thought of yet another one – the list is almost endless. As well as measuring the trait which the scale is designed to measure, a person's response to an item will be influenced by a lot of other things, and there will probably be plenty of random error too as people's view may change from minute to minute for no obvious reason. And some people will just happen to like parties – even though they are not extraverted – an issue which will be picked up in Chapter 10.

If each of the items in a scale is affected by a different set of these nuisance variables, or if the nuisance variables which increase a person's score on one item decrease their score on another item, then there is no problem. Just as measuring the length of the sheet of paper several times increased the accuracy of the assessment, adding together several items, *each of which is affected by a different set of nuisance variables*, will produce a test score which is likely to be more accurate than the score on any single item. The more items which are added together, the more accurate the test score will be. For now, we treat all of the nuisance variables (the things which influence the way in which people answer the item, but which are not the trait we are trying to measure) as being random errors. This means that they will vary from item to item and from person to person.

Each person's answer to an item will thus be influenced by the level of the trait which the scale is designed to measure (their true score) together with some **random errors** of measurement. Spreadsheet 7.1 allows us to vary the extent to which the true score and random error influence people's responses to five items which form a scale. For example, one item might consist of equal amounts of true score and random error. Another (worse) item might consist of three parts true score and seven parts random error and so on. Because this is a simulation, we actually know each person's true score — so the first important thing which this spreadsheet does is show the correlation between responses to an item and people's true scores.

The second thing which this spreadsheet does is add together the responses on several items. We argued that computing a total score for each person by adding together scores on several items should show a large correlation with the true score because all of the random errors will tend to cancel out. So the spreadsheet shows the correlation between scores on the five-item scale and the true score.

Finally, we argued that the more times we measure something, the more accurate the (total) score is likely to be. So the spreadsheet also adds another five items, of equal quality to the original five, to see whether this shows a still-better correlation with the total score.

Spreadsheet name: Spreadsheet 7.1: Summing item scores

Download from: https://routledge.com/9781032146164/

Purpose: To show how the reliability of a test reflects the amount of measurement error. To determine whether test length influences reliability.

Contents of spreadsheet: Data on 10 items from 390 simulated people. Each person's score on each item is influenced by their true score and random error, to an extent which can be varied.

Suggested activity:

- Enter some numbers between 0 and 10 in each green cell: 0 indicates that the true score does not influence the item score at all and 10 indicates that the true score completely determines the score on the item. The number underneath each green cell shows the extent to which random error influences each item. Recalculate several times using f9.
- Note the correlation between each item and the true score in section B.
- Check that entering 0 produces a correlation of about zero and that entering 10 produces a correlation of 1.0. Recalculate several times.
- Set the influence of the true score to a fairly low value (say 2 or 3) for each item. This is typical of those found in real scales. Is the correlation between the sum of scores on items 1–5 larger than the correlation between any individual item and the true score?
- The spreadsheet also generates items 6–10, with identical characteristics to items 1–5. This means that it is possible to see whether using a 10-item test, with the same quality of items as a five-item test, produces better correlation with the total score.
- Find out whether it is possible for a single item scale to perform better than a five-item scale using items of varying quality. Perhaps use one item with a value of 6 or 7 and others with 2 or 3. Examine the correlation between the "good" item and the total score, and compare this with the correlation between the five-item scale and the total score.

Points to note:

- Note that the correlation between the score on the sum of items 1–5 and the true score is much higher than the correlation between any single item and the true score when all items are of equal quality.
- The 10-item test is invariably a better measure of the true score than is the five-item test.
- If the scale consists of one good item and several mediocre ones, it may be better to use just the one good item. See Chapter 16.

Learning outcomes: Readers should now be able to:

- Appreciate that the total score on a scale consisting of several equal-quality items is a better estimate of people's true scores than a single item.
- Realise that longer scales provide better estimates of true scores than do shorter scales – assuming that items 6–10 are of the same quality as the items in the five-item scale.

Although we can never know a person's true score, we can estimate it by using their total score on the items in the scale. We could therefore correlate each person's score on each item with the total score, as the total score is the best estimate which we have of the person's true score. This is a classic method of developing scales (**classical**

item analysis), described in Chapter 16. The best items are those having the largest correlation with the total score on the scale.

We could also look at the quality of the items by examining the correlations between them. An item which has a lot of random error associated with it will show a low correlation with all other items in the scale. An item which is little influenced by random error will show much higher correlations with the other items. So "good" items will show large correlations between them; items which largely consist of random error will intercorrelate feebly. Reliability theory (described later) draws extensively on this idea.

This is a statistical fact. However, there is a major problem with its implementation, for it is not completely obvious how we should define "random error". Most psychologists simply assume that anything other than the trait which one tries to measure is random error (or one of the forms of systematic bias considered in Chapter 8).

I believe that this is incorrect, and this is why I was so scathing in Chapter 2 about scales where the same item is paraphrased several times. For such items, the correlation between the items is not determined just by the trait which the item is designed to measure but by all of the other "nuisance variables" as well, since a person's level of all of these will be the same, too. If the item "Do you agree that a good party is the best way to spend the evening?" appears in the same questionnaire as the item "Do you enjoy lively parties?", it is obvious that the nuisance factors which affect the first item will also affect the second item *in the same way*. They are not random error at all. So the correlation between these two items will overestimate how much people's responses to the two items measure the trait of extraversion, as extraversion is not the only thing which influences how people respond to the two items.

Because the items are so similar in content, all the "nuisance factors" will influence each person's response to both items in the same way and thereby boost the correlation rather than cancelling out. Thus the correlation between the items will arise because the same bunch of traits (not just the one trait which the items are supposed to assess) influence both variables. The correlation between items will be larger than it would be if it reflected extraversion alone. This will make the psychometric properties of the scale appear much better than they would be if better questions had been asked. In addition, adding together scores on several such items will produce a scale which measures more than one trait, and we showed in Chapter 1 that this is a major flaw.

MEASURING RELIABILITY

The **reliability** of a test is defined as the proportion of variance of test scores which is due to the influence of people's true scores. It is usually expressed as a number between 0 and 1, with 0 indicating that the score on the scale is nothing but

measurement error (i.e., no more useful than picking a random number), whilst a reliability of 1 indicates that there is no measurement error associated with people's scores on the scale; they reflect people's true scores with perfect accuracy. The reliability coefficient estimates the square of the correlation between people's scores on the tests and their true scores, and so the *square root* of the reliability coefficient estimates the correlation between scores on the test and people's true scores. A reliability of 0.6 implies that the test correlates about 0.77 with the true score, or alternatively that about 60% of the variation in the test score is caused by the true score; the remaining 40% represents random measurement error. The "other things" that influence one item are generally assumed to be different from the other things that influence each of the other items in the scale – although we have suggested that this is unlikely to be the case in practice. If this is so, reliabilities will be overestimated.

The reliability coefficient is one of the most useful concepts in psychometrics. There are several ways of estimating the reliability of a scale. Reliability has to be estimated rather than measured exactly because in real life we never know a person's true score.

It is vital to remember than when estimating the reliability of a scale, that estimate will change if the scale is administered to a different population of people or for different purposes. A scale which shows high reliability when university students volunteer to take it as part of a research study may show dismal reliability when those same students take it as part of a job selection procedure. All too often, researchers seem to believe that reliability is a fundamental property of a scale, which it is not. The whole point of studying reliability is to estimate how much measurement error is associated with people's scores on a scale, and it is almost certain that different testing settings will cause people to behave differently – for example, trying harder to do well at an ability scale, or trying to create a favourable impression when applying for a job. The make-up of the sample will also affect reliability; if 6-year-olds find many of the items of an ability test too hard for them (and so guess more of the answers) there will obviously be much more measurement error associated with their scores than if the test were given to 8-year-olds.

The range of scores in the sample will also affect the reliability of a scale, in exactly the same way that Spreadsheet 6.5 showed that the range of scores affects the size of a correlation; a scale measuring intelligence will show higher reliability when administered to a sample of the general population than when it is administered to a sample of people identified by their teachers as having above-average intelligence. Whenever anyone justifies using a scale because some other researcher has found that its reliability is some impressive-sounding number, it is vital to check that the context of the assessment is similar and that the demographics of the sample are similar – otherwise the claim is meaningless. One should always be very suspicious. It is also necessary to estimate the reliability of the scale using one's own sample, although we will see later that such estimates are surprisingly inaccurate unless the sample size is astoundingly large.

TEST-RETEST RELIABILITY

One of the most obvious ways of assessing reliability is to give people the same scale on two or more occasions, and by making the (major) assumption that people will forget their previous answers, it is possible to test whether the scores which people obtain on the two occasions are similar. This measures reliability, because if people were just responding randomly to items in the test, the correlation between the scores on the two (or more) occasions would be close to zero. On the other hand, if the items are working perfectly, then each person should obtain the same score on each occasion, and so the correlation between people should be 1.0.

This form of reliability is known as **test–retest reliability**. There are various rules of thumb for the interval which should lapse between the testing sessions, as it is necessary to choose an interval which is long enough to minimise memory effects whilst not being so long that people's levels of the trait or ability will change. Kline (2000a) suggests 3 months, and this fits in with empirical studies of ability tests, such as Catron and Thompson (1979). For personality tests it should be possible to use a shorter interval, and the manuals for many such tests suggest that 2–3 weeks is a common interval; however there appears to be little systematic evidence to support this practice.

There are six issues with this approach to assessing reliability – over and above the logistical nightmare of gathering data from the same group of people on two occasions.

MEMORY

The problem is likely to be more severe for ability tests than for personality tests. If one laboriously works out an answer to some problem, it is likely that this will be remembered (alongside with the strategies which were used) if the test is re-administered within a short time period. If this speeds up the amount of time to solve the test the second time it is administered, it might also free up some time to attempt other problems, which will lead to an increase in scores. This is the so-called practice effect. It is therefore dangerous to administer the same cognitive test more than once, because the processes which are involved may well be different on the second occasion; participants may well remember the answers which they gave before, rather than solving them anew. This is what has been found empirically. Collie et al. (2003) administered the same computerised ability test four times in one day and found a marked difference in performance between the first and second administrations – presumably because the participants remembered their previous answers – but not between the second and third, or third and fourth. This is exactly what one would expect if the cognitive demands of the task are different on the first administration to subsequent occasions.

Memory may also be a problem for personality scales and is particularly likely if the test content is interesting or unusual and is thus processed deeply on the first administration. I would guess that if a participant was asked "Do you like the feeling of soft wool slippers?" (which is an item from a genuine personality test), this item would stick in most people's minds because of its sheer bizarreness. It would not be obvious why this question was asked. Participants might make a mental note of it so that they can marvel at it with their friends afterwards – and many of us who do not possess a pair of soft woolly slippers would need to think carefully about what answer to give! All of these factors would tend to make the item (and one's answer) memorable. Compared to this, an item such as "Do you like meeting new people?" is quite mundane, and one's answer might be more easily forgotten.

Thus although tests may show high test-retest reliability, it is not completely obvious what this means. Whilst high test-retest reliability *could* imply that the test measures the same trait on two occasions and these scores are commendably free of measurement error, it could also imply that the test measures the intended cognitive ability on the first occasion and memory (for the chosen answers, strategies for solving the problems etc.) on the second. There is no easy way to be certain which. Thus although low test-retest reliability indicates that the test is flawed because it produces inconsistent scores, high test-retest reliability does not necessarily imply that the test scores are free of measurement error. Polit (2014) gives a useful discussion of these issues from the perspective of a health researcher.

PEOPLE'S LEVELS OF THE TRAIT MAY CHANGE

Problems arise if people's levels of a trait change between two administrations of a scale. This will reduce the test-retest reliability, wrongly suggesting that there is something wrong with the test. This is a particular problem if the interval between test administrations is very long, or the test is given to children or to adults during a period of transition (e.g., before and after therapy). Here it is quite possible that some people's scores will increase, other people's might decrease and some might stay the same. This will lead to a low estimate of reliability. That said, the test-retest reliability of a scale measuring general intelligence is above 0.7 over a 66-year period (Deary et al., 2000), showing that this trait, at any rate, stays remarkably stable over long time periods.

HIGH TEST-RETEST RELIABILITY DOES NOT MEAN THAT THE ITEMS MEASURE A SINGLE TRAIT

It would be possible to devise a scale containing items measuring completely different things – for example, one item measuring extraversion, one measuring neuroticism etc. If they answer the items in the same way on each occasion, each person should achieve the same score on each occasion leading to a correlation of 1.0 between the two sets of scores. However, the correlation between the items will be close to zero, and the scale score would be meaningless. Test-retest reliability cannot show whether the items in a scale or test are sampled from some well-defined domain.

STATES

Test-retest reliability is only appropriate for traits. In order to measure states (moods or motivations which vary over time and from situation to situation), other methods would need to be devised, as the test-retest reliability of a state should be close to zero. (If it is not, it is probably measuring a trait.)

THE SAMPLE MATTERS

Like any other form of reliability, test-retest reliability will vary depending on who is being assessed and why. If student participants are asked to take the test on two occasions, they may feel bored or resentful when presented with the same items a second time and may start to answer randomly in order to get the loathsome process finished as soon as possible. This will obviously reduce the test-retest reliability. On the other hand, applicants for a job which they really want might be expected to try their best on both occasions. Problems may also arise when administering tests to children. It is possible that some young children may not understand all of the words in a personality test, for example, and so may choose an answer at random each time they take the test, which will reduce the test-retest reliability.

The size of the sample also matters. Like any statistic, the intraclass correlation (a statistic which is commonly used to assess test-retest reliability – see below) has a certain "standard error of measurement" – which basically shows us how closely the intraclass correlation which we have calculated from the sample of people we have available is likely to resemble its "true" value – the value which we would obtain if we were to test everyone in the population. The larger the sample, the better this estimate is likely to be – but determining significance levels for comparing several intraclass correlations (for example, to check whether one test is significantly more stable than another) can be surprisingly complicated (Pal et al., in press).

GROUP DIFFERENCES CAN INFLATE TEST-RETEST RELIABILITY

We showed in Chapter 6 that group differences can influence correlations. As test-retest reliability simply involves correlating scores on two occasions, it follows that if the sample contains two groups of people whose mean scores on the scale are appreciably different, this can lead to the overestimation of test-retest reliability.

MEASURING TEST-RETEST RELIABILITY

There are two commonly used options – the usual Pearson correlation coefficient with which readers of this book will be familiar and the intraclass correlation coefficient which is probably less familiar. It is important to appreciate that they measure rather different things, and which one is used will depend on the purpose of testing.

A researcher might not be too concerned whether people who are assessed twice perform better on the second occasion. They might just be interested in the extent to which scores on the second occasion are proportional to the scores which people obtain on the first occasion. According to this definition of test-retest reliability, the researcher would not care in the slightest if everyone's score on a scale of reasoning ability went up by (say) 10 marks, or if there was more or less variability in scores the second time that they took the test. If the researcher is happy to ignore the possibility that scores might all go up (or down) on the second occasion that people are assessed or that the standard deviation might change, then the usual Pearson correlation may be used as an index of test-retest reliability. It shows the extent to which the scores which people obtain the first time that they are assessed are proportional to the scores which they obtain on the second occasion. These researchers look at the test-retest reliability to convince themselves that scores on the test are not random; they are happy to accept that any change in the test scores between the two occasions might be attributed to some environmental influence which affects everyone similarly.

However, suppose that an educational or clinical psychologist wants to assess people on two occasions – perhaps to check whether their reading skills or level of self-reported pain has improved after some intervention. Or a researcher might wish to determine whether some intervention influences scores on a scale which is administered on multiple occasions. They would analyse differences in the mean scores on each occasion using analysis of variance or something similar, and they too would need to be confident that in the absence of any intervention, people's scores would be the same on each occasion.

These researchers obviously need to use a different definition of test-retest reliability to the one described in the previous paragraph when selecting a test, for they need to identify a test where each person obtains the *same score* on each occasion when there is no intervention. This allows the person's first score to be compared with their second score. To assess how well a particular scale provides replicable scores, the intraclass correlation would be used, following the advice of Shrout and Fleiss (1979). Other possibilities exist too, and Vaz et al. (2013) explore some of them.

It is possible to use the intraclass correlation to test stability on more than two occasions, and the statistic can also be used to check whether different raters give the same assessments when rating personality characteristics etc.

> **Spreadsheet name:** Spreadsheet 7.2: Pearson and intraclass correlations for test-retest reliability on two occasions
>
> **Download from:** https://routledge.com/9781032146164/
>
> **Purpose:** To show how Pearson and intraclass correlations behave differently when scores increase or decrease on retesting.
>
> **Contents of spreadsheet:** Data from 18 people, each administered the same scale on two occasions.
>
> **Suggested activity:**
>
> - With "multiply by" = 1, add various values (e.g., −0.5, +0.5, 1, 5) to each person's score on the second occasion using the setting in section A. Compare the Pearson and intraclass correlations (right of section B) to their original values (left of section B).
> - With "add" = 0, try multiplying everyone's Time 2 score by a constant – e.g., 2 or 0.5 – and note what happens to both correlations.
>
> **Points to note:**
>
> - Experiment by changing entries in the *green* areas. Results are in the *yellow* areas. Simply download another copy if you accidentally change formulae.
>
> **Learning outcomes: Readers should now be able to:**
>
> - Demonstrate an understanding of how a positive intraclass correlation becomes closer to zero or negative if the mean score on the first occasion differs from the mean on retesting.

Unlike the Pearson correlation, the intraclass correlation decreases if there is any change in the average level of scores on the second occasion, or if the variance of these scores changes. This is why it is widely used to assess test-retest reliability. If a test manual or journal article instead only gives a value for the Pearson correlation, it is necessary to check that there is no change in mean score (or variance) between the first and second administration – for example, using a paired-sample t-test, or the Levene test for equality of variance (Levene, 1960).

ALTERNATIVE FORMS RELIABILITY

One occasionally finds scales which have two (or more) **alternative forms**. In other words, there are two versions of a test of the same length but with different items, both measuring the same trait or state, and designed to be used in the same population. These can be useful in practice – for example, if it is necessary to measure the same ability trait on several occasions, and one wants to ensure that participants do not simply remember the answers previously given. People are normally given just one version of the scale. However, if people are given *both* versions, it is possible to correlate them together to draw some inferences about the amount of measurement error associated with each test score. When correlating the two scores together, each person's score on each scale is assumed to be determined by their true score (the score which they would obtain if they were administered all possible items) plus measurement error, which is exactly the same scenario as for test–retest reliability. So once again, the correlation between the two forms estimates the reliability of either form.

SPLIT HALF RELIABILITY

What if a scale does not have alternative forms, and is administered just once? One way of estimating the amount of measurement error in such a scale would be to divide the items into two halves and correlate scores on these two halves together. This is known as **split half reliability**. For example, if a scale consists of 20 items, one could work out each person's score on just the first 10 items and correlate this with their score on the final 10 items. This seems as if it ought to tell us something useful about the amount of measurement error in the test scores, but there are three obvious problems with this approach.

1. It is possible that people respond differently to the later items in a questionnaire than they do to the earlier ones; they may get bored or careless. And if the test has time limits, it is possible that some people might not reach the end of the test; when the test is scored, their score on the second half would be lower or more "error-ful" than their score for the first half, depending on how missing data are treated when the test is scored. For this reason it is normal to calculate each person's score on the odd-numbered items, and correlate this with their score on the even-numbered items.
2. If a test consists of n items, we correlate the score based on half the test items with another score based on half the test items. If the formula for estimating test-retest reliability were used, it would tell us what the reliability of the scale comprising $n/2$ items is – whereas we need to know the reliability of a scale which consists of n items. The **Spearman-Brown formula** may be used to achieve this. To estimate the reliability of a scale based on the correlation between two "half-length scales", simply double the correlation and divide this by 1 plus the correlation. For example, if the correlation between two "half-length-scales" is 0.7, the reliability of the full scale is $\frac{2 \times 0.7}{1 + 0.7}$ or 0.82.
3. Correlating the odd items with the even-numbered items is arbitrary. One would obtain a different answer if one correlated the sum of items 1 and 2, 5 and 6

etc. with the sum of items 3 and 4, 7 and 8 etc. As we are trying to establish the property of the test, we should not really base this on the arbitrary decision of how to divide the items into two groups. One solution might be to calculate all possible split-half reliabilities and average them – and fortunately there is a statistic (coefficient alpha) which does just this.

INTERNAL CONSISTENCY

Thus far we have focused on the relationship between scale scores. Measures of internal consistency instead look at the behaviour of individual items within the scale. In what follows, we assume that the test items are independent – that is, the only thing which influences the way in which a person responds to each item is the single trait which all of the items are supposed to measure. For example, items such as "Do you enjoy teasing animals?" and "Are insurance schemes a good idea?" (Eysenck et al., 1985) are fine, whilst items such as "On the whole, I am satisfied with myself" and "I take a positive attitude toward myself" (Rosenberg, 1965) are not, because the way in which a person answers the first question determines how they must answer the second one.

The phrase "internal consistency" is a misnomer, however. Its name seems to suggest that it measures the extent to which a set of items all measure the same thing (i.e., whether items in a set all measure a single trait). It does not. Factor analysis or network analysis is needed for this (see Chapters 10 and 14). Instead, if it *assumed* that all of the items measure the same trait, internal consistency reliability tries to estimate the extent to which scores on the test reflect people's true scores – the scores which they would obtain if they completed an infinitely long test.

Suppose that we have four test items, each of which measures the same trait with complete accuracy. The average correlation between different items will be 1.0. This is the best-case scenario – a test with no measurement error at all. How about a ghastly test where none of the items has any relationship at all to the trait? Here all of the correlations between different items will be zero. One *could* simply look at the average correlation between different items in the test and infer from this how much measurement error there is. However, the more items we add together when calculating a person's score on a test, the more likely that test score is to be accurate, as was seen in Spreadsheet 7.1. There is some good statistical theory underlying this claim (and we have also acknowledged this when estimating split-half reliability from the correlation between two half-scales using the Spearman-Brown formula). It should also be intuitively obvious from the example of measuring the page using a ruler with which we began this chapter. It is possible that the first measurement might overestimate the true length of the paper. But if we take 15 measurements, it is highly unlikely that they will *all* overestimate the length. So given that we are trying to estimate the amount of measurement error in test scores, it makes sense to devise a statistic which:

1. Is influenced by the number of items in the scale (more items implying higher accuracy)
2. Is influenced by the average correlation between the items.

The overwhelmingly popular choice for this measure is known as **alpha, coefficient alpha** or **Cronbach's alpha** (although as Cronbach only popularised an earlier formula, this is a misnomer). Note that this is nothing to do with the use of alpha in statistical significance testing. Coefficient alpha can be computed from people's responses to a set of items, and under certain conditions it can give some indication of how closely people's scores on a particular scale reflect their true scores – the scores which they would have obtained had they been administered all of the items that could possibly be constructed to measure the trait. This is possible *even though we never know what their true scores are*.

There are several formulae available for calculating coefficient alpha.

$$\text{Coefficient alpha} = \frac{\text{number of items}^2 \times \text{average correlation between different items}}{\text{sum of all correlations in the correlation matrix (including 1's)}}$$

Equation 7.1

This ties in well with the approach developed earlier. It is obvious from this formula that both the number of items (squared) and the average correlation influence alpha; the term at the bottom of the equation just ensures that the value usually stays between 0 and 1. (If the test items are truly awful, with an average correlation less than 0, alpha can be negative.)

The equation which is more often used is:[1]

$$\text{Coefficient alpha} = \frac{\text{number of items}}{\text{number of items} - 1} \times \left(1 - \frac{\text{sum of variances of items}}{\text{variance of total score}}\right)$$

Equation 7.2

This is rather easier to calculate because there is no need to compute the correlation matrix.

Like any statistic, the value of coefficient alpha which one calculates will never be entirely accurate; it all depends on the number of people in the sample, and the number of items in the scale. There is little point in quoting a value of coefficient alpha unless one also includes "confidence intervals". These indicate that we can be 90% (or some other percentage) certain that the value of alpha lies between two values. That said, I have yet to see a paper in which anyone actually does report confidence intervals. Feldt, Woodruff and Salih (1987) show how this can be achieved, and also how it is possible to test whether coefficients alpha from two different samples are significantly different. Spreadsheet 7.3 calculates these confidence intervals.

> **Spreadsheet name:** Spreadsheet 7.3: Confidence intervals for coefficient alpha
>
> **Download from:** https://routledge.com/9781032146164/
>
> **Purpose:** To compute confidence intervals for coefficient alpha.
>
> **Contents of spreadsheet:** Example data.
>
> **Suggested activity:**
>
> - Explore entering some values of alpha (e.g., 0.5, 0.7, 0.9), and for each, adjust the sample size (e.g., 50, 10, 1000) and note what happens to the confidence intervals.
> - Perhaps also adjust the length of the scale – e.g., 5 or 20 items.
>
> **Points to note:**
>
> - The confidence interval for alpha is much wider than most people expect, unless the sample size is large (several hundred).
> - The length of the scale has a fairly small effect on the size of the confidence interval.
>
> **Learning outcomes: Readers should now be able to:**
>
> - Appreciate the need to cite confidence intervals when reporting alpha and have the means to do so.

There are several issues to consider when calculating and interpreting coefficient alpha.

First, there are common rules of thumb for determining "acceptable" values of coefficient alpha. These usually suggest that values of alpha lower than 0.7 are unacceptable (e.g., Kline, 2000a; Nunnally, 1978), whilst values of 0.9 or above are necessary for using tests for individual assessments. To my mind these are not very helpful, given that alpha combines two very different types of information: the number of items in a test, and the average correlation between these items. As Cortina (1993) observes, "For a 3-item scale with alpha = .80, the average inter-item correlation is .57. For a 10-item scale with alpha = .80, the average inter-item correlation is only .28".

So when an author quotes "alpha is 0.7", it is hard to know what to conclude! It could be from a long test where each item is only feebly related to the trait it is designed to measure, or a short test where the trait being measured has a huge influence on the way in which people respond to each of the items. Cortina's paper is not technical and can be warmly recommended.

Second, extremely high levels of alpha can indicate that there are real problems with a test. If some test items are so similar in content that they basically mean the same thing, a person who answers one question in a particular way is *bound* to answer another item similarly. This finding is not an interesting empirical discovery and indeed has nothing to do with psychology. It is a pure consequence of the meaning of the words in the items. The items are thus not independent. They will correlate very substantially indeed, and this will lead to a huge alpha.

In addition, as discussed, two items which are similar in meaning will not just correlate because they both measure the same trait; they will also tend to share all of the other things which influence how a person responds to the item. So items such as "Do you like lively parties?" and "Do large social gatherings appeal to you?" will probably be influenced by extraversion – but they will also reflect social desirability, previous experiences with parties, liking for alcohol etc. Thus whilst a large coefficient alpha is desirable, I would be wary of a short scale (under about 10 items) with a very high coefficient alpha (above 0.8, say). In such a case the large alpha probably means that the scale contains items which are virtual paraphrases of each other. This can only be detected by reading the items and reflecting on their meaning. Blindly performing psychometric analyses of such items is a waste of everyone's time.

Next, as mentioned earlier, a large coefficient alpha does *not* imply that all of the items in a scale measure a single trait. Because it is based on the average correlation between items, a large alpha can arise when some of the correlations are large and others are near zero – as would be the case if the items which formed the "scale" actually measured several different traits. The same average correlation would be found if half of the correlations between items were 0.8 and the rest were 0.2, or if all the items correlated 0.5, and it is the average correlation which determines coefficient alpha. Thus it makes little sense to compute coefficient alpha without first using factor analysis or network analysis to check that all of the items measure a single trait.

Finally, coefficient alpha makes the usual assumptions that the variable being measured is quantifiable, and that the numbers produced by Likert scales and others behave much like numbers in the physical world, meaning that they can be added, multiplied and so on. We pointed out in Chapter 3 that these are very worrying and important assumptions which cannot be tested, and which are very likely to be incorrect.

THE RELATIONSHIP BETWEEN COEFFICIENT ALPHA AND TRUE SCORES

We argued earlier that coefficient alpha is important because it can show how accurately test scores can reflect people's true scores on traits. Now is the time to explore these relationships in a little more detail – but it is necessary to start by defining some terms which psychometricians sometimes use.

Parallel, tau-equivalent and congeneric scales

The idea of alternative forms of a test was introduced earlier; **parallel tests** take this idea to its extreme form. If the same sample of people take both versions of two scales, those scales are "parallel" if each form of the scale produces the same score for each person (which is an estimate of the person's true score), where the true score has the same amount of influence on each of the items in the test for each person, and where the standard deviations of all of the items are the same. This also implies (as we shall see) that all of the correlations between the items are identical. I have never seen a pair of tests where this held true.

Tau-equivalent scales are similar to parallel scales. Here two scales measure the same trait on the same scale with the same degree of precision – but the items may have different amounts of measurement error associated with them. Because the total score is measured on the same scale, the same norms etc. may still be used. The standard deviations of the items are different. (This should be obvious if you think about it, for if people's scores on a particular item are greatly influenced by random error, the more variable they will be, hence the standard deviation will be larger.) The correlations between items may also be different, as will be seen later.

Congeneric measures do away with the assumption that a person's true score on a trait influences every item to an equal extent. This is far more like the sorts of tests which are encountered in real life; it might well be possible to devise two scales both of which measure the same trait but where the standard deviations (and means) of the items are different, and where some items are better measures of the trait than are others.

Assessing the reliability of a parallel or tau-equivalent test is straightforward, which is why these are of interest to psychometricians.

Spreadsheet 7.4 demonstrates this. This spreadsheet simulates the responses of up to 5000 people on four test items – and allows us to construct parallel, tau-equivalent and congeneric scales. It also calculates coefficient alpha for each type of scale by the two formulae given earlier, and (crucially) shows how closely alpha resembles the square of the correlation between the total score on the test and each person's true score.

The simulation allows us to establish this – unlike in real life, where the true score is unknown.

It is necessary to decide whether to explore the "standardised" or "unstandardised" version of coefficient alpha. The unstandardised version calculates each person's total score on the scale to be the sum of their scores on the individual items. The standardised version calculates the standard deviation for each item and divides each person's score on each item by the standard deviation of the item before adding them together. If the items have very different standard deviations, the item with the largest standard deviations will have more impact on the total score. In practice, when tests are scored there is almost never any attempt made to standardise the item scores before summing them, and so using the unstandardised version of coefficient alpha is more realistic. In addition, whilst unstandardised alpha is a "lower bound" for reliability (the true reliability may be higher than alpha), the same may not be true of the standardised version. It is tempting to report the standardised version as it will generally be larger. However, doing so is inadvisable.

The purpose of using this spreadsheet is to demonstrate what happens to coefficient alpha when it is calculated from items which are parallel, tau equivalent or congeneric; how to recognise a set of items which are (nearly) tau equivalent when one sees them; and why doing so aids the interpretation of coefficient alpha.

It is necessary to explain a little about how this spreadsheet generates data. It generates a normally distributed "true score" for each person, the mean and standard deviation of which can be specified. It also generates an "error term" for each person's score on each item; these too are normally distributed with a mean of zero and a standard deviation which is specified. The model assumes that a person's score on a test item is influenced in part by that person's true score and in part by that person's random error.

Spreadsheet name: Spreadsheet 7.4: Coefficient alpha

Download from: https://routledge.com/9781032146164/

Purpose: This spreadsheet shows how closely coefficient alpha resembles the actual relationship between people's scores on a scale and their true scores for parallel, tau-equivalent and congeneric scales, whether alpha systematically over- or underestimates this "true reliability" and how sample size influences the accuracy of alpha.

Contents of spreadsheet: When scales are given to real people, we never know their true scores, but by simulating data each person's true score can be decided in advance. From this a score on each "item" in a scale can be generated – the method in which this is done determines whether the items form a parallel, tau-equivalent or congeneric scale.

Coefficient alpha can be calculated from these "items", and as we know the total score on the scale and the true score, we can show how closely alpha represents the "true reliability" – the square of the correlation between the scale score and the true score. The simulation shows how accurate coefficient alpha is for each of these three types of scale, and whether it over- or under-estimates the relationship between the scale score and the true score. It also shows how inaccurate alpha can be when calculated from small samples.

This spreadsheet generates a four-item scale. Pressing f9 (Windows) or alt/f9 (Mac) generates a new version of the scale, given to a new group of "people".

Suggested activity:

(a) Decide on the number of "people" in the sample. 5000 perhaps?
(b) Set the type of scale to be "parallel".
(c) Decide on the standard deviation and average for the "true scores". 25 and 100, perhaps?
(d) Decide what the standard deviation of the error terms for all items should be – enter a number for sd in "error for all variables". 20, perhaps?
(e) Some rows and columns do not apply and are flagged in red. Numbers in these rows/columns will be ignored.

Section B shows the values used for the simulation. For parallel analysis, all error standard deviations are the same. Error terms always have a mean of zero.

Section C shows the actual means and standard deviations.

Section D shows the correlations and the standardised coefficient alpha (from Equation 7.1).

Sections E and F show unstandardised coefficient alpha calculated in two different ways.

Section G shows the squared correlation between the actual true scores and the total scores on the scale. Coefficient alpha is designed to estimate this when the real value is unknown.

Press f9 (Windows) or alt/f9 (Mac) several (20?) times to generate new simulated scales. Examine the squared correlation in Section G and alpha from Section H. Are they similar? Does alpha consistently over- or under-estimate the square of the correlation?

Try this again after altering the number of "people" in Section A (50? 200? 5000?). Is alpha a closer estimate of the true reliability if the sample is large? Does it consistently over- or under-estimate the true reliability?

Now repeat the above by selecting the type of scale to be tau-equivalent and specify a different standard deviation for each of the error terms (5, 10, 15, 20 perhaps) in Section A. Is the correlation in Section G more or less similar to alpha for this type of scale? Once again, does its accuracy depend on the sample size?

Repeat this for the congeneric scale. Here you specify two additional parameters for each item: d is a constant which is added to each person's score for an item, and b is a number between 0 and 1 which determines how strongly the true score influences the response to each item.

Learning outcomes:

Readers should now be able to appreciate the difference between parallel, tau-equivalent and congeneric items, and note that:-

- coefficient alpha is almost identical to the true reliability for parallel and tau-equivalent items if the sample size is large and the true reliability is large.
- If the true reliability and sample size are large, coefficient alpha consistently underestimates the true reliability for congeneric items.
- for small samples and/or low levels of reliability, alpha can seriously over- or under-estimate the true reliability of all types of scale.

This exercise shows something rather important. For most real-life datasets (which are congeneric), coefficient alpha will underestimate the true reliability of a scale: it is a "lower bound" for reliability. How much it underestimates the reliability is unknown, for in real life we never know the correlation between the test score and the true score. However, what you saw from this exercise is that coefficient alpha resembles the true reliability of the test only when alpha is fairly large and the items are parallel or tau equivalent; that is, when all of the items are equally influenced by the true score. So before interpreting coefficient alpha, it is sensible to test whether the items can be assumed to form a tau-equivalent scale. Graham (2006) suggests how this may be done.

When looking at the table of covariances computed in the spreadsheet (the covariance between items A and B is simply the correlation between items A and B multiplied by the standard deviation of both items), it seems that these covariances are similar if the data are tau equivalent. But whether or not it is possible to develop this into some technique for easily identifying tau equivalent data I leave to interested readers to pursue.

A CONTRARIAN VIEW OF RELIABILITY

The previous sections argued that reliability indicates how much measurement error is associated with scores on a scale. Coefficient alpha resembles (or equals) the amount of measurement error. Coefficient alpha is also influenced by the average correlation between the items. Therefore, large correlations between items lead to accurate scales.

Suppose, however, that a clinician decides to develop yet another scale to measure depression. The relationship between depression and the test items might be as shown in Figure 7.2. The circle labelled "depression" corresponds to all of the characteristics measuring depression – change in mood, feelings of hopelessness, changes in eating and sexual behaviour etc. Each of the items measures a slightly different aspect of depression; the correlation between each item and depression is indicated by the amount of overlap between an item and depression; the correlation between items is indicated by the amount of overlap between items.

Clearly, the scale *should* measure all aspects of depression if at all possible. In other words, the area of the "depression" circle covered by the items should be as large as possible to ensure that the correlation between the true score and the sum of the items is as large as possible. It can be seen that whilst item 1 does tap some aspect of depression, item 2 does nothing extra – it overlaps substantially (correlates appreciably) with item 1. It overlaps appreciably with depression. But it does not explain any more of the variance of depression than item 1 does. Item 3 makes a very modest additional

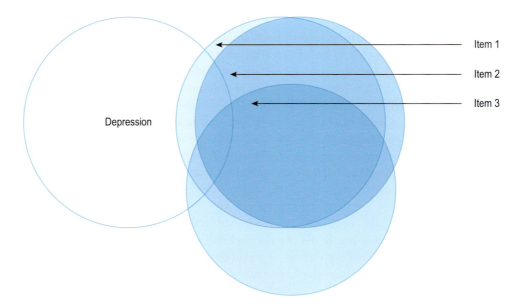

Figure 7.2 Three highly correlated items measuring a small aspect of depression

contribution. Here is an example of three items which correlate substantially together but which fail to measure the full breadth of the construct which they are designed to assess. They will have a very substantial coefficient alpha, each item will correlate with depression, and from a psychometric point of view they look ideal. Yet they manifestly fail to measure the full breadth of the construct – and item 2 is clearly useless, as it does nothing more than duplicate item 1.

Cattell (1973, p. 359) argues that it would be much better if the correlations between the items were small – but that each measured a different aspect of the trait which they are designed to assess. In other words, it would be much better if the items measuring depression resembled those shown in Figure 7.3.

Here each item measures a different (and substantial) chunk of the variance of depression – but there is zero correlation between the items. It is clear that these three items do a better job of assessing depression than the items in Figure 7.2; the total score on these three items will correlate better with depression, which is, after all, the whole purpose of designing a scale. However, as all the correlations between the items are zero, coefficient alpha will be zero!

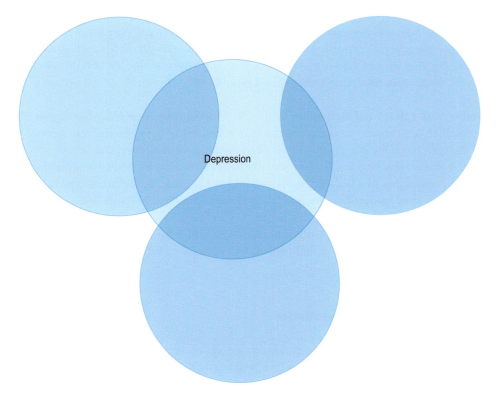

Figure 7.3 Three uncorrelated items, each measuring a different aspect of depression

This is a powerful argument and reminds us of the importance of ensuring that the items in a scale are carefully chosen to represent the full breadth of the construct being measured. Having several highly correlated items in a scale may not be desirable. The problem is, as Kline (2000b) observes, that items such as those in Figure 7.3 prove to be almost impossible to find in practice.

OTHER MEASURES OF INTERNAL CONSISTENCY RELIABILITY

Almost every study reports coefficient alpha, but other measures have been devised too, and a strong case can be made for reporting omega-total (ω_{total}), discussed below.

ORDINAL ALPHA

A major problem with coefficient alpha is that it assumes that the numbers which are being used form an interval scale – which they almost certainly do not, even if the trait being measured is quantitative. One of the more obvious alternatives is to compute something like alpha but using polychoric correlations rather than Pearson correlations. You will remember from Chapter 6 that polychoric correlations are rather like tetrachoric correlations, only with more than two values for each variable. If their underlying assumptions are met, this allows us to assume that the numbers being analysed form an ordinal scale rather than a ratio scale.

Zumbo et al. (2007) and Bonanomi et al. (2015) developed an ordinal coefficient alpha which appears not to underestimate the relationship between the test score and the true score for congeneric items. The problem is, however, that it says nothing about how well one's scale actually behaves. It instead estimates what the internal consistency of a scale probably would have been had a different type of test format been used to measure the trait. This is therefore terribly hypothetical and divorced from reality. In addition, a paper by Chalmers (2018) points out several misconceptions and issues with the simulated data which Zumbo et al. used to justify the use of this coefficient. It would probably be unwise to rely on it until these issues have been resolved.

MacDonald's omega (ω) statistics

Be careful not to confuse the omega reliability coefficient with the omega-squared statistic used to represent effect size when performing regressions. They are quite different. Why mathematicians have to use the same Greek letters for different statistics when there are many other languages to choose from baffles me!

To make matters still more complicated, there are actually two versions of omega, both of which involve performing a factor analysis as an intermediary stage to calculating reliability. What follows will make more sense after reading Chapters 10–13.

The good thing about omega is that performing a factor analysis forces one to check that all of the items do, indeed, measure a single trait. The simplest form, omega-total (ω_{total}), simply determines how well the first principal component describes the data – that is, how much of the variation between the items can be described by the single trait which the scale is designed to measure.[2] The second version ("hierarchical omega" or ω_H) assumes that the items form not just one factor but a set of several (three or more) correlated factors, with a single second-order factor above them. (Such models will be discussed in Chapter 13.) Those familiar with the five-factor model of personality will be aware of such a model. If all of the items from the NEO extraversion scale were factor-analysed, they should form six correlated factors, each factor corresponding to one of the six facets of extraversion. Because these six facets are correlated, a general factor may be extracted; see the Schmid-Leiman procedure in Chapter 13.

Raykov's composite reliability, rho (ρ)

Raykov (1997) developed a statistic which is identical to coefficient alpha when applied to tau-equivalent or parallel scales, but which does not underestimate the size of the relationship between the scale score and the true score when applied to congeneric scales. There are also techniques available for calculating confidence intervals, comparing different coefficients for equality and so on (Raykov, 2004). Like coefficient alpha it shows how much of the variance in the item scores is due to variation in the true scores of various items. (It should not be confused with the other meanings of rho – the Spearman correlation or the population correlation.)

Raykov's technique requires some knowledge of structural equation modelling. For readers who have such skills, rho assumes that people's true score on the scale influences their true score on each of the items; the observed score on each item is also influenced by some error variance. The true score on the scale also influences the observed score on the scale (which is also affected by error variance). What makes this model interesting is the suggestion that it allows the sum of the observed scores on the items to be correlated with the true scale score; the value of this parameter (squared) is the composite reliability coefficient.

The technique seems sound, but in order for the reliability estimates to be accurate, large samples are needed – and each item needs to use as large a number of levels as possible. It is also important that the data fit the model – which can by no means be guaranteed. Raykov (1997) provides code for computing composite reliability using the EQS or LISREL packages.

THE H INDEX

The H index (Hancock & Mueller, 2001, cited by McNeish, 2018) is interesting because rather than weighting the items equally, it gives more weight to the more reliable items in a test when calculating reliability. For this reason it is known as a maximal reliability index. We earlier pointed out that when items in a scale are not tau equivalent (which is usually the case) coefficient alpha will underestimate reliability. As it does not assume tau equivalence, H (along with ω_{total} and ρ, for that matter) will generally be larger than coefficient alpha. Unfortunately, it has been shown that H will sometimes *over*estimate the true reliability of a scale and it cannot be recommended for small samples or when there are few items (Aguirre-Urreta et al., 2019).

WHICH RELIABILITY COEFFICIENT TO USE?

Psychometricians are still developing statistics to estimate reliability and discovering which methods are most appropriate for various types of data (e.g., binary scores or Likert scales) and large or small samples (Metsämuuronen, 2022). They also study the impact of "outliers" (extreme values) on reliability estimates (Liu & Zumbo, 2007) and other more esoteric aspects of reliability. However, readers will want to know which coefficients are likely to be the most useful.

Cho (in press) developed a method for evaluating the quality of reliability coefficients and applied this to 30 indices using simulated data. He concluded that there is no single index which will perform optimally in all circumstances. In particular, he notes that although reliability estimates based on factor analysis are often trumpeted as being superior to the older models, with several authors suggesting that older approaches should be discarded, the evidence shows that such differences are often trivially small.

McNeish (2018) shows that coefficient alpha is a special case of the simple version of omega-total (ω_{total}). If the assumption of tau equivalence is met (i.e., when the items in a scale are all equally strongly related to the trait which the scale measures), the two coefficients are identical. However, unlike alpha, it will not underestimate reliability when the assumption of tau equivalence is not met.

It makes sense to use ω_{total} (or Raykov's rho, if the sample size is large) instead of alpha to estimate reliability. However, as journal editors are so familiar with unstandardised coefficient alpha, this should probably be reported as well.

CONCLUSION

Coefficient alpha, and those based on it, are some of the most widely abused statistics in psychology.

- They do not show that all of the items in a scale measure just one trait.
- They are influenced by two quite different things – the number of items in the scale and the average correlation between these items. Thus a long scale whose items have small intercorrelations can have the same coefficient alpha as a shorter scale with high correlations between the items.
- Alpha only estimates the correlation between test score and the true score on the trait if some rather unlikely assumptions are made (tau equivalence).
- Alpha is the "lower bound" for reliability; the true reliability of a test will generally be greater than the value of alpha.
- There is a large margin of error associated with any estimate of coefficient alpha, unless the sample size is huge. So if an author reports that coefficient alpha is 0.7, it could well really be 0.6 or 0.8.
- A very high value of alpha from a short scale (e.g., fewer than 10 items) might suggest that the items are *too* similar in content to measure anything of value; they may well be "bloated specifics", or mere rephrasings of the same item.
- Rules of thumb such as "alpha must be at least 0.7 for a test to be satisfactory" have little or no basis in theory or research, and arise from misquoting Nunnally (1978).

There are far fewer problems with Raykov's composite reliability statistic or the omega statistics, but they are seldom reported or used. Hancock's H index is more problematical and should be approached with caution.

SUMMARY

Psychometricians love mathematics, and there is plenty of scope for interesting mathematics in reliability theory. This is probably why it is so well researched. However, it is clear that whilst almost all test users and developers grasp the importance of estimating the influence of random and systematic errors of measurement, it is less obvious that care is taken to ensure that the items in a scale capture the full breadth of whatever construct the scale is designed to measure. All too often, items in a scale are highly similar, which guarantees high internal-consistency reliability but breaks the assumption of **local independence** and also means that the scores on the scale fail to measure much of interest. This will not show up in the statistical analyses beloved of psychometricians.

It is also clear that coefficient alpha is less useful than many researchers and test users believe. Unless it is estimated from a very large sample of people any single estimate of coefficient alpha can be quite inaccurate. The true level of internal consistency is likely to be larger than coefficient alpha indicates, unless some rather unlikely criteria are met (tau equivalence). And given that alpha is influenced by the size of the correlations between the items, the standard deviation of the item and the number of items in the scale, it is surely better to examine these independently; rather than developing a long, reliable scale where the average correlation between the items is paltry, it might be better to ensure that the correlations between items are fairly substantial and that the standard deviation of the items is appreciable. This will allow shorter scales to be used. And there are far more useful statistics available, such as omega-total or Raykov's rho.

Despite all the research which focuses on reliability, it should be remembered that ultimately reliability is only a tool which may, perhaps, help develop and identify tests which adequately measure what they claim to assess. Cattell's claim that internal consistency of zero can be a good thing is perhaps an extreme example – but if a scale is clearly a good measure of what it claims, then debates about its psychometric properties are an irrelevance. Just because reliability theory produces numbers (and therefore has the appearance of scientific respectability), it is tempting to forget all of the issues raised by Michell, to ignore the problems inherent in adding together scores on items, and to feign ignorance of the problems inherent in calculating correlations (revealed in Chapter 6). Establishing test reliability involves computing correlations (lots of them), and as we have seen, each and every correlation can be affected by a whole range of different variables, most of which are ignored by researchers and test developers. Reliability theory has many problems.

NOTES

1 These two formulae are not quite equivalent. The first one is based on the correlation matrix; it applies when standardised scores on the items are added together to give the total score on a scale and is known as "standardised alpha". The second formula does not make this assumption, as will be seen in Spreadsheet 7.4.
2 Revelle's omega-total implemented in the R psych package is different.

CHAPTER 8
SYSTEMATIC INFLUENCES AND GENERALISABILITY THEORY

When discussing reliability we assumed that the way a person answers a test item is influenced by (a) the trait which the item is supposed to measure and (b) random measurement error. This chapter starts by discussing types of measurement errors which are *not* random and so may distort responses to test items. It then outlines a technique – generalisability theory – which is an alternative way of looking at test reliability. It considers how the reliability of a scale may be estimated by considering the influence of *several* variables on the test scores. These variables could include (but are not limited to) the systematic influences discussed at the start of this chapter.

SYSTEMATIC ERRORS IN PERSONALITY SCALES

Thus far we have considered random errors of measurement – where a person's true level of a trait is as likely to be underestimated as it is to be overestimated. However, it is possible for **systematic errors** of measurement to creep in to any scale measuring personality, mood, emotion or attitude. For example, it has been found that if people are asked to estimate their level of intelligence, some people (often men) overestimate how smart they are whilst others underestimate their intelligence (Beloff, 1992), a finding which will be familiar to anyone who has conducted interviews for academic posts! There are several other types of systematic errors too.

This creates a problem, as it means that a person's score on a test (or test item) will be influenced by both the trait that the scale/item is designed to measure (estimated intelligence) and one or more "systematic errors of measurement", such as overconfidence/humility. If people are asked to estimate their intelligence, their self-rating will reflect both these influences. This means that these ratings are not unidimensional, and we showed in Chapter 1 that this seriously affects the interpretability of scores. We need to identify and find ways of minimising the effects of these systematic influences.

ACQUIESCENCE

Some people tend to agree with whatever statement they are shown, whilst others do not. Known as **acquiescent responding** or "yea-saying" (Trott & Jackson, 1967), this is a problem for Likert scales where the items are all keyed in the same direction (e.g., so that agreeing with each statement, or saying that it is an accurate description, implies a high level of the trait). This means that a person's score on the scale will be a mixture of two things: their true score on the scale plus their tendency to agree. If all of the items are scored such that agreeing with an item corresponds to a high level of the trait, the scores of yea-sayers will be higher than they should be. If it is not measured or controlled, acquiescence will lead to inaccurate test scores. Jackson and Messick's (1958) treatment of the issue is still a classic. They note that acquiescence is a particular problem where the questions in the scale appear irrelevant or silly, which is bad news for many personality scales

Fortunately, however, there is a straightforward solution. All one needs to do is rephrase half of the items so that agreeing implies a *low* level of the trait. For example, a scale measuring neuroticism might ask people to rate themselves (using a Likert scale) as to how well items such as "Do you worry a lot?" and "Are you a calm person?" describe them. Agreeing with the first item and disagreeing with the second one indicates high neuroticism. An acquiescent person's score on the first item might be 1 point higher than it should be, whilst their score on the second item would be 1 point *lower* than it should be. When the scores on the two items are added together, the effects of acquiescence cancel out and the score is accurate. This is why most scales have about half of their items keyed in each direction – though sometimes it can be hard to write items which read naturally. "How much do you dislike . . . ?" is clumsy, for example.

Acquiescence is considerably more common in some countries than others (Rammstedt et al., 2017), with differences between countries being surprisingly large – in the order of one standard deviation. It is more of a problem in Southern Europe than in the North. If individuals within countries have high levels of conservatism and/or lower educational qualifications, this makes it slightly more likely that they will agree with statements (Narayan & Krosnick, 1996; Rammstedt et al., 2017), although these effects are not large.

There is also excellent evidence that acquiescent responding can have a serious effect on the correlations between test scores and external criteria (Danner et al., 2015) and can also influence the correlations between test items. Items which should correlate together may not, and items from different scales may correlate because both are influenced by acquiescence (Bentler et al., 1971). Danner et al. (2015) additionally show that individual differences in acquiescence are comparable in different personality questionnaires; a person's level of acquiescence is very similar across a range of personality and attitude scales, though it is not hugely stable over time. This last finding ties in with research that shows that acquiescence seems to be influenced by situational variables (e.g., Trott & Jackson, 1967). Anyone using Likert scales to measure personality, attitudes or something similar should worry about the influence of acquiescence, particularly if a scale does not contain roughly equal numbers of positively and negatively keyed items. Suggestions as to how to measure and control for acquiescence and reduce its likelihood may be found in the references given.

SOCIAL DESIRABILITY AND PERSONALITY ASSESSMENT

People often claim to have desirable characteristics (e.g., an above-average sense of humour, or honesty) and deny that they have common failings. This problem of **social desirability** arises when people rate themselves, their family and their friends, though not when rating "people in general" (Edwards, 1959; Pedregon et al., 2012). It is thus likely to be a pervasive problem in questionnaire research. Like acquiescence, social desirability could cause items from different scales to correlate, it might cause scores from scales measuring different traits to appear to be correlated, and it can blur the factor structure of questionnaires. Unlike acquiescence, it is not straightforward to eliminate its effects.

If everyone behaved in the same way (for example, if everyone ticked the box one place to the left of the one that reflected their "true" answer to a particular item), then there would not be much of a problem, for the answers given to the question would still be able to do a pretty good job at differentiating those who strongly agreed with the stem to those who disagreed with it. (The only real difficulty arises at the end of the scale; a person who "strongly agreed" with the stem statement has already given the most extreme response possible, so they will be merged with the people who originally just "agreed" with the stem.) Unfortunately, people vary in the degree to which they seem to distort their responses, and this can create problems because it injects error into the measurement process. In theory, it should be possible to identify the extent to which each person distorts their responses and correct their scores for this tendency (or simply to drop them from the analysis). In practice, this turns out to be quite difficult and surprisingly ineffective, as discussed later.

Paulhus (1984) suggested that there are two aspects to socially desirable responding. **Impression management** involves deliberate deception. Sometimes the motivation for this might be obvious; an applicant for a post as an accountant or lawyer would probably deny being slapdash, using recreational drugs or experiencing hallucinations if they were asked to complete a personality scale as part of some selection process. A patient might perhaps want to portray themselves as being more distressed than they truly were. And a prisoner might wish to make it clear that they had truly reformed. But Paulhus also suggests that sometimes people may just have an unrealistic impression of themselves, and this he termed **self-deceptive enhancement**. Someone may be convinced that they have a fine ready wit, even though they are in reality dull and morose.

Having established that socially desirable responding can be either be deliberate or self-deceiving, Paulhus (e.g., Paulhus, 2002) argues that either form of it consists of two components. **Egoistic bias** is the tendency to exaggerate positive characteristics such as intelligence or fearlessness, whilst **moralistic bias** is the tendency to portray oneself as having high moral standards, dependable, and having few frailties or faults.

It may be useful to consider what might influence a person's decision to present a favourable impression when answering a self-report questionnaire and their ability to do so effectively.

The model in Figure 8.1 suggests that when a questionnaire is used in a particular situation, some people may believe that faking is acceptable whilst others do not. This will then interact with various situational influences (e.g., how much they want the

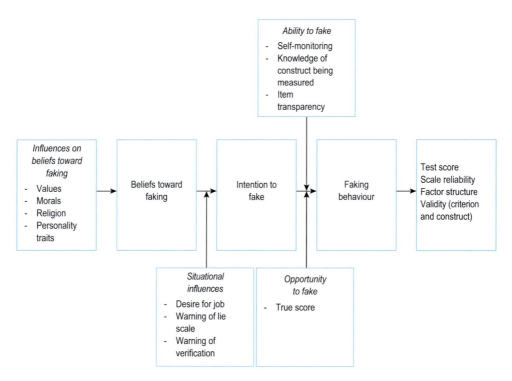

Figure 8.1 Variables which influence faking behaviour

Source: McFarland and Ryan (2000).

job, what sort of image they want to portray to their professor, whether they have been warned that the questionnaire contains a "lie scale" which will detect faking) to determine whether or not they decide to fake their scores. But will they be *able* to fake their scores if they want to? Some studies (e.g., MacCann, 2013) suggest that intelligence may matter here; more intelligent individuals might better discern which responses will create the desired impression, though the "transparency" of personality questions and knowledge of what traits are being measured by the test will also be important. Of course, if someone's true score on a trait is already high (in the desirable direction) they will not be able to improve it much, whereas if someone's score is low, they will have ample room to distort their measures. Hence, a person's true score on the trait will also influence the extent to which they are able to fake their responses on a particular scale. The two variables will interact.

The most obvious way of eliminating socially desirable responses is to write items whose content is not socially desirable. However, this is easier said than done – especially if one is trying to write items for a scale measuring psychopathic traits, aggressive tendencies or anything else which is frowned on by society or one's peer group.

The second method is to administer a scale designed to measure one or both forms of social desirability (e.g., Crowne & Marlowe, 1960; Paulhus, 1998) and use this to either drop people from the sample or perform some statistical corrections to their scores. The Paulhus scales measure both impression management and self-deception and so should reveal the extent to which they are trying to portray themselves in a good light. Alternatively, some personality questionnaires such as the Eysenck Personality Questionnaire (Revised) (Eysenck et al., 1985) include items measuring social desirability (the "Lie Scale") which are scattered throughout the questionnaire rather than being administered as a separate scale. This might make them harder to spot. Eysenck recommends treating the personality scores of anyone with an extreme Lie Score as being untrustworthy and recommends dropping these individuals from any statistical analyses. However, there are three problems with this approach.

- The "cut-off score" above which one eliminates an individual is always going to be arbitrary.
- Removing people with high Lie Scale scores may bias the sample. The Lie Scale correlates with personality traits such as conscientiousness and low neuroticism (McCrae & Costa, 1983); emotionally stable, conscientious people will tend to have high scores on social desirability indices, and so dropping individuals on the basis of their Lie Scale scores will eliminate some stable, conscientious people who just answer honestly.
- One sometimes has to make a decision about an individual even if one knows that they are probably lying, such as when using a questionnaire to help one decide whether a psychopath can safely be released from custody.

There is a very extensive literature in this area; for an overview see Uziel (2010). Other researchers have examined the effects of statistically correcting scores for the effects of social desirability; however doing so may not improve the ability of the test to predict behaviour (McCrae & Costa, 1983; Ones et al., 1996), a finding backed up by Paunonen and LeBel's (2012) statistical simulation.

The third technique for controlling for impression management is a simple warning to participants that the questionnaire contains scales which are designed to detect deceptive responses. This is useful in contexts where questionnaires are administered for some purpose which is important to the individual (such as part of a selection process), as shown by McFarland (2003).

Next, it is worth considering abandoning self-rating scales and instead asking others to rate each individual, although this brings its own set of problems, as noted in Chapter 4.

Finally, Edwards (1953) suggested that it should be possible to eliminate the effects of social desirability by using an ipsatised test. The Edwards Personal Preference Test was constructed by first asking people to rate the social desirability of each item in a personality questionnaire. Pairs of items were identified which had the same level of social desirability but which measured different traits. For example, "People would most often call me (a) unreliable or (b) neurotic". Participants are then asked to choose which of the two items better describes them. However, the problems of ipsatised scales are so major that it is hard to recommend this approach (see Chapters 4 and 6).

Much research suggests, however, that correcting scores for impression management creates as many problems as it solves (Ellingson et al., 1999; McGrath et al., 2010; Ones et al., 1996). Sjoberg (2015) does report considerable success in correcting scores in real-life situations, and this paper is well worth consulting if one uses a scale where social desirability may be a problem.

OTHER RESPONSE STYLES

There are several other response styles which have received less attention. For example, when scoring questionnaires by hand it is obvious that some participants use the whole range of responses available from a Likert scale (plenty of 1s and 7s from a 7-point scale) whilst others rarely if ever use the extremes; most of their responses are 3, 4 or 5. This is reflected in individual differences in the standard deviation of a person's responses, calculated across all scales in a questionnaire. Authoritarian/conservative individuals tend to use the extremes of the response scale more than more moderate individuals – perhaps because they see issues as unrealistically clear-cut, whilst liberals try to see both points of view (Cooper et al., 1986). Thus conservatism may be a confounding variable which affects people's scores on any Likert scale.

Clinical scales cause particular problems, and there is a substantial literature examining how susceptible these are to deliberate distortion – for example, from psychopaths who want to appear as if they have empathy, or from people who want to exaggerate the effects of an illness (e.g., Fugett et al., 2014; Robinson & Rogers, 2015).

Finally, there is the issue of **bias**. This is where a scale *systematically* overestimates or underestimates the scores of particular *groups* of individuals. For example, an ability test might underestimate the IQ scores of participants whose first language is not English; a personality test might overestimate the prevalence of some psychiatric disorder in women but not in men (Kass et al., 1983). This is clearly an important issue, but we cover this in Chapter 9 when considering the validity of tests. It is well worth consulting a review by Podsakoff et al. (2003) which covers social desirability and other forms of bias.

SYSTEMATIC ERRORS IN ABILITY TESTS

We have so far only considered variables which affect performance on personality scales. However, several variables can also affect scores on ability tests.

TEST ANXIETY

Test anxiety is well researched; some people panic whenever their cognitive abilities are assessed, and this may negatively impact their performance. Much of the test anxiety research has been conducted with children or students taking high-stakes examinations, but it is probable that the findings will generalise to those taking psychometric tests as part of a job selection or promotion. Several scales have been developed to measure test anxiety, which is typically found to have four components. Two of these are physiological (tension and bodily symptoms such as headaches), and two are cognitive (worry and test-irrelevant thinking). The cognitive components seem to be most strongly related to performance (Putwain et al., 2010). Some people may "catastrophise" the consequences of underperforming. For example, they may think "if I do badly on this test I will not be accepted onto this course, and if other universities use similar tests I will fail these too so I will be unemployed for the rest of my life or reduced to flipping burgers instead of being a brain surgeon".

Of course, correlational studies cannot show whether the relationship is *causal*. Whilst most researchers assume that test anxiety leads to poor performance on cognitive tasks, it is possible that those who are aware that they do not excel at cognitive tasks (based on previous experience) may start to worry about the consequences when taking a high-stakes assessment. In other words, poor performance may lead to elevated anxiety. Another problem is that I know of no studies which have checked that test anxiety is a *state* (a transient feeling of anxiety) rather than a stable trait; the methods for developing scales measuring states and traits are quite different, as discussed in Chapter 12. Indeed, it has been found that test anxiety is no different from the personality trait of neuroticism (Chamorro-Premuzic et al., 2008).

However, if we assume that test anxiety leads to poor performance (as most researchers do), it is sensible to try to reduce anxiety levels as much as possible when administering a cognitive test. Sample items should be given beforehand (assuming that the test instructions allow for this), and these should be easy so that almost everyone will be able to answer them correctly and gain confidence. The first few items in the main test should be easy for the same reason. In addition, if the test is administered in person (rather than over the internet), the administrator should use their social skills to de-stress participants as much as possible and give a supportive introduction.

PSYCHOLOGICAL AND PHYSICAL VARIABLES

A great many other psychological variables can affect performance on cognitive tasks, depression, aerobic fitness, sleep deprivation, drug/alcohol use, motivation and emotional disturbance. See Martin et al. (2020) for a discussion of how some of these can influence cognition in military personnel; it seems reasonable to suggest that these may also affect performance on other types of cognitive assessments, such as ability tests. The problem is that it is difficult or impossible to control or compensate for these variables in the assessment situation, other than perhaps trying to motivate individuals to perform at their best through an encouraging introduction.

LANGUAGE AND VOCABULARY ISSUES

Many cognitive tests use words: for example, "Spider is to 8 as dog is to . . .", which requires people to remember (or guess) that spiders have eight legs. It is assumed that identifying the link between the first two words and then applying this to the third word will lead to the correct answer; the more obscure the relationship between the first two words, the more difficult the item is assumed to be. However, this may not be the *only* variable which influences the difficulty of the item. "Arachnid is to 8 as dog is to . . ." is will probably be harder than the equivalent "spider" item, as some people may not know what an arachnid is. It is important to ensure that ability tests which use language (rather than just shapes) use simple words throughout. This is vital if the sample includes people who are not answering the test using their first language. It is otherwise possible that the scores on the test will be influenced by language ability, as well as the cognitive ability which the test is designed to assess.

MOTIVATION

Much will also depend on the motivation of participants. If a test is being administered as part of a selection or promotion process, participants will probably try their hardest to perform to the best of their ability. This is also likely if they are friends or colleagues of the experimenter. However, taking long cognitive tests is a tiring experience; one has to focus and concentrate hard, and random volunteers may not do so. One way of overcoming this would be to link test performance to the size of the reward offered (10 cents for every item correctly answered, for example), but this might encourage collaboration and cheating. Once again, testing random people from an internet pool of volunteers may produce low-quality data.

It has been suggested that people vary in their "need for cognition" – the amount of effort they choose to spend performing cognitive tasks. Scales have been developed to measure this (e.g., Blaise et al., 2021) by asking whether people enjoy solving puzzles etc. It is uncertain whether scores on these measures could be used to screen participants for online studies, but it might be worth considering this possibility.

OVERVIEW

If people differ in the way they answer questionnaires or tests, this injects a source of error which can affect the scores on scales and the correlations between items. It is possible to "design out" some of these influences when questionnaires and tests are being constructed. It is possible to detect some influences by administering other scales which measure them, and correcting scores on the basis of this, using regression or a similar technique to estimate how much each person's score on the scale or test is likely to have been overestimated or underestimated given their level of anxiety, social-desirable responding etc. Finally, it may be possible to minimise the effects through careful instructions, empathic introduction to cognitive testing, warnings that personality tests contain items to detect dishonest responding and the like. However, systematic sources of variation remain a problem for the assessment of personality and cognitive abilities.

GENERALISABILITY THEORY

When introducing reliability theory we made two points:

1   Coefficient alpha is estimates how closely people's scores on a particular sample of items ("the scale") reflect the "true score" – the score which they would have obtained had they been given every item that could conceivably have been written to measure the trait.

2. People's responses to an item are assumed to be influenced by their level of the trait which the scale is designed to measure plus other things, termed "error".

The problem with this is that the more sources of measurement error there are, the larger this error term will be, and the less confident we can be that scores on the test accurately reflect people's levels of the trait. Some sources of error are genuinely random – for example, ticking the wrong box or mis-reading a word because of a lapse of attention. However, systematic sources of variation (including but not limited to the systematic errors discussed earlier) also end up inflating the "error" term.

We might hypothesise that children's responses to items measuring anxiety (administered as a pencil-and-paper questionnaire in class) might be influenced by the friendliness of the test administrator, as this affects their motivation to perform well. Under the domain sampling model for reliability, if several groups of children are assessed by people who differ in their friendliness, systematic influences on scores due to the friendliness of the test administrator will inflate the "error" term and will be indistinguishable from random errors of measurement. This inflated "error" term means that the internal consistency (coefficient alpha) of the anxiety scale would be larger than if all the administrators were equally friendly.

Generalisability theory is an extension of reliability theory which can explore the influence of several variables on people's responses to test items. It shows how well scores on a particular set of items (e.g., the 20 items in a certain anxiety scale) are likely to generalise to another test which draws items from the same domain (the set of all possible items that could possibly be written to measure anxiety). This is precisely what reliability theory does, through coefficient alpha; there is nothing particularly exciting about that. However, generalisability theory offers more. It also shows how much variability in a set of scores is due to individual differences between people, how much is due to variations in scores on the various items, and how much is due to measurement error. And it can easily be extended – for example, to show the extent to which the friendliness of the test administrator influences responses to the items, the extent to which responses to the items in the scale vary, and the amount of person-to-person variation in the responses to the items.

Cronbach et al. (1972) developed the theory, which is based on the statistical technique called analysis of variance (ANOVA); readers who are not familiar with this methodology should skip the rest of this chapter. Cronbach et al. argued that every time we measure a person's response to an item, this response can potentially be influenced by several different things (which they called "facets"). These facets are the same as "factors" in analysis of variance. Each facet has a number of levels – possible values or scores.

Suppose that some test items were given to children in several schools. The test items would form one facet. The schools would form another. The gender of the children could form a third . . . and so on. Some facets have a nearly infinite number of levels; for example, if the facet is "items that could be written to measure anxiety", the number of possible levels is almost infinite. Other facets have only a few possible levels.

Each facet can be either fixed or random, as with analysis of variance. So it is possible to treat the set of items as either the only set of items which could possibly be used (as with the pairs of single-digit numbers whose sum is less than 10). This is a fixed facet. Or the items in our scale could be viewed as a random sample of all possible items that could be written to measure anxiety – a random facet.

The simplest model involves just giving a sample of items (randomly sampled from the universe of items) to a random sample of people. It would be useful to know how many items we need to adequately measure the trait and how much variation there is in people's scores on the trait. A repeated-measures analysis of variance can show this, where "items" is the within-subject factor with as many levels as there are items in the scale.

Analysis of variance focuses on the size and statistical significance of differences between facets and levels of facets. Generalisability theory instead focuses on how the error variance is distributed between the various facets. An example will make it clearer. This example uses binary data (0/1) to make it easier to see what is going on, but the technique can also be applied to Likert scales etc.

Table 8.1 shows the scores that eight people obtain on a hypothetical five-item ability test; a correct answer scores 1 and an incorrect answer scores 0. Just look at the different patterns of data in this table by eye.

The data in section (a) clearly shows considerable variation between the items; items 1 and 4 are answered correctly by almost everyone, whilst items 2, 3 and 5 are usually answered incorrectly. There is very little variation between people – persons 2–6 score 2 whilst person 1 scores 1 and person 7 and 8 score 3.

Section (b) shows a lot of variation between *people*. Whilst the items are all of similar difficulty (scores on the 5-item test range from 3 to 5, with all-but-two being 4), people's scores range from zero to five correct. The correlations between the items are therefore large, leading to the large value of coefficient alpha. Section (c) shows what is almost a Guttman scale (see Chapter 4). The items vary greatly in difficulty (scores range from 2 to 7, as you should check). The scores that people obtain also vary greatly – from zero to five items correct. And alpha is fairly high, at 0.77.

Table 8.1 Hypothetical scores of eight people on five ability items, scored 0/1

Data (a)

	Item 1	Item 2	Item 3	Item 4	Item 5
Person 1	0	0	0	1	0
Person 2	1	0	0	1	0
Person 3	1	0	0	1	0
Person 4	1	0	0	1	0
Person 5	1	0	0	1	0
Person 6	1	0	0	1	0
Person 7	1	0	1	1	0
Person 8	1	0	0	1	1
Alpha = 0.109					

Data (b)

	Item 1	Item 2	Item 3	Item 4	Item 5
Person 1	0	0	0	1	0
Person 2	0	0	0	1	0
Person 3	0	0	0	0	0
Person 4	0	0	0	0	0
Person 5	0	0	0	0	0
Person 6	1	1	1	1	1
Person 7	1	1	1	1	1
Person 8	1	1	1	1	1
Alpha = 0.96					

Data (c)

	Item 1	Item 2	Item 3	Item 4	Item 5
Person 1	0	0	0	0	0
Person 2	1	0	0	0	0
Person 3	1	1	0	0	0
Person 4	1	1	1	0	0
Person 5	1	1	1	1	0
Person 6	1	1	1	1	1
Person 7	1	1	1	0	1
Person 8	1	0	1	0	0
Alpha = 0.77					

Data (d)

	Item 1	Item 2	Item 3	Item 4	Item 5
Person 1	0	0	1	0	0
Person 2	0	1	0	1	1
Person 3	0	0	0	1	1
Person 4	0	0	0	0	1
Person 5	1	0	1	0	0
Person 6	0	1	1	0	1
Person 7	0	1	0	1	1
Person 8	1	1	0	0	0
Alpha < 0					

Finally, section (d) shows some random data. People's scores range from 1 to 3, and scores on the items range from 1 to 5.

Coefficient alpha shows how large the variation between people is, compared to the variation between items.

We can perform an analysis of variance on the four sets of data shown in Table 8.1; the results from this analysis are shown in Table 8.2. You may wish to analyse the data

Table 8.2 Analyses of variance of the data of Table 8.1

Dataset (a)

Source	SS	df	MS	Estimated variance	% variance
People	0.575	7	0.0821	0.0018	1%
Items	7.15	4	1.7875	0.2143	74%
Error	2.05	28	0.0732	0.0732	25%
Total				0.2893	
$G_{relative}$	0.11				

Dataset (b)

Source	SS	df	MS	Estimated variance	% variance
People	8.175	7	1.167857	0.225	82%
Items	0.4	4	0.1	0.007143	3%
Error	1.2	28	0.042857	0.042857	16%
$G_{relative}$	0.96				

Data set (c)

Source	SS	df	MS	Estimated variance	% variance
People	3.975	7	0.567857	0.0875	32%
Items	2.35	4	0.5875	0.057143	21%
Error	3.65	28	0.130357	0.130357	47%
$G_{relative}$	0.77				

Dataset (d)

Source	SS	df	MS	Estimated variance	% variance
People	0.975	7	0.139286	0	0%
Items	0.65	4	0.1625	0	0%
Error	8.15	28	0.291071	0.291071	100%
$G_{relative}$	0				

yourself using your favourite statistics package to convince yourself that you get the same answers.

The "mean square" or "MS" columns show how much variation there is between people, how much variation there is between items, and how much random error there is. "Estimated variance" is not usually shown in the output from ANOVA programs, but it is easy to calculate by hand.[1]

The percentage variance due to "people" is important. A large "people" effect shows that people's total scores on the scale vary systematically; not everyone scores the same. Clearly, if the scale is supposed to measure individual differences, this figure should be fairly large. The "items" value shows how much items vary in their average score or difficulty level when averaged across all people. This should probably not be close to zero – particularly for ability items – since we normally want to have some easy and some hard items in an ability scale. Likewise, in a personality scale, we do not want items to which everyone gives the same response – such as "agree" when using a Likert scale. Finally, the "error" term shows how much random variation there is in the data. This term should hopefully be small.

These terms are all relative and show how much variation in the scores is due to systematic differences between people, how much variation is due to systematic variations in the difficulty of the items, and how much is due to other things (treated as random error). The statistic $G_{relative}$, which is calculated from the ANOVA table, is the same as coefficient alpha for these data (see Tables 8.2 and 8.3). However, when generalisability theory is used to identify additional factors which might affect the way in which people respond to the items (gender, for example), $G_{relative}$ controls for these systematic influences rather than treating them as random error.

If you look at the figures in the "estimated variance" column in Table 8.2, you will see that they correspond to what we noticed "by eye" in Table 8.1. Dataset (a) shows a great deal of variation between items (but not between people), dataset (b) shows little variation between items but a good deal of variation between people, and dataset (c) shows variations in the scores of both people and items, whilst dataset (d) shows just random variation.

If ANOVA shows that the percentage of variance due to individual differences between people is appreciable, then the scale is measuring a trait and the reliability (coefficient alpha) is large. If the percentage of variance due to items is large, then some items are appreciably harder (or more often agreed with) than others; there may be some redundancy in the items. For example, in dataset (a) the pattern of responses to item 1 is very similar to the pattern of responses to item 4, raising the question of why we need both of them. The pattern is the same for items 2, 3 and 5.

Whilst exploring relative variance is important, the real power of generalisability theory is its ability to evaluate the importance of several influences on people's responses to items. For example, suppose that a researcher gathers questionnaire data from boys and girls in three schools. Analysing the reliability of the scale using coefficient alpha would involve bundling all of the data together, crossing one's fingers and hoping that gender and school attended do not influence the scores on items – a fairly major assumption. However, this can be thought of as an analysis of variance design with one within-subject of "items" and two between-subjects facets of sex (two levels) and school (three levels). However, repeated measures designs (no between-subjects factors, but potentially several within-subject factors) are preferable (Briesch et al., 2014), and we will explore these from now on.

Consider the data in Table 8.3, from table 3.1 of Brennan (2001). These hypothetical data represent ratings of four aspects of behaviour ("items") made by two independent observers ("observers"). The items might perhaps measure how frequently violent prisoners show violent behaviour when observed over an 8-hour period. Item 1 might be threatening someone else, item 2 swearing at someone else, item 3 physical aggression against a person, and item 4 kicking or punching objects. Ratings ranged from 0 to 9, and 10 people were observed. As each person was rated on each item by each observer, there are two "within-subject" factors to be analysed using repeated measures analysis of variance. The same sort of design could be used for other things too – for example, in exploring test-retest reliability, or the influence of some intervention on behaviour.

It is possible to perform repeated measures of analysis of variance on these data and then work out how much variation there is between the scores of people, how

Table 8.3 Ratings of the behaviour of 10 people made by two independent observers

	Observer 1				Observer 2			
	Item 1	Item 2	Item 3	Item 4	Item 1	Item 2	Item 3	Item 4
Person 1	2	6	7	5	2	5	5	5
Person 2	4	5	6	7	6	7	5	7
Person 3	5	5	4	6	5	4	5	5
Person 4	5	9	8	6	5	7	7	6
Person 5	4	3	5	6	4	5	6	4
Person 6	4	4	4	7	6	4	7	8
Person 7	2	6	6	5	2	7	7	5
Person 8	3	4	4	5	6	6	6	4
Person 9	0	5	4	5	5	5	5	3
Person 10	6	8	7	6	6	8	8	6

much variation is down to differences between the observers, and how much is due to variation between the items. The interpretation of these figures can guide future research; if there is little variation between observers, there is no need to need to use two observers in the future – whereas if there is a lot of variation attributable to observers, it might be wise increasing the number of observers next time to improve the overall accuracy of the ratings. Likewise, if there is little variation between items, it might be possible to drop some – whereas if there is a lot of variation, this suggests that the items are only weakly correlated with the trait, and so more items might be desirable. The analysis also shows the extent to which people behave similarly.

Spreadsheet 8.1 can be used to show the results from this analysis; it can also be used to analyse data from any other analysis where there are two within-subject facets by pasting in the mean squared values from the ANOVA output. It is included to show how the results from a conventional ANOVA may be repurposed to provide generalisability estimates. We use a spreadsheet, for as there are now several interaction terms involved, it is painful to calculate the relative importance of each facet by hand.

Spreadsheet 8.1 is "pre-loaded" with the results from Brennan (2001). It shows that the main source of variation is the error term (33%) – variation which cannot be explained by the person, item or observer effects or their interactions. Next is the person-by-item interaction (20%); people respond in different ways to the items (some may swear but not hit objects, others may threaten people but not swear etc.). The "persons" effect is also substantial (20%), showing that people differ in their levels of aggressive behaviour, whilst the "item" effect (16%) shows that some behaviours are more commonly observed than others. It is possible to estimate what the effect of changing the number of items, the number of observers etc. would have. See, for example, Briesch et al. (2014). These types of studies are called **D-studies** (decision studies), as they attempt to predict the consequences of changing some of the parameters in the future.

It is possible to calculate a **relative generalisability coefficient**. This shows how much measurement error there is as a result of sampling variations in people, raters and items, and it is used when one wishes to look at the rank-order of people – for example, to identify the 20 most violent prisoners. According to the Swiss Society for Research in Education Working Group (2010), values above 0.8 are acceptable. It is called the *relative* generalisability coefficient because only the terms which interact with "persons" contribute to the error term; in this example, items, observers and the item × observer interaction are ignored. (As each person completes each item, any differences in item difficulty affect all persons, and so do not change their rank-ordering.)

There is also an **"absolute" G-coefficient**, sometimes known as phi (not to be confused with the correlation coefficient of the same name), which reports the accuracy with which the items, as rated by the observers, reflect the *absolute value* of prisoners' violent tendencies; this figure should be the same no matter how violent (or non-violent) the other prisoners are. It should therefore be no surprise to discover that there is a literature relating this form of generalisability coefficient to item response theory (Briggs & Wilson, 2004). The absolute coefficient is generally lower than the relative generalisability coefficient (Briesch et al., 2014).

Spreadsheet name: Spreadsheet 8.1: Variance calculation for generalisability theory

Download from: https://routledge.com/9781032146164/

Purpose: To calculate generalisability statistics from the output of a two-within-subjects analysis of variance

Contents of spreadsheet: Output from a two-way analysis of variance of the data from Table 3.1 of Brennan (2001).

Suggested activity:

This spreadsheet is a utility which shows how generalisability coefficients may be derived from analysis of variance results from a statistical package.

(a) Look at the "pre-loaded" output from Brennan (2001) and ensure you understand the explanations given above

(b) Mushquash and O'Connor (2006) used generalisability theory to examine the test-retest reliability of a ten-item scale, administered twice to the same sample of 329 people. The mean-squares output from their analysis of variance is shown below:-

Persons	Items	Occasions	Items x Occasions	Items x Persons	Occasions x Persons	Items x Occasions x Persons
35.961	375.913	7.423	3.128	3.441	5.970	1.810

Enter these results into the spreadsheet and note that the "occasions" and "items x occasions" effects are small (explain little variance). There is considerable variation between persons in their responses to the items, and a moderate degree of variation between items – they vary in how well they measure self esteem – and the reliability of the test on the two occasions is fairly high (0.79). For further details, see their paper.

Points to note:

- Experiment by changing entries in the *green* areas. Results are in the *yellow* areas. Simply download another copy if you accidentally change formulae.

Learning outcomes: Readers should now be able to:

- Calculate generalisability coefficients from a two-within analysis of variance, where a test is administered in two occasions.

Despite its appeal, generalisability theory is not widely used. It is ideal for designs involving test-retest reliability and could also be useful in education (multiple markers of coursework, for example). Perhaps the main problem is practical – with several within-subject facets each requiring data from each person to achieve a fully nested design (e.g., each person being rated on each variable by each rater). All too often, this is not possible. Students may choose to answer different examination questions and so even if the same two markers assess their work, the design is different. Likewise, several different groups of students might answer the same questions (giving a "between-subjects" factor in ANOVA parlance). It is possible to perform generalizability analyses for data from such designs, but the sources of variance cannot all be independently estimated, which rather defeats the main purpose of the procedure.

SOFTWARE FOR GENERALISABILITY ANALYSIS

Whilst it is possible to perform analyses of variance and hand-calculate the various statistics for generalisability theory, specialised packages are much more convenient. Gtheory in R (R Core Team, 2013) is one possibility, whilst EDUG is an elderly stand-alone package for Windows which is fairly straightforward to use and comes with a useful manual (Swiss Society for Research in Education Working Group, 2010). GENOVA (from the University of Iowa) is also widely used.

Briesch et al. (2014) provide a straightforward guide to the use and interpretation of generalisability theory.

SUMMARY

It is probable that a person's score on a personality scale or an ability test is not a "pure" indicator of the single trait which the questionnaire or test is supposed to measure. Several other trait-irrelevant variables have been identified which affect scores. Whilst it is possible to design questionnaires and tests to minimise the effects of some of these influences (for example, by including reverse-scored items and keeping vocabulary simple) this cannot solve the problem completely. Care must be taken when administering the instruments, and selecting the sample, to ensure that these extraneous influences are minimised as far as possible.

Generalisability theory shows the extent to which differences between people, differences between test items, and the interaction between people and test items influence scores – and can be used to predict how changing the test (e.g., by removing items) is likely to affect the amount of measurement error. However, it can do much more than this when there are several variables which may influence people's responses to test items. For example, responses to ability test items might be influenced by the particular individual who administers a test to a group of children (some administrators are calming whilst others are not) and by the gender of the children. Generalisability theory allows the extent of such influences to be quantified.

We should also stress two things. First, generalisability theory assumes that the data are quantitative and interval-scaled – two assumptions which may not be true. Second, although psychometricians enjoy developing mathematical methods such as this, the acid test is whether questionnaire or test scores actually seem to measure what they claim. This is known as *validity*, and is discussed in Chapter 9.

NOTE

1 It is simply the difference between the mean square for people (MS_{people}) and the mean squared error term (MS_{error}) [0.8214–0.0732 for dataset (a)] divided by the number of items (5). Likewise, estimated variance for items is $MS_{items} - MS_{error}$ divided by the number of people; (0.2143 − 0.0732)/8 for dataset (a).

CHAPTER 9
TEST VALIDITY, BIAS AND INVARIANCE

Earlier in this book we set out three criteria for adequate measurement. These are that scores on a scale should only reflect one property of the thing (person) being assessed (unidimensionality), that they should be free of measurement error (show high reliability), and that the scores on the measuring instrument should reflect the thing that the scale claims to measure. A scale purporting to measure anxiety should be directly influenced by anxiety and not anything else. The first two of these issues were dealt with in the previous chapters. The **validity** of a scale addresses the third issue, that of whether scores on a scale actually measure what they are supposed to. Unlike reliability theory, establishing the validity of a scale involves no particular statistical techniques – just common sense, critical evaluation, and a healthy level of scepticism.

Whilst most studies into test validity are correlational, this is dangerous, and I was careful to say "directly influenced" in the previous paragraph. For as with any correlation, it is possible that the scores on the scale and the scores on the criterion (which is used to establish the validity of the scale) are both influenced by some third variable (e.g., social desirability, acquiescence, fatigue, intelligence) which affects scores on both variables.

It is also vital to ensure that validation studies are not **circular definitions**. It is tempting to say that a person enjoys social gatherings because they have a high level of the "sociability" trait, and then "validate" a scale measuring sociability by asking people how often they meet up with friends, correlating scores with another sociability questionnaire and so on. This is nonsensical, as the trait of sociability is used first to describe the behaviour (as a trait) and then to explain it.

We have seen that reliability theory can show how accurately a set of items can measure some underlying trait. What it cannot do is shed any light on the *nature* of that trait, for just because an investigator *thinks* that a set of items should measure a particular trait, there is no guarantee that they actually do so. We mentioned the Repression-Sensitisation Scale (R–S Scale) in Chapter 1. It supposedly measured the extent to which people block out threats rather than keeping alert to any sign of danger, but

DOI: 10.4324/9781003240181-9

it was later found to correlate 0.9 with a test of anxiety. The maximum correlation between two scales is limited by the size of their reliabilities, so *all* of the variance in the R–S Scale could be accounted for by anxiety; the R–S concept was empty of meaning. This tale conveys an important message. Even if a set of items form a highly reliable scale and look as if they measure some theoretical trait such as repression-sensitisation, there is no guarantee that they actually do so. Instead, it is necessary to determine this empirically by a process known as validation.

The philosophical basis of test validation is actually a *lot* more complex than it might appear from this description (Borsboom et al., 2004). These authors provide an excellent discussion of the rationale of test validation of various kinds and suggest that the notion of validation is very simple; is there good evidence that the scores on scales are directly influenced by some (psychological or other) attribute? If so, the test is valid, in exactly the same way that a voltmeter is valid if its readings reflect the difference in electric potential across its terminals.

They also argue that it is vitally important to understand the *processes* by which different levels of some attribute result in different test scores, rather than merely studying correlations (etc.) between scores on some scale and other variables. Gathering some empirical data and discovering relationships between variables is easy: all one needs to do is perform structural equation modelling. Developing a theory about why precisely some concept such as "general intelligence" (assuming it exists) can *cause* some people to react faster than others, show better memory and so on is infinitely more challenging than discovering that scores on one scale correlate with scores on another scale yet fail to correlate with a third!

Borsboom et al. remind us that science demands a grasp of the mechanisms involved. "No table of correlations, no matter how big, can be a substitute for knowledge of the processes that lead to item responses" (Borsboom et al., 2004). The question that we need to address is what is it about the personality trait (ability, mood etc.) which makes people respond to an item in a particular way?

> It is disconcerting to find that a large proportion of test research is characterized by an almost complete absence of theories of response behavior and that so few researchers recognize that the problem of psychological measurement is not a matter of following the "right" methodological rules but of tackling one of the most challenging problems in psychology; how do psychological characteristics relate to empirical observations?
>
> (Borsboom et al., 2004)

The issues raised in this paper are important, but although the work is widely cited, it is not clear that it has yet become mainstream – possibly because developing adequate theories is a lot more difficult than gathering data and developing scales! In addition, many test users are very pragmatic; if using a test of some sort saves them money or provides them with a number (such as a person's IQ) which is less likely to be challenged in court than a subjective opinion, then the niceties of philosophy and scientific measurement are seen as irrelevant. What follows is therefore a fairly conventional view of validity theory.

According to this, a scale is said to be valid if it does what it claims to do, either in terms of theory or in practical application. For example, a scale that is marketed as a measure of anxiety for use in the general UK population should measure anxiety and not social desirability, reading skill, sociability or any other unrelated traits. We can tell this by determining whether scores on this scale correlate with other measures which are also indicators of anxiety – for example, skin resistance or scores on some other questionnaire. We should also determine that it does not correlate substantially with scales measuring sociability, reading skill etc.

The context is crucial; validity depends crucially on the purpose for which the scale is administered and the make-up of the sample being assessed. If we define "aggression" as the number of incidents of physical violence a person performs in a two-year period, the test may work wonderfully well when it is administered to co-operative students, although scores will probably be low. If the same scale is used with a sample of violent offenders who hope to be released early, you might expect the correlation between test scores and behaviour to plummet, because the offenders may be less than keen to admit to violent behaviour.

Rather than asking whether scores on a scale correlate with some other criterion (such as scores on another scale or some behaviour), it is necessary to consider the context in which the assessment is made, and the sample(s) used – together with all of their other individual differences (personality, abilities, hopes, fears, aspirations . . .) before considering whether there is any evidence that scores on the scale are directly influenced by individual differences in the characteristic being measured.

The validity of a scale is related to its reliability. If a scale has low reliability, a great deal of measurement error is associated with each person's score on the scale, and this will reduce correlation between the scale and any other variables. If the validity of a scale is assessed by correlating it with some behaviour or with scores on some other test, the validity of an unreliable scale must therefore be low. On the other hand, if the reliability of a scale is high, there is no guarantee that the validity of the scale will be high; it is measuring *something*, but this may not be what it claims to assess. High reliability is a necessary but not sufficient condition for validity when validity is measured using correlations.

Borsboom et al. (2004) remind us that "a test is valid for measuring an attribute if (a) the attribute exists and (b) variations in the attribute causally produce variation in the measurement outcomes". In other words, we have to be confident that increases in levels of the psychological attribute trait are reflected in increases in the scores on the questionnaire or test. This requires an understanding of the mechanisms involved.

The key to studying is validity is to establish a *causal* relationship between the individual's level of some trait (or state) and scores on some scale. This is a challenge for psychology, because it is difficult or impossible to be sure that a trait exists, let alone ascertain whether levels of that trait directly influence scores on some questionnaire or other measure. Correlations are of little use here, as they obviously cannot demonstrate causality.

Structural equation models (Kline, 2015; Loehlin & Beaujean, 2017) can indicate causal relationships between variables, rather than mere correlations, and so may be well-suited for validating scales. These models consist of two parts. The "measurement model" depicts the relationships between observed variables (scored responses to items or scales) and the hypothesised latent variables (traits). Less-than-perfect reliability is reflected in less-than-perfect relationships between levels of the latent variables and scores on the observed variables. The "structural model" which would be important for validating the scales shows the relationships between the latent variables, unaffected by measurement error. A case can certainly be made for using these models (rather than simple correlations) when validating scales. However, it could well be the case that the structural model would show that the relationships between traits are consistent with some theoretical model, yet the measurement model shows that it is impossible to measure the trait with any accuracy. Pragmatically, it is all very well showing that various traits are interrelated, but if the measurement model shows that a scale cannot accurately assess a trait, what practical use can it possibly be?

The conventional literature suggests that there are six main ways of establishing whether a scale is valid.

FACE VALIDITY

Face validity merely checks that the scale looks as if it measures what it is supposed to. The R-S Scale debacle described earlier shows that scrutinising the content of items is no guarantee that the scale will measure what it is intended to. Despite this, some widely used scales (particularly in social psychology) are constructed by writing a few items, ensuring that alpha is high (which is generally the case because the items are paraphrases of each other), and then piously assuming that the scale measures the concept that it was designed to assess. It is *vital* to ensure that a scale has better credentials than this before using it. It is necessary to establish that the scale has some predictive power, it is causally related to some variable of interest, and that it correlates as expected with other scales before one can conclude that the scale really does measure what it claims to.

Face validity is, however, necessary in order to encourage participants to take a questionnaire or test seriously, and to work hard when attempting it. For example, Chan and Schmitt (1997) found that a video version of a judgement task was perceived as having higher face validity than a paper-and-pencil version of the same task. But crucially members of a minority group performed much better at the video version of the task, and this did not seem to be due to poor reading skills. Perceiving the task as being relevant may have motivated members of the minority group, and this reduced the adverse impact of the test. This seems to be a robust finding, and Ryan and Ployhart (2000) give a useful review of the older literature.

Low face validity can be a problem for some personality scales; in a previous incarnation I was once asked to administer a scale to serving air force officers which included items such as "Do you enjoy the feeling of silk against your skin?" and suchlike. Their reaction was entirely predictable.

CONTENT VALIDITY

Occasionally, it is possible to construct a scale which *must* be valid, by definition. For example, suppose that one wanted to construct a scale to measure spelling ability. Since, by definition, the dictionary contains the whole domain of items, any procedure that produces a representative sample of words from this dictionary has to be a valid measure of spelling ability. This is what is meant by content validity. **Content validity** is (unsurprisingly, perhaps) most common in areas such as educational attainment, where learning outcomes are clearly defined and teachers/students therefore know precisely what the assessment process will cover. For example, a student reading this chapter might be expected to describe and critically evaluate at least four types of test validity.

Although a clinical diagnosis clearly requires a skilled diagnostic interview from a professional, it might be possible to draw on the DSM-5 criteria to help one design a test to measure autism-like traits in the general population by ensuring that the items in such a questionnaire or rating scale cover all of the behaviours listed in DSM-5, and then argue that the test must have content validity. If the test overrepresents some behaviours whilst omitting others, then it cannot have acceptable content validity.

Occupational psychologists sometimes use "work-basket" approaches in selecting staff, where applicants are presented with a sample of the activities that are typically performed as part of the job, and their performance on these tasks is in some way evaluated. Applicants for a customer service role may each be given copies of letters of complaint to deal with. These exercises are not psychological tests in the strict sense, but the process can be seen to have some content validity.

Of course, content validity (like any form of validity) only applies to a particular group of people who are being assessed for a particular purpose; a test which is valid within one population for a particular purpose may well not be valid if it is used within another population or for a different purpose. It is also terribly atheoretical. If several quite different traits, attitudes etc. are required to solve a problem, the work-basket approach will measure them all simultaneously, and it will never be obvious what traits are being measured. We have zero understanding of why some people perform better than others at the task, which ignores the requirement for validity studies to show a sound theoretical understanding of the relationships between the variables (Borsboom et al., 2004).

What happens if the nature of the job changes over time, or people move to different roles? Because we have no understanding of what the task measures, it is impossible to say whether people who performed well in their original role would excel if promoted to a different role. However, if job analyses were used to identify the traits which were important for each task, and these were each measured separately using standard scales, it should be possible to make better predictions. So although tasks can be identified which have content validity, it may not always be prudent to use them.

It is possible to develop tests having content validity for selection purposes by performing some form of job analysis, and ensuring that a selection test measures each of these skills and abilities. For example, it might be found that engineering apprentices frequently flounder because of their lack of mathematical skills. It would be possible to perform a detailed analysis of the tasks performed by these apprentices to identify the precise mathematical skills which are needed for the successful completion of the apprenticeship, and build a screening test to measure these skills. This screening test would then have content for that particular application, when used with samples of applicants drawn from the same population (i.e., with the same mathematical backgrounds).

One of the problems with establishing content validity is that the behaviour which the scale is designed to assess may change over time. This may happen because of a better understanding of the concept (as when DSM-IV evolved into DSM-5, when the indicators for several clinical syndromes were altered) or organisational change (such as when changes in the apprentice training programme alter the list of mathematical requirements). Or a scale might lose its content validity just because of changes in the way in which words are used – the meaning of "wicked" in a personality item, for example. Thus a scale which was content-valid a few years ago may not be content-valid today – a point which should be carefully kept in mind.

A second problem is that it is rarely possible to define the domain of potential test items with any accuracy. For example, how can one ever be sure that a scale measuring leadership covers all the possible ways in which leadership could manifest itself, given that it could cover crisis management, delegation, forward-thinking, and a whole host of other things? Whilst any test developer will often have *some* idea about what their scale is supposed to assess (but see Cattell, 1946), it is unlikely that this knowledge will be sufficiently detailed to allow them to claim that their items form a true random sample of all the items in the domain, and thereby claim that the scale has content validity.

CONSTRUCT VALIDITY

One commonly used way of checking whether a test measures what it claims to assess is to perform thoughtful experiments. This is what is meant by **construct validation**. One simply asks the question "If this scale measures what it claims to measure, how should scores on the scale (or items) relate to other behaviours, measurements or test scores?" Then one performs a series of studies gathering as much data as possible, at the end of which a decision is made as to whether or not the evidence from these studies is sufficiently strong to support the claim that the test measures what it claims to measure.

Suppose that a test is designed to measure anxiety in UK university students. How might its validity be checked through experiment?

The first approach (sometimes called **convergent validation**) determines whether scores on the test relate to other things as expected. For example, if there are other widely used scales of anxiety on the market, a group of students could be given both tests, and the two sets of scores could be correlated together (after checking that none of the items in the two scales are similar in content). A large positive correlation would suggest that the new scale is valid. Alternatively, the scale could be administered to a group of students who claim to have a phobia about spiders, before and after showing them a tarantula. If their scores increase, then the scale might indeed measure anxiety. Scores on the scale could be correlated with measures of skin resistance, which have a known relationship to anxiety levels. Genetic variations linked to anxiety might be reflected in scores on the scale. The list of possible experiments is almost endless.

The basic aim of these convergent validations is to determine whether the scale scores are related to other variables according to some theory. Unfortunately, a failure to find the expected relationships might be due to some problem either with the scale, the theory or with the other measures. For example, the *other* scale of anxiety may not be valid: we might be quite wrong in supposing that anxiety is related to skin resistance, and some of the individuals who say that they are phobic about spiders may not be. However, if scores on a scale do appear to vary in accordance with theory, it seems reasonable to conclude that the scale is valid.

The obvious problem with this approach is that if the novel scale of anxiety correlates substantially with an existing one, why does the world need the new scale? There may be several reasons. The new scale may be shorter. It might be freely available, rather than a commercial product. It might claim to have better content validity. Or it might use a different format (e.g., administered via a mobile device, rather than a clinical interview). But if the new scale does not have any such merits, it is hard to see why it is needed.

Studies of **divergent validity** (sometimes called **discriminant validity**) check that the scale does not seem to measure any traits with which it should, in theory, be unrelated. For example, the literature claims that anxiety is unrelated to intelligence, socio-economic status, social desirability and so on. If a scale that purportedly measured anxiety actually showed a substantial correlation with any of these variables, it cannot be a good measure of anxiety.

One might expect that widely used personality scales would have gone through the construct validation process, and so are known to be distinct from the main personality traits. Unfortunately, this is not always the case. Bainbridge et al. (in press) show that many/most widely used scales are extremely similar to the Big Five personality markers. That is, they lack discriminant validity.

PROBLEMS WITH CONSTRUCT VALIDITY

Studies of construct validity are extremely common because they are ridiculously easy to perform, with scant regard for the need to understand the processes which cause traits to be linked. Without such an understanding, construct validity studies are of little or no value, because they do not and cannot show whether the correlations between variables occur for the reasons that you suppose.

Borsboom et al. (2011) give the example of phlogiston. Alchemists proposed that all substances contained varying amounts of phlogiston which was released when they burned. Sand contains no phlogiston (it does not burn), wood contains some phlogiston and magnesium contains a lot of it. The difference in weight of the substance before and after it was burnt supposedly revealed how much phlogiston it contained. Finding that burning stops when the substance is put into sealed container can be explained by assuming that the air in the container could not absorb any more of the phlogiston and so on.

The theory fits (some of) the evidence – the only problem is that it is quite incorrect. Finding data which is consistent with a theory does not necessarily mean that the theory is correct.

The same could be said about many psychological theories; discovering that scores on one scale are strongly related to two other variables but not to a third does not necessarily show that the scale really measures what its creator claims.

The problem is that the score on any scale or test scores is *assumed* to measure some theoretical trait (intelligence, extraversion, introverted anhedonia). Even if we assume that the trait exists, and that it is quantitative (i.e., can be represented by numbers), the problem is that construct validation only relates scores on this trait to scores on *other* questionnaires which are assumed to measure other theoretical traits, and these have the same problems. Relating scores to physical measures is not much better. We can *assume* that there is such a thing as anxiety, that it is quantitative and that it can be measured by a certain questionnaire. We can *assume* that the more a finger sweats, the higher a person's anxiety is, and so readings from a meter measuring skin resistance may measure anxiety by a different method. Either or both of these assumptions might be quite incorrect. When we find that scores on the questionnaire correlates with skin resistance (construct validation), it *might* be because anxiety is a quantitative trait which influences both variables. Or the correlation might occur for some completely different reason.

In addition, the correlations between measures in validation studies are frequently rather small – in the order of 0.3 or 0.4 – which means that there degree of overlap between them is fairly trivial (9%–16% of the variance is shared). Researchers tend to focus on statistical significance instead, which rather misses the point. It is possible to nudge these correlations up (by using structural equation modelling, or by correcting the correlations for unreliability, as shown in Spreadsheet 6.5) in order to estimate what the correlation would be if both measures were perfectly reliable. However, it is often difficult to know what to make of a construct validity study which shows only modest correlations between variables which are thought to be related and some unexpectedly large correlations with supposedly unrelated variables. Such studies sometimes show enormous creativity. Journal editors are used to receiving papers where authors try to rationalise their findings after finding a few significant correlations (easy, if one has not used conservative significance tests) and use great ingenuity to argue that what they find somehow attests to the validity of a scale. One often suspects that the hypotheses that were tested and then supported were conceived after looking at the data, rather than beforehand.

Construct validation sounds straightforward, but one also needs to consider the context in which the assessments are made and the nature of the sample used. In practice, many authors will "piggyback" their scale onto a larger study in order to validate it, and the scales in the larger study may not really allow for the most appropriate validation.

Given that no-one will have ever tested an identical sample under identical circumstances, it is necessary to use some rather creative thinking (before peeping at the results) to decide precisely which variables should correlate with scores on the scale that one is trying to assess. Should one expect the scale to correlate substantially with another scale which was developed in another culture, or by using a sample with different demographics? Will gender differences moderate the relationships between the variables? There is no way of telling for sure, but it is necessary to make a "best guess" before analysing data and be very aware of how easy it is to rationalise any contrary results after the analyses have been performed. It would be even better if one used structural equation modelling; it would be quite possible to draw up the diagram showing which variables are thought to link which other variables before performing any analyses to check model fit or estimate the various parameters, and a case could be made for journal editors to require such information to be submitted before a study is performed.

Psychologists are only human, and having invested time and effort in developing a scale, it might be hard for them to admit that it is really not very good at measuring anything. Studies which did *not* support the validity of the scale might never be submitted for publication. Confirmation bias is also a matter of real concern; it is easy to pay more heed to evidence which confirms that a test is valid than evidence which suggests that it is not. For all of these reasons, when evaluating the construct validity of a scale, it is advisable to ensure that the hypotheses which are being tested are:

- *Highly appropriate.* The scales which are used to test the construct validity of a novel scale must clearly be the most theoretically relevant ones which can be found. So a new scale measuring working memory needs to be tested against other measures of working memory – not (just) other tests of cognitive ability. There is no point in interpreting gender differences (for example) unless there is a strong theoretical and/or empirical literature suggesting that without gender differences, the scale would be flawed. So gender differences might be used in the construct validation of a scale measuring aggression, but not when validating a scale measuring extraversion or working memory.
- *Independent.* Care should be taken to ensure that correlations between scales cannot arise because some of the items are highly similar in content. We have seen in Spreadsheet 1.1 that if the same (or similar) items appear in both scales, the validation exercise just indicates that participants behave consistently which is not at all what is intended.

    I have shown (Cooper, 2019) that several scales which supposedly measure quite different constructs contain items that are nearly identical in meaning. Respondents are bound to answer these items in the same way. This *guarantees* that the two scales will correlate together. The two scales are not independent, and interpreting the correlation between the scales as part of a validation makes no sense.

Other possible confounds should be explored too, and consideration should be given to removing the influence of other moderating variables through the use of regression, partial correlation, structural equation modelling or other techniques. If scores on a questionnaire correlate substantially with non-questionnaire measures (for example, psychophysiological measures, developmental variables, measures of the family environment or performance on cognitive tasks), this provides particularly strong evidence for its validity. Here there will be little danger of the same "nuisance factors" affecting performance on two questionnaires.

- *Substantial.* Small correlations (e.g., 0.3 or 0.4) may well be statistically significant. However, if the amount of overlap between the two variables is this small (9% to 16%), it is difficult to argue that the study provides strong evidence for the construct validation of a scale. How large does a correlation between two tests need to be to claim that they measure the same trait: 0.5, or 0.7, or another value? Correcting for unreliability (as in Spreadsheet 6.5) may be useful here. Likewise, when establishing the divergent validity of a test, can a correlation of 0.3 be treated as "negligible"? There is no simple answer to these questions.
- *Unambiguous.* There is no point in performing any analysis where a positive, zero or negative relationship between the scale score and another variable could, with sufficient ingenuity, be taken as evidence for the validity of the scale. Every time evidence is cited which supposedly supports the validity of the scale, one needs to ask oneself whether it is at all possible that a null result, or a result in the opposite direction, might also be taken as evidence for the validity of the scale. For example, finding that a scale which is designed to measure satisfaction with therapy actually correlates negatively with the therapist's rating of the effectiveness of the outcome could be explained away by the patient and therapist using different criteria, or by "reaction formation" whereby the patient who is threatened by the depth of their therapeutic relationship turns hostile and denigrates the therapist . . . any data which can be interpreted in many ways are not worth considering.
- *Peer reviewed.* Several authors are notorious for presenting novel theories and/or scales (together with "evidence" for their validity) in books, rather than in peer-reviewed papers in well-regarded journals. The peer review process associated with articles published in good journals is highly detailed, and so validation studies which are reported in a good journal should carry far more weight than studies reported in a book, which will not have been independently reviewed in depth.
- *Impartially evaluated.* All too often, a theory and associated scale are developed by a researcher and used (uncritically) by their graduate students or professionals who are not experts in test design. Eventually everyone assumes that the necessary validation has taken place because so many careers depend on it. Independent validation (ideally by a sceptic approaching the issue from a different theoretical perspective) is very important.

PREDICTIVE VALIDITY

Psychological scales are all designed with some purpose in mind. They all set out to predict some form of behaviour, and their success in doing so is known as their **predictive validity**. For example, a scale might be given to adolescents in an attempt to predict which of them would suffer from schizophrenia later in life. Another might be used to select the most promising candidates for employment as a salesperson. These scales would have predictive validity if their scores were to be related to the later incidence of schizophrenia, or if it could be shown that the people with the highest scores on the scale made the most sales. This method of validating a scale sounds remarkably straightforward but in practice tends not to be.

The first problem is the nature of the criterion against which the scale is to be evaluated. For although noting a diagnosis of schizophrenia or the volume of sales achieved is quite straightforward, many occupations lack a single criterion. A university lecturer's job is a case in point. Mine involved teaching, research, applying for funding, curriculum design, managing colleagues, committee work, the supervision of postgraduate students, providing informal help with statistics and programming, supporting and encouraging undergraduates and so on – the list is a long one, and it is not obvious how most of these activities could be evaluated or their relative importance determined. So even if one's performance could be evaluated in each of these areas, how should these evaluations be combined to produce an overall score?

In other cases (e.g., where employees are rated by their line-manager), different assessors may apply quite different standards. When performance of employees is rated, it is highly advisable to obtain several independent assessments of each person's performance. This allows the reliability of these assessments to be calculated. The correlation between scale score and (averaged) measure of performance can then be corrected for the effects of unreliability.

A second problem is restriction of range, as discussed in Chapter 6. Selection systems generally operate through several stages, e.g., initial psychometric testing to reduce the number of applicants to manageable proportions followed by interviews and more detailed psychological assessments of individuals who get through the first stage. Applicants who are eventually appointed will all have similar (high) scores on all of the screening scales, otherwise they would have been rejected before the interview stage. Thus the range of scores in the group of individuals who are selected will be much smaller than that in the general population. This will create problems for any attempt to validate the screening test, since this restricted range of abilities will tend to reduce the correlation between the scale and any criterion.

The third issue is deciding how large the predictive validity of a scale needs to be in order for it to be valuable. In many cases, this is determined by cost. For example, military flying training is a process which is extremely expensive and time-consuming. Here, even if a scale only has a very modest correlation with the criterion, it may be cost-effective to use it as part of the selection process – as a very small increase in one's ability to predict success at flying training might result in very substantial cost savings. On the other hand, if training and attrition costs are minimal, it might only be cost-effective to use a scale as part of the selection process if its predictive validity is very substantial.

Finally, it is not always reasonable to assume that there is a *linear* relationship between test score and job or school performance. This may make calculating correlations between test scores and performance of dubious value. For example, suppose that a job such as a delivery worker or a sales assistant requires a certain minimum level of numeracy and literacy. It seems unlikely that having a much higher level of numeracy or literacy – a PhD in mathematics or English, for example – would lead to a commensurate increase in job performance. So when assessing the validity of a scale, it is vitally important to examine the scatter diagram between performance and test score, for it might well be that the case that relationship between test score and performance is non-linear. In such a case it might be more appropriate to identify a simple pass mark, rather than using regression or similar techniques to combine the test scores with other information.

ESTABLISHING PREDICTIVE VALIDITY

There are several designs that can be used to establish the predictive validity of scales. Most obviously, the scales may be administered and criterion data gathered later, such as when ability scales are used to predict job performance, or when an intelligence scale is administered to young children whose school performance is measured many years later (e.g., Deary et al., 2007). The advantage of this approach is that the psychological assessment is made a long time before performance is measured. This more or less guarantees that the psychological characteristic(s) measured by the assessment procedure influence performance, rather than vice versa.

The disadvantages of this approach are mainly practical. Administering scales and following up with people over a period of years in order to obtain criterion data requires long-term funding, which may be hard to obtain. Sometimes there is simply no time to perform long-term studies; an organisation may need a selection process to be developed within a few months, which precludes any long-term follow-up to gather performance data. If a long-term study is undertaken, some participants will move house, decide that they no longer wish to take part in the study, change their name or otherwise become difficult to trace. Hence, the administrative overheads of tracking people can be substantial, whilst attrition of the sample also raises statistical concerns. Can it be assumed that the people who drop out of the study before the criterion data are obtained from a random sample of those who were initially tested? If not, the predictive validity of the scale might be inaccurate. For example, if intelligence truly does predict school performance and all the low-intelligence children dropped out of the study, the range of scores on both the ability scale and the measures of educational attainment would be reduced. This will make the correlation between the two variables smaller than it should be.

CONCURRENT VALIDITY

Sometimes the criterion data may be gathered at the same time as the scale is administered, such as when an ability scale is given to students at the same time that their school performance is appraised, or when a firm is considering using a new selection test and decides to see whether it can predict the effectiveness of workers who are already in the organisation. Designs where the test and performance measures (e.g., examination or other grades, supervisors' ratings, sales figures) are obtained at the same time that the test is administered are known as **concurrent validity** studies. These studies have several clear merits. They are easy to perform, for one just needs to assess people and gather criterion data contemporaneously, and so there will be little or no drop-out from the sample. It means that there is no delay in developing a selection test; if a scale shows that it shows a substantial correlation with job performance in an existing sample of employees, it would be possible to consider using it as part of a selection process without delay.

There are several problems with this approach, too. It is hard to be sure that the results from a concurrent validity study will accurately predict how effective a test would be if it were used at an earlier stage as part of a selection process. There are several reasons for this.

- *Situational factors.* As all the data are gathered at one time when performing a concurrent validity study, it might be the case that some situational factor(s) might affect some people's scores on both the test and the measure of performance; these might include lack of sleep, depression, influenza etc. This will tend to inflate the correlation between the scale and the criterion. If the scale were used for selection purposes at an earlier date, these situational factors would not influence both scores.
- *Direction of causality.* Perhaps going to school enhances intelligence, rather than intelligence boosting school performance. Perhaps working in an organisation enhances the abilities or develops the personality traits which are measured by the tests. If so, there is clearly no causal relationship between test score and performance, and so the test would not work if it were used to select children or employees at an earlier date.
- *Attrition.* It might be the case that students who underperform at college or at work drop out or leave at an early stage, and so are not part of the sample when

the test and performance data are gathered. This reduced range of scores will tend to underestimate the correlation which the test would show if it were used for selection purposes at an earlier date.
- *Motivation.* Job applicants and college applicants will generally be highly motivated to perform well on the tests. However, there is no reason or incentive for students or employees who are already in post to answer questions honestly or put much effort into any test which is administered as a part of a concurrent validation exercise; they have nothing to gain or lose by doing so. It seems reasonable to suggest that this might underestimate the potential which a test might have were it used for selection purposes.

Gathering data from concurrent validity studies is quick and easy, whereas true predictive validity studies involves tracking down individuals months or years later and are thus both time-consuming and expensive. However, concurrent validity studies simply cannot be expected to provide accurate estimates of how well a test would predict performance were it administered months or years beforehand.

RETROSPECTIVE VALIDATION

One sometimes encounters studies where the criterion data precede the assessment. These are known as **retrospective** or **postdiction** studies. For example, suppose that a researcher wants to determine whether the extent to which a child was breastfed is associated with IQ in adulthood, or whether the number of friends a child had between the ages of 4 and 6 is related to their adult levels of extraversion. Rather than performing a proper predictive validation, measuring the breastfeeding experience of infants or monitoring their social behaviour and following them up into adulthood, a researcher might decide to simply measure intelligence and extraversion in a sample of adults and then ask their mothers how long they were breastfed, how many friends they had during infancy and so on. Here the criterion data (length of breastfeeding, number of friendships) refer to activities which took place before the psychological assessments were made – a retrospective study.

The problem is that memories are fallible. Quite a lot is known about the accuracy of retrospective reports of traumatic childhood events, as a result of police and other investigations; it turns out that are substantial amounts of error in such recollections (Hardt & Rutter, 2004), which is hardly surprising. Much less is known about how accurate the recall for "normal" events is – and it would be difficult to estimate this with any precision. The fuzzier the behaviour being measured, the more inaccurate the measure might be. For how can anyone accurately gauge their number of childhood friends when the definition of "friend" will vary from person to person?

It is also easy to infer a direct causal relationship where none exists when gathering data about parental behaviour during childhood. For example, it is known that more intelligent mothers choose to breastfeed (Der et al., 2006), and as intelligence is highly heritable, breastfed children may grow up to be intelligent purely because they are related to their mothers. Breastfeeding per se may have zero direct influence on adult intelligence. There is a similar literature on many other aspects of parent-child interaction (Plomin & Bergeman, 1991).

INCREMENTAL VALIDITY

Organisational psychologists may sometimes need to determine whether adding a new scale to an existing battery of selection tests will increase its ability to predict some criterion. Suppose that a retail organisation currently selects its graduate management trainees by means of an interview. It knows that the correlation between interview performance and subsequent job performance is only 0.2. It wonders whether it would be possible to better predict job performance by adding an additional test – for example, a test of written English. If adding an additional scale to a test battery improves its performance, that scale provides **incremental validity**. It is normally established by using multiple regression, determining whether the multiple correlation increases significantly when a new predictor variable (test score) is added. As before, the cost benefit of the additional testing needs to be considered. Is the predicted increase In sales large enough to offset the cost of administering and scoring the test?

Assessing the incremental validity of a test is complicated by the "bandwidth/fidelity trade-off". A very broad trait (such as neuroticism, which is a roughly equal mixture of anxiety, depression, hostility and other traits) may well predict behaviour in most situations – but in some circumstances, a narrower facet may predict better. For example, if trying to predict road rage, it is likely that the hostility facet would be a better predictor than the broad trait of neuroticism. On the other hand, if trying to predict whether a person will undergo psychotherapy in their lifetime, the broader trait will probably be more effective.

Whilst incremental validity has usually been assessed using hierarchical multiple regression, Westfall and Yarkoni (2016) demonstrate that measurement error (imperfect reliability) can play havoc with the estimation of regression parameters' type I error rates. Feng and Hancock (in press) suggest an alternative to regression, based on structural equation modelling, and give examples of how it may be applied in practice.

These approaches are useful to demonstrate whether a trait is unrepresented in an existing battery of tests and questionnaires. Given Borsboom's (Borsboom et al., 2004) argument that in order to understand the *processes* that cause tests to predict behaviour, it is important not to focus just on test scores, but rather on the traits which the test scores represent. The Feng and Hancock paper allows such an understanding to be obtained.

FACTORIAL VALIDITY

A final form of validity refers to the factor structure of the questionnaire or test items. If the odd-numbered items of a questionnaire are supposed to form one scale and the even numbered items form another scale, performing a factor analysis (as described in Chapters 10 and 11) should produce two factors, with the odd-numbered items having large loadings on one factor and the even-numbered items having large loadings on the other. If they do, the two scales have **factorial validity**: the items hang together as expected. The sign of these loadings should reflect whether or not an item is reverse-scored.

Running a factor analysis is quick and useful, and this approach is particularly useful when a test is used in a different culture or age group from the one in which it was designed. (Translating tests is a more difficult issue, one which we consider in Chapter 16.) However, it is difficult to know what to do if the expected factor structure does not appear cleanly. Should some items be dropped from the questionnaire? This is probably not advisable, as it will affect the content validity of the scale. Should the questionnaire be rescored as indicated by the factor analysis? This decision is difficult; my advice would be "almost certainly not". At a minimum, it would be necessary to repeat the analysis on another sample, use confirmatory factor analysis to make sure that any additional factors lead to a significant improvement in fit, make sure that any additional factors do not reflect some sort of response bias (e.g., all the negatively keyed items) and make great theoretical sense – which can only really be discovered by a thorough examination of the items together with a detailed construct or predictive validation process.

Factorial validation is quick and easy to perform, but it should always be remembered that the correlations between items tend to be both small and prone to measurement error; failure to perfectly replicate a factor structure in one sample is quite common, but unless the problems are really substantial, persuading a reviewer or sponsor that it is more appropriate to rescore a test than use the original method is unlikely to be successful.

DEVELOPING AND VALIDATING A BATTERY OF SELECTION TESTS

A common problem in applied psychology is knowing how to combine several very different types of data in order to predict performance. In what follows, we assume that each of the variables we discuss predicts some criterion (e.g., ability to pass some training course); what we need to decide is how to arrange the selection process so as to gather this information in a cost-effective manner and produce a score based on all of the information available which best predicts performance.

MULTIPLE HURDLE METHOD

For example, an organisation may use aptitude data, the results from an interview, and a medical report in order to make a hiring decision. It *could* gather all this data from every applicant. However, aptitude testing is generally cheap (it can be performed in groups or over the internet), whilst medical examinations and interviews are expensive. It might thus make sense to divide the assessments into three blocks. Those who pass the aptitude tests might undergo the medical examination. Those who pass the medical examination might be invited for interview. Those who pass the interview would be hired. This is sometimes called the **multiple hurdle** approach, as applicants need to pass each stage of the selection process before moving on to the next.

But how to decide whether a person "passes" a battery of different aptitude scales? There are two main possibilities. The **multiple cut-off** method involves the employer setting a minimum acceptable score for each scale. Under this model, applicants will only pass the aptitude test battery if they show a certain minimum level of aptitude on each scale – scoring above the mean, for example. Scoring below the mean on just one scale guarantees failure. Whilst this approach is commendably simple and guarantees that each person who passes on to the next stage of the process has a certain minimum competence in each area, it has several problems. The "minimum acceptable score" which is set for each test is arbitrary. Unless the tests which are used are highly reliable, measurement error alone makes it probable that some able candidates will fail one or more of the scales. And unless the cut-offs are kept low, this technique can reject a large proportion of applicants if the correlations between the measures are modest or small.

REGRESSION

The second approach involves using multiple **regression** or logistic regression to weight the scores on the various tests. It assumes that both test and training data are available from a large sample of people (hundreds, at least), and uses regression to combine the scores on the different tests so as to predict how well each person will perform on the training course. Each scale is given a regression weight, and each person's score is multiplied by the regression weight for that test. These values are then summed to give an index score. The scales which best predict training performance will influence the overall aptitude index more than those which have a weaker relationship to this criterion. This aptitude index is then used to decide who should proceed to the next stage of the procedure; it is usual to simply work one's way down the list until all vacancies have been filled.

There are two main problems with this approach. It allows good performance in one area to compensate for poor performance in another. Thus someone with excellent mathematical skills but very weak verbal skills might end up moving to the next stage of the procedure, which might create problems for them later. Hence, in practice organisations sometimes perform a two-stage analysis of the applicants' scores: a multiple cut-off with low cut-offs (e.g., a standard deviation below the mean) to ensure that applicants have some basic competency in each area, with those who pass this stage having their scores weighted according to the regression model. The second problem with regression is that statistical difficulties can arise when the scales are highly correlated (Wainer, 1978).

Under the regression model it is possible to test whether adding a new scale to an existing battery of scales will result in enhanced prediction of the criterion. To do this, a multiple regression is performed using the existing variable to predict the criterion. Then the score from a novel scale is added, and its effect on the multiple correlation coefficient is statistically tested. For example, it might be found that adding a new scale might increase R from 0.4 to 0.45. It is possible to perform statistical significance tests to determine whether this increase is more than would be expected by chance; if adding a new variable does increase the predictive power of a battery of scales, it is said to have **incremental validity**, as discussed earlier. The organisation would need to perform some analyses to determine whether the overheads involved in administering the new scale are cost-effective, but this is a matter of econometrics and so will not be considered here.

Westfall and Yarkoni (2016) however point out some major problems when regression models are used to assess incremental validity – problems which are particularly severe when sample sizes are large. They demonstrate that in this case, a variable can appear to have incremental validity when, in fact, it does not. This paper should be read by anyone who contemplates an incremental validity study.

TEST BIAS AND MEASUREMENT INVARIANCE

Scales may sometimes systematically overestimate or underestimate the scores of groups of people. Suppose that a scale measuring general knowledge was given to random samples of people in different countries. If that scale contained plenty of items asking about cricket and darts, it is probable that British respondents would outperform

Americans, and that men might perhaps outperform women. One obviously should not infer from this that British are more knowledgeable than Americans or that men are more knowledgeable than women; the differences between groups almost certainly arise because some of the items are easier for British men for cultural reasons. In other words, the same test score implies a different level of general knowledge, depending whether one is male or female, British or American. This is precisely what is meant by **test bias**.

It is important to reiterate the concerns outlined in Chapter 3 at this point, as we need to make some quite strong assumptions about whether or not the traits that we are trying to measure actually exist and whether test scores form interval scales.

What do we mean when we say that test scores from different groups of people are "equivalent"? Behaviours and the words used to describe them may have different meanings in different cultures (seeking jobs for family members might be responsible or corrupt behaviour; deference to age may or may not be valued), and so it is quite possible that scores on questionnaires will vary because of this – even if the wording is administered without translation. Fontaine (2005) identifies four aspects of equivalence:

- *Functional equivalence*: Can the same theoretical variable account for test behaviour across groups? Does the trait exist in different cultures, even if it is measured in different ways?
- *Structural equivalence*: Does a set of items measure the same trait in two or more groups?
- *Metric equivalence*: Can patterns of scores be compared between groups? If factor analysis used, are the results similar in each groups – for example, showing that the item which best represents the trait in group A is also the best indicator in group B?
- *Full score equivalence*: Can scores be directly compared between cultural groups? Are the levels of scores comparable, so that a score of 20 in one group indicates the same level of the underlying trait as a score of 20 in another group?

BIAS AND GROUP DIFFERENCES

What if there are genuine differences in scores between groups? Can one infer that any test which shows differences between various groups is biased? The answer is a strong "no". It is always possible that differences between groups are real. Several psychological scales show large gender differences (scales measuring aggressiveness, and those measuring psychopathic tendencies, for example), and this is mirrored in everyday life, with men being more involved in violence and being more likely to be sadistic manipulators of others. Thus few would feel unhappy with the conclusion that the group differences detected by these psychological scales are genuine.

It is therefore impossible to conclude that a scale is biased merely by checking whether different groups obtain different average scores on it, as a scale which shows no group differences might be full of biased items. A moment's thought will reveal why: it is quite possible that half the items in an ability scale could be much harder for men than women, whilst the other half could be much easier for women than men. When administered to a sample of men and women, there would be no difference in the mean score, despite the scale being riddled with biased items.

When group differences are found, determining whether these are genuine or whether they occur because the test is unfair to one or more groups of people becomes a major challenge. It is particularly important in the area of cognitive abilities. Here differences in scores between white and black Americans have been consistently found, differences in the order of a standard deviation. The questions are how much of this difference in performance is due to bias in the tests, and how much (if any) is genuine? Readers who want to explore the psychological literature in this area might like to see the still-relevant review by Brown et al. (1999) and Fagan and Holland's (2007) study, which discuss whether the evidence supports theories that social deprivation, differences in language etc. account for the black-white difference.

Eliminating bias from tests requires some sensitivity when writing items. For example, when writing ability tests, there is much to be said for using items which do not involve language. Several tests such as Raven's Matrices (Raven et al., 2003) follow this approach when measuring general intelligence. Using simple, clear language free of slang or concepts which are likely to be more familiar to members of some cultural or social groups than others will help guard against biased items; guidelines for writing such items are given in Chapter 16. However, proper statistical analyses are required to determine where a scale is biased.

EXTERNAL BIAS

External bias involves detecting bias by relating test or questionnaire scores to other things. By definition, if a test is biased, it will underestimate or overestimate the scores of a group of people. So if criterion data are available, it should be able to test for bias by checking how the scores of a group of people – typically a minority group – relate to some criterion – such as how well children perform in school, job performance or something similar.

It is clear that there are four possibilities, as shown in Table 9.1.

If members of the minority group obtain lower scores on the test, and this lower score is reflected in lower performance, it appears as if the group difference is genuine – as long as there is not some other variable (such as language skills) which influences both score

Table 9.1 Relationship between test scores of a minority group and job performance

	Minority group has lower test score	Minority group has same test score
Minority group shows lower performance	Genuine group difference	Test shows bias in favour of minority group
Minority group shows same performance	Test shows bias against minority group	No bias or group difference

on the test and the measure of performance – a major assumption. If so, the test does not seem to be biased against members of the minority group. It does not underestimate their performance. On the other hand, if a minority group has low scores on the test but their performance is higher than would be predicted by their test score, this is clear evidence that the test is biased. The test scores underestimate their potential performance.

It is also possible to think of this in terms of regression. If the regression line predicting performance from test score is the same for both groups, then there is no evidence that the test is biased, as long as there is no confounding variable affecting both test score and performance for members of the minority group. This is because the regression line shows that the relationship between the test score and the criterion is the same for both groups. If the two groups have regression lines which differ in slope or height, then this suggests that the test is biased.

Spreadsheet 9.1 allows this to be explored. It shows the relationship between test score and performance for two groups of people, identified by red and blue points on a scatter diagram. This scatter diagram also shows the regression lines for each group. Two sliders allow the difference in test score between the red and blue groups to be altered; if the top slider is completely to the left, the two groups perform at the same level on the test. If moved to the right, the red group outperforms the blue group. The bottom slider determines whether there is any difference in job performance. Moving it to the right makes the red group perform better than the blue group. It is also possible to alter the correlation between test score and performance for each group which is initially set at 0.7.

Spreadsheet name: Spreadsheet 9.1: Bias

Download from: https://routledge.com/9781032146164/

Purpose: To show how external bias can be detected.

Contents of spreadsheet: Simulated test scores and measures of job performance from two groups of people.

Suggested activity:

(a) Put both sliders to the left, and note that that the regression lines for the two groups are nearly identical. (As before, press f9 or equivalent to generate a different sample of data.)

(b) Move the top slider to the right. Here the blue group perform better on the test, but the work performance is the same for both groups. Note that the two regression lines are at different heights but parallel (press f9 etc. to confirm).

(c) Move both sliders to the right. Now the blue group perform better at the test, and also better at the job – a genuine group difference. Note that the two regression lines are almost identical.

(d) Move the top slider to the left whilst keeping the bottom one to the right. Here both groups perform equally well on the test, but the blue group perform better at work.

Try experimenting with changing the correlation between test score and performance for the two groups.

Points to note:

- Look upwards to see what a test score of (say) 120 would imply about job performance for members of each group in each of the four scenarios.
- Convince yourself that scenario (a) implies no bias and scenario (b) implies bias against members of the red group (their performance is better than what the regression line for the blue group would predict). Scenario (c) implies a genuine group difference, where differences in test scores are reflected in differences in work performance. Scenario (d) implies bias against the blue group.
- Note that differences in the height of the regression lines implies bias.
- If the correlation between the test and performance is different for the two groups, note that the direction of bias changes depending on whether the test score is low or high.
- Therefore, differences in the height or slope of the regression line indicates external bias.
- Experiment by changing entries in the *green* areas. Results are in the *yellow* areas. Simply download another copy if you accidentally change formulae.

Learning outcomes: Readers should now be able to:

- Appreciate that regression can be useful in detecting external bias in test scores.
- Recognise that differences in the slope and/or height of the regression lines can imply bias.
- Appreciate that group differences do not necessarily indicate bias; a group difference may be accompanied by a difference in job performance, as in scenario (c).

Because this form of bias is inferred by looking at the relationship between scale scores and some external criterion, it is known as "external bias".

INTERNAL BIAS

Very often there is no external criterion against which to test the scale, but it may be possible to check for evidence of **internal bias** by analysing the differences between the items in the questionnaire or test. This assumes that if all items in a test are slightly harder for one group than another, this probably indicates a genuine difference between the groups, the reasons for which need to be investigated. However, if some items in a test are much harder for one group, then these items may be biased. Studies of internal bias therefore explore whether people's responses some items in a test or scale are unduly influenced by group membership.

Detection of biased items by analysis of variance

One very simple approach is simply to gather some data from members of two or more groups and perform an analysis of variance,[1] where "items" are the within-subject variable, and "group" is the between-subjects variable, reflecting group membership. The output will show three things. The item effect will just show whether the mean scores for all of the items are the same. It is of no interest. The group effect will show whether the average score (computed across all items) is the same for each group. This may be of some interest. However, the item × group interaction is the really interesting term. This shows whether some items are appreciably more difficult for members of some groups than others. It is then possible to identify these items by analysing simple effects etc. and consider removing them from the scale. The whole process can then be repeated until the item × group interaction term is non-significant. The obvious problem with this approach is that the size of the sample will influence the significance of the interaction; a huge sample is able to identify tiny amounts of bias, and so will end up removing almost all items. Rather than relying on significance tests, it might be more prudent to decide beforehand what effect size indicates that items are biased and use this (rather than the significance level of the interaction) to decide whether to eliminate items. Osterlind (1983) identifies other problems with this technique, too – but the method is both quick and simple.

Detection of biased items using factor analysis

A second approach is simply to factor-analyse the data from each group separately and check that the factor loadings are similar (see Chapter 13). If one item is so inappropriate for members of the group that it simply fails to measure its intended factor, this analysis will show it. However, it will *not* reveal whether an item is more difficult for members of one group rather than another. It is possible to check this using a form of structural equation modelling known as multiple group analysis, but this is beyond the scope of this book.

Detection of biased items using transformed item difficulties

If there are just two groups, another straightforward method is to create a scatter diagram showing the difficulty of the item for each group. For statistical reasons (Angoff & Ford, 1973) it is usual to transform the item-difficulties into z-scores and then change these into a statistic called delta (Δ). These **transformed item difficulties** (TIDs) follow a normal distribution with a mean of 13 and a standard deviation of 4. Possible values of delta thus range from about 0 to 26.

> **Spreadsheet name:** Spreadsheet 9.2: Transformed item difficulties
>
> **Download from:** https://routledge.com/9781032146164/
>
> **Purpose:** To plot transformed item difficulties in order to detect biased items.
>
> **Contents of spreadsheet:** Item difficulties (mean scores) from 16 items.
>
> **Suggested activity:**
>
> - Notice that with the default dataset, items of middling difficulty the difficulty (mean score) of the red group is lower than for the blue group.
> - Change the difference in difficulty of one of the items for and note that the graph shows that the item moves away from the line. The perpendicular distance of a point from the line is an estimate of its degree of bias.
>
> **Points to note:**
>
> - Note that the data points are items, not people.
> - Note that the line is *not* a regression line, as neither set of TIDs can be regarded as the independent variable.
>
> **Learning outcomes: Readers should now be able to:**
>
> - Detect biased items by plotting transformed item difficulties.
> - Appreciate the difference between internal and external bias.

This approach to detecting bias is very straightforward and intuitive; it also works well in practice. However, problems can arise if the items vary in their discrimination power, and some critics may worry about how far from the line an item needs to be in order to be regarded as biased.

Detection of biased items using item response theory

These days, the most popular method for detecting biased items is through the use of **item response theory**. Chapter 15 outlines how this technique may be used to assess bias. However, this requires large samples, makes some rather strong assumptions about the relationship between test scores and ability, and requires specialised software. Hence, many practitioners will be content with the methods outlined here. For those who wish to read further, the definitive (older) text on detecting bias is Jensen (1980). Reynolds and Suzuki's (2013) chapter provides an excellent short summary of more recent research.

SUMMARY

Establishing whether a scale accurately reflects some underlying attribute of people is clearly of vital importance. Borsboom's suggestion that psychology needs to focus on understanding how, precisely, individual differences in the attribute influences the way in which people respond to items is surprisingly radical; most validation studies focus on relating scores on scales to behaviour, or to scores on other scales. This is problematical. For a scale might predict behaviour even if it does not measure the trait which it supposed to (the R-S Scale mentioned at the start of this chapter would probably predict behaviour, but because it measured anxiety rather than anything more esoteric). We also saw that if scales contain items which are similar in meaning, this can cause surprisingly large correlations between them – which could easily confuse those performing studies of construct validation. It is also important to check whether scales are equally valid for all groups, which is where the notion of test bias becomes important.

Whatever its form, validation is an incremental process – gathering data from a variety of sources to help one determine whether a trait or state actually exists, how the state or trait causes people to respond differently to items in a scale, and/or whether it is useful for anything. All too often, though, researchers act as if the existence of a trait is a given, just because they have developed a scale. A strong dose of scepticism is needed whenever any psychologist proposes a "new" trait.

NOTE

1 Or presumably a multivariate analysis of variance.

CHAPTER 10
INTRODUCTION TO FACTOR ANALYSIS

Few techniques in psychometrics are as useful as **factor analysis**. It can be used to determine whether all of the items in a scale measure the same trait. It can be used to check whether the items in a test work properly – whether they all form scales as they are supposed to. It can help us check whether several different traits do in fact measure the same thing – for example, whether scales supposedly measuring anxiety, emotional instability, depression and defensiveness really do measure four distinct (but possibly correlated) traits, or whether some of these traits are identical to others. It can be used to generate theories of personality, cognitive abilities and suchlike. And (with a little ingenuity) it can be used to develop scales which measure mood, and to develop hierarchical models of personality, ability, mood etc. This chapter introduces the broad concepts of factor analysis. Details of how to perform and interpret factor analyses are covered in Chapter 11. Chapter 13 suggests how hierarchical models may be useful – particularly when analysing questionnaires which may contain items which are near synonyms. And Chapter 12 considers how factor analysis can be used for other purposes – e.g., to develop scales which measure moods, to identify groups of *people* (rather than items) and thus clinical syndromes, or to analyse longitudinal data.

"Factor analysis" can refer to two very different statistical techniques. **Exploratory factor analysis** is the older (and simpler) technique and forms the basis of Chapters 10–12 and the first part of Chapter 13. **Confirmatory factor analysis** and its extensions (sometimes known as "structural equation modelling", "latent variable analysis" or "LISREL models") are useful in many areas other than individual differences and are particularly popular in social psychology. A brief outline of **this** technique is given at the end of Chapter 13. Authors do not always make it clear whether exploratory or confirmatory factor analysis has been used. If the term "factor analysis" is used in a journal, it normally refers to an exploratory factor analysis, so called because it explores the structure of the data. The great thing about exploratory factor analysis is that it does not try to test any preconceived model about the structure of a set of data. Instead, it lets the data speak for themselves.

DOI: 10.4324/9781003240181-10

Chapter 1 showed why it is important that the items in a scale all measure one (and only one) psychological variable, and Chapter 7 introduced coefficient alpha as a measure of the reliability of a scale. This *assumes* that all of the items in a test form one scale; we showed that a large reliability coefficient can be obtained even if a set of items measure two or more completely different traits, as alpha is based on the average correlation between a set of items. If items 1–3 intercorrelate 0.8 and items 4–6 also intercorrelate 0.8 but all the other correlations are zero, it is obvious that the scale measures two things, but coefficient alpha will be substantial (it is 0.74).

The factor-analytic approach does away with the dangerous assumption that a set of items forms a single scale. It analyses people's responses to a sample of items and *discovers* how many distinct scales that set of items measures and which items belong to which scale(s).

Suppose that a psychologist administered 20 vocabulary items, 20 comprehension items and 20 anagram problems to a group of volunteers. Do they all measure a single "verbal ability"? Or because the anagram items involve thinking (rather than just knowing the meaning of words in and out of context), perhaps the items involving anagrams might measure one trait and the comprehension/vocabulary items might form another? Or do the items measure three quite distinct (but perhaps correlated) traits? Factor analysis can tell us this, and so it is a very useful technique for determining how many different constructs are measured by a set of variables. All one needs to do is make some assumptions about the data (for example, whether the responses to the items should be regarded as interval or ordinal measurements), gather some data from a fairly large sample (normally several hundred people) and find a computer program to perform the factor analysis. The computer program is necessary because factor analysis involves a lot of computation, and most analyses would take weeks to perform by hand. However, excellent free software is available, as outlined in Chapter 11.

Rather than factor analysing responses to individual items, it is also possible to factor-analyse total scores on scales. One might simply score the three tests mentioned earlier, as described in Chapter 4. Then these scores on the vocabulary, comprehension and anagram scales can be put into a factor analysis, perhaps alongside some other variables.

In factor analysis, the word "factor" is usually used instead of the word "construct" or "trait", and we shall follow this convention from now on. Exploratory factor analysis essentially does two things:

- It shows how many distinct psychological constructs (factors) are measured by a set of variables. Do the 60 ability items measure one, two, three or perhaps more distinct abilities?
- It shows which variables measure which constructs. In the first example, it might show that the vocabulary items and the comprehension items all measure the same thing, whilst the anagram items measure something different. It can even show how

well each of the items measure each construct. For example, it might be found that the 1st, 5th and 16th vocabulary items and the 4th and 11th comprehension items do not really measure anything – perhaps because they are so easy that almost everyone gets them correct, or so hard that everyone gets them wrong (or guesses randomly). Thus factor analysis can also be a very useful tool for scale construction.

The technique is not restricted to test items or test scores. It would be possible to factor-analyse reaction times from various types of cognitive test in order to determine which (if any) of these tasks were related. Alternatively, suppose that one took a group of schoolchildren who had no specific training or practice in sport, and assessed their performance in 30 sports by any mixture of coaches' ratings, timings, mean length of throw, percentage of maiden overs obtained, goals scored or whatever performance measure is most appropriate for each sport. The only proviso is that each child must compete in each sport. Factor analysis could reveal whether individuals who were good at one ball game tended to be good at all of them, whether short-distance and long-distance track events formed two distinct groupings (and which events belonged to which group) and so on. Thus instead of having to talk in terms of performance in 30 distinct areas, it would be possible to summarise this information by talking in terms of half a dozen basic sporting abilities (or however many abilities the factor analysis revealed). The technique is used outside psychology, too – for example, in spectroscopy (chemistry) and genetic research. Basically, factor analysis is a powerful tool for data reduction; if we measure a large number of variables, it tells us whether and where there is appreciable overlap between them.

EXPLORATORY FACTOR ANALYSIS BY INSPECTION

The top section of Table 10.1 shows a six-item questionnaire. Six students were asked to answer each question, using a 5-point rating scale as shown in the table; their responses are shown towards the bottom of the table.

Eagle-eyed readers may notice some trends in these data. Individuals' responses to questions 1, 2 and 3 tend to be similar. Stephen tends to agree with all three of them, Olivia tends to disagree with them, whilst the others feel more or less neutral about them. These are rough approximations, of course, but you can see that no one who rates themselves as "1" or "2" on one of these three questions gives themselves a "4" or "5" on one of the others. This may suggest that enjoying socialising, acting on impulse and having a cheerful disposition correlate together, and so these three items might be expected to form a scale. Much the same applies to items 4 to 6. Again, people such as Stephen or Olivia who give themselves a low rating on one of these three questions also give themselves a low rating on the other two questions, whilst Christine gives herself high ratings on all three questions.

Table 10.1 Six-item personality questionnaire and the responses of six students

Q1	I enjoy socialising	1	2	3	4	5
Q2	I often act on impulse	1	2	3	4	5
Q3	I am a cheerful sort of person	1	2	3	4	5
Q4	I often feel depressed	1	2	3	4	5
Q5	It is difficult for me to get to sleep at night	1	2	3	4	5
Q6	Large crowds make me feel anxious	1	2	3	4	5
For each question, please circle ONE NUMBER which describes your reaction to each statement.							
Circle "5" if you strongly agree that a statement describes you very accurately.							
Circle "4" if it describes you fairly accurately.							
Circle "3" if you are neutral or unsure.							
Circle "2" if you feel that the statement does not really describe you accurately.							
Circle "1" if you feel strongly that the statement definitely does not describe you accurately.							

	Q1	Q2	Q3	Q4	Q5	Q6
Stephen	5	5	4	1	1	2
Olivia	1	2	1	1	1	2
Paul	3	4	3	4	5	4
Janette	4	4	3	1	2	1
Michael	3	3	4	1	2	2
Christine	3	3	3	5	4	5

Thus there seem to be two clusters of questions in this questionnaire. The first group consists of questions 1, 2 and 3, and the second group consists of questions 4, 5 and 6. However, spotting these relationships by eye is very difficult. Nor is it particularly scientific, as different people might come to different conclusions. Fortunately, some simple statistics can help.

If we make the common, but probably unwarranted assumption that the thing we are trying to measure is quantitative and the numbers representing the responses to the questionnaire behave in much the same was as numbers corresponding to physical measurements (see Chapter 3), we might think it appropriate to calculate Pearson correlations between the six variables. These correlations are shown in Table 10.2. They confirm our suspicions about the relationships between the students' responses to questions 1 to 3 and questions 4 to 6. Questions 1 to 3 correlate strongly together (0.933, 0.824 and 0.696, respectively) but hardly at all with questions 4 to 6 (−0.096 etc.). Similarly, questions 4 to 6 correlate highly together (0.896, 0.965 and 0.808, respectively), but hardly at all with questions 1 to 3. Thus it is possible to see from the table of

INTRODUCTION TO FACTOR ANALYSIS

Table 10.2 Correlations between scores on the items from Table 10.1

	Q1	Q2	Q3	Q4	Q5	Q6
Q1	1.000					
Q2	0.933	1.000				
Q3	0.824	0.696	1.000			
Q4	−0.096	−0.052	0.000	1.000		
Q5	−0.005	0.058	0.111	0.896	1.000	
Q6	−0.167	−0.127	0.000	0.965	0.808	1.000

correlations that questions 1 to 3 form one natural group and questions 4 to 6 form another – that is, the questionnaire actually measures two constructs or "factors", one comprising the first three questions and the other consisting of the final three questions.

Whilst it is easy to see this from the correlations in Table 10.2, it should be remembered that the correlations shown there are hardly typical.

- The data were constructed so that the correlations between the variables were either very large or very small. In real life, correlations between variables would rarely be larger than 0.5, with many in the range 0.2–0.3. This makes it difficult to identify patterns by eye.
- The questions were ordered so that the large correlations fell next to each other in Table 10.2. If the questions had been presented in a different order, it would not be so easy to identify clusters of large correlations.
- Only six questions were used, so there are only 15 correlations to consider. With 40 questions there would be $\frac{40 \times 39}{2} = 780$ correlations to consider, making it much more difficult to identify groups of intercorrelated items.

Well-known mathematical methods can be used to identify factors from groups of variables which tend to correlate together, and even the very largest factor analyses can now be performed on a desktop computer.

A GEOMETRIC APPROACH TO FACTOR ANALYSIS

It is possible to represent correlation matrices geometrically. Variables are represented by straight lines which are of equal length and which all start at the same point. These lines are positioned such that the correlation between the variables is represented by the cosine of the angle between them. Table 10.3 shows a few cosines to give you a general idea of the

Table 10.3 Table of cosines

Angle (in degrees)	Cosine of angle
0	1.000
15	0.966
30	0.867
45	0.707
60	0.500
75	0.259
90	0.000
120	−0.500
150	−0.867
180	−1.000
210	−0.867
240	−0.500
270	0.000
300	0.500
330	0.867

concept. When the angle between two lines is small, the cosine is large and positive: the lines point in much the same direction. When two lines are at right angles, the correlation (cosine) is zero: the lines point in different directions. When the two lines are pointing in opposite directions, the correlation (cosine) is negative: the lines point in opposite directions.

It is sometimes possible to represent entire correlation matrices geometrically. A line is drawn anywhere on the page representing one of the variables – it does not matter which one. The other variables are represented by other lines of equal length, all of which fan out from one end of the first line. The angles between the variables are measured in a clockwise direction. Variables which have large positive correlations between them will fall close to each other, as Table 10.3 shows that large correlations (or cosines) result in small angles between the lines. Highly correlated variables point in the same direction, variables with large negative correlations between them point in opposite directions, and variables which are uncorrelated point in completely different directions. Figure 10.1 shows a simple example based on three variables. The correlation between V1 and V2 is 0.0; the correlation between V1 and V3 is 0.5, and the correlation between V2 and V3 is 0.867. The correlation between V1 and V2 is represented by a pair of lines of equal length joined at one end; as the correlation between these variables is 0.0, the angle between them corresponds to a cosine of 0.0; that is, 90 degrees. The correlation between V1 and V3 is 0.5, corresponding to an angle of 60 degrees, and that between V2 and V3 is 0.867 (30 degrees), so V2 and V3 are positioned as shown.

INTRODUCTION TO FACTOR ANALYSIS

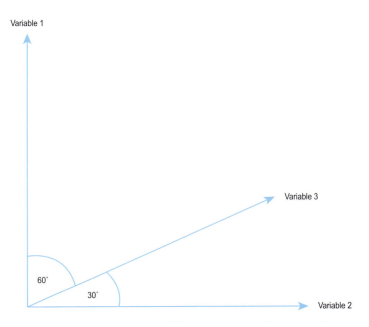

Figure 10.1 Geometric representation of the correlations between three variables

It is not always possible to represent correlations in two dimensions (i.e., on a flat sheet of paper). If the correlations represented in Figure 10.1 had not been chosen carefully, one of the lines would have to project outward from the page to some degree. This is no problem for the underlying mathematics of factor analysis, but it does mean that it is not possible to use this geometric technique to perform real-life factor analyses.

Figure 10.2 is a fairly good approximation of the data shown in Table 10.2. Ignoring lines F1 and F2 for the moment, the correlations between variables 1, 2 and 3 shown in this figure are all very large and positive (that is, the angles between these lines are small). Similarly, the correlations between variables 4 to 6 are also large and positive. As variables 1 to 3 have near-zero correlations with variables 4 to 6, variables 1, 2 and 3 are at 90 degrees to variables 4, 5 and 6. Computer programs for factor analysis essentially try to "explain" the correlations between the variables in terms of a smaller number of factors. It is good practice to talk about **common factors** rather than just "factors" – later on we will encounter "**unique factors**", and it is safest to avoid confusion. In this example, it is clear that there are two clusters of correlations, so the information in Table 10.2 can be approximated by two common factors, each of which passes through a group of large correlations. The common factors are indicated by the lines labelled F1 and F2 in Figure 10.2.

It should be clear that, from measuring the angle between each common factor and each variable, it is also possible to calculate the *correlations* between each variable and each common factor. Variables 1, 2 and 3 will all have very large correlations with factor 1 (in fact variable 2 will have a correlation of nearly 1.0 with factor 1, as factor 1

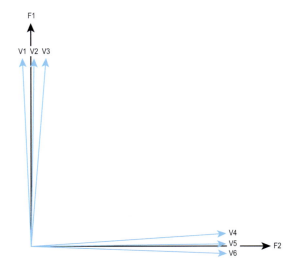

Figure 10.2 Graphical illustration of the data in Table 10.2

lies virtually on top of it). Variables 1, 2 and 3 will have correlations of about zero with factor 2, as they are virtually at right angles to it. Similarly, factor 2 is highly correlated with variables 4 to 6, and is virtually uncorrelated with variables 1 to 3 (because of the 90-degree angle between these variables and this factor). Do not worry for now where these factors come from, or how they are positioned relative to the variables, as this will be covered in Chapter 11. It is possible to show all the correlations between every item and every common factor in a table, called the **factor structure matrix**. The correlations between items and common factors are usually known as **factor loadings**. By convention, the common factors are shown as the columns of this table and the variables as the rows. The values in Table 10.4 were obtained by looking at the angles between each common factor and each variable in Figure 10.2, and translating these (roughly) into correlations using Table 10.3.

In the example, the two groups of variables (and hence the common factors) are at right angles to each other – what is known technically as an **orthogonal** solution – an important term.

HOW TO NAME FACTORS

Factors can be tentatively named by noting which variables have loadings that are more extreme than some arbitrary value. By convention, the cut-off value is 0.4 or 0.3, which implies an angle of 60–75 degrees between the variable and the common factor. The easiest way to see which variables "belong" to a factor is thus to underline

INTRODUCTION TO FACTOR ANALYSIS

Table 10.4 Orthogonal factors showing the correlations from Figure 10.2

Variable	Factor 1	Factor 2	Communality
V1 (enjoy socialising)	0.90	0.10	0.82
V2 (act on impulse)	0.98	0.00	0.96
V3 (cheerful)	0.90	−0.10	0.82
V4 (depressed)	0.10	0.85	0.73
V5 (sleep disturbance)	0.00	0.98	0.96
V6 (anxious)	−0.10	0.85	0.73
Eigenvalue	2.60	2.42	

those that have loadings higher than 0.4 or less than −0.4. Table 10.4 shows that factor 1 is a mixture of V1, V2 and V3 (but not V4, V5 or V6). Likewise, factor 2 is a mixture of V4, V5 and V6. Thus the factor matrix can be used to give a tentative label to each common factor. Suppose that the variables represent the six test items shown in Table 10.1. Finding that V1–V3 form a factor allows us to suggest that F1 may be "extraversion" or something similar, whilst F2 might be "neuroticism". There is no guarantee that labels given like this are necessarily correct. It is necessary to validate the factor exactly as described in Chapter 9 in order to ensure that this label is accurate.

It is important to appreciate that factor analysis has actually shown us that V1–V3 form a factor, as do V4–V6. We have not just looked at the names of the variables and decided to group them together. Factor analysis shows us what structure really exists in the data – without any need for us to specify any sort of theory.

EIGENVALUES AND COMMUNALITIES

For orthogonal solutions, the square of the correlation shows how much variance is shared by two variables – or in simpler language, how much they overlap. Two variables which correlate 0.8 share 0.8^2 or 0.64 or 64% of their variance. As factor loadings are merely correlations between common factors and items, it follows that the square of each factor loading shows the amount of overlap between each variable and the common factor. This simple finding forms the basis of two other main uses of the factor matrix.

EIGENVALUES

It is possible to calculate how much of the variance each common factor accounts for. A common factor that accounts for 40% of the overlap between the variables in the original correlation matrix is clearly more important than another, which explains only 20% of the variance. Once again it is necessary to assume that the common factors are orthogonal (at right angles to each other). The first step is to calculate what is known as an **eigenvalue** for each factor by squaring the factor loadings and summing down the columns. Using the data shown in Table 10.4, the eigenvalue of factor 1 is $0.90^2 + 0.98^2 + 0.90^2 + 0.10^2 + 0.0^2 + (−0.10)^2$, or 2.60. If the eigenvalue is divided by the number of variables (six in this instance), it shows what proportion of variance is explained by this common factor. Here factor 1 explains 0.43 or 43% of the information in the original correlation matrix.

COMMUNALITIES

If the common factors are at right angles (an orthogonal solution), it is also simple to calculate how much of the variance of each variable is measured by all of the factors (combined), by merely summing the squared factor loadings across factors. It can be seen from Table 10.4 that $0.90^2 + 0.10^2 = 0.82$ of the variance of test 1 is "explained" by the two factors. This amount is called the **communality** of that variable.

A variable with a large communality has a large degree of overlap with one or more common factors. A low communality implies that the common factors do not overlap much with that variable. This might mean that the variable measures something which is conceptually quite different from the other variables in the analysis. For example, one personality item among 100 ability test items would have a communality close to zero. A low communality might also mean that a particular item is heavily influenced by measurement error or extreme difficulty, e.g., an ability item which is so easy that everyone chose the same answer, or where no one could understand the question and so everyone guessed. Whatever the reason, a low communality implies that an item does not overlap with the common factors, either because it measures a different concept, because of excessive measurement error or because there are few individual differences in the way in which people respond to the item.

OBLIQUE FACTORS

Thus far we have assumed that the factors are at right angles to each other; however this need not always be the case. Consider the correlations in Figure 10.3. Here it would clearly make sense to allow the factors to become correlated, and to place one common factor through each cluster of variables; if the factors were kept at right angles, they would not pass through each cluster of variables.

Here the two factors are correlated with each other, and each factor is correlated with each variable. Factor analyses where the factors are themselves correlated (i.e., not at right angles) are known as **oblique solutions**. The correlations between the factors

INTRODUCTION TO FACTOR ANALYSIS

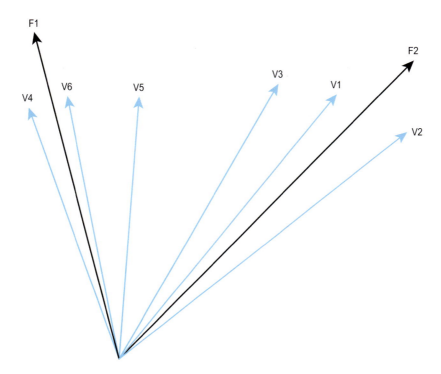

Figure 10.3 Correlations between six variables showing two correlated factors

form what is called a **factor correlation matrix**. In this example the correlation between the two factors is about 60 degrees, so (using Table 10.3) the correlation between them is approximately 0.5.

There is a problem when interpreting oblique rotations. It was easy to see which variables belonged with each of the factors when the variables and the factors were orthogonal (Table 10.4), because the correlations between each variable and each factor were either close to zero or quite large. When the factors are correlated, it is harder to see which variables belong to which factor. For example, as V1–V3 are appreciably correlated with factor 2 (as well as having large correlations with factor 1) the factor structure matrix will be as shown in Table 10.5. Variable 5, for example, is reasonably close to both factors and so has a fairly appreciable correlation with both of them in the factor structure matrix.

It is therefore usual to interpret a different table known as the **factor pattern** matrix. This too is shown in Table 10.5. The pattern matrix essentially corrects for the correlations between the factors and makes it easier to see which variables belong with each factor. The numbers in the pattern matrix are actually regression coefficients (not correlations) and they can, occasionally, be greater than 1.0.

Table 10.5 Approximate oblique factor structure and factor pattern matrices from Figure 10.3

	Factor structure matrix		Factor pattern matrix	
Variable	Factor 1	Factor 2	Factor 1	Factor 2
V1	0.56	0.31	0.52	0.12
V2	0.76	0.22	0.78	−0.06
V3	0.51	0.17	0.51	−0.02
V4	0.01	0.67	−0.16	0.73
V5	0.43	0.60	0.24	0.51
V6	0.35	0.58	0.16	0.52

FACTOR ANALYSIS AND PRINCIPAL COMPONENTS ANALYSIS

In Table 10.4, we calculated that 82% of the variation of people's scores on test 1 was explained by the first two factors. What happened to the remaining 18%? It turns out that the answer depends on what sort of assumptions we want to make.

PRINCIPAL COMPONENTS ANALYSIS

It should be obvious that if we have three variables (V1–V3), then whatever the correlations are between the variables, it is possible to represent them in three dimensions. (Imagine three pencils with the points all touching – whichever the angles between them, they can be represented in three dimensions.) The number of dimensions used to represent a set of data corresponds to the number of factors. Thus a factor matrix showing as many factors as there are variables could look like the one shown in Table 10.6.

Note all of the communalities (h^2) are 1.0. However, if we only considered the first two factors, the communality of each variable would obviously be less than 1 (it would be 0.85 in the case of V1). So one possible reason why the two factors did not explain all of the variance is simply because there were fewer factors than variables. Putting it another way, some of the lines in Figure 10.2 will not fit exactly onto the two dimensions defined by these two factors; some of the lines will need to stick out of the page or go behind the page to properly represent the correlations. Thus some of the lines are slightly shorter than others when projected onto the two dimensions of Figure 10.2. If we had used six factors rather than two, then all the communalities would be exactly 1.0.

Table 10.6 Loadings of three variables (V1–V3) on three orthogonal factors (F1–F3) from a principal components analysis

	F1	F2	F3	h²
V1	0.6	0.7	0.38	1
V2	0.7	0.7	0.14	1
V3	0.8	0.5	0.33	1

So according to this model, the reason why we lost 18% of the variance when calculating communalities is because we are trying to squeeze the information which needs to be represented in six dimensions into two dimensions; some information will be lost by doing so. Of course, this trade-off is often worthwhile. Knowing that two traits do a very good job of approximating six means that it is possible to shorten the time taken to make assessments, and it may also be useful for theoretical purposes – for example, to debunk the idea that the items in a newly devised scale really measure anything different from those in older scales, or to discover that ratings based on a sample of all the adjectives in the English language typically produce five personality factors (McCrae & John, 1992).

This model is known as the **principal components** model. The key thing to note is that if as many factors are extracted as there are variables, then the communality of each variable will be exactly 1.0. In other words, the principal components model can potentially explain all of the variance in a set of data – though by choosing fewer factors than there are variables, we may sometimes decide that a smaller number of factors will provide a good enough approximation.

More formally, the principal components model states that, for any variable being analysed,

total variance = common factor variance + measurement error

Suppose we construct a test in which 10 items inquire about worries and negative moods: "My moods vary a lot", "I feel agitated in confined spaces", "I get embarrassed easily" etc., with each item being answered on a 5-point scale ranging from "very like me" to "not at all like me". Suppose that we know that all these items form a single factor of "neuroticism". The principal components model therefore states that the way a person answers an item depends only on their level of neuroticism plus some measurement error. It is the same assumption that was made in Chapter 6 when discussing reliability, and it implies that when as many factors are extracted as there are variables, these common factors can explain all of the information in the correlation matrix.

FACTOR ANALYSIS

The assumption that anything that is not measured by common factors must just be measurement error is rather a strong one. Each test item may have some morsel of **unique variance** that is special to that item but which cannot be shared with other items. Factor analysis suggests that each variable has a "unique factor" associated with it, which describes variation in scores which is not measurement error but which is not shared with any other factors. The extent to which people fear enclosed spaces may not be completely determined by their level of neuroticism; people may just vary somewhat in the extent to which they show fear of being shut in, perhaps as a result of childhood experiences. So to predict how a person would respond to the item, you would need to consider:

- Their level of neuroticism (common factor loading)
- Their level of this particular fear of being enclosed (unique factor loading).

You also need to recognise that there will always be some random measurement error.

When performing a factor analysis (rather than a principal components analysis), it is therefore necessary to estimate how much unique variance is associated with each variable before performing the factor analysis. We explore how to do this in Chapter 11.

Readers familiar with multiple regression might like to think of the issue in these terms. If we gather data on six variables and try to predict people's scores on one of the variables from their scores on the other five, then the multiple correlation could, in principle, be 1.0. On the other hand, the factor model suggests that there is something special about each variable which cannot be predicted by knowing people's scores on any other variables – and so the multiple correlation will be less than 1.

The *factor-analysis* model thus assumes that for any variable or item being factor-analysed,

total variance = common factor variance + unique factor variance + measurement error

The amount of unique factor variance in an item is reflected in its communality. The more variance an item shares with the other items in the test, the higher are its correlations with both them and the common factors, therefore the higher its communality will be. (Remind yourself how communality is calculated in order to check this.) Thus whilst some of the "missing 18%" of variance in the previous example will be due to extracting two factors instead of six, some of this 18% will also reflect the fact that the communalities are less than 1.0. An item with some unique factor variance will therefore never have a communality as large as 1.0, even if the factor analysis extracts as many factors as there are variables. Some people are just more (or less) afraid of enclosed spaces than you would expect from knowing their level of neuroticism.

It follows that factor analysis is a more mathematically complicated process than principal components analysis. Whereas principal components analysis merely has to determine the number of factors to be extracted and how each variable should correlate with each factor, factor analysis also has to estimate how much of a variable's variance is "common-factor" variance and how much is unique to that particular variable and cannot be shared with any other variable.

In practice, it does not seem to matter too much whether one performs a principal components analysis or a factor analysis, as both techniques generally lead to similar results. In fact, the authorities on factor analysis can be divided into three groups. Some believe that factor analysis should never be used. According to B. Stamm (personal communication, 1995), Leyland Wilkinson fought to keep factor-analysis options out of his SYSTAT statistics package, although commercial pressures eventually won. On the other hand, some maintain that a form of factor analysis is the *only* justifiable technique (e.g., Carroll, 1993), and finally, some pragmatists argue that, as both techniques generally produce highly similar solutions, it does not really matter which of them one uses (Tabachnick & Fidell, 2018).

One slightly worrying problem is that the loadings obtained from component analyses are always larger than those which result from factor analyses, as the former assume that each variable has a communality of 1.0, whereas the latter computes a value for the communality which is generally less than 1.0. Thus the results obtained from a principal components analysis always look more impressive (i.e., have larger common factor loadings) than the results of a factor analysis. This has clear implications for many rules of thumb, such as regarding factor loadings above 0.4 (or less than −0.4) as being "salient" and disregarding those between −0.39 and +0.39. It is also vitally important that authors of papers should state clearly whether they have followed the factor-analysis or component-analysis model. Some authors mention "factor analysis" in the text even though they have performed principal components analysis.

USES OF FACTOR ANALYSIS

Factor analysis has three main uses in psychology.

TEST CONSTRUCTION

First, it may be used to construct tests. For example, 50 items might be written more or less at random; we do not have to assume that they all measure the same trait or state. The items would then be administered to a representative sample of several hundred individuals and scored (in the case of ability tests) so that a correct answer is coded as 1 and an incorrect answer as 0. Responses that are made using Likert scales (as with most personality and attitude questionnaires) are simply entered in their raw form – 1 point if box (a) is endorsed, 2 if (b) is chosen etc. The responses to these 50 items are then correlated together and factor-analysed. The items that have high loadings on each factor measure the same underlying psychological construct, and so form a scale. Thus it is possible to determine how to score the questionnaire in future simply by looking at the factor matrix; if items 1, 2, 10 and 12 are the only items that have substantial loadings on one factor, then one scale of the test should be the sum of these four items and no others.

It is likely that some items will fail to load substantially on any of the factors (i.e., show low communalities). This could happen for a number of reasons; in the case of ability tests the items could be so easy (or hard) that there is little or no variation in people's scores. Personality items may refer to uncommon actions or feelings where there is again little variation – e.g., "There are occasions in my life when I have felt afraid", an item with which *everyone* is likely to agree. Or items may fail because they are severely influenced by measurement error or because they measure something different from any of the others that were administered. Test constructors do not usually worry about precisely why items fail to work as expected. Items that fail to load a factor are simply discarded without further ado. Thus factor analysis can show at a stroke:

- How many distinct scales are present.
- Which items belong to which scales (so indicating how the test should be scored).
- Which items in a test should be discarded.

Each of the scales then needs to be validated, e.g., by calculating scores for each person on each factor and examining the construct validity and/or predictive validity of these scales. For example, scores on the factors may be correlated with scores on other questionnaires, used to predict educational success etc.

CONCEPTUAL SIMPLIFICATION

The second main use of factor is in conceptual simplification. Huge numbers of tests have been developed to measure personality from different theoretical perspectives, and it is not at all obvious whether these overlap. If we take six scales that measure personality traits, it is useful to know how much overlap there is between them. Do they really each assess quite different aspects of personality? At the other extreme, might they perhaps all measure the same trait under different names? Or is the truth somewhere in the middle? To find out, it is simply necessary to administer the test items to a large sample, then factor-analyse the correlations between the items.
This will show precisely what the underlying structure truly is. For example, two factors may be found. The first factor may have large loadings from all the items in tests 1, 5 and 6. All the substantial loadings on the second factor may come from items in tests 2, 3 and 4. Hence, it is clear that tests 1, 5 and 6 measure precisely the same thing,

as do tests 2, 3 and 4. Any high-flown theoretical distinctions about subtle differences between the scales can be shown to have no basis in fact, and any rational psychologists seeing the results of such an analysis should be forced to think in terms of two (rather than six) theoretical constructs – a considerable simplification.

REFINING QUESTIONNAIRES

As mentioned in Chapter 9, the third main use of factor analysis is for checking the psychometric properties of questionnaires, particularly when they are to be used in new cultures or populations, or prior to calculating their reliability. For example, suppose that the manual of an Australian personality test suggests that it should be scored by adding together the scores on all the odd-numbered items to form one scale, whilst all the even-numbered items form another. When the test is given to a sample of people in the UK and the correlations between the items are calculated and factor-analysed, two factors should be found, with all the odd-numbered items having substantial loadings on one factor and all the even-numbered items loading substantially on the other. This is known as establishing the factorial validity of a scale. If this structure is *not* found, it shows that there are problems with the questionnaire, which should not be scored or used in its conventional form.

SUMMARY

It is easy to see why factor analysis is so important in psychometrics. The same statistical technique can be used to construct tests, resolve theoretical disputes about the number and nature of factors measured by tests and questionnaires, and check whether tests work as they should or whether it is legitimate to use a particular test within a different population or a different culture. You may even have wondered whether the size of the eigenvalue obtained when factoring a test that has just one factor running through it has any link to the test's reliability; see omega on page 160.

This chapter provided a basic introduction to the principles of factor analysis. It left many questions unanswered, such as:

- How does one decide how many factors are needed to describe a set of data?
- How can computer programs actually perform factor analysis?
- What types of data can usefully be factor-analysed?
- How should the results obtained from factor-analytical studies be interpreted and reported?
- Is it possible to correlate *people* together, rather than correlating items together?
- What happens if the correlations between factors are themselves factor-analysed?

These and other issues will be explored in the next three chapters.

CHAPTER 11
PERFORMING AND INTERPRETING FACTOR ANALYSES

Whilst Chapter 10 gave an overview of the basic principles of factor analysis, it deliberately omitted the detail needed to either perform factor analyses or evaluate the technical adequacy of published studies. This chapter provides such detail.

Factor analysis involves a serious amount of computation, making it unfeasible to perform calculations by hand. Nor is it straightforward to perform factor analyses using spreadsheets, unless these use macros or matrix algebra extensions. Because the underlying mathematics is rather more complex than for the straightforward analyses encountered so far, even if we *were* to write spreadsheets to perform factor analyses, it would be difficult for readers to amend them. To learn how to perform and interpret factor analyses it makes more sense to actually perform different analyses (for example, using different numbers of variables and participants, different types of correlations, different methods of factor rotation and/or different methods for determining the optimal number of factors to rotate), rather than getting into the computational minutiae which are likely to baffle any readers who do not have a strong mathematical background.

Fortunately, there is an excellent (and free) factor analysis package available for users of Windows (Lorenzo-Seva & Ferrando, 2006), and I will assume that readers have access to this; Macintosh and Linux users can run it using an emulator. It can be downloaded from https://psico.fcep.urv.cat/utilitats/factor/index.html along with support materials (manuals, video etc.).

Confirmatory factor analyses (see Chapter 13) requires a different package. Free versions include the student version of LISREL (although this has limitations on the size of analyses which can be performed) or Onyx (also known as Ωnyx), which is Java-based and so should run on most systems (von Oertzen et al., 2015). Readers who are familiar with the R statistical environment (R Core Team, 2013) can perform all the analyses described in this chapter using Bill Revelle's superb "Psych" package for R (Revelle, 2017c) for exploratory factor analysis or the Lavaan package for confirmatory analyses – though R can hardly be described as user-friendly. Other statistical packages such as SPSS, SAS and SYSTAT can be used by aficionados, but with difficulty. For example, it will be necessary to roll up one's sleeves and use syntax commands to persuade SPSS to perform anything but the most basic analyses.

DOI: 10.4324/9781003240181-11

There are 10 basic stages involved in performing an exploratory factor analysis. The first nine are discussed in what follows, and the final one in Chapter 13.

- Planning
    - Stage 1. Ensure that the data are suitable for factor analysis.
    - Stage 2. Ensure that the sample size is large enough.
- Analysing
    - Stage 3. Decide how to calculate correlations.
    - Stage 4. Decide on the model: factor analysis or component analysis.
    - Stage 5. Decide how many factors are needed to represent the data.
    - Stage 6. If using factor (rather than component) analysis, estimate the communality of each variable.
    - Stage 7. Produce factors giving the desired communalities (factor extraction).
    - Stage 8. Rotate these factors so that they provide a replicable solution ("simple structure").
    - Stage 9. Optionally compute factor scores.
    - Stage 10. Optionally perform hierarchical analyses, if appropriate.

One of the problems with factor analysis is that the computer programs used will almost always produce an answer of some kind, and by trying to analyse the data using many different techniques, taking out different numbers of factors and concentrating on different subsets of variables, it is possible to pull something semi-plausible from the most ghastly study. Indeed, there are some areas of the discipline, such as the repertory grid technique, where this is the norm. It is vital that those who use the technique or read the literature should have an understanding of the design and execution of factor-analytical studies. Hence, this chapter begins with a look at the types of data which may usefully be factor-analysed.

STAGE 1: SUITABILITY OF DATA FOR FACTOR ANALYSIS

Notwithstanding Michell's (1997) critique, most psychologists regard the numbers which they analyse (scores on questionnaires, rating scales, responses to individual items and so on) as having the same properties as real, physical measures. In other words, it is probably safe to assume that anyone reading this far has decided to be pragmatic; readers may need to perform analyses on data from questionnaires and tests in order to pass examinations or to use tests in the real world, and so whilst they may acknowledge these issues at an intellectual level, they do not have the luxury of taking a stand on it. The rest of this chapter (and indeed, this book) therefore makes the major assumption that psychologists can measure quantities using tests.

However, even the most cavalier test user must sometimes recognise that the numbers which they so revere may give rise to misleading results. Chapter 6 dealt with correlations and showed that the following (amongst other things) can influence the size and in some cases even the direction of the correlation between two variables:

- Differences in scores between sub-groups of people
- Variables having different distributions of scores – for example, where one is skewed and the other is not
- Measuring variables which are discrete rather than continuous, particularly when the number of categories is small as when responses to ability items are coded as correct or incorrect
- Using a sample where the range of scores differs from what is normally found in the population – for example, basing an analysis of cognitive tests on scores from university students and people with learning difficulties, or IQ with just a sample of university students
- Making errors when handling missing data.

As the first step of a factor analysis involves correlating all of the variables together, there is plenty of scope for these problems to creep in – an issue which has the potential to make the results of the analysis meaningless.

VARIABLES MUST BE INDEPENDENT

It is also necessary to ensure that all the variables being measured are independent; in other words, there is no reason (other than perhaps something to do with personality, mood, ability, knowledge or some other psychological variable) why the response made to one item should influence the response made to another variable. Readers of Chapter 2 will be familiar with my acerbic views about questionnaires which essentially repeat the same item several times – a clear example of data which are not suitable for factor analysis (and where the use of factor analysis will seem to give a thin veneer of scientific respectability to what is patently obvious to anyone who bothers to read the items). However, it can also happen when items are combined to form several different scales – as with the old Minnesota Multiphasic Personality Inventory (MMPI; Hathaway & McKinley, 1940). Here one item could contribute to several different scales, and so it makes no sense to factor-analyse these scale scores. For example, if individuals produce scores on four test items, it would be permissible to create and factor scales such as:

(item 1 + item 2) and (item 3 + item 4)

or (item 1 + item 2 – item 3) and (10 – item 4)

but not (item 1 + item 2 + item 3) and (item 4 + item 1)

or (item 1 + item 3) and (item 2 + item 3 + item 4)

As in the latter two cases, one of the observed test items contributes to more than one scale score.

Similar problems can arise when analysing data from behaviour checklists, electrophysiological responses or otherwise coding mutually incompatible behaviours. For example, if a "time sampling" method is used to record what a child is doing in various 30-second periods, the variables might include "playing alone", "playing with other children", "sleeping" etc. The problem is that when a child is sleeping, they cannot also be playing – either with other children or alone. When they are playing with other children, they cannot be sleeping or playing alone . . . and so on. The variables are not independent. Likewise, when coding responses to a projective test, one could not have items such as "says that central figure is their mother" and "says that central figure is their father". One has to be careful to ensure that the variables being factor-analysed are genuinely independent; in other words, that a person's response to one of the variables does not affect their response to any other variable other than through the influence of the developmental, psychological social or physiological process which the test/assessment is trying to measure.

THE VARIABLES MUST NOT COME FROM IPSATISED SCALES

It is not possible to factor-analyse all of the scores from any test where it is impossible for a person to obtain an extremely high (or extremely low) score on *all* of its scales (known as "ipsatised tests", discussed in Chapter 4), as all of the scales of such tests are bound to be negatively correlated. Advocates of these tests claim that it is possible simply to drop one of the scales before factoring. However, the interpretation of the results will be affected by the (arbitrary) choice of which scale to omit, which makes the whole exercise rather pointless.

THE CORRELATION MATRIX SHOULD CONTAIN SOME NON-ZERO CORRELATIONS

Although not strictly a requirement for factor analysis, it is usual to check whether the correlation matrix shows several reasonably large correlations – normally by looking at it – and ensuring that some are larger than about 0.3. If all of the correlations are tiny, then one should seriously question whether any factors are there to be extracted – and if an analysis of such a matrix *is* attempted, it follows that because correlations are minuscule, the communalities of the variables will also be small which means that huge sample sizes will be needed, as described later.

If correlations are small because of the use of tests with low reliability, it may be appropriate to correct the correlations for the effects of unreliability, as shown in Chapter 7. Likewise, if poor experimental design led to data being collected from a group of restricted range (e.g., ability scores being obtained from a sample of university students rather than from a sample of the general population), it might be appropriate to correct the correlations for this using the formula of Dobson (1988), as discussed in Chapter 6. However, such pieces of psychometric wizardry should be used with caution and are really no substitute for sound and thoughtful experimental design.

There are statistical tests (such as Bartlett's Test of Sphericity and the Kaiser-Meyer-Olkin [KMO] measure of sampling adequacy; Bartlett, 1950; Kaiser, 1970; 1981), which show whether the correlation matrix contains many non-zero correlations. A useful discussion of their use is given by Dziuban and Shirkey (1974). The Bartlett test is very sensitive to sample size, and minuscule correlations between variables from a large sample will lead the test to indicate that factor analysis is appropriate – a point made by Bartlett (1950) himself. This makes it of limited (if any) use. In addition, there is no way of interpreting the KMO statistic other than by using rules of thumb rather than anything based on empirical data or statistical theory. To misquote Alice in Wonderland, "What is the use of a statistic . . . without effect sizes or significance levels?" The Bartlett and KMO statistics are often reported, probably because they are calculated by popular statistical packages, and quoting them gives authors the appearance of statistical expertise. But at the end of the day, if the correlations are all close to zero, implying that there are no factors to extract, this is what the factor analysis will show. I cannot see the point of statistical tests such as these.

MISSING DATA

Missing data can be a curse. If a small amount of data is missing and this is scattered randomly throughout the data matrix (for example, if a few people have forgotten to answer the occasional question in a personality questionnaire), there are few problems. There are three options for dealing with it. The first is to drop from the analysis everyone who has any missing data. This is (perhaps) the safest option, though it is worthwhile checking demographics and other test scores of people who omit items to ensure that they are, indeed, a random sample of the population. Second, one can ignore missing data and base the correlation between two items on the scores of people who have answered both of them; this means that the correlations will be based on slightly different numbers of cases. This can be a problem, as discussed in the next paragraph. Finally, the missing data could be estimated, as described in Chapter 4.

It would not be wise to factor-analyse data where a proportion of the sample omitted to take complete tests, or blocks of items. For example, some people may have taken tests A, B and C. Others may have taken tests A and C only, and others may have taken only tests B and C. Because of this, it would not be legitimate to factor-analyse these data, although several statistical packages will do so without a murmur.

Ability tests with time limits are particularly problematical, as only the most able (and fast!) people are likely to answer the last few items in the scale. This restriction of range will tend to reduce the size of the correlations between these difficult items (see the discussion of attenuation in Chapter 5). For this reason it is wise to allow participants (nearly) unlimited time to complete ability tests when developing (and factor-analysing) items, and only afterwards impose time limits.

STAGE 2: SAMPLE SIZE FOR FACTOR ANALYSIS

Each factor analysis is based on a correlation matrix – and when the number of variables is large, the number of correlations in these matrices becomes huge; it is $N \times (N - 1)/2$, where N is the number of variables. Thus if 50 variables are being factor-analysed, the analysis is based on 1225 correlations. These correlations are calculated from a sample, which we hope and pray will be sufficiently large and representative to produce correlations which are fairly close to the correlations which we would obtain were we to test all the people in the population. But because we just test a sample, rather than the population, each of these correlations will vary a little from the true (population) value. For example, suppose that the correlation between two variables is 0.25 in the population; if we calculate the correlation between these two variables from a sample of (say) 100 people, we might find that the correlation was 0.22. In another sample of 100 people it might be 0.28 and so on. The problem is that if just one of these 1225 correlations is quite a lot larger or smaller than the value in the population, the factor structure will be inaccurate – and with so many correlations being calculated, the chances are high that some of the correlations will be quite a lot larger or smaller than their true values in the population.

There is some good statistical theory underlying this. Every time we calculate a correlation, we can also calculate a statistic known as its "standard error". This shows how much larger or smaller than its true value a correlation is likely to be, given the size of our sample. For example, if the true value of a correlation is 0.25, and we gather data from several samples each containing data from 100 people, we should not be surprised if the correlation is as small as 0.06 or as high as 0.43 in some of these samples – it can be shown that such extreme values will be found in about 5% of the samples.

Of course, when we calculate a great many correlations (as when performing a factor analysis), the problem becomes worse. This is because when we calculate hundreds or thousands of correlations, the chances of *at least one* of them being quite a lot larger or smaller than it should be, just because of chance variations in the people we sampled, will obviously be larger than the chances of *just one* of them being quite a lot larger or smaller than their true value.

Spreadsheet 11.1 is very simple-minded and shows how much the correlations are likely to deviate from their "true" values by taking a sample of a particular size. For example, if the true correlation between two variables is 0.6 (in other words, the correlation calculated from all members of a particular population is 0.6) but we sample just 10 people from that population, the correlation calculated from those 10 people could be as low as −0.48 or as high as 0.89. More specifically, the values of the correlation will be more extreme than these values in 0.05 of the samples we draw, which is what alpha = 0.05 means. So if we believe that the correlation between two variables in the population is (say) 0.3, it is possible to see how much larger or smaller a single correlation might be. If it is assumed that all the correlations are zero in the population, the spreadsheet also shows what range of correlations are likely to be found.

Spreadsheet name: Spreadsheet 11.1: Confidence intervals for correlations

Download from: https://routledge.com/9781032146164/

Purpose: To show what variation in correlations should be expected by chance.

Contents of spreadsheet: Typical values for the number of variables, population correlations and type I error rate.

Suggested activity:

- Note what happens when the sample size increases for several values of correlation; for example, when the population correlation is 0.1, 0.25 and 0.5. How large does the sample size need to be in order to be fairly sure that the correlation calculated from one sample of people (which is what psychologists normally analyse) is fairly close to the true (population) value? You might like to explore this for various sample sizes by drawing on your "intuition" and/or knowledge of the sample sizes used in published factor-analytic studies.
- If all of the correlations are zero in the population, there are no factors to find. However, sampling variations mean that some quite large correlations may emerge, and it is quite possible that factor-analysing data from a small sample of people will cause these to be mistaken for genuine factors. When the population correlation is set to zero, the spreadsheet also shows how large the largest correlation in the matrix is likely to be. For example, if 20 variables are correlated based on a sample size of 70, there is a 1-in-20 chance that one of the correlations in this matrix will be as extreme as ±0.418, rather than zero. Alter the number of people in each sample to see how large the sample needs to be to avoid misleading oneself.

Points to note:

- Alpha here refers to the probability of making a type I error, *not* reliability.

Learning outcomes: Readers should now be able to:

- Appreciate that performing factor analysis with small samples is unwise.

So how large should the sample be in order to perform a factor analysis? Experts vary in their recommendations, but factor analysis should not be attempted if the number of subjects is fewer than several hundred, otherwise the correlations computed from this sample of people will differ substantially from those which would have been obtained from another sample, giving results which are unreplicable and which are not good approximations of what the relationship between the variables really is in the population.

It used to be thought that it is also necessary to relate sample size to the number of variables being analysed. For example, Nunnally (1978) advocated that there should be at least 10 times as many cases as variables. Later studies (Barrett & Kline, 1981; Guadagnoli & Velicer, 1988) show that, so long as there are more people than variables, the ratio of subjects to variables is not as important as absolute sample size and the size of the factor loadings. Thus if the factors are well defined (e.g., with loadings of 0.7, rather than 0.4), one needs a smaller sample to find them. If the data being analysed are known to be highly reliable (e.g., test scores, rather than responses to individual items), it should be possible to relax these guidelines somewhat. However, attempts to factor-analyse small sets of data are doomed to failure, as the large standard errors of the correlations ensure that the factor solution will be both arbitrary and unreplicable.

MacCallum et al. (1999) offer one of the best treatments of this issue that I know. Their analysis based on simulated data shows that the following variables influence the replicability of factor analyses.

1. The size of the loadings (or communality of the variables). A set of variables yielding factors with small loadings (e.g., 0.4, rather than 0.6) will be harder to find/replicate for a given sample size. The guidelines given in the paper assume a factor analysis has been performed – not a component analysis. (If a component analysis is performed, the criteria outlined by MacCallum et al. would presumably need to be made more stringent.)
2. The number of variables per factor. If the analysis produces factors, each of which consists of (say) six variables with large loadings, this structure will be easier to find/replicate than a model where factors of only (say) three variables have large loadings.
3. The size of the sample, which interacts with the other two influences.

The problem is that until one has performed the analysis, one cannot know how large the communalities of the variables will be. If the study is *truly* exploratory, then one will not know how many variables will have large loadings on each factor either. So when designing a study, it seems sensible to stick to these authors' recommendation of a minimum sample size of 500, bearing in mind that even this will not be adequate if the communalities of the variables are low, which is often the case for personality items. On the other hand, if the communalities of the variables are large (above about 0.7 when performing factor analysis, not principal component analysis) smaller samples and smaller numbers of variables per factor will be acceptable. However, it must be said that I have rarely encountered communalities this large when performing real-life factor analyses. Factor analyses of test items pose a particular problem here; as responses to individual items are severely affected by measurement error, in my experience finding items having a communality greater than about 0.3 is unusual. Factor-analysing test items will almost always require huge samples, and even then there is no guarantee that the findings would be replicable.

Performing and interpreting factor analyses with small samples and identifying factors on which only a few (say three or four) variables have large loadings is a waste of everybody's time unless the communalities of the variables are large. And unless there is excellent reason to suppose that the number of variables per factor and the communalities of these variables will be large, it would be foolhardy to perform a factor analysis with fewer than about 500 participants – and even this may not be sufficient, according to MacCallum et al. (1999).

STAGE 3: CALCULATING CORRELATIONS

RATIO-LEVEL DATA

Most statistics packages assume that factor analyses are to be performed on interval or ratio-scaled data, numbers representing proper physical measurements. For example, if we measured the amount of time it took people to correctly solve a set of visualisation puzzles, their heart rate, their skin resistance, the number of books they say they read last year, the amount of time it takes them to recognise a threatening (rather than an unthreatening) word and so on, there would be no problem performing a factor analysis using Pearson correlations, provided that the variables are not too skewed in opposite directions.

ORDINAL DATA

Responses to Likert scales can probably best be regarded as ordinal data – where we can be fairly confident that one response (strongly agreeing versus agreeing, for example) indicates a higher level of some behaviour than another, but we cannot be sure whether the change in the level of the trait between a rating of "strongly agree" (coded 5) and "agree" (coded 4) is the same as between, say, "agree" and "neutral" (coded 3).

Some psychologists thus used to perform factor analyses using non-parametric correlations, such as Spearman's rho, rather than Pearson correlations. In practice this can be a laborious process, as many popular statistical packages assume that anyone performing a factor analysis will want to use Pearson correlations, and so offer no other options. And opinions were divided about the legitimacy of such analyses; Gorsuch (1983, p. 309) argued that non-parametric correlations might be useful, whilst Cattell (1978, p. 473) and Nunnally (1978, p. 138) argued against their use in factor analysis – although these comments were, of course, made before Michell's (1997) critique. That said, it should be remembered that Spearman's rho is identical to a Pearson correlation performed on ranks, and so it shares all of the desirable properties of the Pearson correlation – lying between −1 and 1 and producing a correlation matrix where none of the eigenvalues is negative.

We have already encountered the tetrachoric correlation for correlating together two dichotomous (two-valued) variables – for example, responses to ability items where "1" indicates a correct answer and "0" an incorrect answer. In Chapter 6 we showed that calculating the Pearson correlation was not a good idea for these variables, for if the items differ in difficulty, the correlation falls. The same problem also affects scores on Likert scales, only to a somewhat smaller extent. It is possible to extend the idea of the tetrachoric correlation to deal with Likert-scaled variables or similar. For example, scores on a 5-point Likert scale may be used to give a rough approximation of people's scores on some normally distributed trait. The polychoric correlation between two Likert-scaled variables estimates what the correlation between the two underlying normal variables would have been. This process is mathematically and computationally complex. Furthermore, it is necessary to *assume* that some continuous variable underlies the scores which we observe – and of course there is normally no way of testing whether this assumption is correct.

In addition, Kampen and Swyngedouw (2000) argue that items which ask respondents to rate how much they agree with statements (the format used in most personality questionnaires) are singularly inappropriate for analysis using polychoric correlations, because there may not be just one variable which determines how a person will rate their level of agreement. "A respondent may have one set of arguments for not-agreeing and another set of arguments for agreeing, some of which could be additive, but others may have the effect of a veto (by nature a boolean variable). This implies that not one, but several underlying variables may exist which may or may not be metric". So whilst polychoric correlations may be suitable for some variables, they may not be for others; the assumption of a single normally distributed underlying variable just may not apply.

Psychologists are generally uninterested in exploring the cognitive processes which cause a person to answer a personality item in a certain way (but see Arro, 2013; Rosenbaum & Valsiner, 2011). However, without knowing these it is hard to know whether it is sensible to make strong assumptions about the presence of some underlying continuous variable. I have less of a problem using the data for computing Pearson (or Spearman) correlations, for in that case if people use very different criteria for answering a question, the analysis will show that it does not load cleanly on one factor. It is when one needs to make assumptions (on the basis of zero evidence) about these processes before calculating the correlations that I start to feel uneasy.

If polychoric correlations are calculated and factor-analysed, it will sometimes be found that the factor analysis program fails because the matrix of polychoric correlations yields some negative eigenvalues. Choosing an option such as "unweighted least squares", also known as "ordinary least squares" or "principal axes factoring", should solve the problem; failing that it is possible to "smooth" the correlation matrix (e.g., Knol & TenBerge, 1989) – adjusting the correlations slightly to eliminate the negative eigenvalue(s). The R environment has routines which will do so, though one might perhaps worry about whether the polychoric correlations cause more problems than they solve if smoothing is necessary.

So what should happen in practice?

It has been shown empirically that if scores on a normally distributed variable are split into categories, the correlations based on the categorised data are rather close to the correlations based on the original, uncategorised data so long as the number of categories is larger than about 4 (Bollen & Barb, 1983). If a variable is measured on a 5-point scale or larger, there is arguably little point going to the trouble of computing polychoric correlations, smoothing them etc.

I take a rather pragmatic view about whether or not to use polychoric correlations. Doing so is unlikely to do harm, provided that one is happy with the assumption that the underlying variable is indeed both continuous and normally distributed, and that one is happy to discount the issues raised by Kampen and Swyngedouw (2000). In practice, the difference between the polychoric and Pearson correlations is likely to be fairly small by comparison with the other effects noted (differences in distributions, sub-groups with the samples etc.), and if the number of categories is five or more, it is probably not necessary to compute polychoric correlations.

The Factor program (Lorenzo-Seva & Ferrando, 2006) will calculate either Pearson or polychoric correlations, and it can be fun to compute both and notice if and when they differ appreciably. I would certainly recommend computing polychoric (tetrachoric) correlations when factor-analysing binary data – such as ability items which are coded as correct or incorrect. In this case it is evidently reasonable to suppose that the underlying ability is continuous, but that items differ in their difficulty (proportion of people who answer them incorrectly). Computing Pearson correlations in this instance is misleading, as large Pearson correlations can only arise when two items have similar levels of difficulty.

EXERCISE 11.1

Dataset name: "1 factor 3 levels of difficulty.dat"

Download from: https://routledge.com/9781032146164/

Purpose: To show a situation where Pearson and polychoric correlations can be very different.

Contents of data file: Answers to nine ability items, where 1 indicates a correct answer and 0 an incorrect answer. Three of the items are easy, three are of average difficulty, and three are difficult. Roughly a third of the 272 participants are highly able, a third have average ability, and a third have low ability.

Suggested activity:

- Use the Factor program (Lorenzo-Seva & Ferrando, 2006) or similar to analyse the data file "1 factor 3 levels of difficulty.dat" using both polychoric and Pearson correlations.

Points to note:

- The polychoric correlations are much larger than the Pearson correlations (for example, the correlation between item 1 and item 9 is 0.657, vs. 0.252, as you should verify).

Learning outcomes: Readers should now be able to:

- Appreciate that if the items in a test differ considerably in their level of difficulty, and the people in the sample differ appreciably in their level of ability, then Pearson correlations will tend to be considerably smaller than tetrachoric correlations.
- The choice of which coefficient to use can therefore have a major impact on the factor structure which is found.

NOMINAL (CATEGORICAL) DATA

It should be obvious, but categorical data, where numbers are assigned arbitrarily to levels of some variable, are not suitable for factor analysis. For example, suppose that a researcher gathered data from several towns and decided (quite arbitrarily) to code location as London = 1, Chicago = 2 and Toronto = 3. Because these codes are arbitrarily assigned, it makes no sense to correlate them with anything, because different results would be obtained if the codes had been assigned differently.

STAGE 4: FACTOR ANALYSIS OR COMPONENT ANALYSIS?

One school of thought maintains that factor (rather than component) analysis should never be used because of the difficulty in estimating communalities – the estimation of a score for each person on each factor (factor scores) when performing factor analysis also turns out to be surprisingly unpleasant. The second school of thought maintains that, as the factor model is a priori much more likely to fit the data, any attempt to estimate communalities is better than none. Interested readers should see Velicer and Jackson (1990) for a more detailed discussion of this topic. My personal preference would normally be to perform factor analysis; journal reviewers will be unlikely to complain if you perform factor analysis, but they might object if you perform principal components analysis.

When performing components analysis, the communality of each variable is 1.0 because variations in the scores on each variable are assumed to be explained entirely by all of the common factors (apart from measurement error). When performing factor analysis the communality of each variable is assumed to be less than 1 – because the common factors themselves are thought not to explain all of the variation in the scores of the variable. Part of the variation is due to the unique factor belonging to that variable. So if a variable has a unique factor loading of 0.6, $0.6 \times 0.6 = 36\%$ of the variation in scores on that variable is due to that unique factor. Therefore, the variance available to be explained by the common factors (its communality) is only 64%.

There are several ways of estimating the communality of each variable, and these are explored in the section on factor extraction.

STAGE 5: TESTS FOR THE NUMBER OF FACTORS

Several tests have been developed to help analysts to choose the "correct" number of factors. These tests require careful consideration, and one cannot rely on computer packages to make this important decision, as many (including SPSS) use a technique which is known to be flawed and fail to incorporate some of the more useful tests.

Determining the number of factors to be extracted is probably the most important decision that one has to make when conducting a factor analysis. A faulty decision here can produce a nonsensical solution from even the clearest set of data. There is no harm in trying several analyses based on differing numbers of factors, and in using several different tests to guide the choice of factors.

The first guides are theory and past experience. One may sometimes want to use factor analysis to ensure that a test is performing as expected when used within a different culture, patient group or whatever. Confirmatory factor analysis can be used for this purpose (see Chapter 13), but if exploratory factor analysis is preferred, the previous results can be used to guide one in deciding how many factors to extract. For example, if a (technically adequate) factor analysis of a test in the UK revealed seven factors, any attempt to factor-analyse the tests in the US should at least consider the seven-factor solution.

Theory and past practice are all very well, but many factor analyses are truly exploratory in nature. The researcher may have no good theoretical rationale for deciding how many factors should be extracted. There are several tests which can be used in such circumstances, all of which seek to determine the number of factors which should be extracted from a correlation matrix. The problem is that few of them have been implemented in the computer packages likely to be encountered by non-expert users. Second, the various techniques do not always yield consistent results. One test may point to six factors, another to eight, and previous research to nine! In circumstances such as this, it is safest to consider a number of solutions and check them for psychological plausibility. Users should also consider the following:

- Whether increasing the number of factors increases the "simplicity" of the solution (such as decreasing the proportion loadings in the range of −0.4 to 0.4). If increasing the number of factors does little or nothing to increase the simplicity of the solution, it is arguably of little value.
- Whether any large correlations between factors emerge when using oblique solutions. These can indicate that too many factors have been extracted and that two factors are trying to pass through the same cluster of variables. Correlations between factors larger than around 0.4 could be regarded as suspect.
- Whether any well-known factors have split into two or more parts. For example, if a myriad of previous studies show that a set of items form just one factor (e.g., extraversion), yet they seem to form two factors in your analysis, it is likely that too many factors have been extracted.

That said, it seems that if there *is* any doubt as to how many factors to rotate, it may be better to extract too many rather than too few.

THE KAISER-GUTTMAN CRITERION

One of the oldest and simplest tests for the number of factors is that described by Kaiser (1960) and Guttman (1954), and known as the **Kaiser–Guttman criterion**. It has the advantage of being very straightforward. One simply performs a principal components analysis on the data, extracting as many factors as there are variables but without rotating the factors. The eigenvalues are calculated as usual by summing the squared loadings on each component. One then simply counts how many eigenvalues are greater than 1.0 – this is the number of factors to be used.

There are many problems with this technique, the most obvious being its sensitivity to the number of variables in the analysis. As each eigenvalue is simply the sum of the squared factor loadings, if the number of variables is large, so too will be the eigenvalue. A test for the number of factors should give the same result whether or not there are 4 or 40 variables representing each factor, and the Kaiser-Guttman test obviously will not do so. Furthermore, Hakstian and Mueller (1973) observed that the technique was never intended to be used as a test for the number of factors. Because it is extremely easy to implement automatically, most statistical packages will perform a Kaiser-Guttman test by default. It should *always* be overridden.

THE SCREE TEST

The **scree test**, devised by Cattell (1966), is also conceptually simple. Like the Kaiser-Guttman criterion, it is based on the eigenvalues of an initial unrotated principal components solution. However, it draws on the *relative* values of the eigenvalues and so is not sensitive to variations in the number of variables being analysed. Successive principal components explain less and less variance, and so the eigenvalues decrease. The scree test is based on visual inspection of a graph showing the successive eigenvalues, such as that illustrated in Figure 11.1.

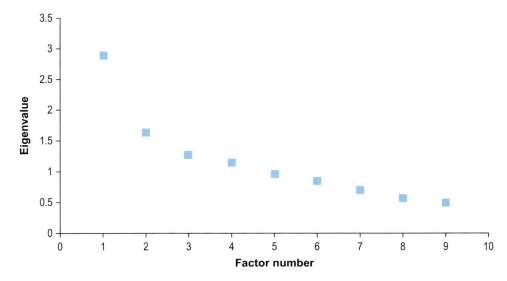

Figure 11.1 Scree test showing eigenvalues from an unrotated principal components analysis of nine variables. The graph indicates that two components should be extracted.

The basic idea is simple. It is clear that the points on the right-hand side of Figure 11.1 form a straight line, known as a "scree slope". It is possible to put a ruler through these points and determine how many eigenvalues lie well above this line. This is the number of factors which should then be extracted. Thus Figure 11.1 depicts a two-factor solution. Further examples of the interpretation of scree tests are given in the literature (Cattell, 1966; 1978; Cattell & Vogelman, 1977). Several popular texts on factor analysis describe the scree test incorrectly, by asserting that the number of factors corresponds to the number of eigenvalues above the scree line *plus 1*. They would thus advocate extracting three factors from the above solution. It is not obvious where this confusion arose, as Cattell's papers and 1978 book are quite clear on the matter: "the last real factor is that before the scree begins" (Cattell & Vogelman, 1977).

A problem with the scree test is that it does rely on subjective judgement and may sometimes have several possible interpretations, particularly when the sample size or the "salient" factor loadings are small (Gorsuch, 1983). Sometimes more than one clearly identifiable straight scree slope is found. In such cases, one simply looks for the eigenvalues which lie above the leftmost scree slope.

PARALLEL ANALYSIS

Simulation studies show that Horn's method of **parallel analysis** (Horn, 1965) is the most accurate way of determining the correct number of factors to extract (Velicer et al., 2000; Zwick & Velicer, 1986), provided that the data being analysed are measured on a continuous scale, or a Likert scale with more than two values (Tran & Formann, 2009). Now that computers are powerful enough to enable its use, it should be the method of choice. The basic principle is quite simple. It involves checking whether each of the eigenvalues that emerges from a principal components analysis is larger than you would expect by chance. (Some implementations use factor analysis instead.)

Suppose that you gather data on 10 variables and 100 people and conduct a principal components (or factor) analysis. The program will produce a list of eigenvalues, as many eigenvalues as there are variables.

Now perform another analysis, but rather than using the data that you have collected, just analyse random data (again using 10 variables and 100 people). You could literally type in numbers at random into the computer. Then run the component (or factor) analysis again, based on this random data. You would expect the correlations between these random variables to be roughly zero – though some will be a little larger than zero and some smaller than zero by chance. (The size of your sample will affect how close to zero they are; with a small sample, you might find that some correlations are as large as 0.3 or as small as −0.3; with a large sample, few if any will be above 0.1 or less than −0.1.) This approach, generating lots of sets of data and seeing what happens when you analyse them in a particular way, as with many of the spreadsheets in this book, is known as **Monte Carlo** simulation. There are several variations possible — for example, rather than generating random data, one can simply mix up the rows of the data matrix — so one person's response to item 1 is followed by another person's response to item 2 and so on. This has the advantage of making sure that the frequency distribution of the variables is always the same, although the correlations between them should be close to zero.

It should hopefully be obvious that if all the correlations are zero, no factors are present in the data. But some of the correlations will be greater or less than zero, just because of chance sampling variations. The question is whether the eigenvalues from the data are larger than would be expected from chance, by factor-analysing correlations from random data.

The problem is that we have only looked at one set of random data — and of course the correlations (and the eigenvalues) will vary depending what set of random numbers we typed in. So it is necessary to repeat the factor analysis many times — a thousand times, for example — using a different set of random data each time to get an idea how large the eigenvalues typically are; a statistician would say that you find the "sampling distribution" of the eigenvalues. Then you simply work out the average size of the first eigenvalue, the second eigenvalue etc. by averaging across all 1000 analyses. You also find the 95% confidence limit; that is, the value of each eigenvalue that is only exceeded on 5% of the 1000 trials. We call this the critical value.

That is all there is to performing parallel analysis. The first eigenvalue from the analysis of the real data is compared with the critical value found from the random data. If the real eigenvalue is larger than critical value for the first eigenvalue from random data, there is at least one factor in the real data, and the process is repeated for the second, third, and fourth factors etc. — until one of the eigenvalues is smaller than the corresponding critical value.

For example, suppose that when correlations between 10 variables derived from 100 participants were analysed using factor analysis, the first few eigenvalues were 2.9, 1.63, 1.27, 1.14 and 0.97. Scores on 10 random variables were also generated from 100 participants, a factor analysis was performed, and the 10 eigenvalues were calculated. This procedure was repeated 1000 times, and the average value for each eigenvalue was found — and also the value for each eigenvalue which was only exceeded in 5% (50) of the 1000 replications. How many factors are present in these data? To answer this question using parallel analysis, the critical values in the final column of Table 11.1 should be compared with the eigenvalues from the real data. The first eigenvalue from the real data (2.9) is larger than the critical value for the first eigenvalue in the table

(1.68), so it is unlikely that one would find such a large eigenvalue by chance (i.e., by factor-analysing random data). There is at least one factor in the data. Likewise, the second eigenvalue (1.63) is bigger than 1.47, so there are at least two factors present. The third eigenvalue (1.27), however is smaller than the critical value of 1.31; it is therefore quite possible that a third eigenvalue as large as 1.27 could have arisen by chance. So one would conclude that there are just two factors in the data.

You should be concerned about where the numbers in Table 11.1 came from. I did not spend weeks typing 1000 sets of random numbers (each involving 10 variables and 100 participants) into a spreadsheet and performing 1000 factor analyses, laboriously tabulating the results. The Factor computer program (Lorenzo-Seva & Ferrando, 2006) will perform this analysis. It generates the table of simulated eigenvalues automatically, and will use the parallel analysis[1] method to advise on the number of factors in the data. Several other computer programs and websites (search for "parallel analysis") also perform parallel analysis. It is just necessary to specify the number of variables and participants in your real data, and the number of replications to be performed, and the program or website will produce a table such as that shown in Table 11.1 within a few seconds. This may be used to determine the appropriate number of factors, as shown. It is then necessary to analyse your "real" data using your favourite statistical package, and specify that it should extract this number of factors (rather than using the default test).

Table 11.1 Average eigenvalues obtained from 1000 random correlation matrices based on 10 variables and 100 participants

Eigenvalue number	Average eigenvalue from the analysis of 1000 sets of random data	Critical value based on the 95% confidence limit; only 5%, or 50, of the random eigenvalues were larger than the values shown here
1	1.53	1.68
2	1.36	1.47
3	1.23	1.31
4	1.12	1.20
5	1.02	1.09
6	0.93	1.00
7	0.84	0.91
8	0.75	0.82
9	0.66	0.74
10	0.56	0.64

One word of warning. The critical values for the eigenvalues depend on the number of variables and the number of participants in the factor analysis. The values shown in Table 11.1 will only be correct should you want to find the number of factors present when analysing 10 variables and you have gathered data from 100 participants. It will be necessary to produce your own version of this table for every set of real data that you need to analyse.

OTHER TECHNIQUES

The **minimum average partial (MAP) test** (Velicer, 1976) is another consistently accurate technique for estimating the appropriate number of factors (Zwick & Velicer, 1986), and the Factor package (Lorenzo-Seva & Ferrando, 2006) is one of the few programs which will also perform it. If too many factors are extracted from a correlation matrix, the last ones tend to have only one or two large loadings. The MAP test tries to identify when this happens by looking at the size of the partial correlations between the variables after extracting successive principal components. When the average of the partial correlations reaches a minimum, this indicates the point at which all the common factors have been removed.

Another useful (but straightforward) technique is Revelle and Rocklin's (1979) **very simple structure** (VSS) test for the number of factors. The rest of this paragraph will probably only make sense after reading the "factor rotation" section of this chapter. If there are n variables, the VSS test involves performing n factor analyses, extracting and rotating[2] one, two, three . . . n factor solutions. In each case a simplified factor pattern matrix is calculated from the factor pattern matrix, where each variable's largest loading[3] is kept unchanged, but all other loadings are changed to zero. This resembles the way in which factor matrices are generally interpreted. A statistic is calculated which evaluates how well this simplified factor matrix fits the original correlation matrix; the authors demonstrate when too many factors are extracted, the goodness of fit becomes worse. The solution where the simplified pattern matrix best fits the data thus indicates the optimal number of factors. It can be run from the R environment (Revelle, 2017b).

EXPLORATORY GRAPH ANALYSIS (EGA)

Preliminary studies suggest that **exploratory graph analysis** (EGA) may be useful when the correlations between factors are large – a condition where some other techniques struggle. This is a very new and largely untested method which is based on network analysis – a technique discussed in Chapter 14, which should be consulted before reading the rest of this section.

The logic is this. The graph analysis package first represents variables as "nodes" whose closeness to each other is determined by the inverse of the partial correlation matrix. Two variables which correlate substantially after their correlations with all other variables are taken into account will thus be close to each other. All this is fairly standard.

What is needed next is a method of determining how many clusters of nodes there are. The Walktrap algorithm (Pons & Latapy, 2005) is used for this. It merges the closest pair of nodes together and recalculates the partial correlations. The process continues until combining nodes causes too much distortion to the system. The underlying mathematics is not pleasant, and is based on graph theory. The process is described in more detail by Golino and Epskamp (2017), though this paper too is rather technical. It is possible to perform these analyses using the R-package (Golino et al., 2020).

There are other methods too, and the Factor program (Lorenzo-Seva & Ferrando, 2006) implements some other, little-researched techniques whose value is uncertain. So how to choose between them?

CHOOSING A METHOD

Many of these tests have been applied to the same sets of simulated data, where the number of "actual" factors is known. If we assume that these artificial data behave in much the same way as any set of real-life data, it is possible to determine which of these tests can best identify the true number of factors. There are several such studies (Golino & Epskamp, 2017; Velicer et al., 2000; Zwick & Velicer, 1986), the most recent being Cosemans et al. (in press) which is well worth consulting, as it is not particularly technical, and considers data from 20 simulated variables. It includes the analysis of both continuous and dichotomous (two-valued) data, the latter being analysed using both Pearson and tetrachoric correlations. Two sample sizes (100 and 1000) were used, two levels of correlation between the factors were examined (0.0 and 0.5) and communalities were either in the range 0.2–0.4 or 0.6–0.8. These last communalities are unusually large. They are arguably unlikely to be encountered in real life.

The study does not consider the VSS method, although Golino and Epskamp (2017) did, and found that it underestimated the number of factors when the correlations between them were small. However, Cosemans et al. did analyse two variants of parallel analysis. They also used an experimental computerised version of the scree test, but as it is not known how well this corresponds to the "eyeball" version (Cattell, 1966), I do not consider the scree results here.

To summarise their findings, as expected the Kaiser-Guttman test proved ineffective (despite being commonly used). When communalities were low (0.2–0.4), no test worked for small samples ($N = 100$). For large samples ($N = 1000$) EGA proved somewhat effective, with a 65% chance of identifying the correct number of factors, no matter whether the correlations between the factors were low or high. None of the other methods was at all effective; the next best was a version of parallel analysis with a 0.18 probability of identifying the correct number of factors. This is very odd, given the considerable literature showing the effectiveness of parallel analysis, and that Golino and Epskamp (2017) found that EGA only outperformed parallel analysis when there were several, strongly correlated factors.

To précis the main findings from these papers, parallel analysis, the minimum average partial technique and the very simple structure criterion seem to generally perform fairly well. The scree test sometimes does, whilst the Kaiser-Guttman test is of little use. The VSS method does not work well if variables have large loadings on more than one or two factors or if correlations between factors are small. EGA looks as if it has great promise, though it is new and little tested.

Thus when performing a factor analysis, it is advisable to use parallel analysis (because of its sound statistical basis and its proven utility) in conjunction with one or two other techniques, such as EGA, the MAP test or VSS. The VSS and EGA procedures are not particularly accessible (other than to users of the R package), whilst Lorenzo-Seva and Ferrando's (2006) Factor package performs parallel analysis and the MAP test.

STAGE 6: COMMUNALITY ESTIMATION

The previous chapter deliberately oversimplified the process by which factors are positioned through the clusters of variables. In practice, this is performed in two stages. First, communalities are estimated and the factors are placed in some arbitrary position relative to the variables (*factor extraction*); the factors are almost invariably at right angles at this point, and will probably *not* pass neatly through the clusters of variables. Then another procedure (called *factor rotation*) is used to move the factors through the clusters of variables, possibly allowing the factors to become correlated.

The estimation of communalities is a process which worries factor analysts, as there is no easy way of checking that one's estimates are correct. Indeed, the problems associated with this can drive some researchers to use the simpler component model, which assumes that the communality of each variable is 1.0. My own preference is clear. When analysing psychological data, it is better to try and estimate communalities rather than to make a completely unrealistic assumption about the data for the sake of mathematical convenience. That said, it would be unusual for the two techniques, factor analysis and component analysis, to give radically different results.

It used to be assumed that the square of the largest correlation between a variable and any other variable in the correlation matrix would give an estimate of the variable's communality. This is because that the correlation between a variable and anything else cannot possibly be larger than the square root of the communality of the variable. (The obvious problem is that if the variables measure different things, this will lead to a serious underestimation of the communality. And if all of the *other* variables in a correlation matrix have a lot of measurement error associated with them, this will also underestimate a variable's communality.)

Then it was appreciated the multiple correlation might be the way to go; the square of the multiple correlation obtained when trying to predict scores on a variable from all the other variables in the correlation matrix might be better. Since the communality is defined as the proportion of a variable's variance that can be shared with the other variables in the analysis, it has been claimed that this gives the lower bound for the communality – the smallest value that the communality could possibly have, although a paper by Kaiser (1990) challenges this view.

Then an iterative process was developed – one starts off with some guess as what the communalities might be (such as the largest correlation each variable has with any other variable, the squared multiple correlation – or just a number such as 0.8). Then one performs a "principal axes" factor analysis, as described below, and calculates what the communality is from the number of common factors extracted. This replaces the original estimate of communality, and the factor analysis is repeated. This sequence is repeated again and again until the estimate of communality does not change – or something goes hideously wrong and the communality exceeds 1.0 or becomes negative. This last situation is known as a **Heywood case** – a term which will occasionally be seen in an error message when performing factor analysis.

Two things should be noted about this iterative procedure.

First, the iterative process often seems to need far more steps than are specified by the default settings in computer packages before the communalities become stable, so it is well worth changing the default values used by packages such as SPSS to something large, such as 1000.

Second, according to Gorsuch (1983), "no proof has yet been presented to show that [the communalities] either must converge or that the value to which they converge is either the theoretical communality or less than the variable's reliability". In other words, the estimate of each variable's communality might not be accurate.

These days, the communality of each variable can also be estimated without iteration by using maximum likelihood estimation when performing the factor analysis, and this is arguably the most appropriate procedure.

STAGE 7: FACTOR EXTRACTION

There are plenty of techniques for performing factor analysis, rejoicing in names such as **maximum likelihood**, principal factors, generalised least squares, weighted least squares, alpha factoring, and image analysis. They all use different mathematical methods to estimate communalities and position the factors relative to the variables before rotation takes place. The good news is that it does not matter much which method is used; Harman (1976; still a classic) demonstrated this by analysing the same sets of data by just about every conceivable method, and the consensus view about this has not changed.

Maximum likelihood estimation is useful for two reasons: it is mathematically elegant and it provides statistics which show how well the factor model fits the data, although the interpretation of these statistics is still contentious, as some of them are heavily influenced by sample size. The technique also has two disadvantages. It requires the assumption of "multivariate normality" and it will sometimes not work when analysing polychoric/tetrachoric correlations. Principal factors/principal axis or unweighted least squares/ordinary least squares are good substitutes; the other methods are a little more esoteric and so might require some justification for their use. The details of the mathematical methods described here are somewhat complex and so will not be explored further. Any good text on factor analysis such as Harman (1976), Gorsuch (1983) or Tabachnick and Fidell (2018) will allow the mathematically astute reader to master these issues.

All of the aforementioned techniques for factor extraction therefore place the factors in essentially arbitrary locations relative to the variables. Typically, the factors are positioned so that each successive factor is placed:

- At right angles to previous factors
- In a position where it "explains" a substantial proportion of the variance of the items (i.e., so that it is close to as many variables as possible; this means that the correlations between the factor and at least some of the variables will be appreciable, and so the eigenvalue of the factor will also be large).

However, as these factors are placed in arbitrary positions, it makes no sense to interpret this **unrotated factor matrix**.

STAGE 8: FACTOR ROTATION

Factor rotation changes the position of the factors relative to the variables so that the solution obtained is easy to interpret. As was mentioned in Chapter 10, factors are identified by observing which variables have large and/or zero loadings on them. The solutions which defy interpretation are those in which a large number of variables have "mediocre" loadings on a factor – loadings of the order of 0.2 or 0.3. These are too small to be used to identify the factor yet too large to be treated as if they were zero. Factor rotation moves the factors relative to the variables so that each factor has a few substantial loadings and a few near-zero loadings. This is another way of saying that the factors are spun round until they pass through the clusters of variables, as was seen in Chapter 10.

Thurstone (1947) was probably the first to realise that the initial position of the factor axes was arbitrary and that such solutions were difficult to interpret and harder to replicate. He suggested that factors should be rotated and coined the term "simple structure" to describe the case in which each factor has some large loadings and some small loadings, and likewise each variable has substantial loadings on only a few factors. Specifically he suggested that:

1. Each variable should have at least one near-zero loading on a factor.
2. Each factor should have at least as many near-zero loadings as there are factors.
3. Every pair of factors should have several variables whose loadings are near zero for one factor but not the other.
4. Whenever more than about four factors are extracted, every pair of factors should have a large portion of variables with zero loadings in both factors.
5. Every pair of factors should have few variables with nonzero loadings in both factors.

For example, if two factors are extracted from the correlations between six variables, the correlations between each of the variables and each of the tables could resemble one of the five models shown in Table 11.2. Here a "large" loading (one greater than

Table 11.2 Five different two-factor solutions, only one of which demonstrates simple structure

	Simple structure		Fails Rules 1 and 2		Fails Rule 2		Fails Rule 3		Fails Rule 5	
	F1	F2	F1	F2	F1	F2	F1	F2	F1	F2
Var. 1	*		*		*	*	*		*	*
Var. 2		*	*	*		*			*	*
Var. 3		*	*			*			*	*
Var. 4	*		*	*	*				*	
Var. 5		*	*	*		*				*
Var. 6	*		*		*	*	*	*	*	

Note: An asterisk denotes a large factor loading. A blank entry denotes a near-zero loading.

0.4 or less than −0.4 by convention) is shown as an asterisk and a "small" loading (between −0.39 and +0.39) is shown as a blank.

It is worth spending a little time to see what simple structure looks like by perusing this table, as it is important to recognise it when interpreting factor matrices.

Table 11.3 demonstrates how much easier it is to interpret rotated rather than unrotated factor solutions. The unrotated solution has several loadings in the order of 0.2 or 0.3 which are too large to ignore but not large enough to get excited about. After rotation, the solution could not be clearer. The first factor looks as if it measures language ability (because of its substantial loadings from the comprehension and spelling tests), whilst the second factor corresponds to numerical ability. The eigenvalues and communalities of the variables are also shown. This indicates that, during rotation, the communality of each variable stays the same but the eigenvalues do not. However, the sum of the communalities (which equals the sum of the eigenvalues) stays the same. The rotated solution explains exactly the same amount of variance as the unrotated solution; it just distributes it differently between the factors.

One crucial decision has to be made when rotating factors. Should they be kept at right angles (an "orthogonal rotation"), or should they allowed to become correlated (an "oblique rotation")? Since one never knows whether factors will be correlated, it is good practice to always perform an oblique rotation. However, the computation and interpretation of orthogonal solutions is considerably more straightforward, which accounts for their continued popularity.

Kaiser's (1958) **VARIMAX** algorithm is a method of rotation which MAXimises the VARIance of the squared factor loadings in order to find the best orthogonal

Table 11.3 Rotated and unrotated factor matrices

Variable	Unrotated solution			VARIMAX rotated solution		
	F1	F2	Communality	F1	F2	Communality
Comprehension	−0.766	0.170	0.616	0.780	0.086	0.616
Spelling	−0.717	0.288	0.597	0.772	−0.042	0.597
Vocabulary	−0.718	0.143	0.535	0.725	0.096	0.535
Multiplication	−0.148	−0.684	0.489	−0.080	0.695	0.489
Matrices	−0.364	−0.524	0.408	0.176	0.614	0.408
Geometry	−0.244	−0.602	0.422	0.037	0.649	0.422
Eigenvalue	1.830	1.237	Sum = 3.067	1.769	1.300	Sum = 3.067

simple structure rotation. Variance is maximised when each factor contains some large and some very small loadings – in other words, when simple structure has been reached. It is the overwhelmingly popular choice for orthogonal rotations, and many computer packages will perform it by default. Its rationale is quite straightforward and is best demonstrated using Spreadsheet 11.2, which allows you to perform a factor rotation "by eye" and compares these results with the VARIMAX solution. It should provide evidence that the VARIMAX solution finds the same answer as eyeballing the data.

Note that when performing a rotation in Spreadsheet 11.2, we keep the axes in the same place and move the variables around rather than keeping the variables in the same place and rotating the axes. The two procedures are of course equivalent.

Spreadsheet name: Spreadsheet 11.2: VARIMAX rotation

Download from: https://routledge.com/9781032146164/

Purpose:

- To show how VARIMAX works.
- To demonstrate that it produces the same solution as rotating factors by eye.
- To introduce the hyperplane count.

Contents of spreadsheet:

Four datasets (A–D), each showing an unrotated factor matrix with six variables and two factors.

Suggested activity:

(a) Copy and paste dataset A into the unrotated factor loading matrix. The rotated factor matrix is shown, and a graph also shows a plot of the rotated factor loadings. The blue squares on the graph represent the arrowheads in Figure 10.2. You should convince yourself that the blue squares on the graph represent the values in the rotated factor matrix.

   o Does the unrotated matrix meet the criteria for simple structure shown in Table 11.2?
   o Underneath the graph is a green slider. Moving this sideways will rotate the variables relative to the factor axes.

PERFORMING AND INTERPRETING FACTOR ANALYSES 255

- o Adjust the slider to identify the best "simple structure" solution by eye – that is, find the position where each variable has a large loading on one factor but a small loading on the other. Note down the "normalised VARIMAX" figure, below the slider.
- o Now adjust the slider without looking at the graph; instead, find the position where the value of the "normalised VARIMAX" statistic is at a maximum. Does your eyeball come to the same conclusion as this statistic?
- o Check Table 11.2 to determine whether the solution has reached simple structure.

(b) Repeat the process for datasets B–D. For each dataset, notice how the information in the diagram is reflected in the rotated factor matrix. This is important, as computer programs do not usually print out diagrams, and so the interpretation of the results from a factor analysis relies entirely on how well one can understand the factor matrix.

Points to note:

- Dataset B clearly requires an oblique solution; it is impossible to position the variables on top of the right-angled factors.
- Dataset C represents random data without any real factor structure; it is hard to decide whether one position is better than another. None of the loadings in the rotated factor matrix is above 0.4.
- Here two factors are used to represent a one-factor solution; once again, the loadings fail to reach simple structure. The best solution places the variables at 45 degrees to each of the factors.
- There is a correlation matrix at the bottom of each spreadsheet. Copying and pasting this into a text document allows the datasets to be analysed using the Factor program or similar.

Learning outcomes:

Readers should now be able to:

- Recognise simple structure when they see it.
- Appreciate that the VARIMAX criterion positions factors sensibly and tries to ensure that they reach simple structure.
- Appreciate that when the wrong number of factors, or if orthogonal rotation is performed when oblique rotation is required, the solution may not reach simple structure.

Table 11.4 shows four sets of unrotated factor solutions which can usefully be rotated as described in Spreadsheet 11.2.

Table 11.4 Four sets of factor loadings for rotation using Spreadsheet 11.2

Dataset A: Two orthogonal factors		
	Factor 1	Factor 2
Var. 1	0.63	0.47
Var. 2	0.53	0.56
Var. 3	0.59	0.43
Var. 4	0.42	−0.56
Var. 5	0.55	−0.33
Var. 6	0.47	−0.45

Dataset B: Two oblique factors		
	Factor 1	Factor 2
Var. 1	0.42	−0.54
Var. 2	0.63	−0.43
Var. 3	0.43	−0.27
Var. 4	0.54	0.08
Var. 5	0.60	0.20
Var. 6	0.54	0.24

Dataset C: No factors		
	Factor 1	Factor 2
Var. 1	−0.20	0.22
Var. 2	0.00	−0.30
Var. 3	−0.20	−0.27
Var. 4	0.15	0.22
Var. 5	0.23	0.00
Var. 6	0.17	−0.32

Dataset D: One factor		
	Factor 1	Factor 2
Var. 1	−0.46	0.12
Var. 2	−0.59	0.02
Var. 3	−0.44	−0.03
Var. 4	−0.48	−0.08
Var. 5	0.42	0.10
Var. 6	0.43	−0.16

Computer programs for factor rotation simply find the solution which maximises some mathematical criterion, such as the normalised VARIMAX criterion shown on the spreadsheet. They can deal with more than two factors (imagine a third axis sticking out from the spreadsheet, with another slider under it). However, you may have noticed that when rotating the factors using the spreadsheet, the normalised VARIMAX criterion sometimes does not change very much even though the factor loadings do. In other words, there can be a range of almost equally good solutions with slightly different factor loadings. Worse still, there may be two almost equally good solutions which have very different patterns of loadings. Computer programs will not warn you if or when this happens. It is therefore important to realise that factor loadings are really fairly crude; it would make no sense to argue that a variable with a loading of 0.5 is in some sense "better" than one with a loading of 0.45, for example. All one can sensibly say is that both are reasonably large.

Sometimes it makes little sense to keep the factors at right angles; in the second dataset it is not really possible to position the factors close to the clusters of variables. Examining the rotated factor matrix shows that rather than having a large loading on one factor and a near-zero loading on the other factor, variables sometimes have one large and one moderate loading −0.2 or so. Seeing this in the VARIMAX rotated factor matrix can indicate that an oblique rotation is needed.

In the third case, there is no discernible simple structure – all of the data points are scattered around, and it is impossible to rotate the axes anywhere sensible. Again this is reflected in the rotated factor matrix; just note how large the factor loadings are.

The fourth case is interesting. Here we have extracted too many factors; the correlation matrix contains one factor, but we attempt to rotate two factors. Rotating the factors to maximise the normalised VARIMAX criterion does not place the variables where one might expect if performing the rotation "by eye". Instead the rotation algorithm places the variables along a line midway between the two factors, as you should determine. This is reflected in the factor matrix, where there are no near-zero loadings, indicating that the rotation has not reached simple structure. This is an important point to remember. If a pair of factors have similar loadings and few near-zero loadings, this may indicate that either too many factors have been extracted, or that an orthogonal rotation has been performed where an oblique one would be more appropriate (see dataset B). The analysis should be run again using oblique rotation, or with one fewer factor being extracted.

What is the difference between the "normalised" VARIMAX criterion and the non-normalised one? Where variables have different communalities, the VARIMAX criterion defined earlier will give more weight to the variables with the higher communalities when positioning the factors. Hence, the normalised VARIMAX criterion is generally used; this gives equal weight to all variables when deciding where to position them. The variables in dataset A and dataset B have somewhat different communalities, so it is worthwhile looking what happens when these are rotated using both criteria. For dataset A difference is fairly small; it is larger for dataset B. As Revelle (2017a) observes, some statistical packages use the normalised criterion whilst others do not, and some (e.g., Factor) give users the choice of which to use. It always makes sense to choose the normalised version of any rotation algorithm.

OBLIQUE ROTATIONS

Whilst the factor structure matrix shows the correlations between all of the variables and all of the factors, in Figure 10.3 we showed that, although each factor passes neatly through a cluster of variables, because the factors are correlated it is no longer the case that each variable has a large correlation with just one factor. Alarmingly, opinions are divided as to whether the factor structure matrix or the factor pattern matrix should be interpreted in order to identify the factors, or to report the results of factor analyses. For example, Kline (1994, p. 63) states that "it is important . . . that the structure and not the pattern is interpreted", yet Cattell (1978 chap 8),

Tabachnick and Fidell (2018) and most others hold precisely the opposite view. Brogden (1969) suggests that if the factor analysis uses well-understood tests but the interpretation of the factors is unknown, then the pattern matrix should be consulted. Conversely, if the nature of the factors is known but the nature of the items is not, then the structure matrix should be consulted. Brogden's justification for this position seems to be sound, and so one should normally interpret the pattern matrix.

Readers may wonder how one would ever be able to identify a factor but not the variables which load on it. However, this is possible. For example, a selection of behavioural or physiological measures may be correlated and factored. Each person's score on each factor may be computed (see below), and these "factor scores" may be correlated with other tests. If a set of factor scores shows a correlation of 0.7 with the people's scores on a reputable test of anxiety, it is fairly safe to infer that the factor measures anxiety. Alternatively, a few well-trusted tests may be included in the analysis to act as "marker variables". If these have massive loadings on any of the rotated factors, this clearly identifies the nature of those factors.

Several programs have been written to perform oblique rotations, and Clarkson and Jennrich (1988), Harman (1976) and Sass and Schmitt (2010) are amongst those which discuss the relationships between the various methods and evaluate their usefulness. However, the *important* decisions are whether to perform a component or a factor analysis, how many factors to rotate, and whether to use an oblique or orthogonal rotation. In practice, it does not seem to matter too much which particular rotation technique is used. "In reality, the selection of 'best' rotation criterion must be made by the researcher. In many circumstances, different rotation criteria yield nearly identical rotated pattern loading matrices" (Sass & Schmitt, 2010). Techniques such as (normalised) **direct oblimin** (Jennrich & Sampson, 1966) are among the more useful.

A point which is often overlooked is that oblique rotation programs need "fine-tuning" in order to reach simple structure (Harman, 1976), usually by means of a parameter called delta or gamma which controls how oblique the factors are allowed to become. This is set by default to a value which the program author rather hoped would be adequate for most of the time. Using this value blindly is a dangerous, if common, practice. Harman suggests performing several rotations, each with a different value of this parameter, and interpreting that which comes closest to simple structure. Using normalised direct oblimin from the Factor program, it is possible to adjust gamma in the "configure rotation" section; a large negative value (e.g., -100) will produce a factor pattern matrix which looks very much like the VARIMAX solution. Larger values (e.g., -30, -10, -1, 0, $+0.2$) will allow the factors to become more and more correlated. Values of delta larger than about $+0.2$ can cause problems, as the program may try to place the factors on top of each other, which will crash the program. It is sensible to rotate the factors several times, using several different values of delta, and then interpret the solution which shows the best simple structure. One method for determining the "best" solution might be to monitor the hyperplane count, as described later (Nguyen & Waller, in press).

FACTOR ROTATION BY MONITORING HYPERPLANE COUNT

An alternative to the so-called analytic methods of factor rotation, such as VARIMAX or OBLIMIN which rely on finding the maximum of some mathematical function, is to simply position the axes so that as many variables as possible have near-zero loadings on the factors. Variables with near-zero loadings are "in the **hyperplane**". It is possible to perform such a rotation using Spreadsheet 11.2. One simply specifies how wide the hyperplane should be (in other words, what value of factor loadings should be regarded as trivially small. Figures such as 0.1 or 0.2 are usual, implying that loadings between −0.1 and +0.1 or −0.2 and +0.2 are "in the hyperplane". One then rotates the solution to simply maximise the hyperplane count. What could be simpler?

EXERCISE 11.2

Purpose: To explore rotation by maximising hyperplane count.

Suggested activity:

- Use Spreadsheet 11.2 to rotate factors so that the hyperplane count (shown below the graph) is maximised.
- Does this generally suggest the same rotation as normalised VARIMAX?

Points to note:

- Several rather different patterns of loadings have similar hyperplane counts, which may make the technique of limited use when the number of variables and factors is small.

Learning outcomes: Readers should now be able to:

- Appreciate that maximising hyperplane count is a simple method of rotation to simple structure.

There are two main problems with this technique:

- The width of the hyperplane is arbitrary. If one gets a different set of factor loadings by maximising the number of variables in the 0.1 hyperplane and 0.2 hyperplane, how does one decide which solution is better?

- Several very different factor matrices can sometimes give the same (high) hyperplane count. This can be seen by rotating dataset B. How does one decide which is the best?

This approach to factor rotation has not received much attention in the literature. This is partly because it was developed at more or less the same time as the mathematically elegant analytical solutions (e.g., VARIMAX, PROMAX) beloved of psychometricians, and it also required a great deal of computational power given the facilities then available. It also had the annoying habit of producing *very* highly correlated factors unless care was taken to prevent factors from piling up on top of each other.

Cattell's "Maxplane" technique (Cattell & Muerle, 1960) was the first program to attempt this form of rotation, and it appears to give similar results to other methods of rotation (Gorsuch, 1970). Functionplane (Katz & Rohlf, 1974) is a later development which seems to overcome the two problems shown. However, it does not seem to be implemented in any popular statistical packages. The good thing about hyperplane maximisation programs is that they do not now involve as much mathematical "work" as analytic rotation algorithms, and so if one has concerns about whether it is appropriate to treat psychological data as interval-scaled, this type of approach may still be useful.

STAGE 9: FACTOR SCORES

Suppose that one factor-analyses a set of test items which measure some mental ability, e.g., the speed with which people can visualise what various geometric shapes would look like after being rotated or flipped over. Having performed a factor analysis on these data, one might find that a single factor explains a good proportion of the variance, with many of the test items having substantial loadings on this factor. It is possible to validate this factor in exactly the same way as one would validate a test (as discussed in Chapter 9). For example, one can determine whether people's scores on the factor correlate substantially with their scores on other psychological tests measuring spatial ability, measures of performance etc. How, then, to work out each person's score on the factor – their **factor score**?

Most readers will never need to compute a factor score and so can safely skip the remainder of this section. In any case, if factor analysis is being used to identify a group of items which will be put together as a scale, it makes more sense to determine how well scores on this scale correlate with behaviour rather than dealing with scores on the "factor".

One obvious way of calculating a factor score is to identify the items which have substantial loadings on the factor and to simply add up each person's scores on these items, ignoring those with tiny loadings on the factor. For example, suppose that four

Likert-scaled items were factor-analysed and that these had loadings of 0.62, 0.45, 0.18 and 0.73 on a factor (after rotation). This suggests that items 1, 2 and 4 measure much the same trait, whereas item 3 measures something rather different. In this case, adding together each person's scores on items 1, 2 and 4[4] might be sensible. There is a lot to be said for this simple approach, which is exactly equivalent to identifying which items form a scale and then adding the scores on these items together. It is simple to perform and easy to understand.

An alternative way of writing the same thing is to say that each standardised variable should be multiplied by a weight to give the score for each factor. In the example, the weights for variables 1–4 are 1, 1, 0 and 1. These are known as *factor score coefficients*. If more than one factor is extracted/rotated, then each factor will have a separate set of factor score coefficients.

It is, however, possible to have factor score coefficients which are not just 0 or 1. For example, if one variable 2 has a larger loading on the factor than variable 1 (meaning that it is a better measure of the factor), it might be sensible to give it a larger weight; the first two factor score coefficients might be 0.6 and 0.8, for example. All the factor score estimation procedures described next are different ways of achieving this end.

In the case of principal components analysis and orthogonal rotation, the calculation is straightforward; one simply divides the factor loadings by the sum of the squared loadings of the *rotated* factor (its eigenvalue) to obtain the factor score coefficients for that factor. Then to calculate each person's score on that principal component, one simply standardises the scores on each of the variables (divides each person's score on each variable core by the standard deviation of the variable) and multiplies these standardised scores by the appropriate factor score coefficient. Then one adds together each of these scores for each person to obtain a factor score.[5] Spreadsheet 11.3 "Calculating component scores following orthogonal rotation" gives a worked example, for those who are interested.

The process is slightly more complex when performing oblique rotation, but the same basic principles apply: one obtains a matrix of factor score coefficients, standardises the raw data, and multiplies a person's standardised scores on all variables by the component score coefficients for a principal component. Summing these gives the score of that person on that component.

Deriving the factor score coefficients from a factor analysis is more complex than for principal components, and there are several different ways of estimating factor scores – often yielding rather similar results (McDonald & Burr, 1967), though Bartlett's method is arguably the best. Good discussions are given by Harman (1976 chap 16), Comrey and Lee (1992 sec 10.3) and Harris (1967), for those who are interested. A useful (though somewhat mathematical) history of methods of calculating factor scores is given by Bartholomew et al. (2009).

SUMMARY

Factor analysis is a tremendously useful technique for clarifying the relationships between interval-scaled or ratio-scaled variables. It can be applied to any such data — from physical and physiological measures to questionnaire items. This chapter described how to perform a technically sound factor analysis and highlighted some common errors which occasionally creep into published papers.

NOTES

1. Actually a choice of two slightly different methods.
2. Except in the case of the one-factor solution.
3. Or in some implementations, two largest loadings.
4. It is better to add together the standardised scores rather than the raw scores for each variable. This is because if the variables have different standard deviations, the variables with the largest standard deviations will have a greater influence on the total score, an issue we encountered when considering coefficient alpha. This is rarely done in practice when computing scale scores from several Likert items. However it should definitely be done when combining scores from several different scales if the standard deviations vary considerably.
5. It is common practice, though not necessary, to subtract the mean of each variable from each person's score before dividing by the variable's standard deviation.

CHAPTER 12
ALTERNATIVE FACTOR ANALYSIS DESIGNS

Thus far we have seen how factor analysis can be a useful tool for analysing the correlations between test scores, item responses or other variables. We have assumed that a large sample of people provide data on a smaller number of tests or items, and that these test scores or items are correlated together. Factor analysis can then be used to examine the correlations between the tests and determine whether they all measure different things or whether they instead measure a smaller number of factors.

The vast number of analyses in the literature perform analyses in this way. However, there are plenty of other possible designs for using factor analysis. This chapter explores some of these and gives some examples of how and why they may be useful in a wide variety of settings – including case studies of individuals, classification of people and the study of mood and motivation. In particular, the idea that factor analysis can provide valuable insights when studying individuals (for example, in clinical work or case studies) does not seem to be well known. What follows draws heavily on the work of Cattell (1946; 1978), who seems to have been the first to see the huge potential which these techniques offer for academic and applied psychologists.

The basic idea is very simple. So far we have used factor analysis to analyse the correlations between a number of pieces of data (e.g., scores on tests, responses to items) obtained from a sample of people. The number of people is larger than the number of variables. Cattell suggests that this form of factor analysis is termed **R-technique** ("R" for "regular") – simply because it is the most familiar and most popular form of factor-analytic design.

It should be obvious from the diagram that there are other possible designs, too. What if a lot of data were gathered from a few people on one occasion? For example, suppose that a developmental psychologist has data on 30 children whose behaviour has been measured on one occasion using the Child Behaviour Checklist (Achenbach & Rescorla, 2001). Typical items on this checklist are "eats things which are not food or drink", "gets in many fights" and "acts too young for age", each of which is scored using a 3-point scale.

DOI: 10.4324/9781003240181-12

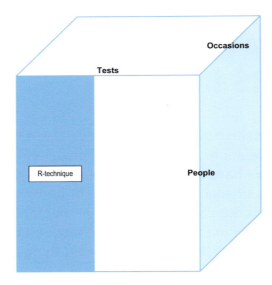

Figure 12.1 Regular (R-technique) factor analysis in context. This involves factor-analysing the correlations between a moderate number of variables based on the responses of many people on one occasion. Putting R-technique in context, the cube shows people, variables and occasions. As R-analysis involves testing a lot of people on a few variables on one occasion, R-analysis can be represented by the dark blue rectangle as shown. The fact that it is taller than it is wide indicates that the number of people exceeds the number of variables.

This checklist consists of 113 items, and so it would clearly be impossible to perform an R-factor analysis in order to determine which of the checklist items form factors, because there are more items in the checklist than there are people in the sample. Anyway, this might not be the question which the child psychologist wants to address. They might be much more interested in knowing how many different "types" of children there are in the sample. For example, does the checklist allow the children to be categorised in terms of disruptive behaviour, or can it also identify children who are anxious/depressed?

One possibility would be to perform what Cattell terms a **Q-technique** factor analysis. Instead of correlating the items together, *people* are correlated together on the basis of their scores on the items, as shown in Figure 12.2. People who respond similarly to the test items correlate substantially, and will form a factor. For example, five children might have large loadings on factor 1 and four might have very low loadings; this tells us that these children are on the opposite ends of some continuum. And on studying the results, the psychologist might realise that the five children with large positive loadings are disruptive, whilst the four at the other extreme are co-operative. A second factor might separate out the children who are diagnosed as having affective disorders (anxiety etc.) from those who are not . . . and so on. It is also possible to calculate factor scores to identify which items in the checklist led to the particular groupings of children which are found.

ALTERNATIVE FACTOR ANALYSIS DESIGNS

There are other possible designs too, and rather than drawing many more figures like Figures 12.1 and 12.2, these are all shown together in Figure 12.3. In each case, the variables to be correlated are represented by the smaller end of a rectangle. Thus T-technique involves administering one test to many people on several occasions

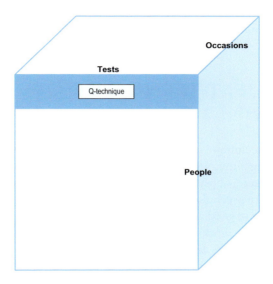

Figure 12.2 Q-technique factor analysis involves factor-analysing the correlations between a moderate number of people based on their responses to a large number of variables

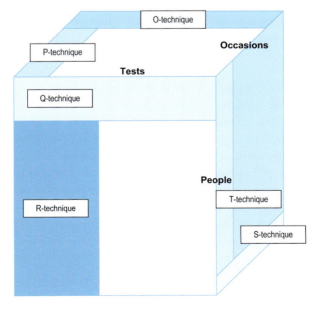

Figure 12.3 Cattell's classification of factor-analytic designs

and correlating/factor-analysing the occasions. Methods which are particularly useful in psychology include P-technique and S-technique. P-technique involves gathering data from just one person on a large number of occasions – although as we shall see next, it can be modified to allow data from several people to be used. It is very useful in studying mood or motivation, as it shows which mood variables change together from occasion to occasion. The other techniques are rarely – if ever – used, even though they may be useful in some contexts. These are described briefly.

S-TECHNIQUE, T-TECHNIQUE AND O-TECHNIQUE

Like Q-technique, S-technique involves identifying types of individuals – but based on their responses to a single test, which is administered on a large number of occasions. Suppose that an occupational psychologist wanted to discover how stress affected members of a university psychology department, with the objective of discovering which individuals were stressed at which periods of the year, so that additional support and/or changes to working practices might be put in place. A key question is whether all members of staff experience stress at the same times, and so a sample of undergraduate students, graduate students, professors, clerical support staff, teaching staff, technical staff and administrators might each be given a stress questionnaire to complete once a day for a year. The total score on this scale is analysed; S-factor analysis might show that the undergraduate students, some administrators and some clerical staff all load on the same factor, indicating that they experience stress at much the same times of the year, whilst professors might fall onto a different factor, indicating that they experience stress at different times. The key point is that the factor analysis will show how many distinct groups of people exist within the sample and which people belong to which group.

On the other hand, T-technique is more likely to be of interest to those who study moods or are interested in the psychometric properties of a particular test which measures a personality trait of some sort – conscientiousness, for example. (It would make little sense to use it to explore an *ability* trait such as general intelligence because T-technique involves measuring the trait on multiple occasions, and participants would remember how they solved the various items in an ability test.) T-technique involves giving a large group of people the same test on a smaller number of occasions; the correlations between the scores which the people obtain on the various occasions are then are inter-correlated and factor-analysed. The size of these correlations says something about the temporal stability (test-retest reliability) of the scale, and if just one factor is found it will indicate that the test produces consistent scores on every occasion.

Several mood induction techniques have been developed to change people's moods, and one way of testing their effectiveness would be to administer a mood scale on several occasions, some of which followed a mood induction. If the mood induction was generally successful, a factor should emerge consisting of the occasions on which the mood induction took place; as the participants lived different lives, one would not expect their mood scores to be correlated on the other occasions. That said, I know of no studies which have used T-technique.

O-technique involves one person completing a large number of tests (or test items) on a smaller number of occasions – corresponding to different situations, perhaps. The scores obtained on the various occasions are then correlated together. It could therefore show which situations similarly influence a person's entire personality profile, or their entire range of mood states. Being based on a single individual, it could conceivably be useful in clinical psychology, although I am not aware of any published research (clinical or otherwise) which uses it.

P-TECHNIQUE AND ITS VARIANTS

P-technique is very useful in developing and evaluating scales which measure moods, emotional states, motivational states, and anything else which is likely to vary over time. Whilst the definition of P-technique given here allows for the analysis of a single individual (for example, discovering which items in a questionnaire measuring mood or behaviour tend to change together), two other techniques – called Chain-P technique and dR or differential R technique) have been developed which allow the use of larger samples of people.

Regular (R-technique) factor analysis should *not* be used when designing a questionnaire to measure states such as mood or motivation. Any scales which are developed in this way should be treated with scepticism. The reason is simple. R-technique only considers the correlations between variables which are measured on one occasion. The key thing about moods and levels of motivation is that they vary over time. So to measure mood, it is necessary to discover whether (for example) the days in which a person feels energetic are also the days in which they feel apprehensive, healthy, alert, confident and strong, and to find that on days when someone's score on one of these variables dips, their scores on all of the others decrease too. If so, these behaviours go together and form a mood state. Only by studying which items vary together over time within an individual can we be sure that the test is measuring states rather than stable personality traits.

P-technique is ideal for this purpose. Suppose that one person is given a 20-item mood questionnaire to complete at random times of the day on 50 or more occasions. It might be found that when the person's responses to the items are intercorrelated and factor-analysed, whenever the person feels healthy they also tend to feel alert, confident and strong; on occasions when their scores on one of these variables dips, the scores on the other variables dip too. In other words, these four items form a factor of mood. Much the same can be done with a test of motivation.

The reason why many psychologists (it would be unkind to give a reference) try to construct mood scales using R-technique is probably just expediency. It is very easy to administer a set of items to a group of students in a class on one occasion, whereas gathering data from a person on multiple occasions requires more effort. In addition, completing a mood scale (and possibly a bundle of other questionnaires too) in a classroom is a pretty grisly experience for anyone, and this will surely have an impact on the very moods which the questionnaires try to assess! It really is far better to administer the questionnaires on a mobile device as people are living their normal lives and identify groups of items which inter-correlate from occasion to occasion.

When analysing data using P-technique there should be more occasions than items. Any of the usual factor-analytic methods may be used (e.g., using parallel analysis to identify the optimum number of factors, plus some form of oblique rotation).

The interpretation of the results is quite straightforward. Each of the factors which emerges corresponds to a group of items which tend to rise and fall together over time, and so which measure the same mood or level of motivation. Scrutiny of the items will allow each factor to be tentatively identified, and each factor should then be validated in the usual way.

There are, however, some problems with P-technique. The most obvious is that it analyses the responses made by a single person. Whilst this may sometimes be extremely useful – for example, in clinical psychology – many researchers will want to reassure themselves that the results obtained from this analysis will generalise to other people. One possibility might be to perform several different P-technique factor analyses, each based on a different person, to determine whether the same mood items have substantial loadings for each individual. However, it would be hard to decide what to do if there were substantial differences between the number or nature of factors found for each person. Or one could use a technique called multiple-group structural equation modelling to determine whether the same factor structure fits the data from all of the participants.

The second issue is more practical. If the mood questionnaire is long, then it will be necessary to administer it on a great number of occasions to perform the factor analysis, given that there needs to be more occasions than items. This may create practical difficulties, as it might be hard to find volunteers who will diligently answer the mood items on (say) 100 occasions. If there are more items than occasions, one solution might be to use item parcelling – grouping items together to reduce the number of variables to be factored (Little et al., 2013). However, in a truly exploratory study, deciding how to form the parcels may be difficult. Unless parcelling is performed very carefully, the results of the factor analysis can be misleading or hard to interpret, and of course the problem with an exploratory analysis such as we describe here is that very little evidence is available about the psychometric properties of the items. It is therefore hard to decide how or whether to combine them into parcels.

Two modifications of P-technique may therefore be more useful.

CHAIN-P TECHNIQUE

Chain-P technique involves gathering data from each of several people and stacking their data on top of each other before performing the factor analysis. For example, if a mood questionnaire consists of six items, the data file might resemble Table 12.1.

Here the first person provided data on four occasions: for this example we pretend that the six mood items have been answered using a 5-point scale, so the responses are numbers from 1 to 5. The second person provided data on just three occasions and so on. The factor analysis would be performed on the whole data file.

Table 12.1 Stacked data for a Chain-P factor analysis

		Item 1	Item 2	Item 3	Item 4	Item 5	Item 6
Person 1	Occasion 1	2	3	5	3	4	3
	Occasion 2	1	2	3	4	3	3
	Occasion 3	4	2	2	5	2	1
	Occasion 4	4	5	2	1	1	4
Person 2	Occasion 1	5	4	5	4	4	5
	Occasion 2	4	3	5	5	4	5
	Occasion 3	5	5	3	4	5	4
Person 3	Occasion 1	5	2	5	1	2	3
	Occasion 2	4	3	3	3	2	3
	Occasion 3	2	3	2	3	3	3
	Occasion 4	2	5	5	3	2	2
	Occasion 5	3	3	4	2	4	1
Person 4	Occasion 1	5	4	5	5	5	4

This method is widely recommended – but there can be a problem with analysing the scores as shown. A cursory look at the data in Table 12.1 shows that person 2 tends to use the 4s and 5s on the rating scale far more than the other participants. This might be because of some sort of response style, such as the tendency to agree with statements. It could be because they have higher scores on a trait which is related to mood; indeed Cattell (1973) has suggested that each trait may have a corresponding mood state. This is hardly surprising. If items are written to measure the state of anxiety, people who are habitually highly anxious (a trait) will tend to rate themselves higher on these "mood" items than will people who are low on trait anxiety. This causes problems with Chain-P analyses.

> **Spreadsheet name:** Spreadsheet 12.1: P-technique
>
> **Download from:** https://routledge.com/9781032146164/
>
> **Purpose:** To show why data must be standardised by person before performing Chain-P technique factor analysis.
>
> **Contents of spreadsheet:** Table 12.1 shows data from a 6-item Likert scale administered to one person on 11 occasions.
>
> **Suggested activity:**
>
> - Scroll down and note the correlations in Table 12.2, which show that items 1–3 measure one state and items 4–6 another state. (You may wish to factor-analyse the correlations to check.)
> - Table 12.4 shows the same data – plus the data from four additional people; a chain-P design. By some huge coincidence all of the people have exactly the same scores on the questionnaires, and so the correlations between the items in Table 12.4 are identical to the correlations in Table 12.2. A moment's thought will reveal why. The scatter diagrams for these two sets of data would look identical; the only difference is that each data point is based on five people, not one.
> - What happens if some people have higher average scores than others on one or both of the moods? For example, if one of the moods is state anxiety, what if some of the participants are more anxious in all situations than are other people? Adjusting the values on the green "Offset" cells in Table 12.3 adds a constant to a person's scores on items 1–3 and/or their scores on items 4–6 on every occasion. Entering an offset of 1 for person 2 on items 1–3 will add 1 to each of that person's scores on these items; it will increase their average score (but not their standard deviation). Do this now and check its effect on the data by comparing the scores of person 1 and person 2 in Table 12.4 and the means and standard deviations in Table 12.6!

- Just slightly increasing all of one person's scores on items 1–3 affects the correlations between items 1–3 more than one might perhaps expect; for example, the correlation between items 2 and 3 rises from 0.39 to 0.56. Now choose some more offset values for items 1–3 in Table 12.3 and note what happens to the correlations between the items in Table 12.5. It can be seen that the more that people's mean scores (offsets) vary, (a) the correlations between items 1–3 become considerably larger and (b) the correlations between items 1–3 and items 4–6 do not change much. Try entering some different values for the offsets for items 1–3 to convince yourself of this.
- If people's scores on items 4–6 are also allowed to vary, the correlations between items 4–6 will also increase. You may want to enter some values in the offsets for items 4–6 in Table 12.3 to check this. But what if the mean scores of the participants are correlated? What if the person with the largest offset (highest mean score) for items 1–3 also has the largest offset for items 4–6? This is quite likely to happen in practice. For example, suppose that items 1–3 measure state anxiety and 4–6 measure state depression. Although the biological mechanisms for anxiety and depression appear to be distinct, people who tend to be anxious also tend to be depressed, and so it is highly likely that in real life data, people with elevated scores on one mood will also have elevated scores on the other. Observe what happens to the correlations between items 1–3 and 4–6 (towards the bottom left of the correlation matrix in Table 12.5) if the offset for items 1–3 is chosen to resemble (or be roughly proportional to) the offset for items 4–6. For example, the offsets for persons 2–5 on items 1–3 might be 1, 2, 3 and 4; their offset for items 4–6 might be 1, 2, 2 and 3. It can be seen that this causes the correlations between items 1–3 and items 4–6 to increase dramatically. For example, using the values suggested, the correlation between items 2 and 5 rises from zero to 0.76! This will completely change the factor structure from what it should be.

Points to note:

- It is essential to re-scale the data so that each person has the same mean score when performing Chain-P analyses.

Learning outcomes: Readers should now be able to appreciate that:

- If people differ in their mean scores, this can influence the number of factors found in the correlation matrix when performing chain-P factor analysis.
- To avoid this, it is necessary to standardise scores on each item for each person before performing the factor analysis.

When people who have elevated scores on one set of items also happen to show elevated scores on another set of items:

(a) Correlations within a set of items which measure the same mood state will increase.
(b) Correlations between items which measure *different* mood states will increase.

Point (a) just suggests that the correlations between items which measure the same mood state – and hence their factor loadings – will become larger. But point (b) implies that the number of mood factors identified by P-technique will be incorrect. In the examples given, factor analysis will identify one mood factor, not two, as the correlations between items which measure different mood factors can become large.

There is an easy way to avoid this problem. If the mood scores for each person are standardised (so that each person's scores on each item, averaged across occasions, have the same mean), the problem vanishes. It is also normal to ensure that each person's scores are brought to the same standard deviation, as consistent differences in standard deviations from person to person can also influence the correlations. It is conventional to standardise scores such that each person's scores on each item have a mean of zero and a standard deviation of 1.

DIFFERENTIAL R TECHNIQUE

If moods are measured on just two occasions, a simpler technique known as **differential R (dR) technique** can be used.

This technique simply involves subtracting each person's score on an item on occasion 2 from the score which they gave on occasion 1. Items which move in the same direction will be identified as states when these difference scores are correlated together and factor-analysed.

The problem with difference scores is that it is necessary to assume that each person in the sample uses the scales in the same way, and that someone whose score on an item shifts from 7 to 6 (on a Likert scale for an item) shows the same amount of mood change as someone whose mood changes from 2 to 1 – which Michell argued is unlikely to be the case. Person 6 in Spreadsheet 12.2 shows massive shifts in mood between the two occasions. This is not unusual; some people's moods swing enormously, whilst other people's moods are extremely stable (McConville & Cooper, 1992) – plus we may not know the situations under which the participants filled in the mood scales, which might explain their extreme shift in moods. But does this matter?

Spreadsheet name: Spreadsheet 12.2: dR technique

Download from: https://routledge.com/9781032146164/

Purpose: To show how individual differences in mood variability can affect the factor structure found using dR technique.

Contents of spreadsheet: Sample data from seven people, each of whom completed some mood items on two occasions. Table 12.1 shows the raw data and Table 12.2 the difference scores. Table 12.3 shows the correlations between these difference scores.

Suggested activity:

- Looking at Table 12.3, it is clear that one or mood factors are found. (Factor analysis reveals a one-factor solution where all variables except for variable 4 have large loadings on the factor.)
- Figure 12.1 of the dR technique spreadsheet plots the scatter diagram showing the correlation between item 1 and item 2. It can be seen that the huge mood shifts experienced by person 6 make them an outlier, and their data alone is responsible for the massive and statistically significant correlation between these two items.
- It is therefore clear that if some people's moods shift more than others, this will affect the correlations between the difference scores.
- It might be prudent to recode the mood-shift data as showing an increase, decrease or no shift between the two occasions. Tables 12.4 and 12.5 and Figure 12.2 of the dR technique spreadsheet show how this affects the correlations. Analysing the data this way would lead the researcher to a completely different conclusion about the number and nature of the mood factors.

Points to note:

- If people vary in the extent to which their moods change, this can affect the correlations and factor structure found using dR technique.
- Possible solutions might include recoding scores as negative, zero or positive, or standardising scores within individuals before calculating correlations.

Learning outcomes: Readers should now be able to:

- Appreciate that if some people's moods vary more than those of others, it is unwise to perform dR technique on raw difference scores.

The purpose of this is to show that correlating and factor-analysing difference scores in dR technique requires considerable care. Individual differences in mood variability mean that some people will show larger mood shifts than others, as will the fact that some people's lives are more eventful than others. There is a danger that these variables – which have nothing at all to do with the structure of moods – will tend to inflate correlations between items which are based on difference scores. One safe solution would be to code difference scores as just −1, 0 or +1.

Q-TECHNIQUE

Q-technique involves correlating people together on the basis of their scores on a large number of variables. For example, suppose that a group of undiagnosed psychiatric patients answered a large number of items in a questionnaire. The depressed patients would answer all of the items which enquired about low mood, sleep disturbances, concentration difficulties etc. in much the same way; the schizophrenic patients would answer items enquiring about hallucinations, delusions, feelings of being controlled etc. in much the same way. So when people are correlated together on the basis of these responses and a factor analysis is performed, then two factors should emerge – one with large loadings from all of the people with depression (remember that it is people, not variables, who show factor loadings in Q-factor analysis) and the other with high loadings from all of the people with schizophrenic symptoms.

Historically Q-technique has often been applied to a form of data known as the **Q-sort** (Stephenson, 1953). Here people are presented with a large number of printed cards, each with a statement written on it (e.g., "sociable"). Each participant decides how accurately the word or phrase on each card describes them, and shows this by sorting them into piles – typically along a scale from "extremely inaccurate" to "extremely accurate". They are usually given instructions to put a certain number of cards in each pile, with most near the centre. (The order of the cards within each pile does not matter.) Figure 12.4 shows an example where a person was asked to sort 22 cards so that there was one card in the leftmost pile, two cards in the next pile, then 4, 8, 4, 2 and 1 cards in subsequent piles.

Each card is given a score corresponding to the number at the bottom of the table: this score reflects how well the person believes that the description on the card describes them. These data are then put into a table rather as shown in Table 12.2. Here the *people* form the columns, and the *items* (*cards*) the rows – unlike the data tables used for R-factor analysis. The column titled "Person 1" holds some of the data from Figure 12.4, as you should verify.

That is the Q-sort. However, it is not necessary to perform a Q-sort in order to conduct a Q-factor analysis. All that is needed is a large number of quantitative variables which are administered to a rather smaller number of people. These variables might be responses to questionnaire items, test scores, physiological measures, ratings of

ALTERNATIVE FACTOR ANALYSIS DESIGNS

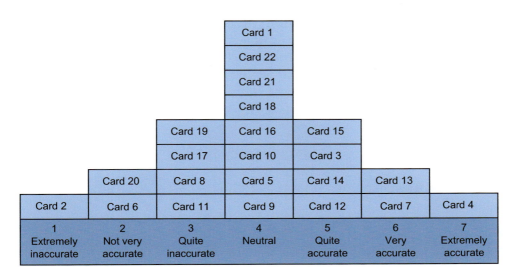

Figure 12.4 Diagram of how one person might arrange 22 cards describing themselves when performing a Q-sort

Table 12.2 Data matrix for Q-technique factor analysis

	Person 1	Person 2	Person 3	etc.
Card 1	4			
Card 2	1			
Card 3	5			
Card 4	7			
etc.				

behaviour or a whole host of other things. The aim of the Q-factor analysis will be to determine how people vary in the way in which they respond to these variables: that is, which people show similar profiles of responses to all of the items.

In order to perform a Q-analysis there should ideally be rather a lot of data from each person, and of course these pieces of data should be independent: the way in which a person responds to one item should not determine how they must respond to another, unless this correlation is caused by some personality trait, ability trait or other psychological phenomenon. For example, whilst "Do you believe in ghosts?" and "Do you believe in fairies?" would be fine, "Do you believe in the supernatural?" and "Do you believe in ghosts?" would not, as people who said that they did not believe in the supernatural could not, by definition, believe in ghosts.

It is also vitally important that the variables should be selected carefully, so that no variables are answered in the same way by (almost) all people in the sample. Any such variables will increase the correlations between *all* people: there will be a general factor of "humanness" (because all of the humans in the sample answer these items in exactly the same way). This is demonstrated in Spreadsheet 12.3. This generates some simulated data for Q-factor analyses for use with a statistical package such as Lorenzo-Seva and Ferrando (2006).

> **Spreadsheet name:** Spreadsheet 12.3: Q-technique
>
> **Download from:** https://routledge.com/9781032146164/
>
> **Purpose**: To show why non-discriminating items should be removed before performing Q-factor analysis.
>
> **Contents of spreadsheet:** Simulated data from three groups with different psychiatric diagnoses (depressive, schizophrenic and psychopathic). Each group contains three people, and everyone answered the same 21 questionnaire items.
>
> **Suggested activity:**
>
> - The first set of data (Table 12.1) in this spreadsheet shows the responses from 9 people (columns) who have each answered 21 questions (rows) on a 9-point Likert scale. The spreadsheet is constructed such that person D1 is given a random score on each item. Person D2's score and person D3's score are based on person D1's score: they are just randomly nudged up or down a little. A similar procedure is followed for persons S1–S3 and P1–P3. Thus the scores
> obtained by persons D1–D3 scores are similar; so too are the scores from S1–S3 and P1–P3. But the correlation *between* people from the different groups should be small. The correlations are shown in Table 12.2 of the spreadsheet., and a scatter diagram showing the correlation between persons D1 and P3 is shown next to Table 12.2. (The correlation between other pairs of people from different groups should be similar.)
> - Cut and paste the scores of the 9 people into a text file and use a program such as Lorenzo-Seva and Ferrando (2006) to convince yourself that Q-factor analysis can identify three groups of people. However, as such programs are designed to perform an R-factor analysis (correlating items together rather than people), when specifying the model it is necessary to specify 9 variables and 21 cases – not 21 variables and 9 cases. After rotation, the factor analysis will reveal three factors, with the first three people having large loadings on one factor, persons S1–S3 having large loadings on the second factor, and persons P1–P3 having large loadings on the third.

- What happens to the correlations between the people if more variables are added which are (a) extreme and (b) which do not discriminate between people? In other words, what if there are some items with which (almost) everyone strongly agrees or strongly disagrees? With Table 12.2 visible on screen, add some more values in the green cells below the existing data – but put the same large (or small) value in each column – 1s or 9s.
- As a row or two of such data are added, it is clear that the correlations between people from different groups (e.g., D1 and P3) increase quite rapidly, as can be seen in the scatter diagram to the right of the correlation matrix in Table 12.2. Factor-analysing the data now shows that the number of factors is fewer than 3 and that the structure is not nearly as clear-cut as previously.

Points to note:

- Non-discriminating items reduce the number of Q-factors.
- Non-discriminating items should be dropped, or the bifactor model or Schmid–Leiman technique might be used (see Chapter 13).

Learning outcomes: Readers should now be able to:

- Identify a problem with performing a Q-technique factor analysis.

It is therefore important to remove any items to which all participants give extreme and similar answers before performing a Q-factor analysis. Such items are not uncommon: any item with which virtually everyone strongly agrees, or with which almost everyone strongly disagrees, will affect the clarity of the results by increasing the correlation between the factors and/or reducing the apparent number of factors. The easiest way of identifying and removing them is to examine the mean and standard deviation of each item, to identify those which (a) do not discriminate between people and (b) have a very high or very low mean. The bifactor model or Schmid–Leiman technique could also presumably be used to eliminate the effects of the general factor; these methods are discussed in Chapter 13. However, I know of no studies which have done so.

G-ANALYSIS

G-analysis is simply a form of Q-analysis, which is based on dichotomous (two-valued) data. It is useful when a checklist is used to describe a person's responses to some stimulus, or when their behaviour is assessed using a true/false format. One of the earliest uses of the technique was to objectively score people's responses to a projective test, such as the Rorschach inkblots: a series of checklist items could be drawn up, perhaps (but not necessarily entirely) based on some theoretical or practical considerations. For example, if people are shown a black-and-white inkblot and one starts by saying that they see "two witches dancing round a bright red fire", it would be possible to code this data by using items such as:

- Item 1 mentions colour.
- Item 2 mentions movement.
- Item 3 mentions an alligator.

etc.

It is normal to gather the data first and then develop a coding system to capture its most salient characteristics: in the example, the aim would be to capture all the richness of the participants' descriptions in a list of features, each of which is coded as present or absent from each person's response to the picture.

For reasons discussed by Holley (1973), it is inappropriate to use the more usual Pearson correlation when correlating people together from binary-coded data. A different correlation called the G-coefficient overcomes the problem: it is shown on Spreadsheet 6.5. It is very simple to calculate. Suppose that two people are to be correlated together based on their responses to 20 two-value items. To calculate G, all one needs to know is how many times they give the same response: multiply this by 2, divide by the number of items, and subtract 1. For example, if the two people give the same responses to 13 of the 20 items, $G = (2 \times 13) / 20 - 1 = 0.3$.

More data are shown in Table 12.3. In part (a), the responses of two people to 16 items are shown. It can be seen that $G - (2 \times 8)/16 - 1 = 0$, which looks eminently sensible. However, suppose that the checklist contains some items to which everyone gives the same answer: for example, suppose that no-one reported seeing an alligator in the inkblot, and there were three more items like this. The data would be as shown in part (b), and G would be $-(2 \times 12)/20 - 1 = 0.2$. Including items which do not discriminate between people will increase the correlation between people, and consequently affect the factor structure in much the same way as shown in Spreadsheet

Table 12.3 Tables showing agreement between two people based on items coded 0/1

Part (a)		Person 2	
		0	1
Person 1	0	4	4
	1	4	4

Part (b)		Person 2	
		0	1
Person 1	0	8	4
	1	4	4

12.3. For this reason, G-analysis is best used when the items show a similar split – where the proportion of people coded as "1" is roughly similar for all items.

Fortunately, it is not that difficult to achieve this, especially if the data are being coded without much in the way of theoretical knowledge. In the example, rather than coding "mentions an alligator" (when virtually no-one ever does so), it might be possible to change the item to "mentions any non-human animal", which might perhaps be endorsed by 50% or so of the sample.

When faced with few theoretical expectations, plus a mass of data on a rather small sample of people – a not uncommon problem in clinical or educational research – it can make sense to perform a G-analysis because the usual R-technique factor analysis would not be appropriate as there are more variables than people. However, care must be taken to ensure that all of the items show individual differences, otherwise a large general factor will mask any more subtle groupings of people unless bifactor analysis etc. are used as described in Chapter 12.

IDENTIFYING Q-FACTORS

When performing a normal R-technique factor analysis, identifying the factors is straightforward, as one merely observes which variables have large positive or negative loadings on the factor. These can then be used to tentatively name the factor; the large-loading items can be put together to form a scale, and this scale can be administered alongside other tests to different samples and cross-validated as discussed in Chapter 9. But Q-technique merely reveals that certain people show similar responses to certain other people. How then can one tell which of the many items that were analysed are responsible for these groupings? How can one tell which items cause several people to correlate together?

There are two main options. The first is to rely on other sources of information about the participants. If factor analysis reveals that participants 2, 5 and 8 all show large loadings on a factor, it might be appropriate to consult case notes, diagnoses and so on in order to hypothesise what they have in common. The problem with this approach is that it is not terribly scientific and does not give any hint as to which particular items *cause* these people to form a factor. If the factor analysis is based on a hundred or more items, it might well be the case that only a couple of dozen of these are responsible for differentiating these people from the rest – and it would clearly be useful to know which these are so that the list of items can be shortened for future applications.

Another way of identifying which items cause people to correlate together and form a factor is to calculate factor scores and note which items have the most extreme (positive or negative) factor scores for each Q-factor. These are the items which are largely responsible for grouping people together on the factor. Alternatively (and more pragmatically), one could just perform many independent sample t-tests using each of the items as the dependent variable. For each variable, one would first test whether the mean score of everyone who had large loadings on factor 1 differed appreciably from the mean score of everyone else in the sample. Then the analysis would be repeated to find out which items differentiated the people who formed factor 2 from the rest of the sample and so on. Having identified which items best discriminate the groups, it should be possible to provisionally name the Q-factors – although as with any form of factor analysis, validation and replication on different samples is necessary.

THREE-MODE FACTOR ANALYSIS

The techniques outlined in this chapter have used factor analysis to analyses the responses of several *people*, each of whom yields scores on several different *variables* on multiple *occasions*. These are known as the three modes. Rather than use messy approximations (such as stacking people together when performing a Chain-P analysis), it might be possible to analyse variables, people and occasions together. Tucker (1966) and Bloxom (1968) developed a technique called three-mode factor analysis to analyse just this sort of data. It reduces the number of variables to a smaller number of factors, as in standard R-technique factor analysis: the reduced number of variables is known as the *attribute factor matrix*. But it simultaneously reduces the number of people, as does Q-technique factor analysis, forming the *object matrix*. And the number of occasions is also reduced, into the *occasion matrix*. The basic aim of three-mode factor analysis is to estimate values for the attribute matrix, the object matrix and the occasion matrix together with what Tucker terms a *core matrix*, which shows the size of the relationship between each of the factors in the attribute matrix, the occasion matrix and the object matrix, such that each person's score on each test on each occasion can be closely approximated by multiplying these four matrices together. The underlying mathematics is quite complex, computational and estimation issues are still being addressed, and so despite recently celebrating its 50th birthday, the technique has rarely been used except by avid psychometricians. It is possible to use it in the R environment (Giordani et al., 2014).

SUMMARY

It is clear from this chapter that factor analysis can do far more than just identify groups of items which form scales. It can help to identify items which measure moods and may be useful in differentiating various groups of people within a heterogeneous sample. It can also help us understand how test scores vary over occasions, even when there is no regular (periodic) pattern in these changes.

Of course all of the normal caveats apply: the need for proper sampling of people and/or variables and/or occasions, together with independence of measures, adequate sample sizes and so forth. It is also clear that there is plenty of scope for statistical artefacts to creep in to such analyses – e.g., by not standardising variables (P-technique) or having items which most people answer in the same way (Q-technique, G-analysis).

One of the most important lessons to emerge from this chapter is, I think, the importance of keeping close to one's data. It is all too easy to run numbers through a powerful statistical package without thinking too much about the legitimacy of what one is doing. When performing any unusual form of analysis it makes huge sense to ask "What if . . . ?", particularly if one stacks data from several participants who may show different average scores or different levels of variability. But these research designs can be useful when performing exploratory analyses in a wide range of variables.

CHAPTER 13
DEVELOPMENTS IN FACTOR ANALYSIS

Chapters 10 and 11 introduced the basic procedures of exploratory factor analysis; many readers will find this sufficient to understand how to develop a scale, or interpret the results from an analysis of several different variables. However, these chapters did not consider one very important and very popular extension of factor-analytic methodology, namely **hierarchical factor analysis**.

This chapter therefore considers this technique (plus some variants) and also briefly outlines a technique known as **confirmatory factor analysis**, which is useful when the researcher has clear expectations about what factor structure should emerge. For example, previous research may have shown that items 1, 3 and 5 of some questionnaire form one scale, whilst items 2, 4, and 6 form another. Confirmatory factor analysis allows this hypothesis to be tested and produces a wealth of statistics showing how well the theoretical model actually fits the data.

HIERARCHICAL FACTOR ANALYSIS

The basic idea behind hierarchical factor analysis is very simple. If many test items (or other measures) are administered to a still-larger sample of people, and the results are factor-analysed, then as long as oblique rotation is performed, some of the factors may well be correlated. For example, a researcher might administer a huge range of ability items to a vast number of people, and then ask how many distinct ability factors there are. Carroll (1993; 2003) reports the results from a great number of studies which show that the results can best be represented as shown in Figure 13.1.

The bottom layer of Figure 13.1 represents individual test items. Above these items are factors – labelled P1, P2, P3 etc. – measuring different cognitive abilities. ("Primary mental abilities" is the usual name for them in intelligence research; hence the labels P1, P2 etc.). Once again there are hundreds of these primary mental abilities – far more than can be shown in the figure. Each of these is measured by a large number of variables (perhaps 20 or 30 per factor), so there would be several thousand boxes on the lowest level of Figure 13.1.

DOI: 10.4324/9781003240181-13

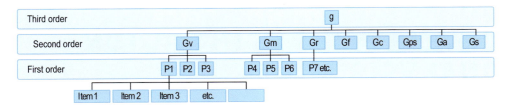

Figure 13.1 Part of a very large hierarchical model of abilities

Lines linking items to factors represent large factor loadings. Thus items 1–4 (for example) have large loadings on factor P1 and near-zero loadings on the other factors as there is no line linking them to other factors. If the items have been carefully developed, each item should only measure one factor, and so each item should be linked to only one primary mental ability.

If an oblique rotation is used when factor-analysing the correlations between the items, the primary factors can themselves be correlated and all factor analysis programs will show the correlations between the factors as part of the output from an oblique factor analysis.

It is possible to factor-analyse the correlations between the rotated primary ability factors. This produces "second order" factors, of which eight are shown in Figure 13.1. What if these eight second-order factors are also correlated? The factor analysis process can be repeated at each level until either (a) all of the factors are uncorrelated or (b) only one factor remains. In the case of human abilities, a single factor ("general ability") can be extracted from the correlations between the second-order factors, as shown in Figure 13.1. However, this is not invariably the case; when factor-analysing the correlations between personality traits, most (though not all) theorists identify five major personality traits and stop there rather than extracting a single "general factor" of personality.

Hierarchical factor analysis is basically the process outlined in the previous paragraphs. However, it is rarely performed as I have described it, starting with a large number of items, factor-analysing the correlations between them, and then factor-analysing the correlations between the first order factors . . . and the second-order factors . . . and so on. Instead it is more usual to work at the structure piecemeal and to investigate the correlations between *tests* measuring the various primary factors (P1, P2 etc. in Figure 13.1) rather than the correlations between *factors*, which stem from factor-analysing a large number of items.

Rather than trying to write items measuring every possible cognitive ability, one researcher might focus on measuring abilities which seem to involve visualisation (sometimes called Gv in the literature). They may develop six different tests which appear to involve different aspects of visualisation – for example, finding routes through mazes, imagining what landscapes of blocks, cylinders and cones would look like if viewed from another position, or being able to identify the outline of a simple shape hidden inside a more complex line drawing. Factor-analysing the correlations between people's scores on several such tests might reveal that they all intercorrelate and form a single visualisation factor. Another researcher might do the same with eight puzzles which involve reasoning – and might perhaps find that *two* factors emerge – one from puzzles which involve unfamiliar content and another which rely more on knowledge gained at school. (These abilities are sometimes called fluid ability, or Gf, and crystallised ability, or Gc.) A third researcher may explore performance on seven tasks measuring memory, and find evidence for a single memory factor, Gm. It is then necessary to check that when some or all of the visual tests, reasoning tests and memory tests are given to the same group of people, the factors emerge as expected. This is necessary because it is possible that some of the second-order factors identified by different researchers might be identical.

REASONS FOR NOT PERFORMING A SINGLE, HUGE, HIERARCHICAL FACTOR ANALYSIS

PRACTICALITY

According to Carroll (1993, p. 197), there were 241 factors of reasoning ability, plus many others measuring memory, attention, language ability etc. – well over 500 in total. To understand the structure of human abilities using hierarchical factor analysis, it would be necessary to give items measuring these 500 factors to a sample of people. Even if there were a mere 10 items measuring each factor, this exercise would involve each participant completing 5000 items – a process which would take several days, once instructions and rest breaks were included: it is not at all obvious how one would recruit volunteers who would solve such problems conscientiously for such a long time.

When diverse items are factor-analysed, the communalities are usually rather low, indicating that each of the items is only weakly related to the factor(s). As a consequence of this, vast samples of people are required in order to correctly identify the number and nature of the factors: the number of people would, in any case, need to be larger than the many thousands of items. This would turn into a massive and expensive research project.

Then there would be the problem of how to factor-analyse a 5000 × 5000 correlation matrix; the amount of time taken to perform a factor analysis is (very roughly) proportional to the cube of the number of variables (Press et al., 1993, p. 97), so analysing such a large correlation matrix is likely to take a very long time.

ESTIMATION OF CORRELATIONS BETWEEN FACTORS

Estimating the correlations between factors with precision becomes particularly important when performing hierarchical analysis, as the correlations between the factors will form the correlation matrix to be analysed at the next-highest level of the hierarchy. We mentioned in Chapter 11 that rotation algorithms generally include a parameter which determines how oblique the factors are allowed to become; see Harman (1976, p. 321). In the case of oblimin, this parameter is known as gamma; SPSS calls it delta, for reasons best known to itself. So how does one go about choosing a value for gamma? Most computer programs will simply use a default value (zero for oblimin, in the case of SPSS), but when performing the rotation neither the rotation algorithm nor the user can know in advance how oblique the factors really are. There is no theoretical rationale or empirical data to suggest choosing a gamma value of 0 rather than (say) 0.4 or −100 for a particular set of data, and this matters because it will influence the size of the correlations between the factors. It is clearly important to estimate these correlations as accurately as possible when performing a hierarchical factor analysis.

Paul Barrett (e.g., Barrett & Kline, 1980) came up with a good solution to this problem. He conducted hundreds of rotations, each with a different value of gamma, and chose the one which gave the best approximation to simple structure. For each rotation, he calculated the percentage of loadings which were between −0.1 and +0.1 ("the hyperplane") and chose the solution with the largest hyperplane count. This was repeated for several hyperplane widths to make sure that all solutions gave similar results.

The bottom line is that it is hard to determine the correlations between factors with great accuracy, and errors in these correlations may well influence the higher-order factor structure – the number and nature of the second-order factors. Given that factor-analysing items is known to be problematical, it might make more sense to replace the primary factors with scores on well-constructed tests and correlate these together in order to explore the higher-order factor structure.

FACTOR-ANALYSING SMALL DATASETS

One problem which is often encountered when performing hierarchical factor analyses is that the number of variables becomes small as one approaches the apex of the pyramid, for the number of variables being factored is equal to the number of factors at the next level down the pyramid. In Figure 13.1, *g* is found by analysing the correlations between just eight second-order factors, which should present few problems (as long as the factor analysis suggests no more than one or two factors!). However, it can be the case that the researcher needs to extract and rotate higher-order factors from the correlations between even fewer lower-order factors, and when the number of variables is small, it is sometimes hard to know where to position the factors relative to the variables.

Hendrickson and White (1966) provide a useful technique to overcome this problem. Rather than using factor rotation to align the (small) number of first-order factors relative to the second-order factors, as shown in the top part of the spreadsheet, it expresses the loadings of the *original variables* on the second order factors. There are two advantages in doing this.

First, deciding where to place the variables relative to the factors can be tricky when the number of variables is small. In the present example, there are only just four first-order factors, and deciding how to rotate the loadings of these four first-order factors on the two second-order factors will be problematical. It is a particular difficulty for those who use the hyperplane count to judge the goodness of fit, because the proportion of loadings in the hyperplanes with four variables can only be 0, 25%, 50%, 75% or 100% – and there may be several rather different rotations which give the same hyperplane count. Showing how the original variables map onto the second-order factors allows for a much larger range of hyperplane counts, which may prove useful in identifying the most appropriate solution.

The second problem with positioning first-order factors relative to second-order factors is the issue of interpretation. It might be that the psychological meaning of one or more of the first-order factors is unclear. If this first-order factor (plus another) shows large loadings on a second-order factor, it can be very difficult indeed to attempt an interpretation of what the second-order factor might represent. On the other hand, if one can see which of the original *variables* show large and small loadings on each second-order factor, it can be much easier to interpret what the second-order factor might mean.

> **Spreadsheet name:** Spreadsheet 13.1: Hierarchical factor analysis
>
> **Download from:** https://routledge.com/9781032146164/
>
> **Purpose**: To demonstrate the Hendrickson-White technique.
>
> **Contents of spreadsheet:** Direct-oblimin rotated factor solution – 24 variables, 4 factors.

Suggested activity:

- Section A of the spreadsheet shows the direct-oblimin rotated first-order factor matrix. It also shows the correlations between these first-order factors.
- Section B and the top chart show the conventional second-order factor loadings; the first-order factors have loadings on two second-order factors. Adjust the top slider and note how difficult it is to decide where best to place the axes.
- Section C performs the Hendrickson-White transformation and shows the loadings of the variables on the two second-order factors. Adjust the bottom slider and note how much easier it is to position the factors now that more data points are present.

Points to note:

- The Hendrickson-White procedure shows the loadings of variables on *second-order* factors.

Learning outcomes:

Readers should now be able to:

- Perform a Hendrickson-White transformation using the spreadsheet and appreciate its usefulness in performing hierarchical factor analyses.

SCHMID-LEIMAN TRANSFORMATION

The **Schmid–Leiman technique** (Schmid & Leiman, 1957) is conceptually very similar to the Hendrickson-White methodology. The main difference from the user's point of view is that it produces a factor matrix showing both the second-order factors and the first-order factors; the influence of the second-order factors has been partialled out from each of the first-order factors. (See the description of partial correlations in Chapter 14.)

Take the example of ability tests. It might be found that four tests of verbal skills (reading, comprehension, anagrams, vocabulary) which correspond to first-order factors in Figure 13.1 form a second-order factor when these tests plus a lot of other tests are given to a sample of people, correlated and factor-analysed. A hierarchical analysis might produce a third-order factor of general intelligence. Some part of the correlation between the verbal tests will arise because of general intelligence which by definition influences performance on all tasks which are below it in the hierarchical model. Someone with a high level of general intelligence will tend to perform well at all the verbal (and all the other) tasks; someone with a low level of general intelligence will probably perform less well at all of the tasks. So if the average correlation between the verbal tasks is (say) −0.5, how much of this is due to general intelligence and how much is due to differences in verbal ability alone? This is the question which the Schmid-Leiman technique addresses.

It produces a factor matrix which shows all of the first-order factors plus all of the second-order factors, third-order factors etc. in one table. The difference between this and a traditional hierarchical factor analysis is that the factor loadings on the first-order factors are corrected for the influence of the second- and third-order factors. The Schmid-Leiman technique shows the relationship between the variables and the second-order factors, rather like the Hendrickson-White method discussed. So it shows the loadings of each of the variables on each of the second-order factors – after correcting for the influence of any third-order factors. (The Hendrickson-White technique does not partial out the influence of the higher-order factors.)

The practical advantage of this technique is that it allows users to see how important primary and second-order factors are, after controlling for higher-order factors. To select a paper at random, Dombrowski and Watkins (2013) factor-analysed the correlations between adolescents' scores on a widely used battery of ability tests. Table 13.1 shows a part of their results. They analysed 42 tests which corresponded to first-order factors and extracted five second-order factors, then one general factor (*g*).

Table 13.1 Part of a Schmid-Leiman analysis of scores on various ability tests (adapted from Dombrowski & Watkins, 2013)

Tests corresponding to first-order factors	Second-order factor	Results from Schmid-Leiman analysis	
	F1	g	F1
Picture vocabulary	.85	.60	.52
Verbal comprehension	.83	.76	.51
General information	.82	.69	.50
Academic knowledge	.79	.70	.48
Story Recall	.72	.56	.44
Oral comprehension	.68	.60	.41
etc.			
% variance	38.9	33.1	5.0

The initial factor analysis, which showed that the 42 variables formed five factors, indicated that the first factor (F1) was impressively large; it explained 39% of the variance in the correlation matrix. As the test scores which were factor-analysed seemed to involve language, most users of this test would probably conclude that this is some sort of verbal ability factor. However, the Schmid-Leiman analysis shows the presence of a large general ability factor. It explains 33% of the variance. Tellingly, this general intelligence factor was largely responsible for the variance explained by the first-order factor, F1. For the Schmid-Leiman analysis shows that after correcting for the effects of general intelligence, F1 only explains 5% of the variance in the correlation matrix.

Why is this important? The most obvious reason is to help practitioners understand what they are measuring. It would be very tempting for educational psychologists or others to give children the picture vocabulary test, the verbal comprehension test etc. in the belief that they are measuring their verbal skills – whereas the Schmid-Leiman test shows that these tests are rather better measures of general intelligence than verbal ability (their loadings on the *g* factor are higher than their loadings on F1). The tests which have large loadings on F1 are not "pure" measures of language skills at all. They instead measure a mixture of general intelligence and language skills – and so if scores on these tests predict school performance, it is impossible to tell whether language skills, general ability or both are responsible for this correlation.

The Factor program (Lorenzo-Seva & Ferrando, 2006) for Windows and the Psych package in R (Revelle, 2017c) both perform Schmid-Leiman analyses.

BIFACTOR MODELS

Psychologists have recently rediscovered **bifactor models** – originally due to Holzinger and Swineford (1937). Confusingly, perhaps, "bifactor" models do not involve just two factors – but instead two *levels* of factors. Each variable is presumed to be influenced by both a general factor and one of several group factors, as shown in Figure 13.2. (Each variable may also have a unique factor associated with it, but these have been omitted for the sake of clarity.) A key assumption is that the general factor is uncorrelated with all of the group factors, which is rather different from the hierarchical model considered above. In addition, all of the group factors are assumed to be uncorrelated; there is no curve denoting a correlation between F1 and F2 in Figure 13.2. Third, it is assumed that each variable is influenced by the general factor plus only one group factor; it is not possible for two different group factors to influence a variable. A final difference from the hierarchical model described earlier is that the loadings on the general factor and the loadings on the other factors are all estimated together, rather than sequentially after factor rotation. Reise (2012) gives an excellent introduction to these models.

DEVELOPMENTS IN FACTOR ANALYSIS

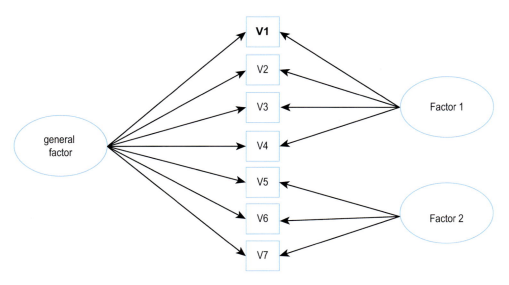

Figure 13.2 The bifactor model; unique factors are omitted for the sake of clarity

When and why can this technique be useful? One possibility is to check for social desirability. Suppose that the variables being analysed are from a questionnaire measuring several personality scales. One scale might consist of items asking about how good one's sense of humour is, a second scale might ask about honesty and so on. Social desirability is likely to influence responses to all the items in the questionnaire; some people will be more likely to make socially desirable responses than others, and this will lead to all tests loading a general factor of social desirability. It might therefore make sense to fit a bifactor model to the data. The general factor would represent social desirability, which should influence every test. The group factors would represent the relationships between the variables after controlling for the effects of social desirability.

In this example, the general factor is a "nuisance", and the interesting part of the analysis centred on the group factors. However, it is also possible to treat the general factor as being the one of main interest. Suppose that a large national sample of children were given two stories to read, and their comprehension was assessed in each of them. One of the stories involved life on the farm, and the other dealt with travel in the city. To their horror the researchers then realised that children who lived in the country might be more familiar with farming terms, whilst urban children might perhaps find the city-based items easier. To see whether all of the items form a general "verbal comprehension" factor after allowing for this, a bifactor analysis could be performed; factor 1 and factor 2 would control for the influence of the two different scenarios on comprehension.

Whether to perform a bifactor analysis or Schmid-Leiman analysis of correlated factors is not a straightforward decision to make; in many cases they seem to yield broadly comparable results. However, Mansolf and Reise (2016) outline some problems with Schmid-Leiman analysis, which may make some form of bifactor model preferable.

Jennrich and Bentler (2011; 2012) have made an important methodological advance by developing a technique where the user does not need to specify beforehand which group factors influence each variable; their software allows this to be determined empirically, rather than on a priori grounds as with the comprehension example. The technique is known as exploratory bifactor analysis (EBFA); their 2012 paper is a development which allows the group factors to be correlated. More recently, Lorenzo-Seva and Ferrando (2019) have developed a bifactor model where the general factor is uncorrelated with the group factors but the group factors may be correlated. Their simulations show that a large sample size is necessary for the "true" factor structure to be recovered (at least 500 people) with at least 12 variables, when the group factors are uncorrelated. When dealing with real data it is possible that much larger samples will be needed, as their simulated data specified that variables should have large loadings (0.5 to 0.65) on the group factors. This may be unrealistic unless one is factoring highly reliable scale scores. In addition, the ability of the technique to identify the "correct" factor structure was best when loadings on the group factor were also 0.5 or above. This too may be unlikely in real life.

When the group factors were correlated, a similar pattern emerged. However, the general factor was recovered better as the number of group factors increased; the two-group-factor case was problematical. Lorenzo-Seva and Ferrando (2019) then go on to describe in detail how the approach may be applied to real-life data. The results from these analyses seem eminently sensible, although it is difficult to tell whether the factor solutions they found are actually correct, as the true structure is unknown.

EBFA is incorporated in the latest version of the Factor program (Lorenzo-Seva & Ferrando, 2006). However, it is a very new and experimental technique which should be used with great caution when analysing real data whose underlying structure is unknown. It seems that large samples probably matter, but we simply do not know how it performs when loadings on the group factors are modest.

ARE HIGHER-ORDER FACTORS IMPORTANT?

My view is that it makes far more sense to explore and interpret higher-order factors (second-order, third-order factors and above) rather than primary abilities. There are two reasons for this.

First, the literature seems to show that higher-order factors can have considerable explanatory power in practical settings. Take general intelligence, for example. The paper mentioned in the previous section is typical of a large number of studies showing that g is the "active ingredient" which allows ability tests to predict performance at school or at work (Thorndike, 1985) and that lower-order ability factors are generally of lesser use for the prediction of behaviour. Suppose that one used a range of ability tests to predict who would perform best when learning to fly by selecting some tests which look as if they resemble the skills needed to fly an aircraft – perhaps performance in a simulator, co-ordination, spatial awareness, planning, mathematics etc.

Suppose that one administers 20 such tests to recruits and that they each show some correlation with flying performance. Without performing some sort of hierarchical or bifactor analysis, it is impossible to tell whether these correlations arise because each of the tests measures general intelligence to some extent, or whether the narrower skills (co-ordination etc.) are more important. If g is far more important than the lower-level skills, then any test which is a good measure of g should be able to predict flying performance; it need not have any obvious relevance to flying an aircraft at all. So a simple test which is known to be a good measure of g (such as one which asks participants to identify the next shape in a pattern or spot the rules linking groups of objects) might work as well as a larger selection of lower-level tests which *appear* to be relevant to aviation but which may in fact only work because they each measure g to some extent.

Understanding the extent to which a low-level factor is influenced by higher-order factors is therefore of practical use – and it also has major theoretical benefits as it can guide users as to the most appropriate variables to measure – lower-level factors (or "facets" as they are sometimes called) or broader personality traits.

For completion we ought to add that higher-order factors do not *always* predict behaviour better than narrower factors – see, for example, Judge et al. (2013), although this study was not able to perform Schmid-Leiman analyses but instead relied on a meta-analysis of correlations between personality traits and job performance.

Second, the number of primary abilities is virtually infinite. In Chapter 2 we bemoaned the fact that many of the items which are administered in personality questionnaires are very similar in content. Anyone can create a personality trait with wonderful psychometric properties by writing items which essentially ask the same question several times. Coefficient alpha will be enormous, and the items will necessarily form a single factor. Many psychologists spend their careers focused on such trivia. In my opinion such work is of zero value, because the scales which are developed using factor analysis only show that participants recognise the meaning of the words, and respond consistently. These factors are really as narrow in meaning as single items and so should arguably not be interpreted. However, their relationships to other items and/or narrow traits will be of interest.

Hierarchical analysis of items, ignoring the factors at the bottom of the pyramid (which are really just items with similar meanings), seems to be a sensible way of dealing with these extremely narrow factors. Although it is not made explicit, this is what underpins the five-factor models of personality, where each factor involves a number of facets each of which is a bundle of very similar items. The relationships between these *facets* is important – not the relationships between the items that form each facet.

The whole point of using factor analysis in psychology is to identify *unexpected* relationships between seemingly quite *different* variables. If the factor reflects some real characteristic of the individual (linked to individual differences in brain structure or function, developmental history, cognitive skills, social background or whatever) it is likely to influence several rather difference aspects of behaviour. For example, post-traumatic stress disorder involves increased arousal (difficulty sleeping etc.), emotional numbness and intrusive thoughts – three symptoms which look as if they are different yet which we know have a common cause. The strength of factor analysis is that it can identify such unexpected relationships.

It is my firm belief that whilst using factor analysis to map out the primary mental abilities at the bottom of the pyramid shown in Figure 13.1 is probably good sense, as the items in these scales will be so similar in meaning or in the cognitive processes which are required to solve them, they are of little or no intrinsic interest. Instead it is necessary to explore the correlations between the factors derived from these items – the higher-order factors, in other words.

There are two possible solutions to this problem. First, one can try to eliminate all questions which are synonyms. Thus if we were constructing a questionnaire to measure depression, one question might ask about sleep patterns, another about mood, another about changes in eating habits, a fourth about feelings that things will never get better and so on; the number of questions in the questionnaire would reflect the number of behaviours which are thought to be related to depression. In the Beck Depression scale (Beck, 1996), each item is written to tap a different aspect of depression, and if these items form a factor, then there is evidence for a source trait of depression. This is essentially the approach which Eysenck, Cattell et al. (1970) and others claim to have followed when developing their personality scales; items were written, synonyms were dropped, and the remaining items were given to samples of people whose scores were then factor-analysed. There are four obvious problems with this approach.

- Only one item is written to measure each aspect of behaviour, and we discussed the problem of "one item scales" earlier (Chapter 7). Using only a very few items – one for each different aspect of behaviour – means that the occasional "slip of the brain", uncertainty about the meanings of words and other random errors can have quite a marked influence on a person's total score.

- The resulting scales will generally be determined by the number of different behaviours which define the trait – for example, from the DSM-5 definition of depression. Thus they may be quite short.
- Although it sounds very straightforward to "eliminate synonyms", this is a time-consuming and highly subjective procedure. Do "unhappy" and "depressed" and "miserable" mean precisely the same thing? It is difficult to tell; Cattell recruited panels of language specialists and consulted dictionaries, but in the end there is a lot of subjective judgement involved.
- Eliminating synonyms disregards the possibility that items measure different degrees of the same characteristic. For example, the words "happy" and "content" may describe different points along a scale of happiness; someone who says that they are happy must also (logically) say that they feel content, whereas someone who says they are content may or may not describe themselves as happy. Simply identifying words as synonyms (or not) ignores this type of dependency.

The second solution would not require synonyms to be eliminated. Several items could be written to tap each aspect of depression – "Do you sometimes feel 'down' for no good reason?", "Does your mood often feel bleak?", "Do you usually feel depressed?", "Have you lost or gained weight recently?", "Have you noticed yourself eating more or less than normal?", "Have your eating habits changed in the last few months?" and so on. These could all be thrown into a factor analysis. The factor analysis will produce factors consisting of groups of items which are near-synonyms – a "mood" factor and an "eating" factor in the case of the six items in the previous sentence. *However, I suggest that these factors should not be interpreted.* They are bound to emerge because several of the questions are semantically related; someone who "usually feels depressed" *must* "often feel bleak", for example.

Rather than paying much heed to these factors, which will necessarily reflect groups of items whose meanings overlap, one should instead perform a hierarchical factor analysis to determine whether the correlations between these *factors* produce a second-order factor, rather as shown in Figure 13.3.

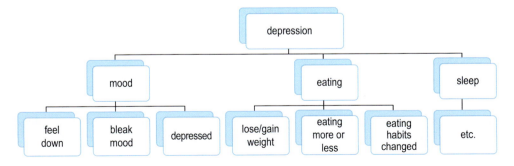

Figure 13.3 Hierarchical factor analysis of semantically similar items related to depression

If a trait represents some physical or psychological characteristic of the individual (rather than a social construction), Cattell argues that it will influence several different behaviours, just as the influenza virus leads to a whole range of seemingly different symptoms (feeling of malaise, aching limbs etc.). From a psychological point of view, it may make sense to use the first-order factors as the building blocks for discovering interesting but unexpected relationships between variables through hierarchical factor analysis. In other words, the lowest-level factors are treated rather as if they were mere items, and only the higher-order factors should be interpreted.

COMPARING FACTORS

Suppose that two researchers have factor-analysed the same variables. Are all (or any) of the factors the same in the two studies? It can be hard to tell just by looking at the factor loadings; if the "replication" of a factor lacks a few substantial loadings, and has a couple of substantial loadings which were not expected, is it the same factor? There is plenty of scope for confirmation bias to creep in when looking at tables of factor loadings, so just looking at the factor matrices cannot be recommended.

There are five main ways of testing whether factors obtained in different samples of people replicate.

CORRELATIONS BETWEEN FACTORS

The obvious procedure is to correlate the factor loadings from the original factor pattern matrix with the factor loadings from the replication. Whilst intuitively appealing, it is best avoided. For example, F1 in the original study does not look much like F1a from replication (a) in Table 13.2. The original factor consists of variable 1 (reverse scored), variable 2, and variable 3 (reverse scored). The substantial loadings on F1a (i.e., loadings above 0.4 or less than −0.4) are variable 2, variable 4 and variable 6. These two factors do not look remotely similar – yet their loadings correlate perfectly together (r = 1.0) as you might care to verify. Correlations will not suffice.

CONGRUENCE COEFFICIENT

Unlike the correlation, the Tucker **congruence coefficient** takes the absolute difference between the factor loadings in the two studies into account; Table 13.2 also shows the congruence coefficients. Lovik et al. (2020) have recently proposed a slightly modified coefficient, although this does not appear to have been much used, and sometimes seems to give strange results, as shown later.

Looking at the congruence coefficients in Table 13.2, it seems at first glance that replication (a) does not provide any factors which resemble the originals, factor 1 from

Table 13.2 Data from an original study plus three "replications", showing correlations and congruence coefficients as measures of factor similarity

| | Original study || Replication (a) || Replication (b) || Replication (c) ||
	F1	F2	F1a	F2a	F1b	F2b	F1c	F2c
Var 1	−0.6	−0.1	0.1	0.7	−0.1	0.7	−0.5	−0.3
Var 2	0.4	0.2	0.6	−0.1	0.1	−0.6	0.3	0.3
Var 3	−0.4	0.1	0.2	−0.5	0.1	0.2	−0.3	0.0
Var 4	0.0	0.8	0.4	0.1	0.4	−0.1	0.2	0.7
Var 5	−0.2	−0.8	0.3	−0.4	−0.4	0.1	−0.3	−0.6
Var 6	0.2	0.4	0.5	0.5	0.2	0.4	0.4	0.4
Correlations with factors from original study	F1		1.0	0.41	0.41	−0.75	.93	.61
	F2		0.4	0.33	0.99	−.20	.62	.96
Tucker congruence coefficients with factors from original study	F1		0.17	−0.08	0.33	−0.75	0.92	0.53
	F2		0.35	0.35	0.99	−.13	0.62	0.97
Lovik congruence coefficients with factors from original study	F1		0.65	0.89	0.48	0.93	0.92	0.53
	F2		0.78	0.56	0.99	0.42	0.67	0.97

replication (b) resembles factor 2 from the first study (congruence of 0.99) and that the factors in replication (c) resemble those found in the first study quite closely. But what value of a congruence coefficient constitutes "good" agreement? No-one knows for sure. "There is general agreement that anything below 0.80 means the factors are incongruent but there is a huge gray area between 0.80 and 1" (Lovik et al., 2020).

> **Spreadsheet name:** Spreadsheet 13.2: congruence coefficients
>
> **Download from**: https://routledge.com/9781032146164/
>
> **Purpose**: To compute congruence coefficients from two sets of factor loadings
>
> **Contents of spreadsheet:** Two columns of factor loadings from different studies using the same variables
>
> **Suggested activity:**
>
> - In the green columns, type in the loadings from different studies which use the same variables (and where the order of the variables is identical).
> - The congruence coefficients show whether or not the two factors are similar.

> **Points to note:**
>
> - The Lovik coefficient is sometimes large, even when the factor loadings appear very different. It is advisable to interpret the Tucker coefficient instead.
>
> **Learning outcomes: Readers should now be able to:**
>
> - Calculate congruence coefficients

There have been attempts to determine significance levels for congruence coefficients, although Davenport (1990) demonstrates that these are inappropriate. Asking experts to identify which factors look similar, and relating this to the congruence coefficient suggests that congruence coefficients larger than about 0.85 indicate that the same factor has been found in two different studies (Lorenzo-Seva & ten Berge, 2006). Although this is hardly the most scientific approach, it is probably the best which is available to date.

Spreadsheet 13.2 computes congruence coefficients to help users decide whether the same factor is found when the same variables are analysed in two different samples. Note that the Lovik and Tucker coefficients are sometimes very different. In Table 13.2, look at the relationship between factor 1 and factor 2a. Here the Tucker coefficient is −0.08 yet the Lovik coefficient is 0.89, indicating either no similarity or acceptable replication of the factor, depending on which coefficient is interpreted.

THE KAISER, HUNKA AND BIANCHINI (1971) CRITERION

This is an alternative to the congruence coefficient, but as Barrett (1986) demonstrated that this technique is both more complicated and less useful than the congruence coefficient, it will not be discussed further.

PROCRUSTES ROTATION

Procrustes rotation[1] (Hurley & Cattell, 1962) allows one to determine whether one set of factor loadings resemble those from another study. One simply specifies the "target" factor matrix from a previous study, and the software rotates the variables to match this as closely as possible (maximising congruence coefficients). However, Procrustes solutions seem to be too powerful, in that almost any set of data – even random data – can be coaxed to fit any model which one wants (Horn & Knapp, 1973; Paunonen, 1997). It cannot be recommended, although the Factor program (Lorenzo-Seva & Ferrando, 2006) allows such rotation to a target matrix to be performed.

CONFIRMATORY FACTOR ANALYSIS

There are several variants of the technique, but its most common use is to determine whether the factor loadings, factor correlations, communalities etc. found in one sample are also found in one (or possibly more) different sets of data. For example, if a set of personality variables are administered to a sample of people, an exploratory factor analysis will reveal their factor structure; this can be a hierarchical model, or something much simpler. Then confirmatory factor analysis can be used to determine whether the same structure is found when the same variables are administered to another sample. It performs a chi-square test to test how well the model fits the data . . . which all sounds very good, except that the significance of the chi-square test depends on the size of the sample. If the sample is large, then a significant chi-square is almost guaranteed, indicating that the fit is poor. If the sample size is small, even rather different structures appear to fit. Fortunately, however, there are also other indices which may be used to check model fit. For details see Byrne (1995) or Kline (2015).

Though I did not make it explicit, the discussion of Procrustes rotations above is an example of confirmatory factor analysis, a method which is used to test whether a particular factor model fits the data. For example, one can use a program such as EQS AMOS, LISREL or MPLUS to analyse a set of data, specifying the model which one wants to fit. Those who are happy using the R-environment may prefer a package such as LAVAAN or OpenMX.

For example, one could specify that the data (10 variables, 200+ cases) should produce a factor matrix with the constraints shown in Table 13.3.

The symbols in Table 13.3 need some explanation. The entries in this table are known as "parameters", and these can be fixed, estimated or estimated with an equality constraint. The value "0" or some other numerical value implies that the factor loading (or correlation between factors) is precisely the value which is shown; a fixed parameter. An asterisk (*) indicates that the value should be estimated by the program. The letter "a", "b" etc. indicates that the value is to be estimated but should be the same as another loading or correlation with the same label. In Table 13.3, variable 4 and variable 5 would both be forced to have exactly the same loading on factor 2. This option is rarely used in practice. The method of specifying these relationships differs between programs, but the basic logic is the same for all of them.

It is also possible to specify communalities for the variables (i.e., test a factor or a component model), and allowing the unique factors associated with each variable to be correlated is common practice. However, this should only be done if it makes psychological sense, and never "blindly" just to improve the fit of the model. Making post hoc modifications to a model purely to improve its fit to the data bad practice

Table 13.3 Examples of model specification for confirmatory factor analysis

	Factor 1	Factor 2	Factor 3
Var 1	*	0	0
Var 2	*	0	0
Var 3	*	0	0
Var 4	0	a	0
Var 5	0	a	0
Var 6	0	*	0
Var 7	0	*	0
Var 8	0	0	0.36
Var 9	0	0	*
Var 10	0	0	0.43
	Factor correlations		
Factor 1	1		
Factor 2	*	1	
Factor 3	0.3	*	1

as it will capitalise on chance variations in the data. This means that another sample of people cannot possibly be expected to show such good fit to the model, and we cannot tell how much we are overestimating the fit of the model by "tweaking" it in this way. Several published papers amend model parameters without then replicating the model using a different sample. These results should be treated with great caution. Many programs encourage this by providing "modification indices" to identify which parameters could be changed to improve the fit of the model – the start of what could be a long and dangerous iterative process. The real danger arises when researchers have clearly modified their model to fit the data but then pretend that this was the model which they planned to test at the outset. Given the pressure to publish positive findings, my advice would be very wary of any study which sets out to test a complex model, because that model may have come from post hoc analyses and so will very probably not be replicable.

It is likewise unwise to perform exploratory factor analysis, drop some variables which do not load as expected and then perform confirmatory factor analysis on the data from the same sample of people. This is because sampling variations will tend to inflate some factor loadings (and underestimate others) when performing the exploratory factor analysis; the factor structure will be somewhat different in another sample. If the confirmatory factor analysis uses the same sample, it will encounter the same sampling variations – and so will appear to fit the data much better than it ought. Papers which do this face automatic rejections from journals – see, for example, Fokkema and Greiff (2017).

Confirmatory factor analysis is a special case of structural equation modelling (Hu & Bentler, 1995), and it is not possible to give a detailed account of the methodology here; my favourite books on the subject are Loehlin and Beaujean (2017) and Kline (2015), whilst David A. Kenny currently provides an excellent online resource at http://davidakenny.net/cm/mfactor.htm. It is essential to consult some of these sources before performing a confirmatory factor analysis.

This is because the technique holds many traps for the unwary. For example, not all models can be tested. If the user specifies too many parameters to be estimated, it is mathematically impossible to find a unique solution. This should be obvious from the previous factor analysis chapters. If all of the factor loadings on all of the factors were to be estimated, an infinite number of solutions is possible. This is why we use factor rotation in exploratory factor analysis – to impose additional constraints to identify the "best" of these solutions. In addition, equality constraints (specifying that one parameter should equal another but leaving the program to estimate the best value for the parameter) can pose problems, though thankfully they are rarely used in confirmatory factor analysis.

All of the software programs mentioned produce a chi-square statistic which shows whether the model is a significantly *bad* fit to the data. This value of chi-squared is proportional to the sample size minus 1; increasing the sample size will increase the value of chi-squared which will make it more likely that the value of chi-squared will be statistically significant, implying that the model is wrong. So (as mentioned earlier in this chapter) a bewildering range of ad hoc indices have been created to measure how well a model fits the data (Hu & Bentler, 1995). There are rules of thumb for interpreting what these mean, but (in my opinion) although it sounds terribly learned to rattle off a lot of values for these indices when publishing a paper using the technique, they actually tell us rather little about how useful the model actually is; see Barrett (2007). Rather than providing an absolute indicator of goodness-of-fit, these fit indices are much better at showing relative fit – in other words, whether one model is better than another.

One sometimes encounters "nested models", which are two models where the simpler model is a special case of the more complex one. For example, an oblique two-factor model can be seen as a special case of a one-factor model. This is because if the correlation between factor 1 and factor 2 of the 2-factor model is 1.0, this is equivalent to a one-factor model where every variable loads the factor. It is possible to conduct a chi-square test to determine whether the two-factor model fits the data significantly better than the one-factor model. To do so, subtract the value of chi-squared for the simple model from the chi-squared value of the more complex model. One also subtracts the degrees of freedom of the simpler model from the degrees of freedom of the more complex model. Then one simply tests whether the difference in chi-square is significant, using the difference in the degrees of freedom.

How then should one use confirmatory factor analysis? If theory or previous research indicates that a particular factor structure should be found, how can one check this in a different sample?

The obvious technique is to simply set all of the parameters to the values from the rotated factor solution reported by the first author; this tests whether each of the factor loadings, communalities and factor correlations are the same in the second sample. Although this is the most straightforward analysis to perform, I have never seen anyone report such a study. We would not expect all the correlations to be exactly the same in a second sample because of sampling variations; the model would probably not fit that data for this reason.

The second possibility is to specify the factors as shown for factor 1 in Table 13.3. In other words, the "small" loadings from the original study are set to zero, and the "large" loadings for each factor (perhaps those above 0.4 . . . or the three largest loadings . . . or whatever criterion the author chooses) are set to be estimated, the expectation being that these are potentially different from zero, the exact value being estimated by the program. It is usual to specify that each variable has a non-zero loading on just one factor.

It is usual to estimate all the correlations between the factors, too, if the original researchers performed an oblique rotation.

Confirmatory factor analysis is extremely popular, although it may not fare well when applied to personality test items (McCrae et al., 1996). This may be because some personality items may load on more than one factor (for example, impulsivity is thought to be related to both extraversion and neuroticism). The obvious riposte is that one should then perhaps consider trying to write better items, which are only influenced by one personality factor, or if such relationships are well known, the factor model should be amended to allow such variables to load more than one factor.

SUMMARY

This chapter addressed some slightly more advanced topics in factor analysis. Key amongst them is the idea of a hierarchy of factors, with factors corresponding to very narrow personality traits, ability traits or behaviours at the bottom of a pyramid, and (assuming that some of these are found to intercorrelate appreciably) second-order factors describing the correlations between these factors . . . third-order-factors describing the correlations between the second-order factors and so on. This approach to factor analysis circumvents what may be one of the major problems in modern research – the proliferation of scales containing items which all mean much the same thing. By focusing on how they relate to other, quite different scales, it is possible to discover interesting, unexpected relationships; simply expanding a list of more and more low-level factors does not seem likely to advance the discipline.

Several useful statistical techniques were introduced, including the bi-factor model and techniques for identifying whether the same factor(s) have emerged in several different exploratory factor analyses. The chapter ended by giving a glimpse of a technique known as confirmatory factor analysis, which can be used to determine whether the factor structure found in one sample also appears in another group.

NOTE

1 Procrustes was a son of Poseidon in Greek mythology who waylaid travellers and forced them to fit his bed – either by stretching them or by cutting pieces off. Procrustes rotations likewise makes factor loadings larger or smaller in an attempt to get them to fit a target.

CHAPTER 14
NETWORK ANALYSIS

Network analysis is a new and very general mathematical technique based on the branch of mathematics known as graph theory. It can be used to explore the relationships between things as diverse as people (social networks), websites (identifying linkages), identifying groups of people who tend to publish together, including who is the "key force", and molecular genetics (understanding gene interactions). Crucially, it can also be applied to test items and test scores and used as an alternative to factor analysis. It can also be used to determine the number of factors to be rotated in factor analysis: see the mention of exploratory graph analysis (EGA) in Chapter 11.

So far we have assumed that the correlations between items (or tests, or facets) arise because that some trait influences all of them; for example, that some people feel negative about the world, negative about themselves and negative about the future, whilst others do not. This can be explained by a trait of depression, or neuroticism – people differ in their levels of this trait, which causes the correlations between these three facets to correlate. However, this is not the only possible explanation. Just because one model (the trait model) fits the data, it does not mean that it is the *only* model that will do so. In order to test the appropriateness of the trait model it is necessary to gather data – for example, to discover whether levels of neurotransmitters are causally associated with all three cognitions, whether they all change following brain damage and so on. However, that is psychology, not psychometrics and cannot be discussed here.

Network analysis attempts to determine which observed variables, such as scores on questionnaire items or facets of a personality questionnaire, influence which other observed variables (or groups of observed variables). For it is possible that there are interactions between these facets which reinforce each other – such as with a cognitive model of depression (Beck, 1976). If there is some external trigger, such as being criticised by a significant other, this may make someone feel that they are worthless. This in turn may lead to negative views about the world, the future and a reinforcement of negative views about themself . . . and so the feeling of being worthless is reinforced, as shown in Figure 14.1. Thus a minor criticism can lead to ever-increasing negative views about oneself and feelings of intense depression.

This is not the place to discuss Beck's theory, which is presented more as a logical possibility than a definitive account of depression. The key point is that there is no

DOI: 10.4324/9781003240181-14

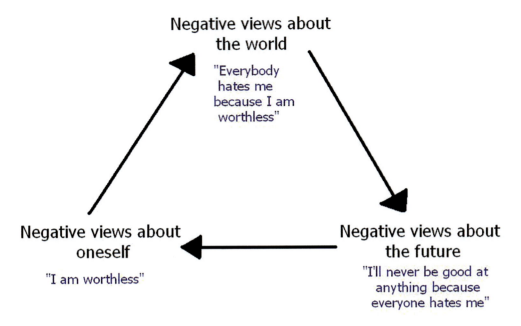

Figure 14.1 Interactions between three items measuring depression

"trait of depression" at work here. The reason why negativity of feelings about oneself, the world and the future are correlated is instead caused by the linkages between observed variables, which reinforce each other and become self-sustaining. There is no need to invoke factors, traits or latent variables at all.

The objects (variables) which are studied in network analysis are known as **nodes**, and the linkages between them are known as **edges**. Nodes are usually represented by circles and edges by straight lines or curves. The thickness of the edge represents the strength of the relationship between two nodes, and edges may indicate positive or negative relationships between nodes (positive or negative correlations).

The basic idea of network analysis is very simple. It explores the extent to which each node (test item) is related to every other node, usually once the influence of all other nodes is taken into account.

PARTIAL CORRELATIONS

We start off with a warning: calculating partial correlations assumes that the data are at least interval scaled, which they quite probably are not. Partial correlations are used to control for the influence of other variables. Suppose that a researcher discovered that the correlation between the quality of children's art and their performance on a reasoning test was 0.5. Reasoning may influence artistic ability (or vice versa). However, suppose they then realised that the children in the sample varied considerably in age – and that age influences both quality of drawings and performance on the reasoning test. A partial correlation estimates what the correlation between reasoning and artistic ability would be if all of the children were the same age.

It is possible to correct for the influence of more than one variable (age *and* parental education, for example), and this is how partial correlations are used in network analysis: if there are 10 variables in a correlation matrix used for network analysis, the partial correlation between variable 1 and variable 3 would correct for the influence of variable 2 and variables 4 to 10. Thus the edges in network analysis usually represent the size of the relationship between two variables after correcting for the influence of all of the other variables. The downside to this is that each partial correlation is computed from as many correlations as there are variables. If some correlations are overestimated or underestimated (for example, because they involve variables which are not interval scaled or are badly skewed in different directions), this will influence many of the partial correlations.

In Figure 14.2 the width of each line ("edge") represents the strength of each correlation, after controlling for the influence of the other variables. Some programs show positive partial correlations in one colour and negative correlations in a different colour.

The partial correlation between each pair of nodes shows how large the relationship would be if everyone answered all of the other items in the same way. It is often said (e.g., Epskamp & Fried, 2018) that network analysis is important because it shows which pairs of variables directly influence each other.

I do not think that this is correct. If the other variables in the analysis (the other nodes) represent every possible influence, then yes – the partial correlations must show direct connections between variables. However, there may be some psychological factor which influences scores on both variables but which has not been included in the network analysis. Intelligence, political attitudes, other personality traits, social desirability etc. might influence performance on a pair of items – but if this has not been measured and included in the network, its influence cannot be removed through the use of partial correlations. It is thus worthwhile including as many variables as possible when performing network analysis for this reason, rather than focusing on a narrow range of items – perhaps including a single measure of intelligence when performing network analysis of cognitive tests, or measures of the main five or six personality factors when performing a network analysis of personality variables. However, this does not seem to be common practice.

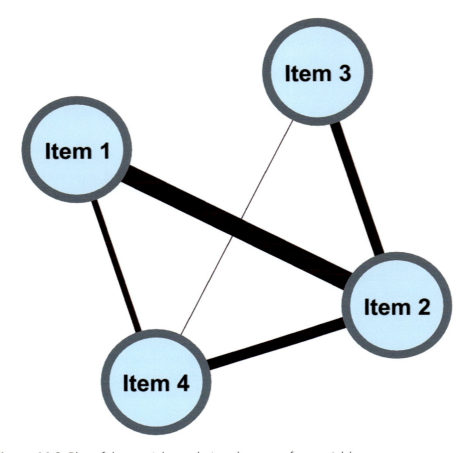

Figure 14.2 Plot of the partial correlations between four variables

NETWORK ANALYSIS AND FACTOR ANALYSIS

Like exploratory factor analysis, but unlike confirmatory factor analysis, moderation analysis, mediation analysis or structural equation modelling, network analysis does not require any model to be specified beforehand. The computer program is basically given a set of data and produces a diagram showing the linkages between nodes. Of course, each node is connected to every other node by an edge, which makes the full diagram horribly complex. It is therefore usual to treat small edges as if they were zero and remove them from the diagram, and several computational procedures have been developed for doing this. Thus network diagrams usually only show the "major" links between variables – though of course how one defines "major" influences what the diagram looks like!

Network analysis represents the connections between nodes (items) graphically, and so it is possible to see groups of connected items. This is in contrast to the factor model, which assumes that each person has a particular level of some trait which influences the way that they respond to all of the items in a scale. Mottus and Allerhand (2018) give an excellent, non-technical account of the similarities and differences between the two techniques. A rather more advanced account of how network analysis may be applied to psychometrics is given by Epskamp and Fried (2018).

APPLICATIONS OF NETWORK ANALYSIS

Network analysis can be applied to both traits and items, and has been of considerable use in elucidating the structure of psychological disorders. For example, it is well known that anxiety and depression tend to occur together, despite having rather different biological and environmental underpinnings. It might be informative to study how different items ("symptoms") influence each other, rather than how they are influenced by some trait. Network analysis can help us understand the relationships between various indicators of depression and anxiety, and can reveal which are at the "core" of affective disorders (e.g., Cramer et al., 2010; Park & Kim, 2020) by showing which are most strongly connected to the others and which are more peripheral.

It can also be used to help develop and refine tests (Christensen et al., 2019) by identifying groups of items (nodes) which form clusters – an alternative to factor analysis. However, this is far from common practice. The method is much used in brain mapping – to determine relationships between activity at different sites. Geneticists use it to study linkages between genes (amongst other things), and it is used to study traffic across computer networks (do those who visit a certain politician's home page also tend to visit conspiracy-theory sites?), model the movement of goods (what is the ultimate destination of packages sent on aircraft?), and explore social networks . . . the applications are legion.

A slightly different form of the methodology which considers directional influences rather than correlations (discussed later) can also be used to explore networks of social connections – to identify clusters of contacts. Such networks can show the *amount* of interaction, or just whether or not it occurs; they can also be designed to distinguish between positive and negative interactions. Although it is a very recent development, network analysis is becoming widely used.

TERMS USED TO DESCRIBE NETWORKS

Network analysis shows how connected each node is to the other nodes in the network (both the *number* of connections and the *size* of these connections), and several statistics can be calculated to represent these. A node's **degree** simply shows the number of other nodes to which it is connected by edges; in Figure 14.2 item A20 has four edges connecting it to other nodes (two of them being very weak), so its degree is 4. Degree therefore shows how well connected the node is, but not how substantial these connections are. Some nodes will be connected to many others; some to only a few. Network diagrams sometimes (but not always) represent the degree of a node by the size of the circle. The **strength** of a node shows the sum of the edges to which it is directly connected. It indicates how *strongly* a node is directly connected to other nodes. A node having a large connection to another node may have greater strength than another node which has only small links to six others. In the case of network analysis of items forming a scale to measure some trait, one would expect the item with the greatest strength to be the one which is the most central to the meaning of the trait. It should be possible to develop short forms of tests by considering this information (choosing items that have the greatest strength), although I am not aware of any attempts to do so.

There are other measures, too. If one measures the distance between a node and every other node in the network (travelling through other nodes if necessary) 1 divided by this distance is the **closeness** of a node, showing whether a node is closely connected to other nodes, or whether the average distance to other nodes is substantial. **Betweenness** measures the extent to which a node acts as a "bridge" connecting other pairs of nodes. It shows the chances that a node lies on the shortest path connecting other pairs of nodes in the network. The size of a node in a network diagram can indicate any of these statistics, so it is important to read the legend under each diagram carefully.

Finally, there are ways of determining the number of distinct clusters of nodes; this is discussed in more detail in Chapter 11, as it can be used to determining the number of factors to extract from a matrix using factor analysis. The idea is that clusters of nodes can be identified by various means; these are known as "partitions" in the network analysis literature. A statistic called the **modularity** is a number between −1 and 1 which shows the density of links inside the various partitions as compared to links between nodes in different partitions. Several algorithms and heuristics have been developed to partition the nodes; see, for example, Blondel et al. (2008). The obvious concern is that not all methods may lead to the same result for every set of data, and it is possible that several different ways of partitioning the data produce almost equally good modularities. In addition, the statistic chosen to define modularity is arbitrary. There is a tendency of end users of the technique to ignore these issues because they are a little technical.

AN EXAMPLE OF NETWORK ANALYSIS FROM A CORRELATION MATRIX

Park and Kim's (2020) paper is typical of studies based on network analysis. We refer to it as it is non-technical and clear for those who wish to explore the issues in more detail. These authors gave tests of depression and anxiety to a sample of depressed people and performed network analysis on the items. Their network diagram for all of the anxiety and depression items is shown in Figure 14.3.

The circles (nodes) represent items; the green nodes are items from the anxiety scale, and the grey ones are from the depression scale. The anxiety and depression items clearly fall into two clusters; the anxiety items are more strongly linked to other anxiety items than to depression items, and vice versa. This indicates that the two scales are fairly distinct. It also shows that items such as A10 and D17 have links to both anxiety and depression nodes. This is not the place to discuss the psychology of anxiety and depression, but it is clear that these relationships generally make good sense.

Items having similar meaning are closely linked. Having "trembling hands" (A12) was strongly linked to "feeling shaky" (A13). If someone says that their hands tremble, then presumably they *must* also say that they feel shaky! However, having trembling hands did not lie at the heart of the anxiety items; once the influence of feeling shaky was taken into consideration, the linkages between having trembling hands and the other items were quite small. "Feeling shaky" is the item which has the strong connections to other items; "trembling hands" only shows links to other items because it reflects "feeling shaky" to some extent. This illustrates the importance of analysing *partial* correlations when performing network analysis.

When the anxiety items were analysed on their own, "feeling shaky" (A13 in Figure 14.3) and "feeling scared" (A17) were the two items which best typified anxiety, as they have the highest **node strength**, or level of connection to other anxiety items. Node strength is basically the sum of the edges linking a node to all other nodes; a large node strength indicates that the total degree of connection between that node and all of the others is substantial; it may reflect a few large connections, numerous small ones or something in between. In diagrams such as Figure 14.3, node strength represents both the number and thickness of the lines joining a node to all the others. The graph to the right of Figure 14.3 shows how connected each node is to other nodes; whilst item D15 is the best connected, D21 ("loss of interest in sex") is only feebly connected to other items. It is linked to D15 ("loss of energy") but not much else.

When the items from the anxiety and depression scales were included in the same analysis, "loss of energy" (D15) and "light-headedness" (A6) were the two items that were most strongly connected to other items. These two items had links to both depression and anxiety items. It suggests that part of the reason why people who are depressed also tend to be anxious tends to be because they feel lightheaded and lack energy. (Other variables also contribute to this overlap, as shown in the right-hand part of Figure 14.3.)

312 NETWORK ANALYSIS

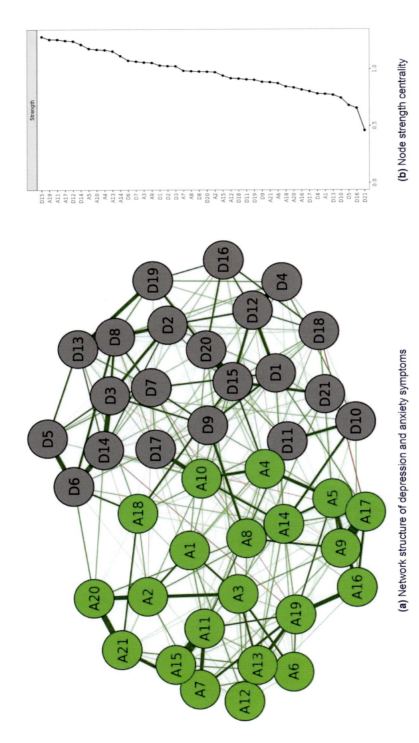

Figure 14.3 Network analysis of anxiety and depression items

Key to selected items: A6 = light-headedness, A10 = nervousness, A12 = trembling hands, A13 = feeling shaky, A17 = feeling scared, D12 = loss of interest, D13 = indecisiveness, D15 = loss of energy, D17 = irritability, D21 = Loss of interest in sex.

Source: Park and Kim (2020).

NETWORK ANALYSIS AND FACTOR ANALYSIS

What information might network analysis provide which cannot be obtained through exploratory factor analysis? Network analysis seeks out interactions between items, whereas most psychometric methods assume a linear model whereby a person's level of some trait is thought to influence the way in which people answer items; items are not thought to directly influence each other. Techniques such as exploratory factor analysis therefore assume that interactions between the items are not important. This assumption may be an oversimplification. For example, consider the following items (adapted from the IPIP50 emotional stability scale):

Item 1. I panic easily.

Item 2. I get overwhelmed by emotions.

Item 3. I often grumble about things.

Factor analysis has shown that these (and other) items all measure the same trait; they intercorrelate and so form a factor. However, correlations do not represent causations and so cannot show the patterns of interactions between the items.

If someone strongly agrees that they panic easily, they must logically also say that they get overwhelmed by emotions. Panic *implies* an overwhelming emotional response, so the way a person answers item 1 should causally determine how they will also answer item 2. However, the reverse linkage is likely to be far smaller. Only a few people who agree that they get overwhelmed by emotions will panic. They might instead feel depressed. Item 3 probably does not have much of a causal link with either item 1 or item 2; panicking or feeling overwhelmed does not imply grumbling, nor is it obvious why grumbling should imply feelings of panic or being overwhelmed.

By calculating partial correlations, network analysis should be able to identify such effects, which factor analysis cannot. However, the acid question is whether network analysis and factor analysis produce very different results when applied to the same set of data.

Few papers perform factor analysis and network analysis on the same data, and this is an issue which needs more research. The two that do seem to find that the two methodologies produce similar results – although of course there is no guarantee that this will be the case for all datasets. Picco et al. (2020) analysed responses to a 26-item questionnaire measuring different aspects of autobiographical memory using confirmatory factor analysis. They found the four-factor structure which they expected, although one item did not load the factor it was supposed to. A network analysis of the same data gave identical results; the item which failed to load as expected in the factor analysis also fell into the wrong (unexpected) cluster in the network analysis.

A network analysis of health-related variables in a sample of gay men (Lee et al., 2020) found that "suicidal ideation, injecting drug use, non-intravenous substance use, and depression were the four most central nodes"; an exploratory factor analysis of the same data found that "suicidal ideation, injecting drug use, depression, social anxiety, IPV [intimate partner violence], non-intravenous substance use, and sexual compulsivity" formed a factor. So the two sets of results are broadly equivalent. The variables which formed the most central nodes also loaded the same factor; some other variables appeared on the factor as well, but this might be because the authors interpreted loadings >0.3 rather than the more usual >0.4.

The whole issue of whether factor analysis or network models are more useful for studying personality structure and function was discussed in a special issue of the *European Journal of Personality* in 2012. The target article (Cramer et al., 2012) and commentaries are well worth reading. For network analysis is not without its share of problems. Like factor models, network models are purely descriptive and require some underlying theory to explain why items interact in the way that they do. In addition, network models (particularly when applied to items) do not consider measurement error. Does one item fail to correlate with another just because it is more susceptible to measurement error? For example, if some respondents moderate their answer to a sensitive question such as "Have you ever stolen anything?" in the socially desirable direction, whilst others do not, the correlation between responses to this question and other questions will be smaller than it should be. Other techniques such as structural equation modelling are able to address the issue of unreliable data and socially desirable responding, and we have seen (Chapter 13) how bifactor models may also be useful in this regard. Finally, as the partial correlation between each pair of nodes in network analysis is influenced by the correlations between these two and all of the other variables, the usual concerns arise. What if the relationships between some of the variables are non-linear? Are any items skewed in opposite directions – and if so, will the reduction in the size of the correlations be large enough to distort the network structure? Is it reasonable to assume that the variables are continuous – or should polychoric correlations be used?

AN EXAMPLE OF NETWORK ANALYSIS AND FACTOR ANALYSIS

Table 14.1 shows a correlation matrix from six questions (Q1–Q6) and the pattern matrix from an oblique, maximum-likelihood factor analysis of it. The items clearly form two factors, with Q1–Q3 forming one factor and Q4–Q6 another.

NETWORK ANALYSIS

Table 14.1 Correlations between six variables, and their rotated factor solution

	Q1	Q2	Q3	Q4	Q5	Q6
Q1	1	0.7	0.5	0.1	0.3	0.2
Q2	0.7	1	0.4	0.09	0.15	0.12
Q3	0.5	0.4	1	0	0.111	0
Q4	0.1	0.09	0	1	0.37	0.44
Q5	0.3	0.15	0.111	0.37	1	0.6
Q6	0.2	0.12	0	0.44	0.6	1
	F1	F2				
Q1	0.932	0.103				
Q2	0.729	0.023				
Q3	0.546	0.064				
Q4	−0.041	0.527				
Q5	0.110	0.695				
Q6	−0.035	0.851				

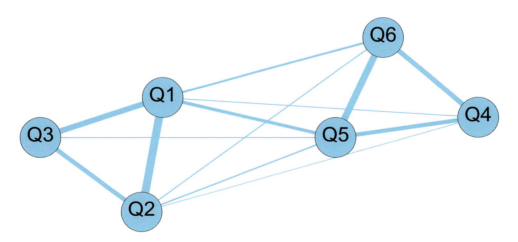

Figure 14.4 A network representation of the data of Table 14.1

The results from a network analysis of this correlation matrix are shown later; the links between Q5 and Q6 and those between Q1 and Q2 seem to be stronger than the others. But the results clearly resemble those of the factor analysis – there are two clusters of variables, the links between which are stronger than the linkages to other variables.

These data are given to encourage readers to start to experiment with network analysis. The figures were prepared using Gephi (Bastian et al., 2009) – a free program available at www.gephi.org which is very easy to use, albeit somewhat limited in scope. In addition, as the width of the edges can be adjusted "by eye" (rather than being specified mathematically), it produces results which may be difficult for others to replicate. Gephi runs on Linux, Windows and MacOS. The igraph package, which is more widely used, runs in the R environment (R Core Team, 2013), though it is considerably more powerful and complex.

POSSIBLE LIMITATIONS OF NETWORK ANALYSIS

We earlier mentioned that it is common practice to treat small partial correlations as if they were zero when performing network analysis. This simplifies the diagram, because treating some edges as zero means they do not need to be represented on the graph – otherwise every node would be connected to every other node. The **lasso** technique (least absolute shrinkage and selection operator) is widely used for this. A choice is made about the value of a parameter (lambda), and the larger the value of lambda that is chosen, the more edges the lasso procedure forces to be zero. "Making the model more sparse" is the technical term for this.

This principle is similar to treating small factor loadings as if they were zero when interpreting rotated factor matrices. It is also rather arbitrary – both in the choice of method and the value of lambda which is used. This is a concern. Whilst psychologists are keen to establish the replicability of their methods, the computer scientists who develop network models pay less attention to this issue. Is the same structure found when the same researcher analyses two samples of data from the same population? There seems to be a meagre literature on this issue, but one study finds that "39–49% of the edges in each network were unreplicated across the pairwise comparisons" (Forbes et al., 2021). There is also the problem of knowing how, and how much, to make a model sparse before fitting it. Epskamp et al. (2017) demonstrate that it is quite possible to fool oneself into "seeing" a structure which simply is not there.

The second problem is that that a node might be influenced by a very large number of other nodes – but each of the individual relationships is small and so may be set to zero when making the network sparse. The obvious example is looking at genetic influences on intelligence. We know that intelligence is substantially influenced by people's genetic make-up – but that this involves a huge number of genes (other nodes), each having a tiny influence. Individually their contribution would be very small (and some could easily be set to zero) – but taken together, their influence can be very substantial.

Next, it is unclear what size samples are needed. There are rules of thumb – for example, Epskamp et al. (2017) suggest it should–be no fewer than $n(n-1)$, where n is the number of nodes – but as these authors then go on to demonstrate that this rule still results in unstable estimates, it is uncertain how useful it is. In any case, it is probable that the sample size needed will be related to the amount of measurement error associated with each variable. Scale scores (computed by summing several items) should have less measurement error than responses to individual items and so may require smaller samples to produce consistent results, for example. Whilst these issues have been dealt with in the context of factor analysis, it does not appear that they have been considered in detail by network analysts.

Fourth, many different algorithms have been developed to represent the structure of the data, and so the appearance of the chart will depend (to some extent) on the arbitrary choice one makes here. For example, Figure 14.4 uses an alternative representation algorithm, and represents density by both the colour (red = low density etc.) and size of the nodes. The structure is exactly the same as in Figure 14.3 – the links between Q1 and Q2 and Q6 and Q5 are large, for example – but Figure 14.4 makes it clearer that any links that Q3 has to other nodes are mainly because it correlates with Q1 and Q2. This is not nearly so obvious in Figure 14.3; one has to notice that the lines linking Q3 to Q4–Q6 are very narrow, indicating weak associations. It is also easy to be seduced by colour; when first looking at Figure 14.4 you may have thought that Q1, Q2 and Q5 were strongly linked because they were the same colour, whereas the colour indicates the degree of connectedness to all other nodes – not groups of connected nodes. Thick edges represent these. Network diagrams look very attractive, but it is important to study the detail of exactly what they represent.

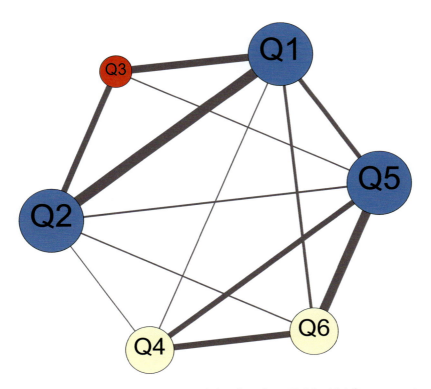

Figure 14.5 Alternative representation of the data from Table 14.1 for comparison with Figure 14.4

DIRECTIONAL MODELS

So far we have considered models based on correlations. These have (at most) only one edge linking each pair of nodes. This is because the analysis starts off with a correlation matrix, and in the network diagram edges represent partial correlations – the size of the relationship between two nodes after all other correlations have been corrected for. However, the relationship between nodes is not always symmetrical. For example, it has been found that IQ, as measured by intelligence tests, is quite strongly related to the number of years of education which a child receives. Why might this be? One possibility is that intelligence influences school performance, so that highly intelligent children perform better, receive positive reinforcement from their high grades, and so decide to continue their studies for as long as possible. Or it might be the case that going to school influences intelligence through developing abstract thinking and language skills, and other things which enhance performance on intelligence tests. Thus a directional model which includes IQ and years of education as nodes may show *two* edges linking these nodes, indicating causal links (probably of different sizes) in each direction. The same principle may apply to test items, too.

Rather than inputting a correlation matrix and computing partial correlations, a similarity matrix can be used as the basis of a network model. This is common practice when mapping social networks using people as nodes; Claire may regard Ryan as a close friend, yet Ryan may see Claire as a mere acquaintance.

Such a "similarity matrix" is shown in Table 14.2, showing responses to three hypothetical extraversion items (e1–e3), three anxiety items (a1–a3) and another unrelated item (a1). The rows show the "source" and the column the "target". Item

Table 14.2 Similarity matrix showing reciprocal influences of seven personality items

		Variables						
		e1	e2	e3	n1	n2	n3	a1
Rows influence columns	e1	0	0.9	0.5	0	0	0	0.1
	e2	0.6	0	0.4	0	0.6	0	0
	e3	0.6	0.4	0	0	0	0.2	0
	n1	0	0	0	0	0.8	0.4	0.1
	n2	0	0	0.2	0.2	0	0.5	0
	n3	0	0.7	0	0.4	0.7	0	0
	a1	0.1	0	0	0	0	0.1	0

e1 has a strong influence on item e2 (1.0), but e2 has a much smaller influence on e1 (0.6). The problem is that estimating what the numbers in such tables should be is not a simple process. Most techniques are based on Bayes' theorem, which estimates the chances of someone agreeing with item e2 given that they have agreed with item e1, and vice versa. This is applied iteratively (McNally, 2016) – a "brute force" approach testing the fit of all possible models in order identify the most appropriate ones. Testing *very* large numbers of models (typically 2^n, where n is the number of nodes) often becomes unfeasible unless shortcuts are taken, which is a potential problem. In addition, the programs which perform network analysis may not be smart enough to flag that several very different models might provide almost equally good fit to the data – and so the choice of which model to report may be essentially arbitrary.

Software to perform Bayesian network analysis includes the GeNIe modeller, which runs on Windows or MacOS and is free to use for academic purposes. It may be obtained from www.bayesfusion.com/. The accompanying manual provides an excellent practical introduction to Bayesian network analysis. The techniques have not yet been applied in psychometrics but will probably soon become influential.

SUMMARY

One of the strengths of network analysis is that it does not require any theoretical input. One simply feeds data into a computer program, specifies what sorts of relationships one expects (directional or non-directional), and a diagram is produced using complex mathematical techniques. Look again at Figure 14.6. You will notice that e1 has a substantial influence on e2, and that e2 influences n2. However, there is no direct link between e1 and n2. Other statistical techniques which explore moderation and mediation require you to specify the model beforehand; network analysis does not.

Network analysis is starting to have a major impact on psychology and other disciplines. It is attractive because it abandons the usual assumption that a trait (which cannot be directly observed) influences responses to some items but not others. It instead computes partial correlations in an attempt to discover which pairs of items influence each other. It can also be used to explore the relationship between traits and between psychiatric symptoms; this might suggest why diagnoses frequently overlap. The danger is that this complex methodology might be treated as a "black box" by psychologists.

In this chapter I have tried to give a conceptual account of the basic methodology so that users have some idea of how the technique works. I have also highlighted

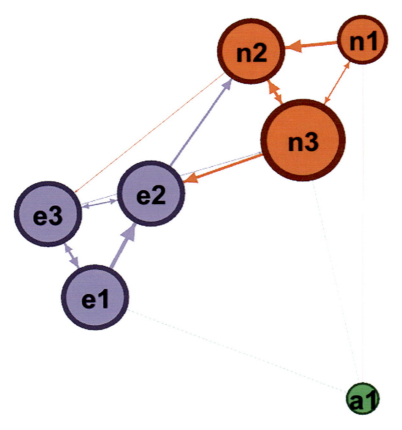

Figure 14.6 Directional model of the data in Table 14.2. The size of each node represents its degree, arrowhead size represents the strength of each directional relationship, and colour indicates the scale to which each item belongs.

some issues which may need careful consideration. The surprising finding (for me) is that the results from network analyses seem similar to the findings obtained by factor analysis – although more evidence is needed to determine how general this claim is. Network analysis is a fairly new methodology whose merits and drawbacks are not yet fully understood. It should probably be explored with caution by enthusiasts.

CHAPTER 15
ITEM RESPONSE THEORY

Thus far we have always assumed that a person's total score on a psychological test provides the best measure of their ability, or endowment with a particular personality trait. We are so familiar with adding up the number of items answered correctly (or totalling up scores on Likert scales) and comparing these scores with norms to interpret their meaning for an individual that it is difficult to see an alternative – despite paying lip service to Michell's criticisms. In this chapter I will mainly refer to ability scales, as the mathematics for these is somewhat easier given that each item is only scored 1 (correct) or 0 (incorrect). However, the principles outlined here apply to Likert-scaled items too – these are known as **ordered response** scales in the item response literature.

One problem with using the total score as a measure of ability is that someone who gets four easy items correct but fails all the hard items ends up with the same score as someone who (through boredom?) gets one easy item and three of the hard items correct. For the total score completely ignores the available information about the difficulty of the test items. A person will obtain a high score given an easy test and a low score if they are given a hard test, even though their level of ability is exactly the same when taking both tests. In other words, a person's level of ability is confounded with the difficulty of the items which they are administered; their score on a scale depends on both their ability and the difficulty of the items which they were given. Because conventional tests cannot separate these two things, it is necessary to use tables of norms to interpret test scores.

Of course this would not be an issue if the items formed a Guttman scale (see Chapter 4). Here, everyone would pass all of the items which were below their ability level and fail all the ones which were above it. But we have seen in Chapter 4 that items simply do not form Guttman scales in real life, unless they differ *enormously* in difficulty. However, Guttman scaling introduces two important principles; it is possible to link each person's level of ability to the pattern of items which they answer correctly.

When plotting the responses to items which form a Guttman scale as in Figure 15.1, a person's ability is defined by their position along the horizontal axis. The three lines (known as **item characteristic curves**, or ICCs) each represent one item. Each line shows the probability that a person with a particular level of ability will answer the

DOI: 10.4324/9781003240181-15

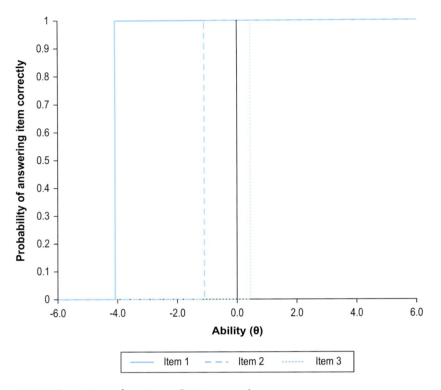

Figure 15.1 Three items forming a Guttman scale

item correctly. So (for example) someone with an ability of zero has a 100% chance of answering items 1 and 2 correctly, and no chance at all of answering item 3 correctly (the three probabilities are 1.0, 1.0 and 0.0).

The difficulty of each item is defined in terms of the ability of the participants. The difficulty level of an item corresponds to the point at which there is a 50% chance that a person will answer it correctly. This can be read off the graph. One simply identifies the point on the y-axis where the chances of passing an item is 0.5, and then reads left or right to find where each ICC crosses this line. For item 1 it is at the ability level of −4, for item 2 it corresponds to an ability of −1, and for item 3 it is an ability of 0.5. Do not worry that some of the abilities are positive numbers and some are negative – this is arbitrary, and we have seen that a person with a zero level of ability will pass two of the three items. When using item response theory, remember that an ability (θ) of zero does not imply that someone scores zero items correct.

Defining item difficulty in terms of ability level is something rather new and rather interesting, because it should be obvious that if these data fit the model, the same graph

ITEM RESPONSE THEORY

will be obtained *no matter how many people in the sample have each level of ability*. It will not matter whether 5% or 90% of the people in the sample have an ability level between (say) −4 and −2. As long as the data fit the model, the ICCs will look the same. In other words, it might be possible to interpret the meaning of a test score without having to use tables of norms. If true, this could be a huge step forward for psychometrics.

To start with, we shall assume that we are dealing with a "free response test" where respondents are asked to produce an answer rather than choose between several alternatives. Otherwise guessing complicates matters, as someone with a very low level of ability may have an above-zero chance of answering an item correctly, just because of lucky guessing.

We pointed out earlier that one of the problems with Guttman scaling is that data simply do not fit that convenient model in real life unless the items differ so enormously in difficulty that administering them would make little sense. But what if the chances of answering an item correctly do not switch suddenly from 0.0 to 1.0? What if there is a more gradual increase in the chances that a person will correctly answer the item, as the

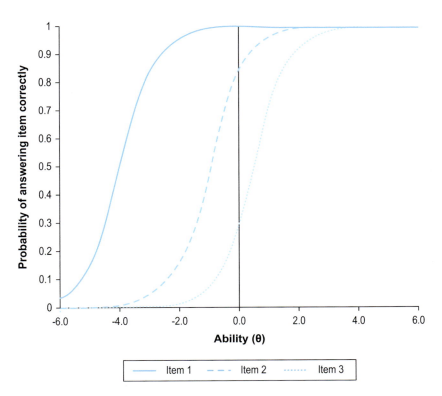

Figure 15.2 Three items following the Rasch model

ability level increases? In this case the curves showing the probability that a person with a particular level of ability will answer an item might be as shown in Figure 15.2. They resemble the Guttman model but have the hard corners smoothed off. For now we will assume that the spread of scores is the same for each curve (i.e., the ICC's all run parallel to each other; they have the same slope – the same "discrimination"), though this assumption will be relaxed later.

Note that the difficulty levels of these items are the same as with the Guttman example (−4, −1 and 1.5), as can be seen by identifying the ability level where there is a 0.5 chance of correctly answering each item.

THE ITEM CHARACTERISTIC CURVE

At this stage we need to make six assumptions about the items in a scale and the ICCs which they produce.

1. The chance of someone getting an item correct depends on both their ability and the difficulty of the test item.
2. All the items in a scale measure just one construct; this can be checked using factor analysis.
3. All of the items have the same "discrimination" – in other words, the ICCs all have the same slope (are parallel). This assumption can sometimes be relaxed, as discussed later.
4. If performing **Rasch scaling**, it is assumed that the discrimination power of each item (the slope of each ICC) is 1.0. For the **one-parameter logistic model**, the slope is assumed to be 1.7 (corresponding to the slope of the normal ogive).
5. The chance of someone getting a particular item correct is not influenced by the correctness of responses to any other items, other than as a function of the person's ability. (This is known as the assumption of **local independence**.)
6. No-one gets all of the items correct, or all of the items incorrect.

The last two assumptions probably need some explanation. The assumption of local independence means that each item should be an entirely novel problem, and there should be no carry-over from one item to the next – either positive (where a correct answer to one question is either necessary or provides a clue for how to answer another) or negative (where it may be necessary to break the "set" used in previous questions to arrive at the correct answer). Thus the assumption of local independence would not hold for items such as:

Item 1. What is 4 + 5?

Item 2. What is the square root of the previous item?

This is because if item 1 is answered incorrectly, so too must item 2. Local independence is important because if the assumption is violated, the parameters (difficulty, ability) of the scale can be inaccurate. However, the Q_3 statistic used to detect whether the assumption is violated (Yen, 1984) is hard to interpret, as the number of items, the sample size and the number of response categories affect it. Commonly used rules of thumb which ignore these variables are thus of little use. See Christensen et al. (2017).

We also need to assume that no-one gets all of the items incorrect, or all of them correct. This is necessary because values of ability can range (in theory) from minus infinity to infinity. If someone answers all three items in Figure 15.2 correctly, we can see from the figure that their level of ability will almost certainly be greater than 4.0. However, there is no way of telling how *much* bigger than 4 it is, because there is no more difficult item in the test. Their ability level could be 4.1, or 4000.

For now, we assume that the ICCs run parallel to each other, with the more difficult items to the right of the ability scale. Since item difficulty is the only thing ("parameter") that makes one ICC different from another, the ICCs shown in Figure 15.2 represent the "one-parameter model". When the value of this discrimination parameter is 1.0, it is also known as the Rasch model, after the Danish psychometrician Georg Rasch who developed it (Rasch, 1960). When performing a Rasch analysis it is necessary to estimate the ability of each person in the sample, together with the difficulty of each item in the scale. So the number of parameters to be estimated increases as the sample size increases – unlike techniques such as factor analysis, where only factor loadings and communalities are estimated. Thus whilst using huge samples is advisable for techniques such as structural equation modelling, because large samples result in smaller standard errors of measurement whilst not increasing the number of parameters to be estimated, the same principle will not apply to Rasch scaling.

The graphs shown in Figure 15.2 can be described by a fairly simple mathematical equation, known as the **logistic function**. There are three main reasons for working with the logistic function. First, the shape of the curve looks sensible according to the criteria outlined; it can be shown that it is almost identical to the cumulative normal distribution, and it guarantees that the probability of a person's passing an item can never stray outside the range of 0.0 to 1.0. Second, it is easy to work with mathematically in that it does not require any integrations or similar messy techniques to be performed. It starts off at zero, moves smoothly upwards at a point determined by the item's difficulty, and then flattens out as it approaches a probability of 1.0.

Rather than plotting graphs, it is possible to calculate the chances that a person with a particular level of ability will correctly answer an item which has a certain level of difficulty. For example, what are the chances that a person whose ability is −1.0 will correctly answer an item whose difficulty is −1.5, when the slope of the ICCs is 1.0 (the Rasch model)?

The equation for the Rasch model is:

$$P_i(\theta) = \frac{e^{(\theta - b_i)}}{1 - e^{(\theta - b_i)}}$$

The left-hand side of the equation reads "the probability that a person will get item 'i' correct given that they have a level of ability that is θ". On the right-hand side of the equation, e is simply a number whose approximate value is 2.718. The value θ is the person's ability, and b_i is the difficulty level of item "i".

So to calculate the chances that a person whose ability is −1.0 will correctly answer an item whose difficulty is −1.5 using the Rasch model, we simply substitute:

$$P_i(1.0) = \frac{e^{(1.0 - 1.5)}}{1 + e^{(1.0 - 1.5)}}$$

$$= \frac{e^{(-0.5)}}{1 + e^{(-0.5)}}$$

$$= \frac{.6065}{1 + .6065}$$

$$= 0.378$$

This agrees with Figure 15.2. The only step that may have given any problem here is the evaluation of $e^{-0.5}$. Many websites or calculators will evaluate it.

For the one-parameter logistic model, we just include the figure of 1.7 to represent the slope of the ICCs:

$$P_i(1.0) = \frac{e^{1.7(1.0 - 1.5)}}{1 + e^{1.7(1.0 - 1.5)}}$$

etc.

We have not so far mentioned what the x-axis scale represents. It is a measure of ability in "logits". Despite some claims to the contrary, this probably does not form an interval scale (Salzberger, 2010) but is instead something rather stronger than ordinal measurement: "linear measurement", which may allow people's abilities (and item difficulties) to be compared so long as the data fit the model. Its scale is set by assuming that all items have a discrimination power of 1.0. A good discussion of these issues is given by Wright and Linacre (1989).

A useful feature of the Rasch technique is that a process called "conditional maximum likelihood estimation" makes it possible to estimate the difficulty of all of the items in the scale *independently of the abilities of the sample of people who took the items*. Thus if the assumptions of the model are met, it should be able to give the same set of items to a group of people who are highly able, and to another group of less able individuals – and the difficulties of the items will be the same in both samples. In other words, the numbers (parameters) which specify the difficulty of the items can be estimated without reference to the abilities of the people who take the items. This is known as **specific objectivity**. Something similar is found when performing a regression. The slope and intercept of the regression line is exactly the same, no matter whether there are a lot of high-ability or low-ability people in the sample. All that matters is that everyone's data fits the model.

Specific objectivity, being able to estimate item difficulties without having to consider the abilities of the people in the sample, is hugely important. For it follows that norms are not needed as pretty much any sample of people can be used to establish the difficulty of the items as long as there are several people who pass and fail each item. Unlike conventional tests, it is not necessary to track down a representative sample of the population, administer the scale and tabulate their scores in order to calculate the proportion of people who answer each item correctly and establish tables of norms. It can be seen that this makes Rasch scaling particularly useful when assessing children, where there is a very wide range of abilities as children mature (Elliott et al., 1996). Then, once the difficulties of the items are known, these items can be used to estimate the ability of a new individual.

RASCH SCALING AND MICHELL'S CRITERIA FOR SCIENTIFIC MEASUREMENT

Because the Rasch model supposedly tests whether data are quantitative (Perline et al., 1979; Wright, 1985) rather than assuming it, a lively debate has arisen about whether Rasch scaling overcomes the objections raised by Michell (1997). Borsboom and Scholten (2008) give an excellent and accessible precis of some of the issues; it is well worth consulting. Their conclusion is that opponents of Rasch scaling have not proved that it does not overcome Michell's objections (with apologies for the triple negative). However, Michell's (2004) view is uncompromising:

> If a person's correct response to an item depended solely on ability, with no random "error" component involved, one would only learn the ordinal fact that that person's ability at least matches the difficulty level of the item. Item response modelers derive all quantitative information (as distinct from merely ordinal) from the distributional properties of the random "error" component. . . . Here, as elsewhere, psychometricians derive what they want most (measures) from what they know least (the shape of "error") by presuming to already know it. . . . By any fair-minded reckoning, our state of knowledge at present does not support claims to be able to measure psychological attributes using item response models.

Paul Barrett (2011) also makes a remarkably clear assessment of the situation:

> The idea that a statistical model of questionnaire item responses can somehow reveal quantitative structure for an attribute constructed by that very same statistical model seems unreal to me. Describing the constructed attribute as a "latent variable" is an attempt to avoid admitting the variable is just something constructed from data observations using a particular form of data analysis. There is nothing "latent" about such variables.

The debate rumbles on without any obvious conclusion in sight, but it certainly seems that (despite what its proponents sometimes claim) the Rasch model is not a statistical panacea which can determine whether or not a set of items measure some quantitative attribute. The problem is that the debate centres on philosophical definitions of "measurement", and ironically enough many of us who were brought up in the tradition of actually trying to assess individual differences may not have the relevant background or inclination to take part in the debate; it is far easier to just carry on as before with one's head in the sand and hope that someone else will decide that what we are doing is justifiable. However, if psychology is to be regarded as a science (rather than a technology which just counts arbitrary things), it is surely necessary to consider these issues in depth.

TWO- AND THREE-PARAMETER MODELS

Thus far we have assumed that every item has an equal "spread" either side of its difficulty value. This is actually quite a restrictive assumption; it seems quite probable that the ICCs of several items may have different slopes (or levels of **discrimination**), as shown in Figure 15.3. A small value of discrimination indicates that people with a broad range of abilities have a reasonable chance of getting the item correct. A high value of discrimination indicates that the ICC is much more upright. (The mathematically minded might like to view the discrimination parameter as being the slope of the ICC at its point of inflection.)

In Figure 15.3, item 1 has a high level of discrimination, item 2 has a moderate level, and item 3 has a low level, indicating that people of a very wide range of abilities have a chance of answering this item correctly. The two-parameter IRT model thus includes a second parameter ("a") denoting item discrimination. As well as estimating the ability of each person and the difficulty of each item, it is possible also to estimate the discrimination power of each item.

The ICCs in Figure 15.3 will be inappropriate for multiple-choice tests. Here even someone with very low ability will have an above-zero chance of getting an item correct, by lucky guessing. But what *should* the probability of correctly answering an item be when a person is offered several alternative answers and is asked to choose the

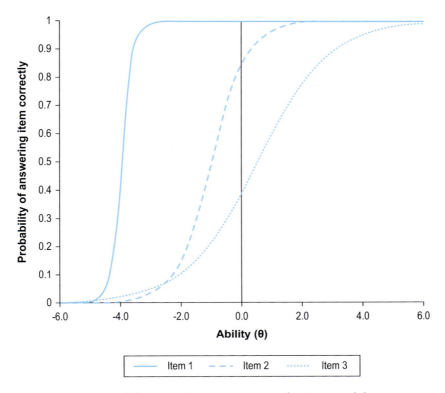

Figure 15.3 Three items following the two-parameter logistic model

correct one? It all depends what one wants to assume. One possibility would be to assume that someone who did not know the answer just guessed one of the answers at random, in which case the probability would simply be $\frac{1}{number\ of\ alternatives}$. However, this may not be realistic. Some of the alternative answers for a multiple-choice item may be so obviously incorrect that even someone of very low ability can eliminate them. It might thus be better to *estimate* what the probability is that a person of very low ability would answer it correctly, rather than assuming that it will be a constant, based on the number of alternative answers offered by a multiple-choice item. This **guessing parameter** ("c") can be estimated using the three-parameter IRT model – although as we shall see it can be difficult to obtain good estimates of its value.

Figure 15.4 shows the same items as in Figure 15.3, only now with guessing parameters of 0.15, 0.2 and 0.25. (Note that when c is not zero, the difficulty of an item is defined slightly differently; it reflects the probability value which is half way between the lower asymptote and 1. Thus in the case of item 2 which has c = 0.2, the difficulty of the item is determined by a probability of passing it which is $0.2 + \frac{1.0 - 0.2}{2}$ or 0.6.)

It is very easy to modify the formula for the one-parameter logistic formula to take account of the discrimination parameter a_i and the guessing parameter c_i. The modified formula is:

$$P_i(\theta) = c_i + (1-c_i)\frac{e^{1.7.a_i(\theta-b_i)}}{1-e^{1.7a_i(\theta-b_i)}}$$

where a_i represents the item's discrimination, b_i its difficulty and c_i represents the probability that a respondent of very low ability answers the item correctly.

The formula is a slight elaboration of the previous one. Thus if $c_i = 0$ and the item discrimination parameter $a_i = 1.0$ we have the equation for the one parameter model.

Although this discussion has been based on an ability model where each person's response to an item is coded as either correct or incorrect, all models have been extended to allow the analysis of responses from Likert scales and similar. These are known as "graded response models" in the case of the one-, two- and three-parameter models and "polytomous models" in the case of Rasch scaling.

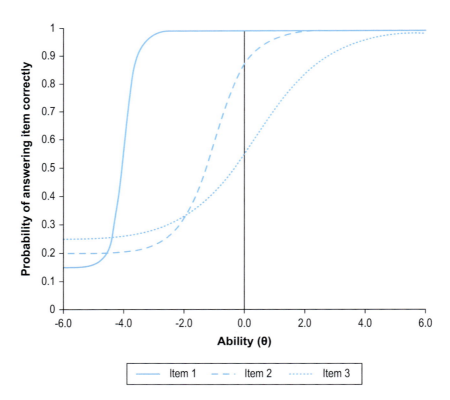

Figure 15.4 Three items following the three-parameter logistic model

ITEM- AND TEST-INFORMATION FUNCTIONS

Suppose that we want to use a scale to discriminate between people who have levels of ability between 2 and 6. It should be obvious that only one of the three items shown in Figure 15.4 can help us distinguish between people whose abilities lie in that range; items 1 and 2 are so easy that everyone with an ability between 2 and 6 will get them correct. Items which everyone passes, or items which everyone gets incorrect, can tell us nothing about individual differences in people's ability. It is therefore necessary to find a way of determining which items will be useful for measuring abilities within a certain range. The **item information function** does this. It shows the precision with which a parameter can be estimated at a particular ability level. For whenever a parameter is estimated using item response theory, the software produces a standard deviation, which shows how much measurement error is present. The information function is simply 1 divided by the square of this standard deviation. Thus the smaller the standard deviation (implying the more accurate the measurement), the larger the information function.

The usual warning applies; if the model does not fit the data, none of these clever statistics has any value whatsoever. But if the data do fit the model, the item information function is a very useful statistic which can show the range of abilities for which a particular item can discriminate between people with accuracy. It shows the precision with which an item can measure the trait at a particular level of ability.

Figure 15.5 shows three ICCs (solid lines) and their associated information functions (dotted lines). The point at which each information function reaches its peak shows for which ability level each item can most accurately measure a person's ability, and its height at any ability level indicates how accurately it can measure an ability of that level.

> **Spreadsheet name:** Spreadsheet 15.1: Information function
>
> **Download from:** https://routledge.com/9781032146164/
>
> **Purpose:** To show how the item information function and test information function can be used to select items to measure a particular range of abilities.
>
> **Contents of spreadsheet:** Item parameters from three items.
>
> **Suggested activity:**
>
> - Try adjusting the three parameters of item 1 to allow it to make as good a discrimination as possible between people whose abilities are in the range of −4 to −2. You might want to start by noticing how varying the item difficulty

affects the information function. Then perhaps vary the discrimination power of the item. Finally, see what effect changing the guessing parameter has on the information function. Note that the maximum value of the information function can be (and often is) greater than 1.
- What do you notice if the c parameter is greater than zero?
- What do you notice if the a parameter is small – i.e., less than 1?

Points to note:

- The width of the information function is determined by the discrimination parameter.

Learning outcomes: Readers should now be able to:

- Appreciate how selecting items with particular parameters may be used to determine the ability range for which a test provides maximum information.

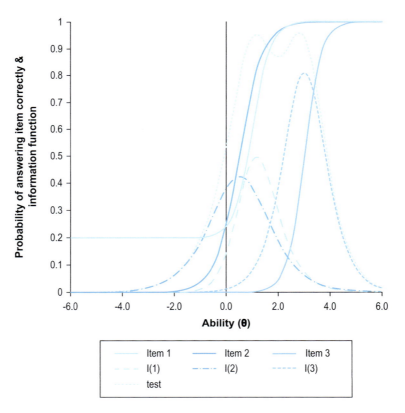

Figure 15.5 Item characteristic curves, item information functions and the test information function from a three-item test

It should be clear that the information function sits (almost) directly underneath the corresponding ICC; the position of its maximum is close to (but not identical to) the difficulty of the item. The width of the information function is determined by the discrimination parameter. In addition, the larger the c-parameter, the lower the information function is. The information functions are not normal distributions (try item parameters of 4, −3 and 0.5 and notice the slight skew of the information function, which peaks at an ability level of −2.9). However, the most interesting thing to come out of this analysis is that an item with low discrimination power is of little use for measuring anything at all, as can be seen by its low information function. Upright ICCs are good ICCs. This is well worth remembering when using IRT to develop scales.

It is also possible to calculate the **test information function** simply by adding together all the item information functions. This shows, for each level of ability, how accurately the scale can discriminate between people of that ability level. The test information function is also shown in Figure 15.5. It shows that for these three items, the test performs best when discriminating between people whose abilities are roughly between 1 and 3.5.

It should now be apparent how massively useful item response theory can be. Once the item parameters are known, it is possible to put together items to form a test with just about any desired test characteristic curve, depending on the purpose of testing. One just estimates the parameters for a large set of items and selects a few items which will produce the desired test information function. For example, an employer might be interested in discriminating between borderline applicants; they may not be particularly interested in accurate assessments of the very best applicants, or the very weakest. They would want a test information function as high as possible towards the middle of the ability spectrum – their experience with previous applicants should give an idea of which levels of ability should be assessed with great accuracy. Or a school may wish to administer items to assess students' progress in mathematics, and in contrast they might want the test to measure all abilities equally accurately – in other words, for this application the test information function should be as high, wide and rectangular as possible.

EXERCISE

Adjust the item parameters in Spreadsheet 15.1 to:

- Create a test which discriminates between people with abilities between 0 and 2.
- Create a test which discriminates between people with abilities between −4 and +4.

Unlike reliability coefficients for conventional scales which attempt to estimate the correlation between scores on a scale and the participants' true scores, item response theory allows the accuracy of measurement to be ascertained *for each particular ability level*.

The test information function in Figure 15.5 is 0.5 for a person having an ability of zero. Therefore, if this three-item test estimates someone's ability to be 0, the standard error of measurement is $\frac{1}{\sqrt{0.5}} = 1.41$. This allows one to say (for example) that there is a 95% chance that this person's true ability lie– somewhere between $(0 - 1.96 \times 1.41)$ and $(0 + 1.96 \times 1.41)$, i.e., between -2.77 and $+2.77$.

RASCH VERSUS TWO- AND THREE-PARAMETER MODELS

Although they are closely related, there are strong differences of opinion about whether it is better to use the Rasch model or adopt the two- or three-parameter models. Those who favour Rasch scaling have outlined their position clearly in working papers and other useful references at www.rasch.org and it is worthwhile browsing these resources to obtain a deeper understanding of the issues outlined later. The (sometimes abrasive) dispute between those who follow the Rasch model and those who favour the more complex models basically hinges on whether one should make a strong assumption about the relationship between item difficulty and ability – namely that every item has exactly the same slope – and ruthlessly remove any items from a scale which do not meet this assumption. Under the Rasch model, differences in the discrimination power of items are regarded as error variance, whereas the two- and three-parameter models estimate these parameters and so they will inevitably provide better fit to the data than the Rasch model.

As will be seen, the one-parameter model does have certain advantages over the two- and three-parameter models which may make its use worthwhile. For example, the ICCs are always parallel under the Rasch model, whereas under the others they can cross each other. Thus a person might be expected to fail an easy item and pass a harder one; this could happen if a person whose ability was −4 took items 2 and 3, whose ICCs are shown in Figure 15.4. However, it means that it is not possible to apply the technique to all sets of items; one will only realise that they do not fit the Rasch model after analysing them, and so it may take several iterations to develop a scale which fits the Rasch model.

Advocates of the Rasch model stress that it has the following merits:

- Only the Rasch model allows the item difficulties to be estimated separately from the person abilities, and so only the Rasch model allows "sample free" estimates of item difficulty to be calculated ("specific objectivity"). In a section titled "Illiterate Theory", Wright (1984) writes: "The estimation virtues extolled by Swaminathan in a chapter featuring the three parameter model apply, in fact, only to the one parameter Rasch model" – strong words, indeed. In addition to specific objectivity, proponents of the Rasch model argue that there are several other reasons to prefer it to the two- and three-parameter models.

- Differences in item discrimination power can be regarded as examples of items failing to fit the model; scales can be constructed by simply removing such aberrant items, making more complex models unnecessary.
- Rasch scaling can be used to analyse multiple-choice data, and when it is, the degree of fit can be surprisingly good (Holster & Lake, 2016). In some cases it seems that estimates of ability are little affected by using the Rasch rather than the three-parameter model.
- Empirically it sometimes seems that item difficulties estimated by the Rasch technique are not very different from those estimated by the three-parameter model (Linacre & Wright, 1995), though it would be naive to assume that this will be the case for all sets of data.
- The Rasch model is parsimonious, which is usually regarded as a virtue in science. Why develop a model requiring the estimation of more parameters if a simple one (which has the advantage of "specific objectivity") will suffice?
- When estimating parameters took hours or days of computer time, it used to matter that Rasch analysis required less computing power than two- or three-parameter models. However, this is now of trivial importance.

Advocates of the two- and three-parameter models counter that:

- No model ever shows perfect invariance because no model (especially the Rasch) ever perfectly fits the data. Invariance is thus not an all-or-nothing phenomenon – there are degrees of invariance, and parameter estimates will thus always show some "drift" from sample to sample. Empirically, item difficulty parameters taken from several different samples fitted by the two- and three-parameter models correlate very substantially indeed, typically with R-squared of 0.9 or above (Rudner, 1974; Rupp & Zumbo, 2006; Lord, 1980), perhaps indicating that two- or three-parameter models show "good-enough" invariance.
- "Common sense rules against the supposition that guessing plays no part in the process for answering multiple-choice items. The supposition is false, and no amount of pretense will make it true" (Traub, 1983).
- Hambleton and Traub (1973) demonstrated that for short tests where items varied in their discrimination power, the two-parameter model provided more accurate ability estimates than the Rasch model; Hambleton and Cook (1983) further found that for scales comprising 20 items, the three-parameter model gave a better fit to the true structure of the data than did the one-parameter model, although this difference became smaller as the number of variables increased.

Pragmatically, the choice of whether to use the Rasch model or something more complex boils down to personal preference, the length of the scale, whether or not one is willing to remove what *look* like good items just because they do not fit the model, and how well the data fit the model – bearing in mind that the statistical significance of goodness of fit indices will be influenced by sample size. An excellent discussion of how to check whether a model fits the data is given by Hambleton et al. (1991).

ESTIMATING ABILITIES AND ITEM PARAMETERS

The basic aim of item response theory is to estimate the difficulty level of each item in the test and (at the same time) estimate the ability of each person who takes the test. If a test comprises 20 items and the responses of 100 children are analysed, it will be necessary to estimate 20 measures of item difficulty and 100 measures of ability for the one parameter model, plus 20 item discriminations if the two-parameter model is used, plus another 20 item difficulty indices if a three parameter model is adopted. How can all these numbers be estimated?

We argued earlier that the item characteristic curve (ICC) shows the chances of a people with various levels of ability passing a particular test item. Perhaps a computer program can be written to first make a rough estimate of the abilities of the various people (perhaps on the basis of the number of items answered correctly) and given these abilities then estimate the difficulty levels of each of the items. Then the same process could be repeated backwards, with the people's abilities being estimated from the item difficulty statistics. This process could be repeated time and time again, obtaining better estimates of the ability and item parameters at each stage, until the estimates of the people's ability and the items' difficulties cannot be improved any more. In other words, the program can attempt to find the most appropriate values for all of the item parameters and abilities. Swaminathan and Gifford (1983) have shown that when the number of items and persons is fairly large, the estimates of the parameters that are obtained in this way are quite close to their true values for the one- and two-parameter models, whilst the three-parameter model is rather more problematical.

It is fairly straightforward to develop a goodness-of-fit statistic which shows how well a particular set of item parameters and abilities fit the data. Altering any parameter will increase or decrease the value of this fit statistic, and so all one needs to do is adjust the several hundred item parameters and abilities until one finds the combination which provides the best value for the goodness-of-fit statistic. Put like this, it sounds a simple enough procedure, though numerically estimating all these parameters is not simple and can go wrong. This is why there is no spreadsheet to perform IRT analyses to accompany this book; it is just too computationally demanding. The whole procedure ("non-linear optimisation") is exactly analogous to a blind explorer wandering through a landscape, trying to find the lowest point. If the landscape consists of gentle slopes downwards all leading a single bowl-shaped crater, this is easy – one just keeps walking downhill until one can go no further. But what if the landscape is fairly flat, with many shallow valleys and depressions? You would need to do a lot of exploring to cover them all – and there is always the danger that although you *think* you have found the lowest point, this is in fact a "local minimum" because there is another, lower point ("global minimum") in an area which has not been thoroughly explored. If a program invites the user to specify the number of iterations to be performed, this is a rough analogy for how much walking should be done in an attempt to find the global minimum. The "tolerance" or "convergence criterion" usually specifies how flat the ground has to be before one is sure that one has reached the lowest point.

This problem affects several types of software, including structural equation modelling, but is a particular issue with the three-parameter model. The "solution" is to repeat the analysis several times, starting from a different point each time, to check that you end up in the same place – though there is no guarantee that this will be the true global minimum, especially if there is a small deep hole with steep sides somewhere in an otherwise flat region. And like the hapless explorer, one has no idea what the terrain looks like. Mathematicians have developed several techniques for performing such numerical optimisations, but one can never be quite certain that they will find the single best solution to a particular problem. And suppose that there are three points on the landscape, all within a hair's breadth of being the same height above sea level. If one is lucky the program will consistently find the lowest point and base the parameter estimates on its location. What it will *not* show is that there are a couple of other, very different, solutions which are almost as good – and which will might yield very different estimates of the parameters in the model. It would be good to know that this is happening, so that one can treat the set of parameter estimates with some scepticism, but as far as I know no programs do this.

Several computer programs have been written to simultaneously estimate abilities and item difficulties (and optionally discrimination and guessing parameters). An internet search will locate the software. Commercial software includes Xcalibre and Winsteps (for Rasch); free student and trial versions are available. Bilog and Multilog are also widely used. All run on Windows. jMetrik is a freeware Java-based program by J. Patrick Meyer at the University of Virginia which runs on a variety of platforms and is fairly straightforward to use. Param by Lawrence Rudner is another Windows freeware offering which is exceptionally straightforward, though it only estimates item and person parameters and their standard errors. Any readers who enjoy using the R environment may find routines such as ltm, TAM, eRm and mirt appealing.

ITEM RESPONSE THEORY AND TEST ITEM BIAS

One important application of item response theory is the detection of **bias** in tests. All one needs to do is estimate the item difficulty parameters for two groups of people – generally a majority and a racial minority group. To determine whether an item is biased against (or in favour of) a minority group, all one needs to do is estimate the item parameters for each group separately. If the item shows no bias, these two item characteristic curves, which show how likely it is that a person of a particular ability from a particular group will pass the item, should be identical. If the item shows bias, they will be different. If a two-parameter model is used, this approach can also show which *level* of ability bias is found. For example, it could be the case that there is no difference at all between the groups at high levels of ability, but that the item becomes much harder for minority group members of low ability than for majority group members of low ability. It is particularly important given that the difficulty parameters are sample-free, and so it should not matter whether one group has higher average scores than the other.

It is possible to calculate a chi-square statistic to test whether the item parameter estimates for a scale differ significantly; this essentially tests whether the test information functions are the same for the two groups. Several other approaches are possible too (Millsap & Everson, 1993; Hambleton & Swaminathan, 1985), but this area can get technical.

One simple way of detecting bias is to analyse the data item by item. One can simply plot the ICCs for two (or more) groups on the same graph. The area between the two graphs can give some indication of the degree of bias shown by that item. For example, suppose that in one group an item has a = 0.8 and b = 1.2, whilst in another group a = 1.0 and b = 0.9; c = 0 for both groups. Plotting these two ICCs (using Spreadsheet 15.1) shows that the two items are unbiased for ability levels less than about 0, but that they show appreciable bias for higher abilities.

Once the parameters defining each curve are known, determining the area between the two curves is a simple problem to solve using calculus or numerical integration. The larger the area, the greater the extent of bias. Of course this approach precludes the use of the three-parameter model, unless the guessing parameter ("c") is fixed to be the same for both groups. This is because as ability scores theoretically range down to minus infinity, if there is any discrepancy between the c-parameters of the two ICCs, the area between the two ICCs will also tend towards infinity.

TAILORED TESTING

The second really important consequence of item response theory is that estimates of the ability of people can be made from different items. For example, Alan might be given items 1, 3 and 6; Joel might be administered items 2, 4 and 5 – but despite having taken quite different sets of items, it would be possible to compare their scores on the ability scale. This is known as **tailored testing**, as the items administered are tailored to fit the ability of each participant.

In order to develop a tailored test it is first necessary to develop an **item bank** – a set of items which form a test or scale, whose difficulties (and perhaps their discrimination powers and guessing parameters) are known, and each of which can be administered by computer. To establish their parameters they are all administered to a sample of several hundred people. Because of specific objectivity it does not matter too much which sample is used to estimate item difficulty, as long as a reasonable number of people (say 30 or more) in the sample pass each item and another 30+ fail each item. This is necessary because – obviously – if everyone passes or fails an item, its difficulty cannot be determined.

The results are analysed using scaling software, and three sets of things are estimated:

- The difficulty (and perhaps discrimination and guessing parameter) for each item
- Its goodness-of-fit to the chosen model (Rasch, two- or three-parameter)
- Ideally, its degree of bias, assuming that the sample comprises two or more reasonably large sets of people.

If the bank of items being developed is large, it might not be feasible to administer them all to the same group(s) of people as the test is being developed. It is possible to administer some of the items to one sample of people and another set of items to a second sample of people *as long as some items are taken by everyone*. A process known as **test equating** may then be used to place all of the items on the same scale – even though just a few of them have been taken by members of both samples. Most scaling software will perform such analyses.

Items which do not fit the model need to be dropped, and as mentioned earlier, more items will be dropped if Rasch scaling is used than if the two- or three-parameter models are employed. Items showing bias should also be dropped at this stage. We now have a database containing the item content, between one and three parameters for each item. All of these items measure a single scale. Specialised software is then used to select items from this database and administer them to a participant.

The test starts by guessing that the participant will be of roughly average ability. An item of average difficulty is selected at random and is presented on screen; the participant's response is recorded and scored (as correct or incorrect), and this is used to refine the estimate of the person's ability. This process is repeated over and over again. As more and more data are gathered, the computer program will be able to predict ever more accurately which not-yet-taken items a person will be able to answer correctly and which they will fail. This allows the person's ability to be determined very rapidly.

The information function guides this process of item selection. It identifies which level of item difficulty will give the most information about a person's ability, given their performance on previous items. The software will then find an item of the appropriate difficulty from the item bank, administer it and recalculate the estimate of the person's ability. The process continues until the program has estimated the person's level of ability with sufficient accuracy.

This process has several advantages over conventional assessments.

One of the problems with conventional testing is knowing which test to select. One has to rely on experience, "gut feeling" or something equally unscientific when deciding which ability test to lift from the shelf, for some are designed for college students, some for young children, some for the general adult population . . . If one chooses an inappropriate test, the participant will either have to take a lot of insultingly easy items (making them bored or careless) or else find that most of the items are impossibly difficult (making them give up). Adaptive testing overcomes this problem. The participant will always be presented with items which feel challenging but not impossible, which makes the whole experience more enjoyable.

The second issue is shorter assessment times. Because participants do not have to waste time taking items which are ridiculously easy or impossibly difficult for them, and so which yield no real information about their ability, adaptive tests can (in theory) gain relevant information about the participant's ability more quickly.

Third, it overcomes problems of test security. It does not matter too much if someone posts online about the items they were asked to answer when applying for a job, for another applicant will probably be given a completely different set of items.

On the other hand, if the item parameters are not appropriate for the person taking the test, the ability estimates will be incorrect – or the program may not be able to estimate ability with accuracy. Random errors ("silly mistakes") can also cause problems. Getting a few easy items incorrect can lead the program into underestimating one's level of ability; it may continue to administer easy items for some time before it re-establishes the correct level of difficulty for that person.

MOKKEN SCALING

How sensible is it to make extremely strong assumptions about the relationship between people's abilities and the way in which they actually perform when answering test items? No-one ever pretends that any model (Rasch or something more complex) ever fits the data exactly – and yet all the desirable properties of item response theory assume that the fit is perfect. So whilst the mathematical sophistication of the technique appeals to psychometricians, it is not entirely clear how useful the techniques are for day-to-day assessments. Also, in many practical applications one does not really need to try to measure people's ability with the sort of precision which item response theory claims to offer; very often an employer will just wish to know which 10 candidates performed best on some scale, without worrying too much about whether the candidate ranked no. 6 is a lot or just slightly more able than the candidate ranked no. 7.

Mokken scaling is a form of item response theory which does not require such stringent assumptions as the Rasch or two- or three-parameter models. Like other forms of item response theory, Mokken scaling can be applied to data which is scored 0/1 (as in most ability-test data) or to data from Likert scales or similar. However, Mokken scaling of Likert (and similar) data raises some theoretical complications; see, for example, the explanations given by Wind (2017).

Mokken scaling (Mokken & Lewis, 1982) is a non-parametric approach to item response theory which orders the items in terms of difficulty and orders the participants according to their levels of ability whilst making far fewer assumptions about the relationship between ability and performance on test items. There are actually two different forms of Mokken scaling, which make different assumptions about the relationship between the ICCs and ability. Rather than assuming that the ICC follows a specified mathematical function such as the logistic curve, the first version of Mokken scaling (known as "monotonic") just assumes that each ICC that the probability of passing an item increases (or stays constant) as one moves from low-ability to higher-ability candidates; it is never the case that the probability of passing the item decreases as ability increases. The second form of Mokken scaling ("doubly monotonic") imposes a second constraint. Like Rasch scaling, it assumes that the ICCs never cross – but unlike Rasch scaling it does not assume that the ICCs follow any particular mathematical function. Only the doubly monotonic model allows the items to be placed in (invariant) order.

All of the ICCs in Figure 15.6 would be acceptable for Mokken scaling, because although they follow no particular function they never move downwards as ability increases. Note that items 1 and 2 fulfil the requirement for double monotonicity.

Mokken scaling also assumes local independence and unidimensionality, as discussed. Local independence means that there is no "carry-over" from one item to the next, whilst unidimensionality assumes that all of the items in a scale measure the same trait. Taken together these imply that the only reason a person produces a particular response to a test item is their level of the trait being measured, plus random error.

Mokken scaling starts off by performing Guttman scaling, as described in Chapter 4. Suppose that eight people take four items and each answer is coded as correct or incorrect. The left-hand side of Table 15.1 shows the responses as they are collected

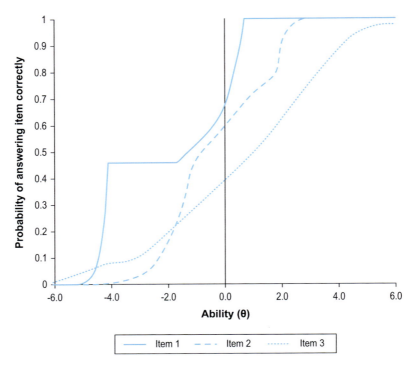

Figure 15.6 Item characteristic curves meeting the demands of Mokken scaling

Table 15.1 Responses of eight people to four test items, unsorted and sorted by item difficulty and ability

Unsorted					Sorted by difficulty and ability				
	Item 1	Item 2	Item 3	Item 4		Item 4	Item 1	Item 3	Item 2
Pers. 1	0	1	1	1	Pers. 4	1	1	1	1
Pers. 2	0	1	1	0	Pers. 5	0	1	1	1
Pers. 3	0	0	0	0	Pers. 1	1	0	1	1
Pers. 4	1	1	1	1	Pers. 8	0	0	1	1
Pers. 5	1	1	1	0	Pers. 2	0	0	1	1
Pers. 6	1	1	0	0	Pers. 6	0	1	0	1
Pers. 7	0	1	0	0	Pers. 7	0	0	0	1
Pers. 8	0	1	1	0	Pers. 3	0	0	0	0
Sum						2	3	5	7

(i.e., in a random order), whereas in the right-hand side of the table the columns have been rearranged so that the hardest item (most incorrect answers) comes first and so on. The right-hand side of the table also roughly orders people so that the most able people (in terms of the number of items answered correctly) are near the top. This does not need any fancy mathematics at all – it just involves sorting the data.

It should be clear from this analysis that the data do not form a Guttman scale. Item 4 appears to be the most difficult one, with only two people passing it. However, one of these (person 1) got item 1 incorrect – and as it is easier, this should not happen if the data form a perfect Guttman scale. There are other anomalies too (look at person 6).

In order to tell how well these data form a Guttman scale it is possible to perform some statistical analyses by looking at the 2 × 2 contingency tables for each pair of items. So for four items there would be six tables, similar to the one shown in Table 15.2.

For a perfect Guttman scale everyone who passed the harder item (item 4) would also pass the other. Table entries which do not fit this model are known as "Guttman errors". It is possible to calculate a statistic called Loevinger's H (Loevinger, 1948), which is simply the value of the phi correlation coefficient divided by its maximum possible value. It can be calculated using Spreadsheet 6.3. It is not obvious why this statistic was chosen rather than (say) the tetrachoric, given its known problems (Davenport & Elsanhurry, 1991). Dividing phi by its maximum possible value provides an index which varies between 0 (randomness) and 1 (agreement which is as good as possible, given any difference in difficulty between the items). Loevinger's H is therefore 1.0 if the two items form a perfect Guttman scale (i.e., everyone who passes one item fails the other) or 0 if there is no relationship between scores on the two items. For the data shown, Loevinger's H is 0.2. If one follows the same logic as Rasch scalers (i.e., removing items that do not fit the model), it might be appropriate to remove items with low H-values from a scale before using it.

Table 15.2 Contingency table showing items 1 and 4 from Table 15.1

		Item 4	
Item 1	Score	0	1
	0	4	1
	1	2	1

It is also possible to average these correlations (six of them, in the case of four variables) to obtain an index for the scale as a whole; this basically shows how well the scale as a whole fits the Guttman model.

Mokken defines a scale as any set of items which all have positive correlations between them, and which also show positive values of H. A quick factor analysis beforehand will ensure that all of the items measure just one trait. A rule of thumb seems to be that a value of H above 0.3 for each item is good enough for the items to form a "satisfactory" Mokken scale (Mokken, 1971), though obviously the larger the value of H the better each item fits the Guttman model. A value above 0.5 is regarded as "good". These figures are arbitrary guidelines, based on experience using the technique rather than any firm statistical theory. However, they seem to be widely used.

Roskam et al. (1986) point out several problems with using H for Mokken scaling:

- The discrimination power of the items (the steepness of the ICC). Items with near-vertical ICCs will lead to larger values of H, all other things being equal.
- The difference in difficulty between two items matters. Items which differ substantially in difficulty will tend to have higher values of H.
- The value of H will be linked to the variance of people's scores on the trait. H will be low if the variance is either very low or very high.

These points seem to have merit, and Sijtsma's (1998) excellent review considers these and other problems with the technique. Several "how to" guides give excellent accounts of Mokken scaling (Sijtsma & van der Ark, 2017; van Schuur, 2003; Wind, 2017), of which Sijtsma and van der Ark is perhaps the most accessible for non-specialists. That paper summarises much recent research on Mokken scaling and gives particular emphasis to the problem of assessing model fit for the doubly monotonic model, which is the one most users would probably want to adopt. It also gives a step-by-step guide of how to perform Mokken scaling, complete with a worked example. As far as software for Mokken scaling is concerned, there are few reasonably modern choices – the Mokken routine which runs in the R statistical environment, or the Mokken or MSP modules for users of Stata.

SUMMARY

This chapter explored several techniques which estimate people's abilities and item difficulties simultaneously. They may allow test scores to be interpreted directly (i.e., without using norms) as the item difficulties can be estimated independently of the distribution of abilities within the sample. It is shown that these techniques have great potential for adaptive testing, and may also be useful for the detection of items which are biased. However, it is not obvious that these techniques are able to produce ability estimates which satisfy Michell's criteria for scientific measurement.

The strong assumptions which they make about the way in which people respond to test items make some psychometricians uneasy. Mokken scaling is a quick, simple technique which makes far fewer assumptions and merits serious attention.

CHAPTER 16
TEST AND SCALE CONSTRUCTION

Creating or modifying a scale or test involves far more effort than students or researchers generally expect, and my advice is always to double- and triple-check that someone else has not already assembled such a scale using the sources listed in Chapter 2. If the scale is to measure a new personality trait, it is advisable to check that it intends to measure some real property of people, and not an imputation or social construction. In addition, it is worthwhile bearing in mind that Bainbridge et al. (in press) found that many "novel" personality scales resemble one, or a combination, of the "Big Five" scales which dominate personality research, and so there may not be a need for a new scale at all.

OVERVIEW

The procedure of creating a new scale include obtaining ethical permission for the study from an ethics committee, writing items, deciding how to check for careless responding or "bot" attacks, deciding whether/how to include additional items to check for social desirability or other forms of response bias, putting the items online or administering them to a large sample of people face to face. Then the responses are put into a computer, missing data dealt with, and careless/malicious responders are identified and removed. All this happens before the hard work of analysing the data and validating the test using another sample of people.

We give an overview of the two phases of test construction before considering the steps in more detail, with a focus on developing and writing items.

PHASE 1 ITEM PREPARATION

This involves deciding on the format of the scale or test (5- or 7-point Likert scale? Multiple-choice or free response ability items?), deciding what domain you plan to

DOI: 10.4324/9781003240181-16

measure, how you plan to sample items from that domain, who will take the scale/test (adults, people with low literacy . . .), how you plan to administer the items (internet, face to face . . .), deciding how many items you need (bearing in mind that some of them will not work) and finally, actually *writing* the items.

PHASE 2: ITEM TRIALS

It is then necessary to give the items to a large sample of people to establish their psychometric properties using factor analysis (Chapter 11), item response theory (Chapter 15), network analysis (Chapter 14) or **classical item analysis** (described later). If the scale measures a state rather than a trait, the methods discussed in Chapter 12, or special forms of network analysis need to be used. The scale or test then needs to be checked to ensure that it is reasonably free from measurement error (Chapters 7 and 8) and that there is a good spread of responses to each item – either by looking at the frequency with which each alternative is endorsed, or by using the item information function and test information function (Chapter 15). If extra items were included to check for social desirability, each item should be correlated with this scale.

These steps will almost certainly show that some items need to be removed or amended. Almost everyone may give the same answer so some items, or they may not load the same factor as the others. They may pull down the reliability of the scale. They may correlate substantially with the social desirability scale. The test information function may show that the scale contains too many easy (or difficult) items. In the case of multiple-choice ability items, some "distractors" may be too popular or too unpopular.

Items will be dropped or amended based on these considerations, but when eliminating items care must be taken to ensure that they cover the full breadth of the trait that is being measured. If a depression scale is being developed, you should not drop all the "change in eating habits" items, for example.

PHASE 3: VALIDATION

It is then necessary to consider how to validate the scale, as discussed in Chapter 9.

If the scale is intended for publication, it is advisable to outline how the measure will be validated, and submit this to a journal as a **pre-registered report** *before validation data are collected*. These registered reports normally consist of just an introduction, method, and pilot data (the results from the Phase 1 analyses). The methods and proposed analyses are pre-registered and reviewed prior to research being conducted.

High-quality protocols are then provisionally accepted for publication before data collection takes place.

The advantage of a pre-registered report are threefold:

- First, it forces authors to make their hypotheses clear before gathering data. This is an important issue for construct validation studies as unscrupulous researchers might otherwise look at the validation data and then write their "hypotheses" so that they fit the findings. Pre-registering the report makes it clear to readers and journal editors that this is not the case.
- Second, as the proposal is reviewed by the journal, reviewers may make helpful suggestions as to how the validation process and/or the proposed statistical analyses might be improved.
- Finally, if there are major problems with the scale which would make it unpublishable, it is good to know before going to the effort of validating it.

If the pre-registered report is accepted in principle, authors next register the approved protocol on the Open Science Framework at https://osf.io/rr/ or other recognised repository. Once registered and timestamped, the method and hypotheses cannot be changed.

Then after the scale is validated precisely as outlined in the pre-registered report, the stage two report is submitted to a journal – the introduction and method being identical (word-for-word) to those in the pre-registered report. The abstract, results, discussion etc. are of course new.

DEVELOPING ITEMS

It is necessary to consult the guidelines for the construction and use of psychological tests and the code of human research ethics of one's professional association (e.g., British Psychological Society, American Psychological Association, Canadian Psychological Association) when designing and developing a test – for example, the use of non-discriminatory language.

Obviously, writing good items is the crucial step in developing a scale. If the items are poorly written, or tested on an inappropriate sample of people, then no amount of psychometric wizardry will ever be able to produce a reliable and valid scale. Kline (1986) and Most and Zeidner (1995) have given some common-sense rules of thumb for writing items and developing scales which might also be useful for those who plan to construct a scale. Gulliksen (1986) is an excellent, non-technical paper on the assessment of abilities and attainment. It considers several other forms of test items and makes vital reading for anyone who is interested in constructing tests in this general area.

SAMPLING ITEMS FROM THE DOMAIN

Specifying the areas of content which a scale should measure is probably the most important, yet overlooked, aspect of test and scale design. Writing items is easy; determining what, precisely, the scale should measure requires some grasp of the theoretical background plus a thorough knowledge of the literature in the area. Any test or scale is simply a sample of items from the domain which the scale seeks to measure. There are two ways of creating this: trying to sample items at random (for example, opening a dictionary and selecting a word at random) or by some sort of stratified sampling. It is best to ensure that the scale is a stratified sample of all of the items which could conceivably be written; that is, a sample where equal numbers of items are drawn from a number of different sub-domains, called "facets".

The simplest example is an attainment test where students are assessed on knowledge and skills which they acquire over a series of weeks. Here the sensible choice of a facet would be knowledge gathered in a particular class, or in a particular week. This will presumably be defined in the course syllabus, and so is easy to access. Ensuring that each facet contains the same number of items is a simple way of ensuring that the assessment covers what was taught. Without this discipline it is very easy to write an item with which one feels proud . . . and so write another which is quite similar to it . . . and then another . . . whilst quite forgetting to cover the whole breadth of the trait.

Items which virtually everyone answers in the same way (personality items) or which almost everyone gets correct or incorrect (ability items) cause problems if they are concentrated in one facet rather than being distributed randomly. Such items cannot discriminate between people and so will mean that facet does not contribute to the test score when the test is scored. Although one does not know for sure how difficult an item will be, or how similarly people will respond to an item when one writes it, it is worth bearing this in mind when writing items.

Constructing ability tests, rather than knowledge-based scales, is harder because it is less obvious how one should sample the whole domain of possible items. Most ability tests contain items which are highly similar in content. Psychologists invent some task (e.g., "What is the next shape in the series . . . ?", "Which three-letter word can be inserted in place of the asterisks to form another word?", "How many words can you think of to describe [an object] within 2 minutes?") and then claim to have discovered a new ability trait by measuring performance on this task. This is why discovering the higher-order traits is far more important than focussing on low-level factors, as was argued in Chapter 13. The number of ability traits will otherwise equal the number of possible cognitive tasks which could be devised, which is nearly infinite.

There is another problem, too. In the case of ability items it is necessary to ensure (as far as possible) that each item involves the same cognitive processes. Just because two items share the same format it does not follow that they are difficult for the same reasons. For example, consider the two items "Food is to mouth as seed is to (a) earth (b) plant . . .", which is difficult because it is necessary to recognise that the relationship between the first two items "goes into" making (a) the correct answer. On the other hand, "Oblimin is to oblique as VARIMAX is to (a) orthogonal (b) eigenvalue . . ." is difficult because only those who know about psychometrics would know what oblimin etc. are. The relationship ("performs this form of rotation") is trivially easy to spot if one knows the meaning of the terms. So although the format of the two items is identical, the first relies on reasoning, whilst the second requires quite detailed knowledge for its successful solution. When writing items it is necessary to consider both the knowledge needed and the cognitive processes which may be required to solve each problem.

DEFINING THE POPULATION WITH WHOM THE TEST OR SCALE IS TO BE USED

It is important to specify this as it determines how difficult ability items should be and how complex the vocabulary of items in personality scales and their instructions may become. If a scale is designed for use in a *very* diverse population, then it may be necessary to ensure that the items are non-verbal. For example, an ability scale might use shapes rather than words, with instructions involving animations (for example, showing that the aim of the test is to identify which piece would not fit into a jigsaw). A personality scale might ask people to show which cartoon figure best depicts how they might react or feel in a certain situation. For examples of how non-verbal personality items may be designed and used, see Paunonen et al. (1990) and Paunonen's subsequent work.

The vocabulary and complexity of sentence structure typically found in personality scales and their instructions are far above the vocabulary level of the average American (e.g., Schinka, 2012). However, this seems to miss the point. The vocabulary and sentence structure used should surely be suitable for the *least* well educated, *least* intelligent individual who will ever be given the scale. Short, common words, short sentences and simple grammar are advisable (no double negatives, passive voice, gerunds etc.) unless the population for whom the scale is designed is well educated and will answer the items in their first language.

Consideration should also be given to what background knowledge each person should be assumed to have. For example, items in some American personality questionnaires refer to concepts ("United Way", "grade point average"), which will be unfamiliar to those outside North America. One can only assume that when these scales were being devised, someone decided that their use would be confined to that continent. Having culturally inappropriate items in a scale is a problem because it will reduce the reliability of the scale as people will need to guess what the concepts mean or respond randomly. Participants may also object to seeing culturally inappropriate items and may not take the rest of the items seriously.

All too often, authors assume that scales which work in one context for one sample of people will miraculously generalise to almost any application with almost any group of people. Simons et al. (2017) suggest that researchers should abandon this naive assumption and be forced to rigorously justify why, precisely, on theoretical or empirical groups, the results from one sample (e.g., UK students) might be expected to generalise to another (e.g., Australian cricketers).

THE METHOD OF ADMINISTRATION

Items should be developed in the same format which they will eventually be used (only excluding time limits, for reasons discussed later). A test which is ultimately designed to be administered orally, person to person by a trained psychologist should also be developed by being administered orally, person to person. One otherwise runs the risk that items may not work properly. For example, words which sound the same but are spelled differently could easily be confused if an item was administered orally but not if the words were written. So it is necessary to think about how the items will ultimately be delivered early in the development process.

Paper and pencil

Paper and pencil scales are still used – largely because little can go wrong when administering them, and it is possible to ask participants to make responses (such as sketches) which are difficult using computers. It is also easy for participants to change their answer at any time and revisit a previously answered question – two things which are generally difficult with computerised items. Questions are printed in a booklet and answers are written on either the test booklet or a separate answer sheet. Using a separate answer sheet means that the booklets are reusable. However, the answer sheets must be carefully designed so that it is easy for the participant to see if their answers have got out of sync with the questions in the booklet – for example, by accidentally skipping a question. Thus the layout of the answers on the answer sheet should mirror the layout of the question booklet; there should be a line or gap corresponding to each page or column break in the test booklet.

The responses then need to be scored as described in Chapter 4. It is essential to record the responses to individual items when developing scales; using templates to calculate the total score will not suffice.

Viewing items on a screen

It is possible to test groups of people where each participant has only an answer sheet, the items being projected onto a screen. It is straightforward to produce a series of slides using standard presentation software, perhaps with a standard time limit for each slide, and a warning tone to indicate how much time is left. This can allow videos etc. to be incorporated if necessary, and professional-looking presentations can be produced very quickly. However, the display must be large enough to ensure that those seated further away are not disadvantaged, and care must be taken to ensure that the image brightness is fairly uniform. Problems can also arise if participants need to change glasses to view the screen and mark the answer sheet.

Stand-alone computers

Item administered on stand-alone computers allow the greatest flexibility. Customised hardware can be used where necessary (e.g., to measure ability to track objects using a joystick, or to display very brief presentations of stimuli). Commercial or in-house software can be written to record responses, along with the time taken to answer each item. This is invaluable when developing ability scales, which will eventually have time limits. Several computer programs allow items which were developed using item response theory to be administered adaptively, as described in Chapter 15. Davey (2011) has produced an excellent guide to the practicalities of computerised assessments.

The internet

As mentioned earlier, internet administration of personality scales is straightforward; internet-based administration of ability scales is less easy, particularly if graphics are required or if time limits are needed, whilst internet-based adaptive testing requires specialised software, such as FastTest. Although several scales which were originally administered using printed booklets also seem to work well whilst administered by computer, guidelines exist for the development and use of computerised scales (Bartram, 2009), whilst those who plan to develop adaptive tests should consult a text such as Wainer et al. (2014) at the outset.

Equipment-based tests

Some scales require hardware — anything from a (standard) toy elephant through cards with inkblots printed on them to a set of small nuts, bolts and screws and washers and a plate into which they are fixed. However, these are so specialised that they cannot be discussed here.

THE FORMAT OF THE ITEMS FOR PERSONALITY SCALES

Chapter 2 introduced Likert scales, the instructions for which can have several forms such as "How much do you agree with each of the following statements?", "How well does each statement describe you?", "How much do you like . . . ?", "I see myself as . . .", and "How much do you usually . . . ?", and there is no real rationale for preferring one to the other.

Ability scales usually just present participants with a set of problems to be solved.

We have not yet encountered situational judgement tests. These are measures which present participants with a standard situation (real or imagined) and ask them what they think, feel or would do. An example of a situational judgement test involving a real situation would be an "in-tray" selection test; a job applicant might be given a set of typical issues which they would be expected to deal with (these could be anything relevant to the job: dealing with letters of complaint, balancing books, filleting a fish, scheduling a delivery round etc.), and as all applicants are given the same problems, it should be possible to compare their performance. Several computerised or paper-and-pencil tests rely on *hypothetical* situations. Participants might be asked how they would probably act in different situations. For example, "If you are walking down the sidewalk (pavement) and a group of children are blocking it, would you (a) walk round them saying nothing, (b) walk round them smiling and reminding them that an elderly or disabled person would find it difficult to pass, (c) push through" etc. This example is of a forced-alternative (ipsatised) scale, for each action will represent a different personality trait; it is also possible to ask people to rate how likely they would be to perform each action.

THE FORMAT OF THE RESPONSES FOR PERSONALITY SCALES

If possible, all of the items in a scale or test should have the same format. Likert scales of either five or seven items are popular for personality scales, though some use just a 3-point scale and some as many as 10. It is sensible to choose an odd number of categories so that respondents have a "neutral" answer, rather than being forced to express a preference one way or the other.

It is important to ensure that a few words are used to give meaning to each level of the scale. Rather than asking people to write a number

| Strongly disagree | 1 | 2 | 3 | 4 | 5 | 6 | 7 | Strongly agree |

or tick or fill in a box or circle

Strongly disagree	○	○	○	○	○	○	○	Strongly agree

corresponding to their answer, it is better to anchor each response, to try to make sure that people use the scale in similar ways. For example, "I like betting":

	Strongly disagree	Disagree	Slightly disagree	Neutral/ unsure	Slightly agree	Agree	Strongly agree
I like betting	○	○	○	○	○	○	○

The problem is that social desirability might taint these responses, and of course different people might understand different things by "like", "strongly" or "slightly". For this reason it is better still if the responses can be tied to actual behaviour; e.g., "I have placed a bet".

	Never in the past year	Once or twice in the last year	3–20 times in the last year	21–50 times in the last year	More than 50 times in the past year
I have placed a bet	○	○	○	○	○

The last example asks people to say what they actually *did*, and unless they choose to deliberately lie or have forgotten, this sort of format will yield better data than simply asking people what they like or dislike. If some items ask about very common behaviours ("How often do you brush your teeth?"), whilst others ask about very rare ones, it is difficult to find a rating scale which suits all items. Using different scales for different items (rather than showing one header which applies to all of the items in a scale) can cause confusion, takes up a lot of space and requires a lot of reading.

THE FORMAT OF THE ITEMS FOR ABILITY TESTS

Ability tests generally either ask people to either write the correct answer to a problem (free response) or choose between various alternatives (multiple-choice), as discussed in Chapters 2 and 4. If item response theory is to be used (see Chapter 15), then estimating the "guessing" parameter for each multiple-choice item may be a problem; pretending that guessing does not happen in order to justify the use of the Rasch model might only be sensible if the number of distractors is large (six or more).

Multiple-choice items

Writing good distractors is difficult. The objective is to produce answers which all sound plausible, so that none can be eliminated as "obviously incorrect" by the test-taker who resorts to guessing. Here are a few examples:

Example 1

Tadpole is to frog as caterpillar is to (a) garden (b) toad (c) pond (d) butterfly.

My rationale for choosing (a), (b) and (c) as distractors was that (a) caterpillars are found in gardens, so if someone thinks that this could be the rule linking tadpole and frog, they might choose this option; (b) frogs and toads are somewhat similar; and (c) both tadpoles and frogs are found in ponds. I deliberately made sure that all of the distractors had some sort of relationship to the first three terms of the analogy; if I had chosen "coal", most people would recognise that this was unlikely to be correct.

Example 2

Which shape completes the pattern? (Figure 16.1)

There is less of an obvious rationale for choosing distractors for items such as this. Distractor (a) was chosen in case they did not notice the shift to the right. Distractor (b) is there in case they thought they may have to combine two shapes somehow.

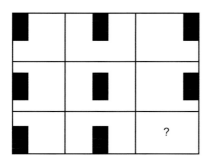
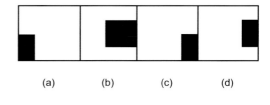

Figure 16.1

Example 3

Which is the odd one out: (a) light bulb (b) radio (c) air conditioner (d) cuckoo clock.

These items are difficult to write, because it is almost impossible to ensure that there is only one correct answer. When writing this item I originally thought that (d) (not electric) would be the correct answer but then realised that light bulbs can be found outside the home, making (a) correct. Or one could argue that (b) is correct: it contains electronic circuits, whereas the others may not. Or perhaps (c) is correct: it cannot easily be lifted. There again, all make a noise apart from the light bulb . . . it may be better to avoid such items.

Example 4

What are the base 3 numbers 0121 + 1112 in base 3 notation? (a) 1233 (b) 2010 (c) 1200 (d) 11011.

Choice (a) is correct; distractor (b) is the answer in decimal; distractor (c) is the answer one would get if one forgot to carry numbers greater than 2; and distractor (d) is a random binary number, on the assumption that such numbers may be familiar to participants who do not understand the concept of base 3.

The key to writing all such items is to try to think flexibly and have *some* sort of hypothesis about the way in which participants might be trying to approach the problem, rather than choosing words or numbers at random. For a more detailed discussion see Gierl et al. (2017).

Free response tests

Free response tests outlined in Chapter 2 involve a person making a response other than selecting from a series of alternatives. These responses might include writing the answer to a problem, drawing, singing, saying a word, arranging wooden blocks, using tools to bolt two objects together, using a mouse to track a dot which moves around the screen, or a host of other possibilities. Such items are sometimes more difficult to score than multiple-choice tests; spoken responses are really only feasible if a test is administered to one person at a time, whilst interpreting the meaning of what is written can be difficult (see Chapter 5). However, some free response tests are straightforward. In the classic Guilford test of divergent thinking, one simply counts how many different words a person can produce in a minute when describing an object; it does not matter what the words are. The computerised tracking task will produce statistics showing the accuracy of performance.

THE ORDER OF THE ITEMS AND ALTERNATIVE RESPONSES

It is usual to randomise the order of items in personality scale or questionnaire. When items are written to measure several different facets, they should all be mixed up together rather than having several items measuring the same facet next to each other, as if several similar items are adjacent to each other, participants may simply check the same answer to each of them to ensure that they are behaving consistently. In addition, the order in which items are presented can affect the scores which people obtain – a finding which has particular implications for the use of adaptive personality scales based on item response theory (Ortner, 2008; Steinberg, 1994). So once an arbitrary order of items has been decided, it is probably wise to keep the same rank-ordering of items in the final version of the scale (i.e., after removing items which do not work).

Ability items are normally ordered in terms of difficulty, with the easiest ones at the start of the scale to give participants confidence. Whilst the difficulty of the items obviously cannot be known before any data is gathered, informal estimates (e.g., from friends or pilot studies) might be better than nothing in helping one to decide on the initial order of the items. However, once the items have been administered to a sample as part of the item analysis procedure, subsequent versions of the scale should arrange them in their actual order of difficulty. It goes without saying that the position of the correct answer in multiple-choice items should be randomised.

If ability tests and personality tests are to be administered in the same session, Akhtar and Kovacs (in press) found that it is best to administer personality questionnaires before ability tests, as there was less careless responding to personality scales when these were administered first, whereas the order of administration did not affect performance on ability tests.

THE INSTRUCTIONS

In this section we describe how a typical group-testing session might be run. In the case of computer-based assessments some (or, if the scale is being administered remotely, *all*) of this information will need to appear on screen. After making introductions, the test administrator should thank the participants for taking part and make it clear that they are welcome to leave at any time without giving any explanation as to why, and any data they have provided will then be destroyed. They should then spell out to participants what they are being asked to do (e.g., complete three personality questionnaires), what the purpose of the study is, how long is it likely to last, whether their responses are anonymous, and who will have access to individual and collated data. There should always be reference to the fact that ethical approval for the study has been obtained, and it is important to give the name and contact details of someone who

TEST AND SCALE CONSTRUCTION

can be approached if the participants have any concerns after participating. Business cards are good for this. A consent form should be signed by every participant, indicating that they agree to take part in the study as described.

This preamble will vary from study to study, and it is important to consult the ethical standards of one's psychological association in case other issues need to be considered. If vulnerable people (children, patients, prisoners etc.) are participating, or if deception is to be used, a more detailed risk assessment will always be needed. This will also be necessary if the scales deal with information which is in any way personal (e.g., sexual or political behaviour, experience of violence or prejudice, attitudes to abortion or rape).

If any of the scales is believed to be valid, feedback should normally be offered on these scales if participants want it. If scales are unvalidated, the reason for not offering feedback on these scales should be explained. It is important to give all this information before gathering data, so that participants can decide to withdraw should they choose to.

It is best to try to make this introduction as friendly as relaxed as possible; rather than using a script, it is better to just consult a list of bullet points to ensure that all of the issues have been mentioned. I usually then explain (apologetically) that assessments need to be standardised so that everyone has the same experience, and so it is necessary to read a standard set of instructions for each scale. And these *should* be read verbatim.

The instructions for each scale should be drafted when the scale is being developed and read verbatim even when the scale is being trialled for the first time. They can then be amended if necessary for any further studies. These instructions should normally make it clear what each scale measures, how participants should indicate their responses (e.g., whether they should use an answer sheet), how quickly they should work, what to do if they are unsure about an answer, whether to turn the page, whether there is a time limit, and whether or how it is possible to change their answer to a question, either immediately or by returning to it if they have time at the end. When group testing, there should also be the opportunity to ask if anything is unclear. All this needs to be couched in clear, simple language.

For personality scales it is also advisable to ask participants to give the first answer which comes naturally to mind, otherwise some people will start agonising about the precise meaning and nuance of every word in the scale. Kline (1986) argues that a well-written item should evoke an immediate response.

A typical set of instructions for a personality questionnaire might resemble the following. Note the short, easy sentences.

> This scale measures personality. The printed sheet contains 50 statements. Please decide how well each statement describes you. To the right of each statement there are five boxes. These are labelled "strongly disagree", "disagree", "neutral or unsure", "agree" and "strongly agree". Please put a tick through the box which shows how well the statement describes how you usually feel or behave. Then move on to the next statement. There are 50 statements in total: 25 on the first page and 25 on the second page. Just turn the page when you reach the bottom. You can take as long as you like to respond to each statement. However, please do not spend too long thinking about the exact meaning of the words. Just give the response which comes naturally to mind. If you are unsure about any response, please just give your best guess. Please give a response for every statement. If you change your mind about a response, cross it out and put a tick to indicate your new response. Does anyone have any questions?

Ability scales sometimes ask people to solve quite complex problems. It may be necessary to check that participants understand what they are being asked to do by showing them an item with the correct answer marked for them, and then asking them to solve a second (very easy) practice item themselves before starting the test proper, marking their answer on the answer sheet or question booklet. The test administrator can check that everyone has answered this item correctly before proceeding. Good examples of this can be seen in the instructions for Raven's Matrices (Raven et al., 2003) and Cattell's Culture Fair Tests series 3 (Cattell, 1965) – though for this test the instructions are so detailed that reading the instructions takes longer than answering the items!

With ability scales it is important to tell participants how fast to work, what their error rate should be, and whether they should guess if they do not know an answer. Unless dealing with a "speeded test", where virtually everyone would score 100% given unlimited time, it is best to give very generous (or unlimited) time when *developing* the test. Otherwise since some candidates may not reach the items at the end of the test, it is very difficult to estimate the difficulty of those items. Time limits can be imposed when putting together the final version.

A typical set of instructions for a multiple-choice ability scale might resemble the following:

> This game measures [some ability]. The printed sheet contains 50 puzzles. To the right of each puzzle there are four possible answers. Only one of these answers is correct. Please put a tick through the box by the correct answer, then move on to the next puzzle. If you are unsure of an answer, please guess. Please work as quickly as you can. You will have 30 minutes to complete the test, though do not worry if you finish long before then. There are 50 puzzles in total, 25 on the first page and 25 on the second page. Just turn the page when you reach the bottom. If you change your mind about an answer, cross it out and put a tick to indicate your new answer. Does anyone have any questions?

WRITING ITEMS

No-one can write perfect items on their first attempt. It is possible that an item may be drafted so that almost everybody will answer it in the same way (who would ever claim that they are miserly?). There may be some ambiguity of meaning which has not been noticed. Sexist language may have crept in. In the case of ability scales, an item may be so easy that everyone gets it correct, or so difficult that no-one does – or worse still, more than one of the answers to a multiple-choice test may be correct. It is also possible that the items simply do not measure the trait or state which they are deigned to assess; indeed, it might be the case that the trait or state simply does not exist! It is therefore necessary to draft the items, administer them to a sample of people similar to that with which the scale will eventually be used, and perform statistical analyses to identify and remove items which do not work properly. What follow are some general guidelines, followed by more detailed guidelines for writing personality and ability items.

1. How many items should be written? This is a commonly asked question to which there is no simple answer. Chapter 7 showed that reliability increases with test length, and so it is advisable to start with as many items as possible. For personality items, 30 per scale is the suggestion given by Kline (1986), in the hope that about 20 of them will eventually work. However, it also depends on the breadth of the concept being measured. Measuring a broad trait such as anxiety will require more items than measuring a single narrow facet such as test anxiety, where there are fewer different questions which *can* be asked without repeating oneself.
2. Items should be short and clear, using simple words. They should be clear enough for anyone to read – which is especially important if formulae are used.
3. Items should be locally independent. In other words, the only thing which should affect a person's response is the trait which the item is supposed to measure – *not* their response to any previous item. We pointed out in Chapter 7 that items which are similar in meaning will inevitably fail this test; item writers should examine every possible pair of items in a scale and check that the way a person answers one item does not force them to answer any other item in a particular way, other than through the influence of the trait that the test is designed to measure.
4. Check words using a dictionary to ensure that an item does not have several possible interpretations. For example, one personality questionnaire used to include the item "Do you enjoy gay parties?", with "gay" then meaning "lively".
5. The cultural appropriateness of each item should be carefully considered. This will typically include the implicit knowledge required to understand the item or solve the problem. Would every 80-year-old know what a vegan is? Would every 18-year-old know what "carbon copy" means?
6. Items should be written so that they measure only the trait which the scale is supposed to assess. They should not require a sophisticated vocabulary and should not be influenced by social desirability or by any other traits.

7   Decide on the response format, as discussed. For multiple-choice ability items there should be three or four alternatives in order to reduce the effects of lucky guessing (Gierl et al., 2017).
8   Write an equal number of items for each facet, taking care to construct good, plausible distractors (possibly based on an analysis of common errors from an earlier, free response pilot version of the test if using a multiple-choice format). Ensure that the items in each facet appear to span a similar and appropriate range of difficulty.
9   Do not test the trivial just because it is easy to do so. When assessing students' statistical knowledge, the easiest type of item to write involve formulae and definitions, e.g., "What is the equation for calculating the sample standard deviation?" The problem is, of course, that the instructor probably *should* be interested in testing how well students *understand* and can *apply* the concepts – parroting definitions is rarely what is wanted. The UK driving test provides another good example. I can remember learning and reciting stopping distances, although the examiners never checked that candidates knew what those distances actually looked like when they were driving, thereby missing the point entirely.

Writing items for personality tests

1   Try to write items that are clear, unambiguous and require as little self-insight as possible. Wherever possible, you should refer to behaviours rather than to feelings.
2   If it is obvious what an item measures, some test-takers will identify what the trait is and respond to the item in the way which matches their view of where they stand on the trait. This may not be the same as where they really stand on the trait. For example, "Are you honest?" is an awful item, as anyone reading it can see that the scale is meant to measure honesty. Respondents will probably all decide that they *are* usually honest, and answer the item accordingly. A better approach might be "I told a lie (a) today (b) within the last week" . . . with possibly more items asking about breaking laws etc. Guilford (1959) argued that the best items will produce scores on traits which the test-taker does not know as a result of asking them questions the answers to which they do know.
3   Ensure that each item asks only one question. For example, do not use a statement such as "I sometimes feel depressed and have attempted suicide", since extremely depressed people who have not (quite) got round to attempting suicide would have to disagree with it, which is presumably not what is intended.
4   Try to avoid negatively phrased items such as "I dislike crowds: yes/?/no", since choosing "no" requires the participant to interpret a double negative. "I enjoy uncrowded places" is better.
5   Try to avoid questions asking about frequency or amount. How frequently is "often"? Different people will probably mean different things by the term. Instead, refer to specific rather than general behaviour. Instead of asking "Do you

read a lot?", try asking "How many books have you read for pleasure in the past month?" – or better still, "List the books that you have read for pleasure in the past month" (which may reduce socially desirable responses).

6. If possible, try to avoid items reflecting feelings, but refer to behaviours instead, e.g., "How many parties have you been to in the last month?", rather than "Do you enjoy parties?"

7. Try to ensure that about 50% of the items in each facet are keyed so that a "yes/strongly agree" response indicates a high score on the trait and the others are keyed in the opposite direction. For example, "I generally fall asleep at night as soon as the light is turned off" would be scored so that "strongly disagree" indicated anxiety. (See Chapter 8.) However, it may be difficult to write such items without using double negatives.

8. If you *must* ask about something socially undesirable, consider phrasing the item from another person's point of view, e.g., "Some people might describe me as mean" or, better still, "My friends have occasionally called me mean" (a fact, rather than anything requiring insight), rather than "Are you mean?"

Writing items for ability or attainment tests

Most readers of this book are students or graduates, with extensive vocabularies and good numerical skills. As such it can be difficult to gauge the difficulty of items written for other groups. It is therefore important to draft some items which appear to be extremely easy, so as not to overestimate the abilities of the general population.

Any test measuring ability or attainment consists of a problem to be solved, some cognitive operations which are used to the problem, and some response. This may sound banal, but it is important to recognise that the difficulty of an item, and its validity, depend on all of these factors. The modality of the problem also varies. Some problems will involve sounds, others words, shapes and behaviours (e.g., video clips of interactions between people), and there are other possibilities, too.

Identifying the precise issue to be addressed is often what makes problems hard to solve in everyday life. For example, one may have a very broad issue to address such as "What should you do if you are running out of money?" To address this issue it is necessary to perform more detailed analyses. Are you *sure* this is the case, or could you have made an error? Is it a temporary glitch for reasons that you understand? Have you been robbed? Can expenditure be reduced? Can income be increased? These are the sorts of questions which need to be asked to identify what the precise problem is.

Most ability scales do not require such high-level thinking, but some do. For example, a free response item could ask for as many answers as possible to the previous question. Or an item might present a picture or video, the task being to see what is wrong with it. This could be anything (inconsistent shadows, water flowing uphill, objects falling at different speeds, parts of objects missing), and so the difficult part of this task is to determine what to look for. However, most problems make the problem to be solved as unambiguous as possible, e.g., "What is the next letter in the sequence?"

The difficulty of ability items generally depends on the cognitive processes needed to solve a well-defined problem. These include how well lists can be memorised whilst performing other cognitive operations on the data (working memory), memory scanning, devising novel uses for objects, solving anagrams, mental rotation, various forms of inductive and inductive reasoning, or indeed any other cognitive processes, singly or in combination. Surprisingly, perhaps, it does not seem to be common practice for item writers to consult research on cognitive psychology or cognitive neuroscience to try to ensure that their items involve fundamental processes – and ideally that all items in a scale focus on just one of them. Instead, items seem to be developed on a much more ad hoc basis. This was obviously necessary in the days before cognitive psychology had a sound theoretical and experimental basis, but now it might not be so appropriate.

A few items are difficult because the response is hard to make. Tracking a moving object on a screen using a joystick, sight-reading a challenging extract of music, flying an aeroplane using a simulator or assembling a small object using tweezers would be examples. However, as most scales are designed to measure cognitive processes rather than co-ordination or adroitness, such scales are in a minority.

When writing ability items, be careful when using colour as some participants will be colour-blind. It is best to avoid using red and green as distinguishing features in an ability item, and ideally avoid using yellow and blue together too. If in doubt, print the item in greyscale and check that the differences between the various parts of the puzzle are clearly visible.

Examples of ability items

There are several widely used types of ability items:

Analogies. These items, such as "Tadpole is to frog as caterpillar is to . . ." (Example 1) can be used either to test knowledge (where the hard part of the item is understanding the meanings of the nouns) or reasoning (where the relationship between the terms is hard to discern). These items require participants to identify the relationship between the first two terms and apply this to the third term in order to find the answer.

Sequences. These items ask participants to identify what comes next in some series. The series can be a list of shapes, numbers, musical notes or virtually any group which forms a logical series. As with analogies, the difficulty of these items can stem from either knowing what the elements in the sequence are, or what the rule connecting them is. For example, to give the next term in the sequence "Helium, Neon, Argon . . ." it is necessary to know that these are chemical elements. And it is also necessary to recognise that these form a column in the periodic table in order to complete the sequence. That said, it is most common to use sequence items to explore how well people can identify the relationships between items – "inductive reasoning".

Matrices. Figure 16.1 shows a matrix, a mixture of two sequence problems – one sequence runs from left to right, and the other from top to bottom. They can be made quite difficult.

Odd one out. This format was mentioned previously. Once again, it is only possible to solve these items if one knows the meaning of all the terms in the question and can think of some rationale for grouping several of them together. As mentioned, the problem with these items is that it is possible to think of an almost unlimited number of groupings. "Helium, Neon, Argon, Iron" looks straightforward until it is appreciated that only one of the words does not end in "n". If such items have to be used, they should be tried out on friends and colleagues before they even enter a draft ability scale. It is possible to create odd-one-out problems using shapes, too. For example, three shapes might have a dot which is inside a circle but outside a square, whilst the other has the dot outside the circle. These unfamiliar items are probably safer.

Linkages. These problems typically ask respondents to identify a word which links two others; for example, back **** mat. The same thing could be done with sequences of musical notes – what four notes end one well-known tune and start another?

Mazes. A printed maze has four entrances and participants identify which one leads to the centre. (The problem here is that people will explore the entrances in different orders, which will add random error to the score, if the scale is timed.)

Embedded figures. A complex geometrical figure has one (but only one) of a list of simple figures embedded within it.

These are just some examples of commonly used item formats for ability tests, but almost anything can be used.

TRANSLATING ITEMS

Translating items – particularly personality items – raises a whole set of interesting issues. The problem is that the nuanced meaning of the words in the item will probably be lost in translation, and may well be culturally specific. Cultural attitudes too will almost certainly affect the way in which people respond to items, even if they translate perfectly. For example, in some cultures it is considered impolite to say "no". So even if the traits being measured are the same in several different cultures, one cannot simply take a questionnaire, translate it and hope that it will yield valid results.

It is instead necessary to have the items professionally translated, and then "back translated" (by a different person, or team). So if a Japanese scale was to be used in England, one would have the items translated into English, and then have each English item translated back into Japanese. If the back-translated item does not closely resemble the original, as will almost certainly be the case for some items, the two teams of translators meet to agree the best possible form of words. Bartram et al. (2018) give detailed guidance on translation procedures, as do van de Vijver and Hambleton (1996).

AUTOMATED ITEM GENERATION

It is sometimes possible to allow a computer program generate ability items so that each person sees a different item, but they are equivalent in terms of their difficulty and the cognitive processes required to solve them. For example, if objects differ in their colour (three levels) and shape (three levels), participants could be presented with either of the two items in Figure 16.2 and asked what shape would complete the pattern.

You can see that though they look different, the two items are equivalent. A star in the first item corresponds to a multiplication sign in the second, a white shape in the first item corresponds to a yellow shape in the second etc. Thus the two items should be equally difficult, as the cognitive processes taken to solve them should be identical. Some people might be given the first item and others the second item, and they would not realise that the two were equivalent. This may be useful when using tests for selection purposes, to stop others being told the answer via social media.

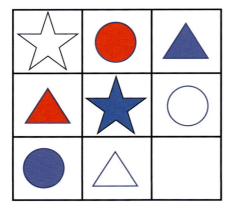 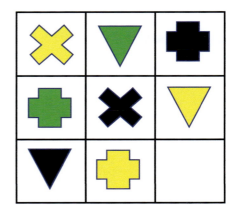

Figure 16.2 Two functionally equivalent ability items. What shapes should fill the empty cells?

Number-series problems may be automatically generated (Sun et al., 2019), and it is also possible to use the technique for individual feedback rather than standardised assessments (e.g., Gierl & Lai, 2018). The obvious problem is ensuring that the difficulties of the computer-generated tests are equal, and this requires either long tests (so that each random sample of items will have the same average difficulty) or a very detailed grasp of what cognitive processes are involved with each item so that the equivalence of the items can be guaranteed.

SPEEDED TESTS AND POWER TESTS

One important decision which needs to be made when developing an ability scale is whether the final form of the scale should have a time limit, and if so, what should it be. Almost all ability tests do have time limits – particularly if people are given the opportunity to go back and revise their answers. This is because a sample of people may contain some who are highly conscientious but with an unexceptional level of the ability which is being assessed. They might therefore spend a great deal of time trying to solve the items which puzzle them, and if the test is administered to a group of people, this will frustrate others who might need to wait until they have finished before moving on to the next task. As discussed in Chapter 2, the time limit can be very generous in which case the scale is known as a "power test" because it really measures *level* of performance rather than *speed* of performance. For example, the time limit could eventually be set to the time taken for 90% of a sample drawn from the target population to complete as many items as they can. On the other hand, the time limit can be rather short, requiring participants to complete as many items as possible in the time allocated. Here it is unlikely that anyone will have time to attempt all items. These "speeded tests" measure the speed with which people can correctly solve problems. These terms stem from Gulliksen (1950a).

Some scales must necessarily be speeded. For example, scales measuring the speed with which people can cross out every "e" in a passage of text or substitute letters for symbols to reveal a coded message clearly need a time limit, for almost everyone could get full marks if they were given unlimited time. There are some problems with measuring the reliability of speeded scales, as discussed by Gulliksen (1950b), because not everyone will reach the later items in the scale, making it hard to compute alpha etc. The "split half" reliability coefficient based only on the number of items each person attempts may be used as an alternative.

Do speeded tests and power tests measure the same things? Vernon (1961) argues that they do in fact correlate so substantially that moderate speeding is not a major issue. However, this was within the context of intelligence research, and matters may be different when measuring other abilities. Subsequent writers suggest that speeded and power tests do tend to load on rather different factors; Partchev et al. (2013)

summarise this later literature and perform a rather sophisticated study which shows that for verbal analogy items, at any rate, speeded and power tests have only a very modest correlation.

ADMINISTERING ITEMS

Instructions should be written, and the items should be administered exactly as you plan to do in the final version of the test or scale (including obtaining written consent to participate) – with one exception. For power ability tests, the time limit should be very generous, so that almost everyone is able to attempt all items (or until they choose to give up). That way you can work out the average time taken per item, which will provide some guidance when setting time limits for the final version of the test.

It is a good idea to seek feedback – afterwards asking if participants were unsure about the meaning of any items, whether they found difficulties making their answers and so on.

ITEM ANALYSIS

Having compiled a draft test, it is necessary to ensure that all of the items measure the same construct before proceeding to check that the test is reliable and valid. In order to do this, the test should be administered to a large sample of people, similar in composition to the individuals who will ultimately use the test. We have seen (Chapter 7) that the standard error of the reliability coefficient is large unless large samples are used, and so developing a scale using a small sample or one which is unrepresentative of the population with which the scale will be used is pure folly. Several hundred people are necessary.

Each person's response to each item is then entered into a spreadsheet.

DISTRACTOR ANALYSIS FOR MULTIPLE-CHOICE TESTS

When analysing the data from multiple-choice ability tests, it is a good idea to plot the number of people who choose each distractor as a function of their score on the other items of the test, as shown in Figure 16.3.

Figure 16.3 summarises the popularity of each of the answers given by a group of people to a single multiple-choice test item. It shows how the popularity of each response varies according to their score on the other items in the test (which is the best-available estimate of their ability level). Choice A was the correct answer and people with high ability are more likely to choose choice A. Choice D is a good distractor because it is attractive to people with low ability; perhaps they do not know enough to discount it as obviously incorrect. Its popularity goes down as the score on the other

TEST AND SCALE CONSTRUCTION

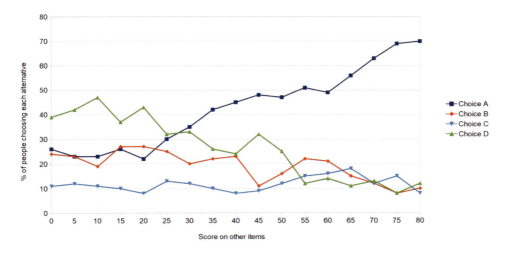

Figure 16.3 Popularity of answers to a multiple-choice test item

items increases. Choice B is generally rather more popular (plausible) than choice C at all ability levels.

Such plots can show whether highly able people can identify the correct answer. If not, the item should probably be dropped. It can also show if any distractors are so rarely chosen as to be useless; a case could be made for removing or amending choice C in the previous example. It can also indicate if two answers may be correct; if so, *two* lines will slope upwards from left to right. We earlier flagged that this may be a problem for "odd-one-out" items.

It is also possible to analyse distractors by item response theory and other means. See Gierl et al. (2017).

DATA CLEANING AND SCORING

If the data were collected over the internet, checks should be made to remove "bots" and careless/malicious responders as described in Chapter 4; all data provided by these individuals should be deleted.

Missing data should be estimated as described in Chapter 4, and people with too much missing data should be dropped from the sample. It is advisable to check their demographic data (and scores on other scales) carefully to ensure that they form a reasonably random sample of the group; obviously, if all the anxious men in a sample left many items unanswered, the sample would no longer be representative of the population which the scale was designed to assess.

The responses are then scored as described in Chapter 4. For ability tests, scoring will typically involve giving 1 point for a correct answer and zero points for an incorrect response or an omitted item. For Likert-scaled items (e.g., strongly agree/agree/neutral/disagree/strongly disagree), the response is converted to a number indicating the strength of the response as described in Chapter 4, remembering to reverse the items where necessary. The easiest way of scoring items is to use a spreadsheet to convert the raw responses into numbers.

The next stage is to examine the mean score. In the case of an ability test (where items are scored 0 or 1), the mean score indicates the difficulty of each item. A mean score of 0.95 would indicate that 95% of the sample gave the correct response to an item. In the case of personality tests, the mean score shows the extent to which individuals tend to agree or disagree with statements. As a rule of thumb, it would be undesirable to have *too* many very easy or very difficult items in the test, so if more than about 10% of ability items have an average score above 0.8 or below 0.2, or if more than about 10% of Likert-scaled items have average scores at the extreme ends of the scales (i.e., from 4.1 to 5 for a 5-point scale scored 1–5), it would be prudent to consider removing some of them.

Examine the standard deviation for each item. This shows the level of individual differences found in participants' responses to it. For example, if an item has a standard deviation of zero, everyone has answered it in the same way, therefore the item is clearly not tapping any kind of individual differences and so should be removed from the scale. (When items are scored using a 2-point scale, such as correct/incorrect, the standard deviation is linked directly to the mean. This step should be skipped in such cases.)

GENERAL ISSUES WITH ITEM ANALYSIS

Although checking the items' means and standard deviations is a necessary first step, this cannot reveal which questions in the test are flawed in content. For example, suppose that one item in a personality test used language that was too difficult for the participants to understand, causing them all to guess an answer. Responses to this item will look good; the mean will probably be near the middle of the scale, and the standard deviation will be large. However, the item is clearly useless. We shall mention four techniques of *item analysis* for identifying items that, for whatever reason, simply do not measure the same thing as the other items in the test.

When using any of the four techniques described later to eliminate items from the test, it is important to try to ensure that the test retains approximately equal numbers of items in all of its facets. Suppose, for example, that a teacher started off by writing five items in each of seven facets of mathematical attainment: long division, long multiplication, geometry/trigonometry, solution of simultaneous equations, finding roots of quadratic equations, differentiation and integration. Item analysis will remove some of the 35 items (those that are too easy, too hard, or simply do not seem to work), but it would clearly be unfortunate if the analysis led to the removal of *all* of the long-division items and *all* of the long-multiplication items, since the teacher believes that these are two important components of the pupils' mathematical attainment. Item analysis is an art as well as a science, and when removing items it is important to try to ensure that approximately equal numbers are left in each of the facets.

METHOD 1: CONSTRUCTING TESTS BY CRITERION KEYING

Suppose that we are asked to construct a psychological test to select individuals who will successfully learn to pilot an aircraft. The goal is to develop a test whose total score will be able to predict the pilots' final score on their training course. Having no clear idea of what may be appropriate personality and ability characteristics for this application, we might put together 600 items that we hope will measure all of the main abilities and personality traits that can be assessed. But which ones actually predict pilot performance?

Suppose that the draft version of the scales have been administered to several hundred trainees. The most obvious way of identifying the good (i.e., predictive) items in the test is to validate each item directly against the criterion. For example, suppose that at the end of their training, each trainee pilot is awarded a mark of between 0 and 100. Surely the item analysis process would simply involve correlating the trainees' scores on each of the items in the test with their scores on the training course. Items that have substantial correlations would appear to be able to predict the criterion, and those that do not would be dropped from the test.

This procedure, which is known as *criterion keying*, has been used in the construction of several well-known scales, including the MMPI and MMPI-2 (Graham, 1990; Hathaway & McKinley, 1967) and the California Psychological Inventory (Gough, 1975), the scales of which can supposedly discriminate between various clinical groups. *Do not use this method of item analysis.* As Nunnally (1978) observes, it has several fatal flaws.

First, it is very likely to produce scales that have very low reliability – that is, scales containing items that measure a number of different things. For example, suppose that success in the training course depended on spatial ability, hand-eye coordination, low neuroticism and extraversion. If criterion keying were to be applied to a large sample of items, it would produce a scale that measured a mixture of all of these things rather than four distinct scales.

Second, it is rarely possible to identify a *single* criterion to be used when selecting items. Consider the activities of a university professor. These will typically include lecturing, obtaining research funding, performing research, taking tutorials, managing other staff, marking essays and examination papers, co-ordinating certain laboratory activities, supervising PhD students and a host of other activities. Which one of these should be used as the criterion against which their performance should be judged? If they are to be averaged in some way, marking how exam scripts or how many dollars of research grants are equivalent to supervising one PhD student, writing a scientific paper or giving a lecture? If one criterion is used, one particular set of predictive items will be identified – if another criterion is chosen, the chances are that quite a different selection of items will be indicated.

The third point is a little more statistical. In order to select the "best" items by criterion keying, one correlates responses to particular items with the criterion – if the test consists of 400 or so items (as does the MMPI), then one calculates 400 correlations. If large numbers of correlations are being calculated, we would expect several of the correlations to be appreciably larger than their true (population) values even if there is really no relationship between the test scores and the behaviour; this is, after all, what "$p < 0.05$" means: 5% of the correlations will be spuriously significant. So if 400 items are correlated with some behaviour and 25 of these correlations are significant (rather than the 20 which one would expect), how can one tell which if any of these correlations indicate a genuine relationship?

Finally, this procedure gives us no real understanding of *why* the test works – it is completely atheoretical. Without an understanding of what psychological constructs are being measured by the "useful" items, it is impossible to tell whether the test is likely to be useful in other applications (e.g., for air-traffic controllers), and it becomes very difficult to "fix" the test if it suddenly stops predicting performance. For all of these reasons, criterion keying should be avoided.

METHOD 2: CONSTRUCTING TESTS BY FACTOR-ANALYSIS OF ITEMS

Here the correlations between the (scored) items are factor-analysed as described in Chapter 11, and the factor(s) that emerge are tentatively identified on the basis of their loadings on the rotated factors. When putting together a set of items to measure one particular construct, we would of course *hope* that just one factor will emerge, and that all of the variables will have large loadings (in the same direction) on that factor. In practice, there may be more than one factor, and some variables may not have loadings above 0.4 on *any* factor, and so should be dropped.

Factor analysis is probably the most common method of developing scale or tests.

METHOD 3: CONSTRUCTING A SCALE USING ITEM RESPONSE THEORY

See Chapter 15.

TEST AND SCALE CONSTRUCTION

METHOD 4: CONSTRUCTING A SCALE USING NETWORK ANALYSIS

Rather than exploring the structure of existing scales and questionnaires, it should be possible to develop a scale test or questionnaire using network analysis or exploratory graph analysis (Golino & Epskamp, 2017) to identify groups of items that directly influence each other, as described in Chapter 14. Items which are weakly linked to other members of a swarm can be dropped, after checking that doing so does not unbalance the content by removing all items measuring one aspect of the trait. That said, those that have mentioned this methodology (Mancini et al., 2022; Mueller, in press) do not show the results of a network analysis and do not appear to have used the technique to refine their items. Exploring the role of network analysis in scale development alongside the other methods described here could make for an interesting PhD.

METHOD 5: CONSTRUCTING TESTS USING CLASSICAL ITEM ANALYSIS

We have left the oldest and easiest method of item analysis until last. This technique *assumes* that a set of items all measure just one scale, and so it is important to perform a factor analysis first, just to check that this is the case. All one needs to do is check that parallel analysis (and possibly other methods) show that the items form just one factor. If not, it will be necessary to use factor analysis to identify which items load each factor, and perform a separate item analysis for each of these sets of items.

High reliability is generally thought to be an excellent feature of a test (see Chapter 7). It therefore seems sensible to try to estimate the extent to which each of the items in a test correlates with individuals' "true scores", which are the scores that each individual would have obtained if he or she had been administered all of the items that could possibly have been written to measure the topic. If we somehow identify items each of which has a substantial correlation with the true score, when we add up individuals' scores on these items, the total scores on the test are bound to show a substantial correlation with the true score. This is, of course, another way of saying that the test has high internal consistency reliability. Thus if it is possible to detect items that show appreciable correlations with the true score, those items that will produce a highly reliable test.

The problem is that we can never know individuals' true scores. However, it is possible to estimate them from their total scores on all of the items in the scale. Thus **classical item analysis** simply correlates the total score on the test with the scores on each of the individual items. Consider, for example, the data shown in Table 16.1, which represent the responses of six people to a five-item test (where a correct answer was scored as 1 and an incorrect answer as 0), together with each person's total score on the test. The row marked "r with total" simply correlates the responses to each of the items with the total scores on the test. You may wish to check one or two of these so that

Table 16.1 Data for item analysis

	Item 1	Item 2	Item 3	Item 4	Item 5	Total
Person 1	1	0	1	1	1	4
Person 2	0	1	1	1	0	3
Person 3	0	0	1	0	0	1
Person 4	0	0	1	0	0	1
Person 5	0	1	0	1	1	3
Person 6	1	0	1	1	0	3
r with total	0.63	0.32	−0.20	0.95	0.63	
Corrected r with total	0.11	0.22	−0.48	0.87	0.50	

you can see how they have been calculated. Here item 4 appears to be the best measure (that is, it correlates well with the total score) whilst item 3 is the worst. It is probable that dropping item 3 will improve the reliability of the scale.

The correlations between each item and the total score are as close as we can get to estimating the correlation between each item and the true score, so it seems sensible to drop those items that have low correlations with the total score – keeping a careful eye on which facet of the trait is measured by a particular item and ensuring that the items that are left contain approximately equal numbers of items from each of the facets. Thus whilst the item analysis procedure involves removing an item which has a low correlation with the total score at each stage, this will not always be the very lowest-correlating item.

There is one obvious problem associated with correlating items with total scores, and this is the fact that each item *contributes* to the total score, so we are to some extent correlating each item with itself. In order to circumvent this difficulty, the item analyses use **corrected item–total correlations**, also called "Guilford-corrected item–total correlations", which are simply the correlations between each item and the sum of the *other* remaining items. In the present example, item 1 would be correlated with the sum of items 2, 3, 4 and 5. Item 2 would be correlated with the sum of items 1, 3, 4 and 5 and so on. Other techniques for performing such corrections have been proposed, but they create as many problems as they solve (Cooper, 1983).

Each time an item is eliminated, the test's reliability (alpha) needs to be recalculated. As items that have low correlations with the total score are eliminated, the value of alpha will rise. As more and more items are removed, the value of alpha will eventually

TEST AND SCALE CONSTRUCTION

start to fall, since alpha depends on both the average correlation between the items and the number of items in the test. Of course, removing a "poor" item boosts the average correlation between the remaining items — but it also shortens the test. Items are successively removed (on the basis of a consideration of their corrected item–total correlations and the facets from which they originate) until the test is short, well balanced and highly reliable.

It is not possible simply to look at the table of corrected item–total correlations and decide from this precisely which items should be eliminated. This is because each person's total score will inevitably change each time an item is dropped, and consequently each of the correlations between the remaining items and the total score will also change. Therefore, it is necessary to decide which item to drop, recompute the total scores and recompute all of the remaining item – total correlations, as well as recomputing alpha at each stage. Spreadsheet 16.1 performs such analyses.

Spreadsheet name: Spreadsheet 16.1: Item analysis

Download from: https://routledge.com/9781032146164/

Purpose: To perform classical item analysis by identifying items having small corrected-correlations with the total score. It can analyse data from 100 variables and 2000 people.

Contents of spreadsheet: Sample data from a five-item scale, with eight participants. Data are in the "Data_only" tab.

Suggested activity:

- Click on the "Data_only" tab to see, amend, or replace the data to be analysed. Each row represents a different person.
- In the "Item analysis" tab, check that the number of cases and items is correct and that the minimum and maximum scores are correct – in case of typological errors.
- Type "1" in the green cell if an item is to be scored normally or "−1" if it is to be reverse-scored.
- Note coefficient alpha, the correlation between each item and the total score, the corrected item–total correlation and other statistics.
- Remove an item by typing "0" into the green cell. Note how alpha and the statistics for the other items change. An item can be replaced at any time by entering "−1" or "1".
- Continue removing items until the scale is sufficiently reliable and sufficiently short.

Points to note:

- The (scored) data are simply pasted into the "Data_only" tab. The calculates how many participants and items there are.

- With the given dataset, item 1 has a large *negative* item–total correlation, indicating that it probably should not have been reverse-scored.
- The corrected correlation between each item and the total score is often modest, showing that each item is only weakly related to the trait which it is designed to measure.

Learning outcomes: Readers should now be able to:

- Perform an item analysis to produce a shorter, more reliable scale.

VALIDATION AND DOCUMENTATION

The test constructor's task is far from finished once the item analysis has been completed. Instructions should be refined and time limits adjusted before the revised (shorter and more reliable) test is given to another sample of several hundred individuals so that its reliability and factor structure may be checked. Validation data should also be gathered at this stage – for example, by administering the scale alongside other standard tests and correlating scores, jointly factor-analysing the items etc. In the case of ability tests, the amount of time that individuals take to complete the test should be noted and a final decision taken as to what time limits (if any) should be imposed.

In the case of item response theory, the sample-independence of the parameters should also be checked – e.g., by splitting the sample into two groups (one predominantly low ability and the other mainly high ability) and ensuring that the item difficulties are similar in each. Its validity should also be established at this stage (e.g., by construct validation). A test manual should be prepared showing the results of these analyses, the administration instructions, the marking scheme and as much evidence as possible that the test is reliable and valid.

SUMMARY

This chapter covered some basic principles of item writing and administration for both ability tests and personality scales and showed how factor analysis, item response theory, network analysis and classical item analysis can be used to refine the initial set of items to create a shorter, reliable scale. Gulliksen (1986) is still essential reading for anyone who is developing a scale measuring abilities or educational attainment, whilst Most and Zeidner (1995) and Spector (1992) are also recommended for all scale developers.

CHAPTER 17
PROBLEMS WITH TEST SCORES

Before considering problems with tests which are used to assess individuals (for example, to check their cognitive development), we look at a research design which frequently leads to misinterpretations of test scores.

CHANGE SCORES

Change scores involve administering the same test (or two alternative forms of a test) to a sample of people on two occasions. A t-test or similar could be used to determine whether there is an overall increase or decrease in scores from one occasion to the next, which is perfectly reasonable. However, researchers sometimes set out to discover which individuals' scores improve the most. This can lead to seriously misleading inferences being drawn.

Suppose that a researcher assessed children's cognitive ability using a multiple-choice test and exposed children to Mozart every day for a week in an attempt to boost their cognitive skills. A parallel form of the multiple-choice test was then administered, and a related-samples t-test determined whether the intervention produced an improvement in scores. It would almost certainly show no significant effect, as the "Mozart effect" is a myth (Pietschnig et al., 2010).

Desperate to salvage something from the study, a change score was then calculated by subtracting each child's first score from their second score to show how much each child had improved. Some of these change scores seemed to be much larger than others, so the researcher then wondered whether the improvement affected children with the lowest levels of cognitive ability. To test this they correlated the change score with the first test score, arguing that a negative correlation would show that children who initially performed worst at the test showed the largest increase in scores. They are delighted to find that this correlation is large and negative, showing (they feel) that listening to Mozart has a major impact for the cognitively disadvantaged.

Unfortunately, they are completely incorrect.

The usual measurement model discussed in Chapter 7 assumes that a person's score on a test is influenced by the trait which the test is designed to measure plus some

DOI: 10.4324/9781003240181-17

random error. The problem is that someone who obtains a very low score on the first administration of the test is likely to (a) have a low level of the trait and (b) be unfortunate in that the random error of measurement also decreased their score on the test on this occasion. When retested, their score is likely to improve. Similarly, someone who obtains a very high score on the test is likely to have high ability plus some lucky guessing. When they are tested again, their scores are likely to get worse.

If the test scores are affected by measurement error, this form of analysis is *bound* to produce a large, significant, negative correlation between the change score and the first score. Not only does this look excitingly significant, the negative correlation suggests that the intervention is most effective for the children who showed the lowest initial scores.

If this is not obvious, consider Spreadsheet 17.1, which shows the true scores of 199 people. These scores follow a normal distribution with a mean of 100 and standard deviation of 15. Each person is tested twice, and their true score is exactly the same on each occasion (the intervention was ineffective). However, on each occasion there is some random measurement error; this mimics exactly what happens when someone is tested twice on a scale. The difference score (their "time 2" score minus their "time 1 score" is then correlated with their score at time 1. The correlation is negative.

Spreadsheet name: Spreadsheet 17.1: Change scores

Download from: https://routledge.com/9781032146164/

Purpose: To show why change scores should never be correlated with a baseline score.

Contents of spreadsheet: Normally distributed true scores of 199 simulated people, plus two random error terms per person.

Suggested activity:

- Note the correlation between the change score and the time 1 score. Altering the standard deviation adjusts the amount of measurement error: 15 corresponds to a scale with reliability of 0.7.
- Recalculate using f9 etc.
- Increasing the standard deviation of the error term is equivalent to reducing the reliability of the scale. Note how this affects the correlation.

Points to note:

- Change scores inevitably show a substantial correlation with the baseline score.

Learning outcomes: Readers should now be able to:

- Appreciate why change scores should not be correlated with the baseline score.

This just gives a flavour of one problem with change scores; there are others too. For example, the amount of error associated with change scores is large, as each of the two scores has measurement error associated with it. Hence, the change score is far less accurate than a single measurement would be.

Rather than subtracting one observed score from the other, it might seem better to estimate each person's true score (as shown previously) – by working out the size of the difference between each person's score and the mean, multiplying this by the reliability of the scale, and adding this back to the mean. This is a step in the right direction – however it fails to recognise that the two scales are correlated . . . there is a substantial literature on this issue. At the end of a still-influential paper, Cronbach and Furby (1970) conclude, "It appears that investigators who ask questions regarding gain scores would ordinarily be better advised to frame their questions in other ways". Researchers who really need to work with change scores will find that this venerable paper gives a good discussion of methods for computing and interpreting them, though they may wish to supplement this reading with more recent work on structural equation modelling (e.g., Kline, 2015). Cascio and Kurtines (1977) give an example of how the techniques outlined by Cronbach and Furby may be applied in practice. Maxwell and Howard (1981) give still-relevant advice about how and when it may be appropriate to interpret change scores using analysis of variance and related designs.

PROBLEMS USING TESTS TO ASSESS INDIVIDUALS

The previous chapters have dealt with the design and interpretation of test scores for research purposes, where scores on tests are related to other things (health or educational outcomes, genetic variations, measures of brain activity and so on). However, specialised tests are also used to help practitioners make important decisions about individuals – for example, whether a child has exceptional ability, or whether someone accused of a crime has the ability to appreciate that they have done wrong or whether they are able to adequately instruct their lawyers. Many of these crucial decisions are based on tests of cognitive ability and tend to focus on the extremes of the distribution. The tests need to be able to assess individuals with very low or very high levels of intelligence.

The issues discussed in this chapter mainly arose during conversations with my psychometrically inclined ex-colleagues in educational and clinical psychology, who focus more on the interpretation of individual scores than on the correlational analyses typically used by researchers in individual differences.

The tests used to assess individuals do not resemble the simple questionnaires and ability tests considered so far. As it is important that the people who being are assessed perform to the best of their ability, assessments are invariably made by a trained psychologist or test administrator, who assesses each person individually and uses their empathy and social skills to try to ensure that each person performs to the very best of their ability. Indeed, such tests are only made available to those who have been trained in their administration, scoring and interpretation. Some tests are designed for children and teenagers, others for adults, and there are many acronyms. The most widely used are probably the Wechsler Intelligence Scale for Children (WISC), the Wechsler Adult Intelligence Scale (WAIS), the Wechsler Preschool and Primary Scale of Intelligence (WPPSI), the British Ability Scales (BAS), the Stanford-Binet scales (SB) and the Kaufman ABC; there are others, too. As if this was not confusing enough, there are several versions of each test – which are often quite different from each other in content and also in interpretation. For example, older versions of the WISC provided scores on "Verbal IQ" (based on tests which involved language) and "Performance IQ" (based on tests which did not) – a distinction which was later dropped.

The testing session generally involves the administration of 10 or more different tests, assessing a range of different cognitive operations. These sub-tests sometimes correspond to the ability factors identified by individual-difference psychologists but are often rather different. The reasons for this divergence are unclear or historical. Tests may measure understanding of social situations, ability to assemble blocks into a certain design, identifying which shape completes a pattern, memory for strings of numbers, mental arithmetic, and a host of other cognitive tasks.

The instructions for administering these tests are complex. As well as obvious things like standardising the instructions, administrators are trained when to give feedback about performance ("That's good!"), whether older children should be started part way through a test for risk of boring them with trivially easy items, when to discontinue a test (as if the later items are clearly too difficult for them, asking them to plough on may make a person feel demotivated), how to lay out the test materials in front of the person, which parts of the procedure are timed, what to do if a person is visually impaired or has motor issues, how and when to decide to suggest taking a break . . . the whole procedure is extremely complicated, and even trained professionals sometimes get it wrong (see Chapter 2 of Kaufman et al., 2016). It is important that the guidelines are followed, as only then can we be confident that the score from this child or adult may be compared with those of others. Kaufman et al. (2016) summarise the instructions and guidelines for a widely used measure of children's cognitive skills.

The remainder of this chapter addresses some commonly encountered misconceptions and mis-uses of psychometric techniques when performing these assessments. Some of the issues are quite fundamental – such as whether scores on tests which comprise several sub-scales and which claim to have coefficients alpha of 0.95 or above are really as accurate as most practitioners assume.

CONFIDENCE INTERVALS

Every time an individual person's score on a test is measured, it is usual to also report "confidence intervals" to show what the range of scores is likely to be. For given that every test score is affected, to some extent, by random errors of measurement, it would be naive to assume that a person would obtain exactly the same score if the test were administered on another occasion. The confidence interval uses the "standard error of measurement" to show the likely range of measurement error for any person's score. This essentially corrects each person's score for the consequences of "lucky guessing" (as discussed at the start of this chapter) or other forms of measurement error.

A practitioner might establish that a someone has an IQ of 100, and given the particular test which was used, we can estimate that if they were to be given the same test on 1000 occasions (!) they would score somewhere between 94 and 106 on 950 of those occasions. This can be deduced by knowing the standard deviation of the test and its reliability; the standard error of measurement is *standard deviation* $\times \sqrt{1 - reliability}$. If a test has a reliability of 0.9 and a standard deviation of 15, the standard error of measurement is $15 \times \sqrt{0.1} = 4.7$. It is possible to use the normal distribution to allow us to decide on the width of this confidence interval; for 95% confidence this would be 1.96 × 4.7 on either side of the person's estimated true score. In the case of someone who scores 100 on the IQ test, this implies that there is a 95% chance that their true score lies between (100 − 9.2) and (100 + 9.2); in other words, between about 91 and 109.

This sort of analysis can be very important indeed, as it may be used to help make legal and other decisions about the individual (fitness to plead, suitability for gifted education etc.). Most of these applications involve assessing people whose scores are either very high or very low − and this presents particular problems.

This will be familiar territory to most professionals, who probably wonder why I am stressing it. The reason is that there are two important issues which are not always properly addressed in test manuals.

What is the best estimate of the person's true score?

Given that:

- Each person's score on every scale is influenced by measurement error.
- The random error follows a normal distribution with a mean of zero.
- The amount of random error is determined by the reliability of the scale.
- Each person's observed score is the sum of their true score plus random error.

we showed at the start of this chapter that someone who obtains an extremely high score on a test is (a) likely to have an above-average score, and is (b) likely to be lucky, in that the random measurement error has boosted (rather than lowered) their score. The next time that they are assessed, their error score will probably be closer to zero, and so their observed score will probably be rather lower on a second occasion. Likewise, a person with a very low score on one occasion will probably achieve a higher score if they are tested on another occasion.

So what *is* the best estimate of the person's true score on the test? A simple equation allows it to be estimated.

Estimated True Score = mean + (observed score − mean) × reliability

It is vital to construct one's confidence intervals on either side of *this* score – not the score which is indicated by scoring the test. It is easy to see if someone has followed this advice by checking that the confidence interval is *not* symmetrical around the observed score – unless the observed score is close to the mean.

Assuming that scores on a scale or test are normally distributed, if its reliability is 0.9 the best estimate of the true score of a person who obtains a score of 80 is 100 + (80 − 100) × 0.9 = 82. It is important that the confidence interval should be constructed around *this* value rather than the observed score of 80, which is likely to be too extreme because of the effects of random error. If the standard deviation of the scale is 15, the standard error is $\sqrt{(1-0.9)} \times 15$ or 4.7. Thus there is a 95% chance that their true score lies between (82 − 1.96 × 4.7) and (82 + 1.96 × 4.7). One would report that their estimated IQ was 80, with a 95% confidence interval from 72 to 92. Had the confidence interval been constructed around the observed score (80), this would have misleadingly suggested that the confidence interval included the value of 70, which might have important practical consequences for the individual.

> **Spreadsheet name:** Spreadsheet 17.2: Confidence intervals around an individual's score
>
> **Download from:** https://routledge.com/9781032146164/
>
> **Purpose:** To calculate confidence intervals around an individual's score on a scale whose scores follow a normal distribution.
>
> **Contents of spreadsheet:** Typical values for the reliability etc. of an IQ test.
>
> **Suggested activity:**
>
> Enter an individual's IQ score, and note the estimated true score and confidence interval. Repeat for values close to the mean and for extreme values (e.g., measured IQs of 60 or 140). Note that the confidence interval is symmetrical only when the IQ is equal to the mean (100).

> **Points to note:**
>
> Some commercial tests do not construct confidence intervals either side of the estimated true score. They may instead advise using the scale score.
>
> In addition, the problems with using coefficient alpha as a measure of reliability (see Chapter 7) should be carefully considered before using it to estimate confidence intervals.
>
> **Learning outcomes: Readers should now be able to:**
>
> Correctly report confidence intervals about an individual's score on a scale whose scores follow a normal distribution.

The other thing to notice from this is that if the reliability of a scale is modest, it is patently useless for saying anything sensible about an individual. For example, if the reliability of the scale were 0.7, the confidence interval for the example extends from 70 to 102 – a massive range of over two standard deviations. So someone with a score of 80 could be either slightly above average, or two standard deviations below the average. It is difficult to see how this says anything useful about that individual – and of course it explains why correlations between such imprecise measures and other things are generally woefully small.

The reliability of the test appears twice in these analyses – once in determining how much to move extreme scores closer to the mean before constructing confidence interval, and once when determining the width of the confidence intervals themselves. It is clearly important that the reliability of the test should be as large as possible – and also that there should be no doubt about its actual value within a particular population. We shall see later that neither of these issues is clear-cut.

Difference scores

Educational psychologists and others often need to decide whether one person's scores on two rather different scales are large enough to suggest that there is some underlying problem which requires further investigation. For example, if a child is found to perform above average at cognitive scales which involve processing shapes and memory for patterns and so on but poorly at cognitive tests involving the use of language, the educational psychologist may then gather other evidence to help them decide whether dyslexia is a possible explanation.

Four things influence the size of a difference score:

- The mean of each scale
- The standard deviation of each scale

- The reliability of each scale
- The correlation between the two scales.

From a psychometric (and statistical) point of view, difference scores can have several different meanings.

Is the difference between a person's scores on two scales statistically significant? In other words, can we measure these traits with sufficient precision to determine that they are different? To answer this question we need to estimate the size of the difference score (after standardising, or using percentiles to get round the problem that the scales will have different means and standard deviations) and perform some sort of statistical test to determine whether a person's difference score is significantly different from zero. This is basically an issue about the precision with which we can measure difference scores. What this analysis does *not* attempt to show is whether a large difference score is at all unusual. For if two highly reliable, well-validated scales measure very different things (extraversion and general intelligence, for example) it will be quite common for people to have a high score on one scale and a low score on the other; this is what a low correlation between the two scales implies. It might be found that 80% of people who take these two scales score significantly higher on one scale than the other; a lot of people may have difference scores which are significantly different from zero. The technical manuals of tests such as the WAIS-III include a table showing how often various difference scores are found for each level of ability, which may help a professional decide whether a particular individual's score is unusual.

Rather than testing whether two scores are *significantly* different, it is more common for a professional psychologist to ask whether a difference in scores is *uncommon*. For example, they may wish to determine whether a child's language skills are markedly lower than one would expect, given their level of non-verbal skills, or whether their educational performance is significantly worse than would be expected given their level of general intelligence. In order to determine whether a child's difference score is so large as to be "unusual", it is necessary to gather data on both scales from a large, representative sample and plot their joint distribution. This might show that only 2% of children who score 100 on one scale score below 80 on another scale, and so a child with a difference score this large might well have some form of language-related issue which needs to be explored further. Details of how to perform such analyses will vary from test to test, and so that test handbook should be consulted.

There are other techniques too. For example, a regression line may be used to predict scores on the language scale from scores on the non-verbal reasoning test. Figure 17.1 shows a simplified example of such a regression line, together with one individual whose language score is far lower than would be expected on the basis of their

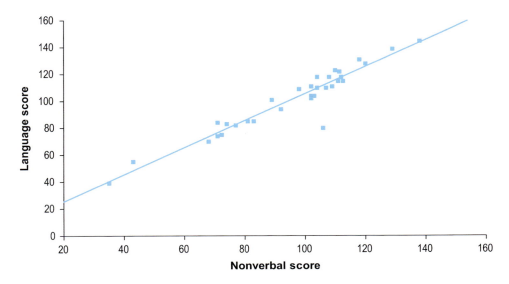

Figure 17.1 Regression to predict language score from non-verbal ability

non-verbal ability. It is a simple matter to use the equation of the regression line to estimate what this individual's language ability would be expected to be, on the basis of their non-verbal reasoning. Then it is straightforward to compute the distance (the vertical distance in Figure 17.1) between that individual and the regression line. The significance of this distance can be easily calculated.

Reliable component analysis (RCA; Cliff & Caruso, 1998) is a more recent development which may perhaps useful when computing difference scores between factors, each of which is measured by several scales. For example, the eight scales measuring the Perceptual Organisation and the Verbal Comprehension scales of the Wechsler Intelligence Scale for Children might be administered to a sample of people. But rather than scoring the Perceptual Organisation scale by averaging the scores on the four perceptual subtests, RCA weights them unequally. These weights are chosen so that each of the two factors (Perceptual Organisation and Verbal Comprehension) contain as much *reliable* variance as possible whilst being uncorrelated with each other. This, of course, maximises the reliability of the difference scores.

The weights are available for several published tests (e.g., Caruso & Cliff, 2000), or they can be computed from data given in the test manual given a little programming skill. The procedure leads to difference scores which are far more reliable than those which are calculated conventionally (Caruso, 2004). However, these components are not identical to the "conventional" Perceptual Organisation and Verbal Comprehension scales, and this will present problems for practitioners. In short, the technique is a neat psychometric technique but one which will affect the validity of the scores to an unknown extent.

HOW RELIABLE IS AN IQ TEST?

This may seem an odd question, given that Chapter 7 considered reliability theory in some detail. However, that chapter dealt with a very simple case, where several items formed a scale, and reliability coefficient(s) could easily be computed from the responses of a sample of people. It was shown that under the domain–sampling model, the reliability of a scale (coefficient alpha) can sometimes estimate the square root of the correlation between the score on a scale and the true score – the score which people would have obtained if they had been administered every item in the domain.

However, most practitioners do not use a single scale to assess an individual person's IQ. Instead they use tests which comprise a dozen or so different sub-scales – comprehension, memory for designs etc. Each of these sub-tests consists of a number of items, and each of the sub-tests is generally reliable (coefficient alpha being typically 0.8 or higher).

Scores on these sub-tests are then combined in some way, usually on the basis of a hierarchical factor analysis. Figure 17.2 shows the factor model which best describes

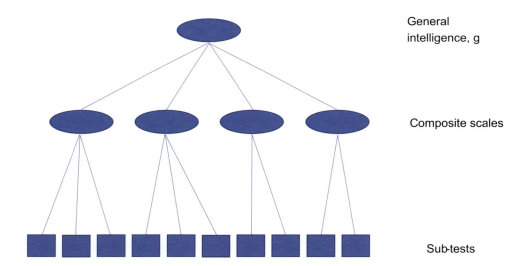

Figure 17.2 Hierarchical structure of the WAIS-IV showing 10 sub-tests, four composite scales and general intelligence (g). Lines represent non-zero factor loadings.

the WAIS-IV. It does not show the names of the variables or factors to improve clarity. Here the scores on the 10 sub-tests intercorrelate to form four factors, known as composites. These four factors are themselves correlated, leading to a single factor of general intelligence (or "g") at the top of the pyramid. This is an example of hierarchical factor analysis, as described in Chapter 13. This g-factor represents the full scale IQ score (FSIQ), on which we will focus. The problem is how one should estimate the reliability when combining scores on several (fairly reliable) scales in order to produce a composite measure, such as FSIQ.

Knowing a test's overall reliability is enormously important for practitioners. If reliability is estimated incorrectly, then the estimates of the standard error of measurement will be inaccurate, and at the start of this chapter we showed that this will affect the size of confidence intervals, the significance of difference scores, as well as other corrections which are performed on data (e.g., for restriction of range). So what *is* the reliability of one of these tests?

I am indebted to Bob Basham and Paul Barrett, who raised this issue in a now-defunct internet forum in 1994, and on whose analysis I have drawn extensively below. Bob's observation was simple. Top-quality tests such as the Wechsler scales and Stanford-Binet all claim to have extremely high reliabilities (alpha of 0.95 or over) – and we know that from Chapter 7 that alpha is probably an underestimate of the true reliability of a measure.

Given that all such tests claim to measure the same thing (general intelligence, rescaled as IQ) you would expect two different tests to correlate very substantially together. If two tests are correlated together, this correlation should equal the product of their reliabilities. As it is a matter of chance which test a professional chooses to administer, to find otherwise would be alarming.

The reliability of the IQ scale of the WAIS-IV is about 0.98 according to the test manual. (The exact figure varies somewhat depending on age.) The reliability of the WAIS-III is about 0.96, and so one would expect the two scales to correlate about $0.98 \times 0.96 = 0.95$. Although Wechsler reports a correlation of 0.94 between the two scales (Wechsler, 2008, p. 75), others find the correlation to be far lower – and indeed Wechsler also reports the correlation between the WAIS-IV and the WISC-IV to be 0.87 (p. 80) in a sample of 16-year-olds whose age means that they can be administered either test. This seems to be a typical finding for the Wechsler tests; the IQ scales of the WAIS-III and the WISC-III correlate 0.88 (Tulsky et al., 2000), and the correlation between the WISC-V and WISC-IV FSIQ is 0.81. The WISC-V FSIQ and the WAIS-V FSIQ correlate 0.84, whilst the correlation between the WISC-V and the Kaufman ABC-II Mental Processing Index is 0.77 (Canivez & Watkins, 2016).

Table 17.1 The 95% confidence intervals for IQ[1] under the assumptions that coefficient alpha is (a) 0.98 and (b) 0.88

Full scale IQ	95% confidence interval assuming alpha = 0.98		95% confidence interval assuming alpha = 0.88	
	Lower bound	Higher bound	Lower bound	Higher bound
60	57	65	55	76
65	62	70	60	80
70	66	75	64	84
75	71	80	68	89
80	76	85	73	93
90	86	94	81	102
100	96	104	90	110

These correlations of over 0.8 are large – but not as large as one might expect from knowledge of the tests' reliability, given that reliability may be defined as the correlation between two parallel tests. They are considerably lower than one would expect from tests that all claim to measure the same thing and which (in the case of the Wechsler tests) sometimes contain sub-tests which are very similar; this will tend to inflate the correlation between the tests, as error variances will be correlated.

Do these discrepancies matter? And how were these reliabilities calculated in the first place?

DOES IT MATTER IF TEST RELIABILITY IS LOWER THAN ADVERTISED?

Whether a test has reliability of 0.98 or 0.88 has major practical implications. When estimating the confidence intervals about a person's score using the formulae given earlier in this chapter, we obtain the results shown in Table 17.1.

If coefficient alpha is 0.88 rather than 0.98, estimates of IQ are not nearly so precise. The 95% confidence interval is then about 20 IQ points instead of about 8 points. If the test is being used to determine whether a child requires special educational support, or whether a prisoner is fit to stand trial using an arbitrary cut-off (such as an IQ of 70) if the true reliability of a scale is lower than assumed, this can easily lead to an incorrect decision being made about a person's true IQ.

PROBLEMS WITH TEST SCORES

HOW WAS RELIABILITY CALCULATED FOR THE WECHSLER SCALES?

Where did the figure of 0.98 come from? The scores on the various Wechsler sub-tests are weighted and combined to produce several "composite scores" – which resemble second-order factors. These are Verbal Comprehension, Perceptual Reasoning, Working Memory and Processing Speed. The composite scores may themselves be combined to give a measure of general intelligence (IQ).

The reliability of the intelligence score of the WAIS depends on the reliabilities of composite scores together with the correlations between them. The reliabilities (alpha) of composite scores shown in the test manual are substantial – all are above 0.9. It is possible to calculate the reliability of a weighted sum of combination of these three variables using formula 7.13 from Nunnally (1978):

$$alpha_{total} = 1 - \frac{\text{no. of variables} - \text{sum of reliability of subscales}}{\text{sum of all correlations between subscales including diagonals}}$$

$$= 1 - \frac{4 - 3.75}{13.96} = 0.98$$

This is presumably where the reliability of the FSIQ came from; it seems likely that the same method was probably used to estimate the reliability of the composite scores from the sub-tests.

INTERPRETATION ISSUES

When discussing coefficient alpha from a sample of items in Chapter 7 we noted that alpha is related to the correlation between the "true score" and the score on the test. The number of items in the test and the average correlation between the items influence alpha, and if the average correlation between the items in a test is zero, alpha is zero, too, as you can check using Spreadsheet 7.4.

This is not the case using Nunnally's formula. If you add together scores on several scales which have little measurement error associated with them, you obtain a score which contains even less measurement error; it does not matter whether or not these scales correlate together. As Bob Basham observed, when calculated this way the reliability is high *even if the correlations between the subscales are zero*.

Suppose that all of the correlations between the composite scales of the WAIS were zero (i.e., they measure completely different things). When they are combined to measure general intelligence (g), alpha would be $1 - \frac{4 - 3.75}{4} = 0.94$. Adding together

Table 17.2 Reliability of the sum of several scales as a function of their average intercorrelation and average reliability

					Average reliability of sub-tests					
	Sum of all correlations	0.10	0.30	0.50	0.60	0.70	0.80	0.85	0.90	0.95
Average off-diagonal correlation between 11 scales	0.0	11	0.10	0.30	0.50	0.60	0.70	0.80	0.85	0.90	0.95
	0.1	22	0.55	0.65	0.75	0.80	0.85	0.90	0.93	0.95	0.98
	0.2	33	0.70	0.77	0.83	0.87	0.90	0.93	0.95	0.97	0.98
	0.3	44	0.78	0.83	0.88	0.90	0.93	0.95	0.96	0.98	0.99
	0.4	55	0.82	0.86	0.90	0.92	0.94	0.96	0.97	0.98	0.99
	0.5	66	0.85	0.88	0.92	0.93	0.95	0.97	0.98	0.98	0.99
	0.6	77	0.87	0.90	0.93	0.94	0.96	0.97	0.98	0.99	0.99
	0.7	88	0.89	0.91	0.94	0.95	0.96	0.98	0.98	0.99	0.99
	0.8	99	0.90	0.92	0.94	0.96	0.97	0.98	0.98	0.99	0.99

accurate measures of four completely different traits will produce a "scale" with exceptionally high reliability! When calculated using Nunnally's formula, coefficient alpha does *not* imply that scores on various aspects of intelligence correlate substantially, although many test users will probably interpret it as such.

Table 17.2 shows some more examples of this effect. Suppose we have some composite scores which have (on average) a reliability of 0.5 – a feeble figure, which would lead to them being rejected as unsuitable by almost every researcher. Suppose the average correlation between these composites is 0.3 – a modest number which does not really suggest that they have a common "core". However, when scores on these error-ridden, modestly correlated tests are combined, Table 17.2 shows that the overall reliability is 0.88 – a highly respectable figure! This method of calculating reliability does not seem to make great sense. It does not appear to show how scores on a bunch of composites reflect the universe of items.

WHAT *IS* THE RELIABILITY OF A FULL-SCALE IQ SCORE?

Perhaps we can estimate the reliability of the FSIQ by simply treating the four composite scales as if they were items and applying the formula from Spreadsheet 7.4. This ensures that the correlations between the composite scales are taken into account. Coefficient alpha from this analysis is 0.84. This is likely to be an underestimate of the true reliability of FSIQ because of the lack of tau-equivalency, but it is a *lot* smaller than the 0.98 quoted in the test manual.

Our final approach to estimating the reliability of the FSIQ scale from this test involves the calculation of hierarchical omega (ω_h) described in Chapter 7 using the psych package in R, using the Schmid-Leiman technique discussed in Chapter 13 and specifying four composite scales between the sub-scales and the general factor. This suggests that the reliability of the full scale IQ is 0.79, with the general factor (FSIQ) explaining 62% of the variation in sub-scale scores. As ω_h is one of the more useful measures of model-based reliability (Revelle & Condon, 2019), this modest value may be cause for concern.

So what is the reliability of this test, which is so important for its correct interpretation?

- The test manual suggests that it is 0.98, which agrees with Nunnally's formula when using the published reliabilities of the composite scales and their intercorrelations. However, we show that this means that the total score has little measurement error associated with it – not that the composite scales are highly correlated, or that the scores on the scale correlate substantially with the true score.
- The correlation between the IQ from this test and the IQ from other, similar tests is in the order of 0.8 to 0.9. The average correlation suggests that coefficient alpha might be about 0.88 or less.

- Treating the composite scales as "items" and calculating FSIQ as if it was a four-item test suggests that its coefficient alpha might be 0.83. This may be an underestimate of its true value because of the lack of tau-equivalence.
- Hierarchical omega is arguably the most relevant statistic (and one which is not quoted in the test manual). After extracting a four-factor oblique solution and performing a Schmid-Leiman transformation to obtain a general factor, the hierarchical omega reliability of the general factor is 0.79.

We should stress again that this is a general issue, and not one which is specific to this particular test. It is important because the way in which professionals use such tests to assess individuals relies on the assumption that the reliability of the composite scores (such as full-scale IQ) is very substantial indeed, and indicates how closely scores on these tests are aligned with the trait(s) which they are designed to measure.

Practitioners purchase these tests at great expense precisely because they do seem to provide highly reliable (therefore presumably accurate) measures of intelligence and other ability traits. The problem is that reliability can be calculated in many different ways. Whilst Nunnally's formula produces the coefficient alpha which is quoted in the test manual, all of the other estimates are far lower. The most telling findings are the modest hierarchical omega (0.79) and the correlations between other, supposedly equally reliable tests that measure the same trait. Almost all this evidence suggests that the true reliability of the scale might be less than 0.90. If true, this may have important consequences for test users.

Given the oft-repeated concerns about whether test scores are suitable for complex statistical calculations (which assume that they are interval scaled, multivariate normal etc.), my instinct would be to focus on the correlations between similar tests which does not rely on such sophisticated analyses. After all, the whole purpose of reliability analysis is to predict the correlation between scores on the test and the true score – and correlating two different tests together is really the simplest way of estimating this.

I mention these issues towards the end of this book in order to inject a note of healthy scepticism. Psychometrics is an inexact science (if indeed it is a science at all). Even if one assumes that the items which we write form scales and tests, it is always necessary to make a lot of rather unlikely assumptions about the data – for example, that the responses form an interval or ratio scale, that we have properly sampled all of the items from the domain, that the item characteristic curve is a certain shape, that people guess alternatives at random, that we base our analyses on a random sample of the population, that it is appropriate to calculate a particular form of correlation from the data which we have collected . . . the list is a long one. Some or all of these assumptions will probably be violated in any study, and no-one can tell what the consequence of this will be. Is it really *likely* that any test can correlate 0.99 with the "true score" it is supposed to measure, which is what an alpha of 0.98 implies? Do the various ways of estimating reliability necessarily give the same results, and imply the same thing? What are the practical consequences of any differences which are found? Whenever one encounters something unusual such as interpreting coefficient alpha from a test based on a hierarchical model of abilities, or seeing a statistic which may imply that a test is an almost perfect measure of the trait it is supposed to assess, it is worthwhile digging deep to check whether the statistics really imply what we think.

Many psychometricians view the subject as a series of interesting mathematical, statistical and computational challenges. It might be more useful to regard psychometric techniques as a set of rather crude tools which researchers use to explore the structure, function and processes which underly traits. The resulting products may help practitioners make informed and defensible decisions which will affect the lives of real people.

SUMMARY

Practitioners frequently use scores on tests to help make decisions about individuals, and this chapter outlined a few issues which are not always adequately addressed in test manuals. The importance of setting confidence limits on either side of the estimated true score (rather than the actual test score) is often not stressed in test manuals, and this could lead to erroneous decisions. We also mentioned some issues with difference scores and change scores, and finally invited readers to worry about how, precisely, one can establish the reliability of a test which consists of multiple sub-tests. Does a test whose manual says its reliability is 0.98 actually *behave* like a test whose reliability is 0.98? And does reliability (in this context) actually mean what we assume it does? It is well to be sceptical; having read this far, readers should have no problems turning to more statistically orientated psychometrics books to find the answers to other issues which start to worry them.

NOTE

1 Mean 100, standard deviation 15.

CHAPTER 18
PSYCHOMETRICS IN CONTEXT

We start by considering what is actually meant by a personality trait.

TRAITS: BEHAVIOUR OR SOCIAL CONSTRUCTIONS?

The first issue concerns what we try to measure with scales, questionnaires or other devices. Do we try to measure how people actually behave, or do we impute some characteristic to them? The difference between these approaches becomes obvious if we consider scales which are developed to measure a person's anxiety, and another which measures their beauty. The anxiety scale has been used in several examples in this book. It assumes that anxiety is a genuine characteristic of people which affects several aspects of their behaviour; they may report feeling nervous, sweat, be vigilant and so on, and the idea of the anxiety questionnaire is to try to measure the strength of each of those behaviours.

We generally assume that our questionnaires and tests measure something inside each person which varies. The reason why people vary in their levels of this characteristic cause can take many forms, and may be unknown. The explanation might be physiological (as with anxiety) psychological (as with post-traumatic stress disorder), developmental (as with theory of mind) or have other origins. The key point is that the questions and problems that we devise try to measure some real characteristic of the person – perhaps linked to brain processes, memories, genetic make-up, physiology or something similar. We then hypothesise why these individual differences arise and use the hypothetico-deductive method to determine whether these theories are (partially) correct, modifying and extending them to better fit in with observation and experimental results. If scores on an anxiety questionnaire are manifestly unconnected to any physiological or psychological variables, then it is clear that the theory is incorrect and must be abandoned or modified. It is falsifiable, hence scientific.

Strangely enough, this is not always the case. Social psychologists argue that we view people in an arbitrary way, determined by society; there is no such "thing" as a personality trait which reflects some internal process. Instead we can choose how we view and categorise behaviour, and we do so according to societal norms. From this perspective it would be perfectly easy to put together a questionnaire measuring beauty. This could assess things such as body mass index, hairstyle and social poise. However, there is no hint of causality. No-one would suggest that a person's beauty

DOI: 10.4324/9781003240181-18

causes them to be slim, with a particular aesthetic. Indeed the definition of beauty will change from society to society and over time; we choose to categorise certain behaviours as indicating beauty, but in a few years' time society might change its mind entirely and look for quite different characteristics. Beauty is a social construction, and we can try to measure people's beauty using whatever definition is currently fashionable.

In case this sounds like a "straw man", a made-up example which would never be encountered in real life, consider self-concept – a variable which has been extensively studied, and which basically measures whether a person likes themselves. However, the *criteria* for liking oneself are likely to change over time, and from culture to culture.

In addition, some theorists have argued that variables which we traditionally regard as rooted in the biological make-up of the individual, such as general intelligence, are themselves social constructions and so are arbitrary. According to this view we can – and should – define intelligence to be anything we want it to be.

> Naming a general category – intelligence, for example – and putting some abilities into it while excluding others is at root another kind of thought, to which the idea of empirical verification is irrelevant. They do not belong together. The first is a judgement, the second a sorting of terms. The confusion between those two entirely different types of thought process is key. To clear it up would be not to relativize intelligence but to annihilate it. Yet abandoning a concept so socially powerful requires a revolution.
>
> (Goodey, 2011, p. 74)

One of the problems with any form of social construction is that it limits the use to which test scores can be put. If general intelligence (or any other trait) does not reflect something which actually occurs within the individual, and is defined in an arbitrary way (e.g., next year society might decide that "intelligence" is all about Morris dancing and gardening, rather than cognitive processes), then it makes no sense to use test scores to try to predict behaviour. Most readers of this book will probably agree that this approach is sterile. Furthermore, it seems to be difficult to falsify, and therefore unscientific. How could one ever show that one's conception of beauty was incorrect, as it is arbitrary in the first place?

It might be more productive to measure the way in which people really behave, and deduce from these measurements which personality and ability traits exist. We might *notice* that some people sweat more than others, are fearsome of heights and so on – and hypothesise that this is because something about their psychological, physiological or other make-up (we call it "anxiety") affects all of these behaviours. We then research why some people are more anxious than others.

TOP-DOWN AND BOTTOM-UP THEORIES

The reason I mention this here is that it seems to impact on the way in which personality scales, in particular, are developed and used. The example of anxiety is a "bottom-up" approach. The traits which are discovered are determined by observation; we observe that several behaviours tend to occur together, and because of this infer the presence of a trait. It is a data-driven process, which takes place without requiring any form of theory or preconceived ideas about the structure of personality. Social constructionism is a top-down approach. Society determines what characteristics it chooses to combine (no matter how arbitrary and diverse these are) and imputes these characteristics to an individual.

Researchers such as Cattell (1946; 1971; 1973) and Costa and McCrae (1992) argue that factor analysis is capable of identifying traits using the bottom-up approach. All one needs to do is measure as many behaviours as possible, perform a factor analysis, and the factor analysis will show whether apparently different behaviours (sweating, avoiding high places) form a factor. There is no theoretical expectation at all: the data drive the theory. On the other hand, social psychologists frequently seem to use the top-down approach. A theorist decides to measure "insecure insubordination" or some other trait which exists only in their own mind, and develops a questionnaire to measure it, without any evidence that it is related to the way in which people actually behave. This is one reason why I have been so repeatedly scathing about attempts to measure personality by inventing traits. This approach to developing a theory of personality seems analogous to trying to build a high wall by continually bringing two or three new bricks to the project and arranging them by the side of the existing structure, rather than trying to do anything useful with the materials which are already there.

This book began by reminding users that psychometric tests and scales are terribly simple. They almost always just involve gathering data from questionnaires or measures of performance, making some dangerous statistical assumptions, converting the responses into numbers, and adding together these numbers. However, many researchers seem to forget how simple this process is and develop grandiloquent theories in which highly abstract concepts are interrelated in complex ways.

To my mind, the scientific study of personality and abilities involves trying to measure how people actually behave, and then trying to determine why these consistencies of behaviour (traits) occur, using the methods of experimental psychology. Inventing traits oneself (unless these are later shown to be linked to actual behaviour, as was the case with emotional intelligence) seems to be a recipe for disaster – although it now seems to be the norm. It seems to me that the discipline is fragmenting as researchers carve out small new niches for themselves and their students to develop, rather than tackling the far more difficult job of developing and testing theories about the processes which cause some people to vary – an essential step in validating any scale according to Borsboom et al. (2004).

For those who still believe that personality is a complex area which requires us to understand more and more distinct but interrelated traits, see Bainbridge et al. (in press), who show that many of these correspond rather closely to "Big Five" personality traits or their facets. The structure of personality (and abilities) seems to be quite well understood and quite simple; developing tests and scales to explore novel traits may be unlikely to drive the discipline forward. What is needed, it seems to me, are sound theories about how and why individual differences in personality and cognition develop, and the mechanisms by which they operate. Developing and testing theories is *much* more intellectually demanding than writing a few items to measure some trivial (or perhaps non-existent) personality trait.

STATISTICAL ANALYSIS OF TRAITS

I finish the book with some comments about the ways in which scores on tests are subjected to statistical analyses, in order to draw conclusions about the structure and interactions between personality traits. Some problems have already been discussed – such as the assumption that attributes are quantitative and can be measured on an interval scale. In addition, there are obvious assumptions which need to be made, such as linear relationships between variables, lack of group differences in means, and freedom from multicollinearity. Here I will focus on how inferences about personality are drawn from scores on tests and scales.

SAMPLE SIZE AND POWER

Large sample sizes are important (a) because drawing a large sample makes it more likely that the sample is representative of the population from which it is drawn, (b) estimates of parameters (such as factor loadings) generally become more accurate as sample sizes increase and (c) the statistical power of almost any design increases as sample size increases; one is more likely to be able to correctly reject the null hypothesis if the sample is large. However, interpreting significance levels is a waste of time with large samples – as even tiny effects will be statistically significant. It is far more important to focus on measures of effect size. If the effect size (correlation, path coefficient etc.) is tiny, then it is of no real theoretical or practical importance, even if it significantly different from zero with $p < 0.0000001$.

STRUCTURAL EQUATION MODELLING

When structural equation modelling is used, there are frequently so many paths and correlations that the diagram resembles a plate of noodles. Models are frequently modified in order to coax them to better fit the data, no matter how psychologically implausible such modifications may be. "Confirmatory" factor analysis can easily turn into an exploration of many different models, by allowing error variances to correlate. This is a concern, as it is vitally important to test any modified model on a new sample as the modified model will almost certainly not fit a second sample of data as well as the original; see, for example, Tabachnick and Fidell (2018) and Hoyle and Panter (1995). However, cross-validations are rarely seen. The pressure to publish at all costs takes precedence over ensuring that the findings are replicable. Indeed, one occasionally reads a journal article which proposes a model which is so complex that one suspects that the "model" arose after many hours of analysing the data every way possible, in the hope of finding *something* which fitted. It is impossible to prove this, of course.

MEDIATION AND MODERATION ANALYSES

Moderation/mediation analyses are simple and popular versions of structural equation models where one or more variables (traits) totally or partially influence the causal relationship between two variables. Once again, again theoretical relevance is a major issue. Does the analysis really test an important aspect of theory, or is it likely that the "hypotheses" only emerged after the data were analysed in every possible way? For moderation analysis it is necessary to assume a *causal* model – and in psychology, it is not always obvious what is cause and what is effect. Does intelligence determine how many years of education you receive, or does the number of years of education you receive determine your intelligence? It is often difficult to tell from cross-sectional studies, and this is a major problem for such analyses – see Judd and Kenny (2010).

OVERLAP OF ITEMS

I have shown (Cooper, 2019) that the correlations between several scales show literally nothing of psychological importance. Instead they arise because two or more scales have items which mean the same thing – "Do you sometimes feel depressed?" or "Do you sometimes feel 'down'?", for example. If participants agree with the first item, they are *bound* to agree with the second, as they have the same meaning. My paper gives several published examples of such overlapping items leading to incorrect interpretations and analyses; it is not difficult to find more. Spreadsheet 1.1 showed that just one or two such items can lead to spurious correlations between scales, which will inevitably affect the factor structure which is obtained, and which might be interpreted as if it was something of psychological interest rather than a statistical artefact.

I suspect (without a shred of evidence) that the problem arises because researchers who design such studies are not the ones who actually administer the questionnaires; these senior figures may have long forgotten the precise content of the items, and so may be unaware of the difficulties which shared items can pose. There is a lot to be said for slowly and thoughtfully reading each item in each scale which is to be administered, and asking oneself whether answering one item in a particular way has to influence the answer which is made to another item. If this happens on just one occasion there is a problem, and it needs to be recognised and addressed during the analysis of the data. Structural equation modelling makes it quite straightforward to do this if item responses (rather than scale scores) are analysed.

OVER-OPTIMISM ABOUT VALIDITY

Part of the problem is probably also having too much faith in psychological scales. After all, the only thing which any scale can do is combine several pieces of information. It cannot tell us anything which is unavailable by other means, or provide deep insights into the soul; it may not even assess what it claims to measure very well. One frequently sees papers justifying the use of a test because it has a reliability of 0.7. This implies that 83% ($\sqrt{0.7}$) of the person-to-person variation is explained by the test, and 17% is due to random error. Would one have much faith in a watch or ruler which provided a fairly crude estimate such as this?

Construct validation studies pose a particular problem. When a new scale ("scale x" is validated by correlating it with other scales, one often reads a conclusion such as "<scale x> correlates as 0.6 with <scale y> showing that they are distinct but related traits. The positive correlation supports the validity of <trait x>". However, this conclusion may be problematical if:

1. There is some overlap of items as discussed; two rather different traits may appear to correlate if one or more items are common to both of them.
2. The reliability of the tests is not taken into account. Two tests measuring exactly the same trait each with reliability of 0.6 will correlate 0.6. Concluding that two traits are "similar but not identical" without correcting for unreliability of measurement is common practice but potentially misleading.
3. Features of the sample such as restriction of range are not corrected for, where necessary.

SCIENCE OR TECHNOLOGY?

Michell's appraisals of psychological measurement make it clear that the scales which we use just count (rather than measure) responses to questionnaires and tests. Test scores therefore do not behave like weight, length and other physical measures, and so even if a highly accurate measure was devised it is not obvious how its scores could ever be used as the basis for quantitative laws. It is hard to see how scores on psychological scales could ever lead to the discovery of mathematically defined relationships – psychological equivalents to Newton's laws of motion in physics or Ohm's law, which state clear mathematical relationships between quantitative variables. The problem is not just that these relationships are viewed through the fog of probability; it is that the scores that are used may simply not be quantitative. Whilst it is sometimes claimed that item response theory is the panacea for all of the issues identified by Michell, it is clear from Chapter 15 that this is certainly not universally accepted.

This does not mean that psychological scales are completely devoid of merit. They can have practical applications. It might be rather useful to be able to say that one person is (probably) more depressed or intelligent than another, and it is empirically true that tests can predict who is likely to perform best if appointed to a job (Schmidt & Hunter, 2004), even if it is difficult or impossible to quantify the extent of the difference between them. Second, it is possible that scores on psychological scales could correlate so substantially with physical measurements that they could be used as a sort of proxy for the physical measurements. The only problem is that there are no such large relationships at present. Intelligence tests show an impressive correlation with "inspection time" (the amount of time for which a shape has to be shown in order to be correctly recognised) but this correlation (approx. -0.6) is not large enough to allow us to use intelligence tests as a sort of proxy for whatever neural processes go on when inspection time tasks are solved.

Despite the sophisticated mathematical underpinnings of some modern developments in psychometric theory, it seems safest to regard psychological assessments as technological, rather than scientific, achievements.

REFERENCES

Achenbach, T. M., & Rescorla, L. A. (2001). *Manual for the ASEBA school-age forms & profiles*. University of Vermont, Research Center for Children, Youth, & Families.

Aguirre-Urreta, M. I., Ronkko, M., & McIntosh, C. N. (2019). A cautionary note on the finite sample behavior of maximal reliability. *Psychological Methods, 24*(2), 236–252.

Akhtar, H., & Kovacs, K. (in press). Which tests should be administered first, ability or non-ability? The effect of test order on careless responding. *Personality and Individual Differences*.

Alf, E., & Abrahams, N. (1971). A significance test for biserial. *Educational and Psychological Measurement, 31*(3), 637–640.

American Psychiatric Association. (2022). *Diagnostic and statistical manual of mental disorders (DSM-5-TR)* (5th ed., text rev.).

Angoff, W. H., & Ford, S. F. (1973). Item-race interaction on a test of scholastic aptitude. *Journal of Educational Measurement, 10*(2), 95–106.

Arias, V., Ponce, F., & Martínez-Molina, A. (2022). How a few inconsistent respondents can confound the structure of personality survey data: An example with the Core-Self Evaluations Scale. *European Journal of Psychological Assessment*. Advance online publication. https://doi.org/10.1027/1015-5759/a000719

Armstrong, T. (1994). *Multiple intelligences in the classroom*. Association for Supervision and Curriculum Development.

Arro, G. (2013). Peeking into personality test answers: Inter- and intraindividual variety in item interpretations. *Integrative Psychological and Behavioral Science, 47*(1), 56–76.

Bainbridge, T., Ludeke, S., & Smillie, L. D. (in press). Evaluating the Big Five as an organizing framework for commonly used psychological trait scales. *Journal of Personality and Social Psychology*.

Baron, H. (1996). Strengths and limitations of ipsative measurement. *Journal of Occupational and Organizational Psychology, 69*, 49–56.

Barrett, P. (1986). Factor comparison: An examination of three methods. *Personality and Individual Differences, 7*(3), 327–340.

Barrett, P. (2007). Structural equation modelling: Adjudging model fit. *Personality and Individual Differences, 42*(5), 815–824.

Barrett, P. (2008). The consequence of sustaining a pathology: Scientific stagnation – a commentary on the target article "Is psychometrics a pathological science?" by Joel Michell. *Measurement: Interdisciplinary Research and Perspectives, 6*(1–2), 78–83.

Barrett, P. (2011). Invoking arbitrary units is not a solution to the problem of quantification in the social sciences. *Measurement: Interdisciplinary Research and Perspectives, 9*(1), 28–31.

Barrett, P., & Kline, P. (1980). The location of superfactors P, E and N within an unexplored factor space. *Personality and Individual Differences, 1*, 239–247.

Barrett, P., & Kline, P. (1981). The observation to variable ratio in factor analysis. *Personality Study and Group Behavior*, *1*, 23–33.

Bartholomew, D. J., Deary, I. J., & Lawn, M. (2009). The origin of factor scores: Spearman, Thomson and Bartlett. *British Journal of Mathematical & Statistical Psychology*, *62*, 569–582.

Bartlett, M. (1950). Tests of significance in factor analysis. *British Journal of Psychology*, *3*, 77–85.

Bartram, D. (1996). The relationship between ipsatized and normative measures of personality. *Journal of Occupational and Organizational Psychology*, *69*, 25–39.

Bartram, D. (2009). The international test commission guidelines on computer-based and internet-delivered testing. *Industrial and Organizational Psychology: Perspectives on Science and Practice*, *2*(1), 11–13.

Bartram, D., Berberoglu, G., Grégoire, J., Hambleton, R., Muñiz, J., & Van de Vijver, F. (2018). ITC guidelines for translating and adapting tests (second edition). *International Journal of Testing*, *18*, 101–134.

Bastian, M., Heymann, S., & Jacomy, M. (2009). *Gephi: An open source software for exploring and manipulating networks* International AAAI Conference on Weblogs and Social Media, San Jose, CA.

Beck, A. T. (1976). *Cognitive therapy and the emotional disorders*. International Universities Press.

Beck, A. T. (1996). *Manual for the Beck Depression Inventory – II*. Psychological Corporation.

Beloff, H. (1992). Mother, father and me: Our IQ. *Psychologist*, *5*, 309–311.

Bentler, P. M., Jackson, D. N., & Messick, S. (1971). Identification of content and style: A two-dimensional interpretation of acquiescence. *Psychological Bulletin*, *76*(3), 186–204.

Birnbaum, M. H. (1973). The devil rides again: Correlation as an index of fit. *Psychological Bulletin*, *79*(4), 239–242.

Blaise, M., Marksteiner, T., Krispenz, A., & Bertrams, A. (2021). Measuring motivation for cognitive effort as state. *Frontiers in Psychology*, *12*, Article 785094. https://doi.org/10.3389/fpsyg.2021.785094

Blondel, V. D., Guillaume, J. L., Lambiotte, R., & Lefebvre, E. (2008). Fast unfolding of communities in large networks. *Journal of Statistical Mechanics: Theory and Experiment*, Article P10008. https://doi.org/10.1088/1742-5468/2008/10/P10008

Bloxom, B. A. (1968). A note on invariance in three-mode factor analysis. *Psychometrika*, *33*, 347–350.

Bollen, K. A., & Barb, K. H. (1983). Collapsing variables and validity coefficients: Reply. *American Sociological Review*, *48*(2), 286–287.

Bonanomi, A., Cantaluppi, G., Ruscone, M. N., & Osmetti, S. A. (2015). A new estimator of Zumbo's ordinal alpha: A copula approach. *Quality & Quantity*, *49*(3), 941–953.

Borsboom, D., Cramer, A. O. J., Kievit, R. A., Scholten, A. Z., & Franic, S. (2011). The end of construct validity. In R. W. Lissitz (Ed.), *The concept of validity* (pp. 135–170). Information Age.

Borsboom, D., Mellenbergh, G. J., & van Heerden, J. (2004). The concept of validity. *Psychological Review*, *111*(4), 1061–1071.

Borsboom, D., & Scholten, A. Z. (2008). The Rasch model and conjoint measurement theory from the perspective of psychometrics. *Theory & Psychology*, *18*(1), 111–117.

Brennan, R. L. (2001). *Generalizability theory*. Springer.

Briesch, A. M., Swaminathan, H., Welsh, M., & Chafouleas, S. M. (2014). Generalizability theory: A practical guide to study design, implementation, and interpretation. *Journal of School Psychology*, *52*(1), 13–35.

Briggs, D. C., & Wilson, M. (2004). *Generalizability in item response modeling* Psychometric Society Conference, Pacific Grove, CA.

Brogden, H. E. (1969). Pattern, structure and the interpretation of factors. *Psychological Bulletin, 72*(5), 375–378.

Brown, R. T., Reynolds, C. R., & Whitaker, J. S. (1999). Bias in mental testing since bias in mental testing. *School Psychology Quarterly, 14*(3), 208–238.

Butler, R. P. (1973). Effects of signed and unsigned questionnaires for both sensitive and nonsensitive items. *Journal of Applied Psychology, 57*(3), 348–349.

Byrne, B. (1995). One application of structural equation modeling from two perspectives. In R. H. Hoyle (Ed.), *Structural equation modeling: Concepts, issues and applications* (pp. 138–157). Sage.

Byrne, D. (1961). The repression-sensitisation scale: Rationale, reliability and validity. *Journal of Personality, 29*, 334–339.

Calvin, C. M., Fernandes, C., Smith, P., Visscher, P. M., & Deary, I. J. (2010). Sex, intelligence and educational achievement in a national cohort of over 175,000 11-year-old schoolchildren in England. *Intelligence, 38*(4), 424–432.

Canivez, G. L., & Watkins, M. W. (2016). Review of the Wechsler Intelligence Scale for Children – Fifth Edition: Critique, commentary, and independent analyses. In A. S. Kaufman, S. E. Raiford, & D. L. Coalson (Eds.), *Intelligent testing with the WISC-V*. Wiley.

Carroll, J. B. (1993). *Human cognitive abilities: A survey of factor-analytic studies*. Cambridge University Press.

Carroll, J. B. (2003). The higher-stratum structure of cognitive abilities: Current evidence supports g and about ten broad factors. In H. Nyborg (Ed.), *The scientific study of general intelligence: Tribute to Arthur R. Jensen*. Elsevier Science.

Caruso, J. C. (2004). A comparison of the reliabilities of four types of difference scores for five cognitive assessment batteries. *European Journal of Psychological Assessment, 20*(3), 166–171.

Caruso, J. C., & Cliff, N. (2000). Increasing the reliability of Wechsler Intelligence Scale for Children – Third Edition difference scores with reliable component analysis. *Psychological Assessment, 12*(1), 89–96.

Cascio, W. F., & Kurtines, W. M. (1977). A practical method for identifying significant change scores. *Educational and Psychological Measurement, 37*(4), 889–895.

Catron, D. W., & Thompson, C. C. (1979). Test-retest gains in WAIS scores after 4 retest intervals. *Journal of Clinical Psychology, 35*(2), 352–357.

Cattell, R. B. (1946). *Description and measurement of personality*. World Book Company.

Cattell, R. B. (1965). *The IPAT Culture Fair Intelligence Scales 1, 2 and 3* (3 ed.). Institute for Personality and Ability Testing.

Cattell, R. B. (1966). The scree test for the number of factors. *Multivariate Behavioral Research, 1*, 140–161.

Cattell, R. B. (1971). *Abilities, their structure growth and action*. Houghton Mifflin.

Cattell, R. B. (1973). *Personality and mood by questionnaire*. Jossey-Bass.

Cattell, R. B. (1978). *The scientific use of factor analysis in behavioral and life sciences*. Plenum.

Cattell, R. B., Cattell, A. K., & Cattell, H. E. P. (1994). *16PF Fifth Edition technical manual*. Institute for Personality and Ability Testing.

Cattell, R. B., Eber, H. W., & Tatsuoka, M. M. (1970). *Handbook for the Sixteen Personality Factor questionnaire*. IPAT.

Cattell, R. B., & Muerle, J. L. (1960). The "Maxplane" program for factor rotation to oblique simple structure. *Educational and Psychological Measurement, 20*, 569–590.

Cattell, R. B., & Vogelman, S. (1977). A comprehensive trial of the scree and KG criteria for determining the number of factors. *Journal of Educational Measurement, 14*(2), 289–325.

Chalmers, R. P. (2018). On misconceptions and the limited usefulness of ordinal alpha. *Educational and Psychological Measurement*, *78*(6), 1056–1071.

Chamorro-Premuzic, T., Ahmetoglu, G., & Furnham, A. (2008). Little more than personality: Dispositional determinants of test anxiety (the Big Five, core self-evaluations, and self-assessed intelligence). *Learning and Individual Differences*, *18*(2), 258–263.

Chan, D., & Schmitt, N. (1997). Video-based versus paper-and-pencil method of assessment in situational judgment tests: Subgroup differences in test performance and face validity perceptions. *Journal of Applied Psychology*, *82*(1), 143–159.

Chmielewski, M., & Kucker, S. C. (2020). An MTurk crisis? Shifts in data quality and the impact on study results. *Social Psychological and Personality Science*, *11*(4), 464–473.

Cho, E. (in press). The accuracy of reliability coefficients: A reanalysis of existing simulations. *Psychological Methods*.

Choi, J., Peters, M., & Mueller, R. O. (2010). Correlational analysis of ordinal data: From Pearson's r to Bayesian polychoric correlation. *Asia Pacific Education Review*, *11*(4), 459–466.

Christensen, A. P., Cotter, K. N., & Silvia, P. J. (2019). Reopening openness to experience: A network analysis of four openness to experience inventories. *Journal of Personality Assessment*, *101*(6), 574–588.

Christensen, K. B., Makransky, G., & Horton, M. (2017). Critical values for Yen's Q(3): Identification of local dependence in the Rasch model using residual correlations. *Applied Psychological Measurement*, *41*(3), 178–194.

Clarkson, D. B., & Jennrich, R. I. (1988). Quartic rotation criteria and algorithms. *Psychometrika*, *53*(2), 251–259.

Cliff, N., & Caruso, J. C. (1998). Reliable component analysis through maximizing composite reliability. *Psychological Methods*, *3*(3), 291–308.

Closs, S. J. (1996). On the factoring and interpretation of ipsative data. *Journal of Occupational and Organizational Psychology*, *69*, 41–47.

Collie, A., Maruff, P., Darby, D. G., & McStephen, M. (2003). The effects of practice on the cognitive test performance of neurologically normal individuals assessed at brief test-retest intervals. *Journal of the International Neuropsychological Society*, *9*(3), 419–428.

Comrey, A. L., & Lee, H. B. (1992). *A first course in factor analysis* (2nd ed.). Lawrence Erlbaum Associates.

Condon, D. M., & Revelle, W. (2014). The international cognitive ability resource: Development and initial validation of a public-domain measure. *Intelligence*, *43*, 52–64.

Conley, J. J. (1984). The hierarchy of consistency: A review and model of longitudinal findings on adult individual differences in intelligence, personality and self-opinion. *Personality and Individual Differences*, *5*, 11–25.

Cooper, C. (1983). Correlation measures in item analysis. *British Journal of Mathematical and Statistical Psychology*, *32*, 102–105.

Cooper, C. (2015). *Intelligence and human abilities*. Routledge.

Cooper, C. (2019). Pitfalls of personality theory. *Personality and Individual Differences*, *151*, Article 109551. https://doi.org/10.1016/j.paid.2019.109551

Cooper, C. (2021). *Individual differences and personality* (4th ed.). Routledge.

Cooper, C., & Kline, P. (1982). A validation of the defense-mechanism inventory. *British Journal of Medical Psychology*, *55*, 209–214.

Cooper, C., Kline, P., & May, J. (1986). The measurement of authoritarianism, psychoticism and other traits by objective tests: A cross-validation. *Personality and Individual Differences*, *7*(1), 15–21.

Cornwell, J. M., & Dunlap, W. P. (1994). On the questionable soundness of factoring ipsative data: A response. *Journal of Occupational and Organizational Psychology, 67*, 89–100.

Corr, P. J. (2008). *The reinforcement sensitivity theory of personality.* Cambridge University Press.

Cortina, J. M. (1993). What is coefficient alpha? An examination of theory and applications. *Journal of Applied Psychology, 78*(1), 98–104.

Cosemans, T., Rosseel, Y., & Gelper, S. (in press). Exploratory graph analysis for factor retention: Simulation results for continuous and binary data. *Educational and Psychological Measurement, 82*(5), 880–910.

Costa, P. T., & McCrae, R. R. (1992). Four ways five factors are basic. *Personality and Individual Differences, 13*(6), 653–665.

Cramer, A. O. J., Van Der Sluis, S., Noordhof, A., Wichers, M., Geschwind, N., Aggen, S. H., . . . Borsboom, D. (2012). Dimensions of normal personality as networks in search of equilibrium: You can't like parties if you don't like people. *European Journal of Personality, 26*(4), 414–431.

Cramer, A. O. J., Waldorp, L. J., van der Maas, H. L. J., & Borsboom, D. (2010). Comorbidity: A network perspective. *Behavioral and Brain Sciences, 33*(2–3), 137–150.

Cronbach, L. J., & Furby, L. (1970). How we should measure "change": Or should we? *Psychological Bulletin, 74*(1), 68–80.

Cronbach, L. J., Gleser, G. C., Nanda, H., & Rajaratnam, N. (1972). *The dependability of behavioral measurements.* Wiley.

Crowne, D. P., & Marlowe, D. (1960). A new scale of social desirability independent of psychopathology. *Journal of Consulting Psychology, 24*(4), 349–354.

Curran, P. G. (2016). Methods for the detection of carelessly invalid responses in survey data. *Journal of Experimental Social Psychology, 66*, 4–19.

Danner, D., Aichholzer, J., & Rammstedt, B. (2015). Acquiescence in personality questionnaires: Relevance, domain specificity, and stability. *Journal of Research in Personality, 57*, 119–130.

Davenport, E. C. (1990). Significance testing of congruence coefficients: A good idea. *Educational and Psychological Measurement, 50*(2), 289–296.

Davenport, E. C., & Elsanhurry, N. A. (1991). Phi-phimax: Review and synthesis. *Educational and Psychological Measurement, 51*(4), 821–828.

Davey, T. (2011). *Practical considerations in computer-based testing.* E. T. Service.

Deary, I. J., Strand, S., Smith, P., & Fernandes, C. (2007). Intelligence and educational achievement. *Intelligence, 35*(1), 13–21.

Deary, I. J., Whalley, L. J., Lemmon, H., Crawford, J. R., & Starr, J. M. (2000). The stability of individual differences in mental ability from childhood to old age: Follow-up of the 1932 Scottish mental survey. *Intelligence, 28*(1), 49–55.

Der, G., Batty, G. D., & Deary, I. J. (2006). Effect of breast feeding on intelligence in children: Prospective study, sibling pairs analysis, and meta-analysis. *British Medical Journal, 333*(7575), 945–948A.

Desimone, J. A., Harms, P. D., & Desimone, A. J. (2015). Best practice recommendations for data screening. *Journal of Organizational Behavior, 36*(2), 171–181.

Dobson, P. (1988). The correction of correlation coefficients for restriction of range when restriction results from the truncation of a normally distributed variable. *British Journal of Mathematical and Statistical Psychology, 41*, 227–234.

Dombrowski, S. C., & Watkins, M. W. (2013). Exploratory and higher order factor analysis of the WJ-III full test battery: A school-aged analysis. *Psychological Assessment, 25*(2), 442–455.

Dziuban, C. D., & Shirkey, E. C. (1974). When is a correlation matrix appropriate for factor-analysis: Decision rules. *Psychological Bulletin, 81*(6), 358–361.

Edwards, A. L. (1953). *Edwards Personal Preference Schedule*. Psychological Corporation.

Edwards, A. L. (1959). Social desirability and the description of others. *Journal of Abnormal and Social Psychology, 59*(3), 434–436.

Ellingson, J. E., Sackett, P. R., & Hough, L. M. (1999). Social desirability corrections in personality measurement: Issues of applicant comparison and construct validity. *Journal of Applied Psychology, 84*(2), 155–166.

Elliott, C. D., Murray, D. J., & Pearson, L. S. (1996). *British ability scales* (2nd ed.). NFER-Nelson.

Epskamp, S., & Fried, E. I. (2018). A tutorial on regularized partial correlation networks. *Psychological Methods, 23*(4), 617–634.

Epskamp, S., Kruis, J., & Marsman, M. (2017). Estimating psychopathological networks: Be careful what you wish for. *PLoS ONE, 12*(6), Article e0179891. https://doi.org/10.1371/journal.pone.0179891

Eysenck, H. J., & Wilson, G. D. (1976). *Know your own personality*. Penguin Books.

Eysenck, S. B., Eysenck, H. J., & Barrett, P. (1985). A revised version of the psychoticism scale. *Personality and Individual Differences, 6*(1), 21–29.

Fagan, J. F., & Holland, C. R. (2007). Racial equality in intelligence: Predictions from a theory of intelligence as processing. *Intelligence, 35*(4), 319–334.

Feldt, L. S., Woodruff, D. J., & Salih, F. A. (1987). Statistical inference for coefficient-alpha. *Applied Psychological Measurement, 11*(1), 93–103.

Feng, Y., & Hancock, G. R. (in press). Model-based incremental validity. *Psychological Methods*.

Ferguson, G. (1941). The factorial interpretation of test difficulty. *Psychometrika, 6*, 323–329.

Feynman, R. P., Leighton, R. B., & Sands, M. (1963). *The Feynman lectures on physics: Vol. 1. Mainly mechanics, radiation, and heat*. Addison-Wesley.

Fokkema, M., & Greiff, S. (2017). How performing PCA and CFA on the same data equals trouble: Overfitting in the assessment of internal structure and some editorial thoughts on it. *European Journal of Psychological Assessment, 33*(6), 399–402.

Fontaine, J. R. J. (2005). Equivalence. In K. Kempf-Leonard (Ed.), *Encyclopedia of social measurement* (pp. 803–813). Elsevier.

Forbes, M. K., Wright, A. G. C., Marko, K. E., & Krueger, R. F. (2021). Quantifying the reliability and replicability of psychopathology network characteristics. *Multivariate Behavioral Research, 56*(2), 224–242.

Francis, L. (1981). Anonymity and attitude scores among 10-year and 11-year old children. *Journal of Experimental Education, 49*(2), 74–76.

Franke, G. H. (1997). "The whole is more than the sum of its parts": The effects of grouping and randomizing items on the reliability and validity of questionnaires. *European Journal of Psychological Assessment, 13*(2), 67–74.

Fugett, A., Thomas, S. W., & Lindberg, M. A. (2014). The many faces of malingering and participant response strategies: New methodologies in the attachment and clinical issues questionnaire (ACIQ). *Journal of General Psychology, 141*(2), 80–97.

Gallitto, E., & Leth-Steensen, C. (2015). Autistic traits and adult attachment styles. *Personality and Individual Differences, 79*, 63–67.

Gierl, M. J., Bulut, O., Guo, Q., & Zhang, X. X. (2017). Developing, analyzing, and using distractors for multiple-choice tests in education: A comprehensive review. *Review of Educational Research, 87*(6), 1082–1116.

Gierl, M. J., & Lai, H. (2018). Using automatic item generation to create solutions and rationales for computerized formative testing. *Applied Psychological Measurement, 42*(1), 42–57.

Giordani, P., Kiers, H., Antonietta, M., & Ferraro, D. (2014). Three-way component analysis using the R package ThreeWay. *Journal of Statistical Software, 57*(7), 1–23.

Godinho, A., Schell, C., & Cunningham, J. A. (2020). Out damn bot, out: Recruiting real people into substance use studies on the internet. *Substance Abuse, 41*(1), 3–5.

Goldberg, L. R. (1999). A broad-bandwidth, public domain, personality inventory measuring the lower-level facets of several five-factor models. In I. Mervielde, I. Deary, F. D. Fruyt, & F. Ostendorf (Eds.), *Personality psychology in Europe* (Vol. 7, pp. 7–28). Tilburg University Press.

Golino, H. F., Christensen, A. J., & Moulder, R. (2020). *Package "EGANET": Exploratory graph analysis: A framework for estimating the number of dimensions in multivariate data using network psychometrics.* https://cran.r-project.org/web/packages/EGAnet/EGAnet.pdf

Golino, H. F., & Epskamp, S. (2017). Exploratory graph analysis: A new approach for estimating the number of dimensions in psychological research. *PLoS ONE, 12*(6), Article e0174035. https://doi.org/10.1371/journal.pone.0174035

Goodey, C. F. (2011). *A history of intelligence and "intellectual disability"*. Routledge.

Gorsuch, R. L. (1970). Comparison of biquartimin, maxplane, promax, and varimax. *Educational and Psychological Measurement, 30*(4), 861–872.

Gorsuch, R., L. (1983). *Factor analysis* (2nd ed.). Lawrence Erlbaum Associates.

Gosling, S. D., Rentfrow, P. J., & Swann, W. B. (2003). A very brief measure of the Big-Five personality domains. *Journal of Research in Personality, 37*(6), 504–528.

Gough, H. G. (1975). *The California Personality Inventory*. Consulting Psychologists Press.

Graham, J. M. (2006). Congeneric and (essentially) tau-equivalent estimates of score reliability: What they are and how to use them. *Educational and Psychological Measurement, 66*(6), 930–944.

Graham, J. R. (1990). *MMPI–2: Assessing personality and psychopathology*. Oxford University Press.

Guadagnoli, E., & Velicer, W. F. (1988). Relation of sample size to the stability of component patterns. *Psychological Bulletin, 103*(2), 265–275.

Guilford, J., & Lyons, T. (1942). On determining the reliability and significance of a tetrachoric coefficient of correlation. *Psychometrika, 7*, 243–249.

Guilford, J. P. (1959). *Personality*. McGraw-Hill.

Gulliksen, H. (1950a). *Theory of mental tests*. Wiley.

Gulliksen, H. (1950b). The reliability of speeded tests. *Psychometrika, 15*(3), 259–269.

Gulliksen, H. (1986). Perspective on educational measurement. *Applied Psychological Measurement, 10*(2), 109–132.

Guttman, L. (1954). Some necessary and sufficient conditions for common factor analysis. *Psychometrika, 19*, 149–161.

Hakstian, A. R., & Mueller, V. J. (1973). Some notes on the number of factors problem. *Multivariate Behavioral Research, 8*, 461–475.

Hambleton, R. K., & Cook, L. (1983). Robustness of item response models. In D. J. Weiss (Ed.), *New horizons in testing*. Academic Press.

Hambleton, R. K., & Swaminathan, H. (1985). *Item response theory: Principles and applications*. Kluwer-Nijhoff.

Hambleton, R. K., Swaminathan, H., & Rogers, H. J. (1991). *Fundamentals of item response theory*. Sage.

Hambleton, R. K., & Traub, R. E. (1973). Analysis of empirical data using two logistic latent trait models. *British Journal of Mathematical and Statistical Psychology, 26*, 195–211.

Hancock, G. R., & Mueller, R. O. (2001). Rethinking construct reliability within latent variable systems. In R. Cudeck, S. E. Du Toit, & D. Sörbom (Eds.), *Structural equation modeling: Present and future – a festschrift in honor of Karl Jöreskog*. Scientific Software International.

Hardt, J., & Rutter, M. (2004). Validity of adult retrospective reports of adverse childhood experiences: Review of the evidence. *Journal of Child Psychology and Psychiatry, 45*(2), 260–273.

Harman, H. H. (1976). *Modern factor analysis* (3rd ed.). University of Chicago Press.

Harman, J. L., & Brown, K. D. (2022). Illustrating a narrative: A test of game elements in game-like personality assessment. *International Journal of Selection and Assessment, 30*(1), 157–166.

Harris, C. W. (1967). On factors and factor scores. *Psychometrika, 32*, 363–379.

Harter, S. (1988). *Manual for the Self-Perception Profile for Adolescents*. University of Denver.

Hathaway, S., & McKinley, J. (1940). A multiphasic personality schedule: I. Construction of the schedule. *Journal of Psychology: Interdisciplinary and Applied, 10*, 249–254.

Hathaway, S. R., & McKinley, J. C. (1967). *The Minnesota Multiphasic Personality Inventory Manual (Revised)*. Psychological Corporation.

Heim, A. W., Watts, K. P., & Simmonds, V. (1970). *AH4, AH5 and AH6 tests*. NFER.

Hendrickson, A. E., & White, P. O. (1966). A method for the rotation of higher-order factors. *British Journal of Mathematical and Statistical Psychology, 19*(1), 97–103.

Hepburn, L., & Eysenck, M. W. (1989). Personality, average mood and mood variability. *Personality and Individual Differences, 10*(9), 975–983.

Holley, J. W. (1973). The Rorschach. In P. Kline (Ed.), *New approaches in psychological measurement*. Wiley.

Holster, T. A., & Lake, J. (2016). Guessing and the Rasch model. *Language Assessment Quarterly, 13*(2), 124–141.

Holzinger, K. J., & Swineford, F. (1937). The bi-factor method. *Psychometrika, 2*, 41–54.

Horn, J. L. (1965). A rationale and test for the number of factors in factor analysis. *Psychometrika, 30*(2), 179–185.

Horn, J. L., & Knapp, J. R. (1973). Subjective character of empirical base of Guilford's structure-of-intellect model. *Psychological Bulletin, 80*(1), 33–43.

Howell, D. C. (2012). *Statistical methods for psychology* (8th ed.). Wadsworth.

Hoyle, R. H., & Panter, A. T. (1995). Writing about structural equation models. In R. H. Hoyle (Ed.), *Structural equation modeling* (pp. 158–176). Sage.

Hu, L.-T., & Bentler, P. M. (1995). Evaluating model fit. In R. H. Hoyle (Ed.), *Structural equation modeling*. Sage.

Hurley, J. R., & Cattell, R. B. (1962). The Procrustes program: Producing direct rotation to test a hypothesized factor structure. *Behavioral Science, 7*(2), 258–262.

Ilagan, M. J., & Falk, C. F. (2022). Supervised classes, unsupervised mixing proportions: Detection of bots in a Likert-type questionnaire. *Educational and Psychological Measurement*. https://doi.org/10.1177/00131644221104220

Jackson, D. N., & Messick, S. (1958). Content and style in personality assessment. *Psychological Bulletin, 55*(4), 243–252.

Jennrich, R. I., & Bentler, P. M. (2011). Exploratory bi-factor analysis. *Psychometrika, 76*(4), 537–549.

Jennrich, R. I., & Bentler, P. M. (2012). Exploratory bi-factor analysis: The oblique case. *Psychometrika, 77*(3), 442–454.

Jennrich, R. I., & Sampson, P. F. (1966). Rotation for simple loadings. *Psychometrika, 31*(3), 313–323.

Jensen, A. R. (1980). *Bias in mental testing*. Free Press.

Jiang, G., Mai, Y., & Yuan, K. H. (2017). Advances in measurement invariance and mean comparison of latent variables: Equivalence testing and a projection-based approach. *Frontiers in Psychology*, *8*, 1823.

Johnson, C. E., Wood, R., & Blinkhorn, S. F. (1988). Spuriouser and spuriouser: The use of ipsative personality tests. *Journal of Occupational Psychology*, *61*(2), 153–162.

Judd, C. M., & Kenny, D. A. (2010). Data analysis. In D. Gilbert, S. T. Fiske, & G. Lindzey (Eds.), *The handbook of social psychology* (Vol. 1, pp. 115–139). Wiley.

Judge, T. A., Rodell, J. B., Klinger, R. L., Simon, L. S., & Crawford, E. R. (2013). Hierarchical representations of the five-factor model of personality in predicting job performance: Integrating three organizing frameworks with two theoretical perspectives. *Journal of Applied Psychology*, *98*(6), 875–925.

Kaiser, H. F. (1958). The VARIMAX criterion for analytic rotation in factor analysis. *Psychometrika*, *23*, 187–200.

Kaiser, H. F. (1960). The application of electronic computers in factor analysis. *Educational and Psychological Measurement*, *20*, 141–151.

Kaiser, H. F. (1970). A second generation little jiffy. *Psychometrika*, *35*(4), 401–415.

Kaiser, H. F. (1981). A revised measure of sampling adequacy for factor-analytic data matrices. *Educational and Psychological Measurement*, *41*(2), 379–381.

Kaiser, H. F. (1990). On Guttman's proof that squared multiple correlations are lower bounds for communalities. *Psychological Reports*, *67*, 1004–1006.

Kaiser, H. F., Hunka, S., & Bianchini, J. C. (1971). Relating factors between studies based upon different individuals. *Multivariate Behavioral Research*, *6*(4), 409–422.

Kampen, J., & Swyngedouw, M. (2000). The ordinal controversy revisited. *Quality & Quantity*, *34*(1), 87–102.

Kanfer, P. L., Ackerman, Y. M., & Goff, M. (1995). Personality and intelligence in industrial and organizational psychology. In D. H. Saklofske & M. Zeidner (Eds.), *International handbook of personality and intelligence*. Plenum.

Kass, F., Spitzer, R. L., & Williams, J. B. W. (1983). An empirical study of the issue of sex bias in the diagnostic criteria of DSM-III Axis II personality disorders. *American Psychologist*, *38*(7), 799–801.

Katz, J. O., & Rohlf, F. J. (1974). Functionplane: New approach to simple structure rotation. *Psychometrika*, *39*(1), 37–51.

Kaufman, A. S., Raiford, S. E., & Coalson, D. L. (2016). *Intelligent testing with the WISC-V*. Wiley.

Kline, P. (1968). Obsessional traits, obsessional symptoms and anal erotism. *British Journal of Medical Psychology*, *41*(3), 299–305.

Kline, P. (1986). *A handbook of test construction*. Methuen.

Kline, P. (1994). *An easy guide to factor analysis*. Routledge.

Kline, P. (2000a). *The handbook of psychological testing* (2nd ed.). Routledge.

Kline, P. (2000b). *A psychometrics primer*. Free Association Books.

Kline, R. B. (2015). *Principles and practice of structural equation modeling* (4th ed.). Guilford.

Knol, D. L., & TenBerge, J. M. F. (1989). Least-squares approximation of an improper correlation matrix by a proper one. *Psychometrika*, *54*(1), 53–61.

Kolen, M. J., & Brennan, R. L. (2014). *Test equating, scaling, and linking: Methods and practices* (3rd ed.). Springer Science + Business Media.

Konstabel, K., Lonnqvist, J. E., Walkowitz, G., & Verkasalo, M. (2012). The "Short Five" (S5): Measuring personality traits using comprehensive single items. *European Journal of Personality*, *26*(1), 13–29.

Kruger, J. (1999). Lake Wobegon be gone! The "below-average effect" and the egocentric nature of comparative ability judgments. *Journal of Personality and Social Psychology*, *77*(2), 221–232.

LaBuda, M. C., deFries, J. C., & Julker, D. W. (1987). Genetic and environmental covariance structures among WISC-R subtests: A twin study. *Intelligence*, *11*, 233–244.

Lalla, M. (2017). Fundamental characteristics and statistical analysis of ordinal variables: A review. *Quality & Quantity*, *51*(1), 435–458.

Lang, F. R., John, D., Ludtke, O., Schupp, J., & Wagner, G. G. (2011). Short assessment of the Big Five: Robust across survey methods except telephone interviewing. *Behavior Research Methods*, *43*(2), 548–567.

Lee, J. S., Bainter, S. A., Carrico, A. W., Glynn, T. R., Rogers, B. G., Albright, C., . . . Safren, S. A. (2020). Connecting the dots: A comparison of network analysis and exploratory factor analysis to examine psychosocial syndemic indicators among HIV-negative sexual minority men. *Journal of Behavioral Medicine*, *43*(6), 1026–1040.

Levene, H. (1960). Robust tests for equality of variances. In I. Olkin (Ed.), *Contributions to probability and statistics: Essays in honor of Harold Hotelling* (pp. 278–292). Stanford University Press.

Linacre, J. M., & Wright, B. D. (1995). How do Rasch and 3P differ? An example from the national adult literacy study. Memo 81, MESA Laboratory.

Little, T. D., Rhemtulla, M., Gibson, K., & Schoemann, A. M. (2013). Why the items versus parcels controversy needn't be one. *Psychological Methods*, *18*(3), 285–300.

Liu, Y., & Zumbo, B. D. (2007). The impact of outliers on Cronbach's coefficient alpha estimate of reliability: Visual analogue scales. *Educational and Psychological Measurement*, *67*(4), 620–634.

Loehlin, J. C., & Beaujean, A. A. (2017). *Latent variable models: An introduction to factor, path, and structural equation analysis* (5th ed.). Routledge.

Loevinger, J. (1948). The technic of homogeneous tests compared with some aspects of "scale analysis" and factor analysis. *Psychological Bulletin*, *45*(6), 507–529.

Lord, F. M. (1980). *Applications of item response theory to practical testing problems*. L. Erlbaum Associates.

Lorenzo-Seva, U., & Ferrando, P. J. (2006). Factor: A computer program to fit the exploratory factor analysis model. *Behavior Research Methods*, *38*(1), 88–91.

Lorenzo-Seva, U., & Ferrando, P. J. (2019). A general approach for fitting pure exploratory bifactor models. *Multivariate Behavioral Research*, *54*(1), 15–30.

Lorenzo-Seva, U., & ten Berge, J. M. F. (2006). Tucker's congruence coefficient as a meaningful index of factor similarity. *Methodology: European Journal of Research Methods for the Behavioral and Social Sciences*, *2*(2), 57–64.

Lovik, A., Nassiri, V., Verbeke, G., & Molenberghs, G. (2020). A modified Tucker's congruence coefficient for factor matching. *Methodology: European Journal of Research Methods for the Behavioral and Social Sciences*, *16*(1), 59–74.

MacCallum, R. C., Widaman, K. F., Zhang, S. B., & Hong, S. H. (1999). Sample size in factor analysis. *Psychological Methods*, *4*(1), 84–99.

MacCann, C. (2013). Instructed faking of the HEXACO reduces facet reliability and involves more Gc than Gf. *Personality and Individual Differences*, *55*(7), 828–833.

Mancini, A., Granziol, U., Migliorati, D., Gragnani, A., Femia, G., Cosentino, T., . . . Mancini, F. (2022). Moral orientation guilt scale (MOGS): Development and validation of a novel guilt measurement. *Personality and Individual Differences*, *189*, Article 111495. https://doi.org/10.1016/j.paid.2021.111495

Mansolf, M., & Reise, S. P. (2016). Exploratory bifactor analysis: The Schmid-Leiman orthogonalization and Jennrich-Bentler analytic rotations. *Multivariate Behavioral Research*, *51*(5), 698–717.

Maraun, M. D. (1998). Measurement as a normative practice: Implications of Wittgenstein's philosophy for measurement in psychology. *Theory & Psychology*, *8*(4), 435–461.

Martin, K., Periard, J., Rattray, B., & Pyne, D. B. (2020). Physiological factors which influence cognitive performance in military personnel. *Human Factors*, *62*(1), 93–123.

Maul, A., Torres Irribarra, D., & Wilson, M. (2016). On the philosophical foundations of psychological measurement. *Measurement*, *79*, 311–320.

Maxwell, S. E., & Howard, G. S. (1981). Change scores: Necessarily anathema. *Educational and Psychological Measurement*, *41*(3), 747–756.

McCall, W. A. (1939). *Measurement*. Macmillan.

McConville, C., & Cooper, C. (1992). Mood variability and personality. *Personality and Individual Differences*, *13*(11), 1213–1221.

McCord, J.-L., Harman, J. L., & Purl, J. (2019). Game-like personality testing: An emerging mode of personality assessment. *Personality and Individual Differences*, *143*, 95–102.

McCrae, R. R., & Costa, P. T. (1983). Social desirability scales: More substance than style. *Journal of Consulting and Clinical Psychology*, *51*(6), 882–888.

McCrae, R. R., & John, O. P. (1992). An introduction to the five-factor model and its applications. *Journal of Personality*, *60*(2), 175–215.

McCrae, R. R., Stone, S. V., Fagan, P. J., & Costa, P. T. (1998). Identifying causes of disagreement between self-reports and spouse ratings of personality. *Journal of Personality*, *66*(3), 285–313.

McCrae, R. R., Zonderman, A. B., Bond, M. H., Costa, P. T., & Paunonen, S. V. (1996). Evaluating replicability of factors in the revised NEO personality inventory: Confirmatory factor analysis versus Procrustes rotation. *Journal of Personality and Social Psychology*, *70*(3), 552–566.

McDonald, R. P., & Burr, E. J. (1967). A comparison of four methods of constructing factor scores. *Psychometrika*, *32*, 381–401.

McFarland, L. A. (2003). Warning against faking on a personality test: Effects on applicant reactions and personality test scores. *International Journal of Selection and Assessment*, *11*(4), 265–276.

McFarland, L. A., & Ryan, A. M. (2000). Variance in faking across noncognitive measures. *Journal of Applied Psychology*, *85*(5), 812–821.

McGrane, J. A. (2015). Stevens' forgotten crossroads: The divergent measurement traditions in the physical and psychological sciences from the mid-twentieth century. *Frontiers in Psychology*, *6*, Article 431. https://doi.org/10.3389/fpsyg.2015.00431

McGrath, R. E., Mitchell, M., Kim, B. H., & Hough, L. (2010). Evidence for response bias as a source of error variance in applied assessment. *Psychological Bulletin*, *136*(3), 450–470.

McNally, R. J. (2016). Can network analysis transform psychopathology? *Behaviour Research and Therapy*, *86*, 95–104.

McNeish, D. (2018). Thanks coefficient alpha, we'll take it from here. *Psychological Methods*, *23*(3), 412–433.

Meade, A. W. (2004). Psychometric problems and issues involved with creating and using ipsative measures for selection. *Journal of Occupational & Organizational Psychology*, *77*(4), 531–551.

Meade, A. W., & Craig, S. B. (2012). Identifying careless responses in survey data. *Psychological Methods*, *17*(3), 437–455.

Metsämuuronen, J. (2022). Typology of deflation-corrected estimators of reliability. *Frontiers in Psychology*, *13*, Article 891959. https://doi.org/10.3389/fpsyg.2022.891959

Michell, J. (1997). Quantitative science and the definition of measurement in psychology. *British Journal of Psychology*, *88*, 355–383.

Michell, J. (2000). Normal science, pathological science and psychometrics. *Theory & Psychology*, *10*(5), 639–667.

Michell, J. (2004). Item response models, pathological science and the shape of error – reply to Borsboom and Mellenbergh. *Theory & Psychology, 14*(1), 121–129.

Michell, J. (2008). Is psychometrics pathological science? *Measurement: Interdisciplinary Research and Perspectives*, *6*(1–2), 7–24.

Michell, J. (2019). Conjoint measurement underdone: Comment on Günter Trendler (2019). *Theory & Psychology*, *29*(1), 138–143.

Michell, J., & Ernst, C. (1996). The axioms of quantity and the theory of measurement. *Journal of Mathematical Psychology*, *40*(3), 235–252.

Miller, G. A. (1956). The magical number seven, plus or minus two: Some limits on our capacity for processing information. *Psychological Review*, *63*(2), 81–97.

Millsap, R. E., & Everson, H. T. (1993). Methodology review – statistical approaches for assessing measurement bias. *Applied Psychological Measurement, 17*(4), 297–334.

Mischel, W. (1968). *Personality and assessment*. Wiley.

Mokken, R. J. (1971). *A theory and procedure of scale analysis with applications in political research*. Mouton.

Mokken, R. J., & Lewis, C. (1982). A nonparametric approach to the analysis of dichotomous item responses. *Applied Psychological Measurement, 6*(4), 417–430.

Most, R. B., & Zeidner, M. (1995). Constructing personality and intelligence instruments: Methods and issues. In D. H. Saklofske & M. Zeidner (Eds.), *International handbook of personality and intelligence*. Plenum.

Mottus, R., & Allerhand, M. H. (2018). Why do traits come together? The underlying trait and network approaches. In V. Zeigler-Hill & T. K. Shackelford (Eds.), *The Sage handbook of personality and individual differences* (pp. 130–151). Sage.

Mueller, T. (in press). Development and testing of the University Student Resilience Scale. *Journal of American College Health*.

Mushquash, C., & O'Connor, B. P. (2006). SPSS and SAS programs for generalizability theory analyses. *Behavior Research Methods*, *38*(3), 542–547.

Narayan, S., & Krosnick, J. A. (1996). Education moderates some response effects in attitude measurement. *Public Opinion Quarterly*, *60*(1), 58–88.

Nettelbeck, T. (1982). Inspection time: An index for intelligence. *Quarterly Journal of Experimental Psychology Section A: Human Experimental Psychology*, *34*, 299–312.

Newman, D. A. (2014). Missing data: Five practical guidelines. *Organizational Research Methods*, *17*(4), 372–411.

Nguyen, H. V., & Waller, N. G. (in press). Local minima and factor rotations in exploratory factor analysis. *Psychological Methods*.

Nunnally, J. C. (1978). *Psychometric theory* (2nd ed.). McGraw-Hill.

Olkin, I., & Finn, J. D. (1995). Correlations redux. *Psychological Bulletin*, *118*(1), 155–164.

Olsson, U. (1979). Maximum likelihood estimation of the polychoric correlation coefficient. *Psychometrika*, *44*(4), 443–460.

Ones, D. S., Viswesvaran, C., & Reiss, A. D. (1996). Role of social desirability in personality testing for personnel selection: The red herring. *Journal of Applied Psychology*, *81*(6), 660–679.

Ortner, T. M. (2008). Effects of changed item order: A cautionary note to practitioners on jumping to computerized adaptive testing for personality assessment. *International Journal of Selection and Assessment*, *16*(3), 249–257.

Osterlind, S. J. (1983). *Test item bias*. Sage.

Pal, S., Luo, R., Bagui, S., & Paul, S. (in press). Alternative tests for the significance of the intraclass correlation coefficients under unequal family sizes. *Communications in Statistics: Simulation and Computation*.

Park, S. C., & Kim, D. (2020). The centrality of depression and anxiety symptoms in major depressive disorder determined using a network analysis. *Journal of Affective Disorders*, *271*, 19–26.

Partchev, I., De Boeck, P., & Steyer, R. (2013). How much power and speed is measured in this test? *Assessment*, *20*(2), 242–252.

Paulhus, D. L. (1984). Two-component models of socially desirable responding. *Journal of Personality and Social Psychology*, *46*(3), 598–609.

Paulhus, D. L. (1998). *Paulhus Deception Scales (PDS): The Balanced Inventory of Desirable Responding: User's manual*. Multi-Health Systems.

Paulhus, D. L. (2002). Social desirable responding: The evolution of a construct. In H. I. Brown, D. N. Jackson, & D. E. Wiley (Eds.), *The role of constructs in psychological and educational measurement* (pp. 49–69). Erlbaum.

Paunonen, S. V. (1997). On chance and factor congruence following orthogonal Procrustes rotation. *Educational and Psychological Measurement*, *57*(1), 33–59.

Paunonen, S. V., Jackson, D. N., & Keinonen, M. (1990). The structured nonverbal assessment of personality. *Journal of Personality*, *58*(3), 481–502.

Paunonen, S. V., & LeBel, E. P. (2012). Socially desirable responding and its elusive effects on the validity of personality assessments. *Journal of Personality and Social Psychology*, *103*(1), 158–175.

Paunonen, S. V., & O'Neill, T. A. (2010). Self-reports, peer ratings and construct validity. *European Journal of Personality*, *24*(3), 189–206.

Pedregon, C. A., Farley, R. L., Davis, A., Wood, J. M., & Clark, R. D. (2012). Social desirability, personality questionnaires, and the "better than average" effect. *Personality and Individual Differences*, *52*(2), 213–217.

Perline, R., Wright, B. D., & Wainer, H. (1979). The Rasch model as additive conjoint measurement. *Applied Psychological Measurement*, *3*(2), 237–255.

Pettigrew, T. F., & Meertens, R. W. (1995). Subtle and blatant prejudice in Western Europe. *European Journal of Social Psychology*, *25*(1), 57–75.

Picco, S., Pedreira, M. E., & Fernandez, R. S. (2020). Psychometric validation of the survey of autobiographical memory: Confirmatory factor analysis and network analysis. *Memory*, *28*(8), 1037–1050.

Pietschnig, J., Voracek, M., & Formann, A. K. (2010). Mozart effect–Shmozart effect: A meta-analysis. *Intelligence*, *38*(3), 314–323.

Plomin, R., & Bergeman, C. S. (1991). The nature of nurture: Genetic influence on environmental measures. *Behavioral and Brain Sciences*, *14*(3), 373–385.

Podsakoff, P. M., MacKenzie, S. B., Lee, J. Y., & Podsakoff, N. P. (2003). Common method biases in behavioral research: A critical review of the literature and recommended remedies. *Journal of Applied Psychology*, *88*(5), 879–903.

Polit, D. F. (2014). Getting serious about test-retest reliability: A critique of retest research and some recommendations. *Quality of Life Research*, *23*(6), 1713–1720.

Pons, P., & Latapy, M. (2005). Computing communities in large networks using random walks. *Computer and Information Sciences: ISCIS 2005*, Berlin, Heidelberg.

Pozzar, R., Hammer, M. J., Underhill-Blazey, M., Wright, A. A., Tulsky, J. A., Hong, F. X., . . . Berry, D. L. (2020). Threats of bots and other bad actors to data quality following research participant recruitment through social media: Cross-sectional questionnaire. *Journal of Medical Internet Research*, *22*(10), Article e23021. https://doi.org/10.2196/23021

Press, W. H., Teukolsky, S. A., Yetterling, W. T., & Flannery, B. P. (1993). *Numerical recipes in FORTRAN*. Cambridge University Press.

Prytulak, L. S. (1975). Critique of S. S. Stevens' theory of measurement scale classification. *Perceptual and motor skills*, *41*(1), 3–28.

Putwain, D. W., Connors, L., & Symes, W. (2010). Do cognitive distortions mediate the test anxiety–examination performance relationship? *Educational Psychology*, *30*(1), 11–26.

Rammstedt, B., Danner, D., & Bosnjak, M. (2017). Acquiescence response styles: A multilevel model explaining individual-level and country-level differences. *Personality and Individual Differences*, *107*, 190–194.

Ranger, J., Kuhn, J. T., & Pohl, S. (2021). Effects of motivation on the accuracy and speed of responding in tests: The speed-accuracy tradeoff revisited. *Measurement: Interdisciplinary Research and Perspectives*, *19*(1), 15–38.

Rasch, G. (1960). *Probabilistic models for some intelligence and attainment tests*. Danmarks Paedogogiske Institut.

Raven, J., Raven, J. C., & Court, J. H. (2003). *Manual for Raven's progressive matrices and vocabulary scales*. Oxford Psychologists Press.

Raykov, T. (1997). Estimation of composite reliability for congeneric measures. *Applied Psychological Measurement*, *21*(2), 173–184.

Raykov, T. (2004). Point and interval estimation of reliability for multiple-component measuring instruments via linear constraint covariance structure modeling. *Structural Equation Modeling: A Multidisciplinary Journal*, *11*(3), 342–356.

R Core Team. (2013). *R: A language and environment for statistical computing*. The R Foundation for Statistical Computing. http://www.R-project.org/

Reise, S. P. (2012). The rediscovery of bifactor measurement models. *Multivariate Behavioral Research*, *47*(5), 667–696.

Reise, S. P., & Henson, J. M. (2000). Computerization and adaptive administration of the NEO PI-R. *Assessment*, *7*(4), 347–364.

Revelle, W. (2017a). *Apply the Kaiser normalization when rotating factors*. Personality Project, Northwestern University. http://personality-project.org/r/psych/help/kaiser.html

Revelle, W. (2017b). *Determining the optimal number of interpretable factors by using very simple structure*. Personality Project, Northwestern University. http://personality-project.org/r/vss.html

Revelle, W. (2017c). *Psych: Procedures for personality and psychological research*. Comprehensive R Archive Network. http://cran.r-project.org/web/packages/psych/

Revelle, W., & Condon, D. M. (2019). Reliability from alpha to omega: A tutorial. *Psychological Assessment*, *31*(12), 1395–1411.

Revelle, W., & Rocklin, T. (1979). Very simple structure: An alternative procedure for estimating the optimal number of interpretable factors. *Multivariate Behavioral Research*, *14*(4), 403–414.

Reynolds, C. R., Chastain, R. L., Kaufman, A. S., & McLean, J. E. (1987). Demographic characteristics and IQ among adults: Analysis of the WAIS-R standardization sample as a function of the stratification variables. *Journal of School Psychology*, *25*(4), 323–342.

Reynolds, C. R., & Suzuki, L. A. (2013). Bias in psychological assessment: An empirical review and recommendations. In I. B. Weiner, J. R. Graham, & J. A. Naglieri (Eds.), *Handbook of psychology: Assessment psychology* (2nd ed., Vol. 10, pp. 82–113). Wiley.

Roberts, B. W., & Yoon, H. J. (2022). Personality psychology. *Annual Review of Psychology*, *73*, 489–516.

Robins, R. W., Hendin, H. M., & Trzesniewski, K. H. (2001). Measuring global self-esteem: Construct validation of a single-item measure and the Rosenberg self-esteem scale. *Personality and Social Psychology Bulletin, 27*(2), 151–161.

Robinson, E. V., & Rogers, R. (2015). Empathy faking in psychopathic offenders: The vulnerability of empathy measures. *Journal of Psychopathology and Behavioral Assessment, 37*(4), 545–552.

Roddy, S., Stewart, I., & Barnes-Holmes, D. (2010). Anti-fat, pro-slim, or both? Using two reaction-time based measures to assess implicit attitudes to the slim and overweight. *Journal of Health Psychology, 15*(3), 416–425.

Roman, Z. J., Brandt, H., & Miller, J. M. (2022). Automated bot detection using Bayesian latent class models in online surveys. *Frontiers in Psychology, 13:789223*.

Rosenbaum, P. J., & Valsiner, J. (2011). The un-making of a method: From rating scales to the study of psychological processes. *Theory & Psychology, 21*(1), 47–65.

Rosenberg, M. (1965). *Society and the adolescent self-image*. Princeton University Press.

Roskam, E. E., van den Wollenberg, A. L., & Jansen, P. G. W. (1986). The Mokken scale: A critical discussion. *Applied Psychological Measurement, 10*(3), 265–277.

Rouse, S. V. (2020). Reliability of MTurk data from masters and workers. *Journal of Individual Differences, 41*(1), 30–36.

Rudner, L. M. (1974). *A closer look at latent trait parameter invariance*. Annual Meeting of the New England Educational Research Organization, May 4–7, Manchester, New Hampshire.

Rupp, A. A., & Zumbo, B. D. (2006). Understanding parameter invariance in unidimensional IRT models. *Educational and Psychological Measurement, 66*(1), 63–84.

Ryan, A. M., Bradburn, J., Bhatia, S., Beals, E., Boyce, A. S., Martin, N., & Conway, J. (2021). In the eye of the beholder: Considering culture in assessing the social desirability of personality. *Journal of Applied Psychology, 106*(3), 452–466.

Ryan, A. M., & Ployhart, R. E. (2000). Applicants' perceptions of selection procedures and decisions: A critical review and agenda for the future. *Journal of Management, 26*(3), 565–606.

Sackett, P. R., & Yang, H. (2000). Correction for range restriction: An expanded typology. *Journal of Applied Psychology, 85*(1), 112–118.

Saint-Mont, U. (2012). What measurement is all about. *Theory & Psychology, 22*(4), 467–485.

Salzberger, T. (2010). Does the Rasch model convert an ordinal scale into an interval scale? *Rasch Measurement, 24*(2), 1273–1275.

Sass, D. A., & Schmitt, T. A. (2010). A comparative investigation of rotation criteria within exploratory factor analysis. *Multivariate Behavioral Research, 45*(1), 73–103.

Schell, K. L., & Oswald, F. L. (2013). Item grouping and item randomization in personality measurement. *Personality and Individual Differences, 55*(3), 317–321.

Schinka, J. A. (2012). Further issues in determining the readability of self-report items: Comment on McHugh and Behar (2009). *Journal of Consulting and Clinical Psychology, 80*(5), 952–955.

Schmid, J., & Leiman, J. M. (1957). The development of hierarchical factor solutions. *Psychometrika, 22*(1), 53–61.

Schmidt, F. L., & Hunter, J. (2004). General mental ability in the world of work: Occupational attainment and job performance. *Journal of Personality and Social Psychology, 86*(1), 162–173.

Schneider, S., May, M., & Stone, A. A. (2018). Careless responding in internet-based quality of life assessments. *Quality of Life Research, 27*(4), 1077–1088.

Shamon, H., & Berning, C. (2020). Attention check items and instructions in online surveys with incentivized and non-incentivized samples: Boon or bane for data quality? *Survey Research Methods, 14*(1), 55–77.

Shearer, C. B. (2007). *The MIDAS: A professional manual*. Greyden Press.

Sheeran, P., & Webb, T. L. (2016). The intention-behavior gap. *Social and Personality Psychology Compass, 10*(9), 503–518.

Shrout, P. E., & Fleiss, J. L. (1979). Intraclass correlations: Uses in assessing rater reliability. *Psychological Bulletin, 86*(2), 420–428.

Sijtsma, K. (1998). Methodology review: Nonparametric IRT approaches to the analysis of dichotomous item scores. *Applied Psychological Measurement, 22*(1), 3–31.

Sijtsma, K. I., & van der Ark, L. A. (2017). A tutorial on how to do a Mokken scale analysis on your test and questionnaire data. *British Journal of Mathematical & Statistical Psychology, 70*(3), 565–565.

Simons, D. J., Shoda, Y., & Lindsay, D. S. (2017). Constraints on generality (COG): A proposed addition to all empirical papers. *Perspectives on Psychological Science, 12*(6), 1123–1128.

Sjoberg, L. (2015). Correction for faking in self-report personality tests. *Scandinavian Journal of Psychology, 56*(5), 582–591.

Slough, N., Kleinknecht, R. A., & Thorndike, R. M. (1984). Relationship of the repression-sensitization scales to anxiety. *Journal of Personality Assessment, 48*(4), 378–379.

Spector, P. E. (1992). *Summated rating scale construction*. Sage.

Steinberg, L. (1994). Context and serial-order effects in personality measurement: Limits on the generality of measuring changes the measure. *Journal of Personality and Social Psychology, 66*(2), 341–349.

Stephenson, W. (1953). *The study of behavior*. University of Chicago Press.

Sternberg, R. J. (2004). Culture and intelligence. *American Psychologist, 59*(5), 325–338.

Stevens, S. S. (1946). On the theory of scales of measurement. *Science, 103*, 677–680.

Stevens, S. S. (1951). *Handbook of experimental psychology*. Wiley.

Stoet, G. (2010). PsyToolkit: A software package for programming psychological experiments using Linux. *Behavior Research Methods, 42*(4), 1096–1104.

Storozuk, A., Ashley, M., Delage, V., & Maloney, E. A. (2020). Got bots? Practical recommendations to protect online survey data from bot attacks. *Quantitative Methods for Psychology, 16*(5), 472–481.

Sun, L. N., Liu, Y. N., & Luo, F. (2019). Automatic generation of number series reasoning items of high difficulty. *Frontiers in Psychology, 10*, Article 884. https://doi.org/10.3389/fpsyg.2019.00884

Sutin, A. R., Costa, P. T., Evans, M. K., & Zonderman, A. B. (2013). Personality assessment in a diverse urban sample. *Psychological Assessment, 25*(3), 1007–1012.

Swaminathan, H., & Gifford, J. A. (1983). Estimation of parameters in the three-parameter latent trait model. In D. Weiss (Ed.), *New horizons in testing* (pp. 13–30). Academic Press.

Swiss Society for Research in Education Working Group. (2010). *EDUG User Guide*. IRDP.

Tabachnick, B. G., & Fidell, L. S. (2018). *Using multivariate statistics* (7th ed.). Pearson.

Thorndike, R. L. (1985). The central role of general ability in prediction. *Multivariate Behavioral Research, 20*, 241–254.

Thurstone, L. L. (1947). *Multiple factor analysis: A development and expansion of the vectors of mind*. University of Chicago Press.

Tran, U. S., & Formann, A. K. (2009). Performance of parallel analysis in retrieving unidimensionality in the presence of binary data. *Educational and Psychological Measurement, 69*(1), 50–61.

Traub, R. E. (1983). A priori considerations in choosing an item response model. In R. K. Hambleton (Ed.), *Applications of item response theory* (pp. 57–70). Educational Research Institute of British Columbia.

Trendler, G. (2009). Measurement theory, psychology and the revolution that cannot happen. *Theory & Psychology, 19*(5), 579–599.

Trendler, G. (2019). Conjoint measurement undone. *Theory & Psychology, 29*(1), 100–128.

Trott, D., & Jackson, D. N. (1967). An experimental analysis of acquiescence. *Journal of Experimental Research in Personality, 2*(4), 278–288.

Tucker, L. R. (1966). Some mathematical notes on three-mode factor analysis. *Psychometrika, 31*(3), 279–311.

Tulsky, D. S., Zhu, J., & Prifitera, A. (2000). Assessment of adult intelligence with the WAIS-III. In G. Goldstein & M. Hersen (Eds.), *Handbook of psychological assessment* (3rd ed., pp. 97–129). Pergamon.

Uziel, L. (2010). Rethinking social desirability scales: From impression management to interpersonally oriented self-control. *Perspectives on Psychological Science, 5*(3), 243–262.

van de Vijver, F., & Hambleton, R. (1996). Translating tests: Some practical guidelines. *European Psychologist, 1*, 89–99.

van Schuur, W. H. (2003). Mokken scale analysis: Between the Guttman scale and parametric item response theory. *Political Analysis, 11*(2), 139–163.

Vaz, S., Falkmer, T., Passmore, A. E., Parsons, R., & Andreou, P. (2013). The case for using the repeatability coefficient when calculating test-retest reliability. *PLoS ONE, 8*(9). Article e73990. https://doi.org/10.1371/journal.pone.0073990

Vegelius, J. (1973). *Correlation coefficients as scalar products in Euclidean spaces*. Department of Psychology Report #145, University of Uppsala.

Velicer, W. F. (1976). Determining the number of components from the matrix of partial correlations. *Psychometrika, 41*(3), 321–327.

Velicer, W. F., Eaton, C. A., & Fava, J. L. (2000). Construct explication through factor or component analysis: A review and evaluation of alternative procedures for determining the number of factors or components. In R. D. Goffin & E. Helmes (Eds.), *Problems and solutions in human assessment: Honoring Douglas N. Jackson at seventy* (pp. 41–71). Kluwer Academic.

Velicer, W. F., & Jackson, D. N. (1990). Component analysis versus common factor analysis: Some issues in selecting an appropriate procedure. *Multivariate Behavioral Research, 25*(1), 1–28.

Vernon, P. E. (1961). *Intelligence and attainment tests*. Philosophical Library.

von Oertzen, T., Brandmaier, A. M., & Tsang, S. (2015). Structural equation modeling with ΩNYX. *Structural Equation Modeling: A Multidisciplinary Journal, 22*(1), 148–161.

Wainer, H. (1978). Sensitivity of regression and regressors. *Psychological Bulletin, 85*(2), 267–273.

Wainer, H. (2014). *Computerized adaptive testing: A primer* (2nd ed.). Routledge.

Wechsler, D. (2008). *WAIS-IV technical and interpretative manual*. Pearson.

Weirich, S., Hecht, M., Penk, C., Roppelt, A., & Bohme, K. (2017). Item position effects are moderated by changes in test-taking effort. *Applied Psychological Measurement, 41*(2), 115–129.

Wessling, K. S., Huber, J., & Netzer, O. (2017). MTurk character misrepresentation: Assessment and solutions. *Journal of Consumer Research, 44*(1), 211–230.

Westfall, J., & Yarkoni, T. (2016). Statistically controlling for confounding constructs is harder than you think. *PLoS ONE, 11*(3), 22, Article e0152719. https://doi.org/10.1371/journal.pone.0152719

Widaman, K. F., & Reise, S. P. (1997). Exploring the measurement invariance of psychological instruments: Applications in the substance use domain. In K. J. Bryant, M. Windle, & S. G. West (Eds.), *The science of prevention: Methodological advances from alcohol and substance abuse research* (pp. 281–324). American Psychological Association.

Wind, S. A. (2017). An instructional module on Mokken scale analysis. *Educational Measurement: Issues and Practice, 36*(2), 50–66.

Wright, B. D. (1984). Despair and hope for educational measurement. Research Memorandum 41, MESA Laboratory.

Wright, B. D. (1985). Additivity in psychological measurement. In E. Roskam (Ed.), *Measurement and personality assessment* (pp. 101–112). North Holland.

Wright, B. D., & Linacre, J. (1989). Observations are always ordinal; measurements, however, must be interval. *Archives of Physical Medicine and Rehabilitation, 70*, 857–860.

Yen, W. M. (1984). Effects of local item dependence on the fit and equating performance of the three-parameter logistic model. *Applied Psychological Measurement, 8*(2), 125–145.

Yu, P. L. H., Lam, K. F., & Lo, S. M. (2005). Factor analysis for ranked data with application to a job selection attitude survey. *Journal of the Royal Statistical Society Series A: Statistics in Society, 168*, 583–597.

Zumbo, B. D., Gadermann, A. M., & Zeisser, C. (2007). Ordinal versions of coefficients alpha and theta for Likert rating scales. *Journal of Modern Applied Statistical Methods, 6*(1), 21–29.

Zwick, W. R., & Velicer, W. F. (1986). Comparison of five rules for determining the number of components to retain. *Psychological Bulletin, 99*(3), 432–442.

INDEX

1PL model 324–336
2PL model 328, 329, 335–338
3PL model 328–330, 334–336

abilities 5, 6, 13–19, 21–29, 33–35, 321–323, 364
ability tests 29–35
acquiescence 166, 167
adaptive tests *see* tailored testing
age norms 104
analysis of variance 3, 88, 130, 147, 174–181, 208, 210, 379
ANOVA *see* analysis of variance
anxiety 1, 6, 13–18, 171–175, 185, 311–314
assessment centres 4, 62
assumptions 17–20, 35, 46–58, 91, 129, 153, 160, 163, 183, 193, 204, 210, 230, 324, 325, 327, 341, 345, 388, 392, 397, 398
attainment tests 1, 16, 25, 29, 31, 43, 68, 82, 189, 198, 349, 350, 363, 370, 371, 376
attitudes 15, 17, 18, 38, 43, 48, 68, 85, 94, 167, 190, 307, 359, 365
attributes 48, 50–57, 328, 398
automated item generation 366

bandwidth/fidelity tradeoff 200
betweenness (of a node) 310
bias 40, 168–211; external bias 205–208; internal bias 206, 208–210, 338, 339
bifactor models 277
blank answers 32, 34, 40, 75, 76, 90, 97, 253
bots 66, 67, 82, 98, 369
bottom-up theories 397

careless responding 35, 65, 66, 97, 347, 358
Chain-P technique 267, 269–272, 269–272, 280
change scores 377, 378
classical item analysis 141, 142, 348, 373–376
cleaning data 82–90, 369, 370
clinical psychology 3, 4, 13, 20, 27, 61, 84, 99, 101, 147, 189–190, 190, 192, 371, 379
closeness (of a node) 247, 310
cognitive abilities 1, 6, 13–15, 21, 23, 48, 173, 205, 283

common factor 217–225
communality 219–225, 230, 236, 241, 249–251
computer administration 34, 35, 61, 62, 67, 353, 366
concatenation 49, 54
concurrent validity 198, 199
confidence intervals 152, 235, 381–384
confirmation bias 296
confirmatory factor analysis 299
congeneric scales 154–157, 160, 161
congruence coefficient 296
conjoint measurement 56
constructs 54, 111, 194, 212, 212–213, 215, 227, 372
correction for restriction of range *see* restriction of range
correction for unreliability 134
correlations 117–135; averaging 134, 135; biserial 128; corrections 131–133; and group differences 129–131; phi coefficient 122–126; point-biserial 126–128; polychoric 126, 128, 129, 160, 239–240, 251, 314; Spearman's rho 128, 237; tetrachoric 126, 128, 129, 160, 238–240, 248, 251, 343
counting 52, 55–58, 96–98
covariance 157
criterion keying 371, 372
Cronbach's alpha *see* reliability, coefficient alpha
cut-off scores 104, 169, 218, 388

degree (of a node) 310
delta 209, 258, 286
density (of nodes) 310
dichotomous variables 122, 126
difference scores 273, 274, 384–387
difficulty 25, 35, 46, 58, 91, 95–97, 100, 104, 106, 139, 172, 178, 180, 209, 220, 239, 322–334, 338, 339–340, 341, 342, 343, 358–364, 367, 370, 374
directional networks 309, 318–319
direct oblimin *see* factor analysis; oblique rotation
discriminant validity *see* validity
discrimination 209, 324–330, 333, 335–337, 344

distractors 31, 32, 62, 90, 348, 355, 356, 362, 368, 369
Dobson's method 132, 134
domain 22, 23
dR (differential R) technique 267, 272–274
dyslexia 4, 13, 383

edges 307–320
educational psychology 4, 99, 109, 132, 279
Educational Testing Service 45
EGA *see* exploratory graph analysis
egoistic bias 168
eigenvalue 219–220, 227, 239, 242–243, 244, 245, 251, 261, 351
emotional intelligence 13
ethics 43, 347, 349
exploratory bifactor analysis 292
exploratory factor analysis *see* factor analysis
exploratory graph analysis 247–248
extreme scores 104, 105

facets 26, 161, 174–182, 293, 294, 305, 350, 358, 370, 371, 374, 375, 398
factor analysis 28, 49, 210–303; communality 219–220, 224–225, 241, 249–250, 253; confirmatory factor analysis 299–303; eigenvalue 219–220, 253; factor comparison 283–303; factor pattern 221, 222; factor scores 258, 260; factor structure 221, 222; hierarchical solutions 283–296; number of factors 241–249; oblique rotation 221, 242, 257, 258, 261, 268, 283–286, 301, 302, 314, 351, 392; orthogonal rotation 219–220, 253–258, 261, 351; parallel analysis 244–247, 248, 249, 268, 373; principal components analysis 222–223, 224, 241, 241, 261; Schmid-Leiman procedure 161, 277, 288–293, 391, 392; scree test 243–244; simple structure 230, 247, 249, 252–259, 286; three-mode factoring 280; unique factor 217, 224–225, 241, 290; unrotated factor matrix 251, 253; uses 225–227; VSS test 247
FACTOR program 126, 239, 239–240, 248, 255, 258, 290, 292
faking 167–170
first order factor 284
Fisher's z *see* correlations, averaging
forced-alternative items 41, 42
free response items 29–33, 68, 91, 96, 101, 103, 347, 355, 357, 362, 363
functional equivalence 204

gamma 125, 258, 286
G-analysis 277–280
general intelligence 14, 19, 145, 288, 290, 389
generalisability theory 165, 174–183
GENOVA program 182

Goodman-Kruskal gamma *see* gamma
group differences 129, 146, 204
group factors 290–292
guessing 32, 68, 86–90, 323, 329, 332, 338, 338–340, 355, 356, 362, 378, 381
guessing parameter 329
Guttman scale 90–96, 100, 175, 324, 341, 343

halo effect 40
Hendrickson and White technique 287
HEXACO model 21
Heywood case 250
hierarchical model 284, 290, 299, 393
hierarchical omega *see* omega
H INDEX 162
Hölder's axioms 57
hyperplane 254, 259–261, 286, 287

ICAR (international Cognitive Ability Resource) 21, 45
ICC *see* item characteristic curve
impression management 167
incremental validity *see* validity
individual testing 4, 5, 78, 88, 379
information function 331–333, 340
instructions 4, 22, 24, 33, 40, 43, 44, 82, 87–90, 172, 173, 274, 285, 351, 354–360, 376, 380
internal consistency 74, 150, 160, 164, 174, 373
internet testing *see* online testing
interpreting test scores 99–115
interval scale 52, 160, 326, 398
intraclass correlation 146–148
invariance 103, 104, 203, 204
IPIP personality scales 45, 46
ipsative scores 77–82
IQ 104, 109
IRT *see* item response theory
item analysis 142, 348–376
item characteristic curve 338, 392
item difficulty 97, 325, 336–342
item information function 331–333, 348
item response theory 12, 35, 49, 90, 181, 210, 322–345, 348, 355, 358, 369, 376, 401
Item-total correlation 373
item writing 349–358, 361–367

job analysis 190

Kaiser-Guttman criterion 242–243

lasso technique 316
latent variable *see* factor analysis
Likert scale 35, 46, 68, 83–85, 121, 166, 170, 238, 244, 270, 272, 276, 347
local independence 163, 325, 341
locating tests 44–46

INDEX

Loevinger's H 343
logistic function 325

magnitude 50, 51
MAP test 247
measurement 47–59
measurement error 1, 39, 131, 137–164, 174, 180–185, 188–203, 331, 348, 378–382, 389, 391
Mental Measurements Yearbooks 44
metric equivalence 204
Michell, J. 2, 19, 47–56, 115, 164, 230, 238, 272, 321, 327, 345, 400, 401
missing data 40, 76, 82, 84, 85, 86, 87, 89, 119, 120, 149, 231, 233–234, 347, 369
modularity 310
Mokken scaling 340–344
moralistic bias 168
motivation 1, 2, 4, 14, 16, 17, 23, 26, 34–36, 61, 167, 172–174, 263, 266–268
multiple-choice tests 32, 33, 68, 75, 329, 357
multiple cut-off method 202, 203
multiple hurdle method 202
multiple regression for selection 3, 86, 100, 200–203, 224

narrative feedback 62
nested models 301
network analysis 305–325, 373
nodes 247, 306–323
non-parametric approaches 56, 59, 113, 128, 238, 341
normal distribution 105–107, 137
norms 4, 51, 99–114, 154, 321, 325, 327, 344, 395; age norms 104; percentile norms 101, 103, 108, 110; quartiles 111; stanines 109; stens 111

oblique rotation *see* factor analysis
omega 160–164, 391, 392
one-parameter logistic model *see* 1PL model
online testing 7, 12, 21, 36, 41, 61–67, 107, 173, 301, 340, 347
optical scanners 75
ordered response scales 321
order of items 24, 358
ordinal alpha *see* reliability
ordinal data 50, 56, 237–238
ordinary least squares 239, 251
orthogonal rotation *see* factor analysis
outliers 119, 162
overlapping items 10, 118, 120, 158, 193, 195, 213, 219–220, 226, 295, 311, 319, 400

parallel analysis *see* factor analysis
parallel tests 154, 388
partial correlations 8, 131, 195, 247, 307, 314
partitions 310

Pearson correlation *see* correlations
peer ratings 40, 41
percentile norms *see* norms
personality scales 6–9, 12–16, 21, 38, 45, 145, 165–171, 354–363
phi coefficient *see* correlations
point biserial *see* correlations
polychoric correlation *see* correlations
postdiction 199
power tests 33, 367
practice items 24, 44
prediction of behaviour 190, 203, 293
pre-registered report 348, 349
principal components analysis 222–223, 224, 241, 261; *see also* factor analysis
Procrustes rotation 298
psychometric assessment 22
P-technique 267–274, 281

Q′-data 38
Q-data 38
Q-sort 274–276
Q-technique 264–266, 274–280
quantitative structure 47–59, 99, 328
quartiles *see* norms
questionnaire 21

random errors 137
random responding 39, 83, 84
Rasch scaling 31, 325–328, 330, 334–336, 339, 340, 341
ratings of behaviour 16, 41, 119
ratio scales 50–52
Raykov's rho *see* reliability
rectangular distribution 111, 121
Relative error *see* generalisability theory
reliability: alternative forms reliability 148, 149; coefficient alpha 12, 131, 150–164, 173–179, 212, 262, 293, 375, 383, 386–393; maximal reliability 162, 163; of multi-scale tests 380, 384, 386, 387, 389; omega 160, 161; ordinal alpha 160; Raykov's rho 161–164; split half 149, 150, 367; test-retest reliability 131, 144–149, 179, 182, 266
reliable component analysis 385
repression-Sensitisation scale 18
response styles *see* systematic errors of measurement
restriction of range 132–136, 196, 233–234, 387, 400
retrospective validation *see* postdiction
Revelle, W. 45, 129, 164, 229, 247, 257, 290, 391
rho *see* correlations; reliability
R-technique 263, 264, 268, 279, 280

sample sizes 120, 134, 203, 232, 235, 248, 281, 398

sampling items from a domain 350
scale 21
scale length *see* test length
scaling scores 105–115
Schmid-Leiman procedure *see* factor analysis
scoring questionnaires 68–82
scree test *see* factor analysis
self-deceptive enhancement 168
self-knowledge 39
self report 16, 36–40
simple structure *see* factor analysis
single-item scales 26
situations 18, 19
skew 121, 122, 231, 333
social constructions 54, 55, 296, 347, 396
social desirability 9, 18, 42, 167–171, 185, 192, 291, 348, 355, 361
social psychology 6, 7, 9, 188, 397
Spearman-Brown formula 149, 150
specific objectivity 327, 339, 339
speeded tests 33, 34, 367, 368
standard error of measurement 146, 234, 334, 368, 381, 382, 387
standardised alpha 164
states 16–19, 146, 267–274
stem 29, 31, 36, 39
strength (of a node) 310
structural equation modelling 7, 8, 49, 100, 161, 186, 189, 193–195, 200, 209, 211, 268, 299–303, 308, 325, 337, 398
systematic errors of measurement 163, 165–182

tailored testing 34, 35, 42, 62, 338–340
tau-equivalent scales 154–157, 161
test 21
test administration 43, 44, 46, 61–68, 358–361
test battery development 201–203
test construction 347–376

test information function 333, 334, 348
test length 28, 29, 140, 361
test manual 43, 376
Test the Nation 12
three parameter logistic model *see* 3PL model
time limits 33–36, 44, 87, 367
top-down theories 397–399
traits 6, 15, 16
transformed item difficulties 209
translations 365, 366
true score 23
truncated normal distribution *see* Dobson's method
T-scaling 109, 112, 113, 114
T-scores 109, 112
two-parameter logistic model *see* 2PL model

unidimensional scales 27, 33, 165
unique variance 224
unit of measurement 49, 51, 53
unreliability, correcting for 131

validity 185–203; concurrent validity 198; construct validity 191–195, 226; content validity 189–191; convergent validity 191–192; discriminant validity 192; divergent validity 192, 195; face validity 189, 189; factorial validity 201, 227; incremental validity 200, 203; predictive validity 196–199, 226
VARIMAX 253–259, 351
VSS *see* factor analysis

Wechsler intelligence tests 102, 380–384, 386–393
work-basket 189, 190
writing items 39, 95, 111, 205, 293, 347–351

z-scores 107–112, 209